Rethinking Chinese Popular Culture

Through analyses of a wide range of Chinese literary and visual texts from the beginning of the twentieth century through to the contemporary period, the thirteen essays in this volume challenge the view that canonical and popular culture are self-evident and diametrically opposed categories, and instead argue that the two cultural sensibilities are inextricably bound up with one another.

An international line-up of contributors present detailed analyses of literary works and other cultural products that have previously been neglected by scholars, while also examining more familiar authors and works from provocative new angles. The essays include investigations into the cultural industries and contexts that produce the canonical and popular, the position of contemporary popular works at the interstices of nostalgia and amnesia, and also the ways in which cultural texts are inflected with gendered and erotic sensibilities while at the same time also functioning as objects of desire in their own right.

As the only volume of its kind to cover the entire span of the twentieth century, and also to consider the interplay of popular and canonical literature in modern China with comparable rigor, *Rethinking Chinese Popular Culture* is an important resource for students and scholars of Chinese literature and culture.

Carlos Rojas is Assistant Professor of Chinese Cultural Studies at Duke University.

Eileen Cheng-yin Chow is Associate Professor of Chinese Literary and Cultural Studies at Harvard University.

Routledge Contemporary China Series

Rethinking Chinese Popular Culture

Cannibalizations of the Canon

**Edited by Carlos Rojas and
Eileen Cheng-yin Chow**

Routledge
Taylor & Francis Group

LONDON AND NEW YORK

First published 2009
by Routledge
2 Park Square, Milton Park, Abingdon, Oxon OX14 4RN

Simultaneously published in the USA and Canada by Routledge
270 Madison Ave, New York, NY 10016

*Routledge is an imprint of the Taylor & Francis Group, an informa
business*

Typeset in 10/12pt Times NR by Graphicraft Ltd., Hong Kong
Printed in the UK by the MPG Books Group.

British Library Cataloguing in Publication Data
A catalogue record for this book is available from the British
Library

Library of Congress Cataloging in Publication Data
Rethinking Chinese popular culture : cannibalizations of the canon /
edited by Carlos Rojas and Eileen Cheng-yin Chow.
    p. cm. – (Routledge contemporary China series)
    1. Chinese literature—20th century—History and criticism.
2. Popular culture—China. I. Rojas, Carlos. II. Chow, Eileen.
PL2303.R45 2008
895.1′09005—dc22
                                                    2008023499

ISBN10: 0–415–46880–9 (hbk)
ISBN10: 0–203–88664–X (ebk)

ISBN13: 978–0–415–46880–0 (hbk)
ISBN13: 978–0–203–88664–9 (ebk)

Contents

Notes on contributors

Michael Berry is Associate Professor of Contemporary Chinese Cultural Studies at the University of California at Santa Barbara. He is the author of *Jia Zhangke's Hometown Trilogy* (2009), *A History of Pain: Trauma in Modern Chinese Literature and Film* (2008) and *Speaking in Images: Interviews with Contemporary Chinese Filmmakers* (2005). He is also the translator of book-length novels by Wang Anyi, Ye Zhaoyan, Chang Ta-chun, and Yu Hua.

Hsiao-hung Chang is NTU Distinguished Professor in the Department of Foreign Languages and Literatures at the National Taiwan University. Her books in Chinese include *Fake Globalization* (2008), *Running into a Wolf in the Department Store* (2001), *Queer Family Romance* (2000), *Sexual Imperialism* (1998), *Queer Desire: Gender and Sexuality* (1996), *Narcissistic Women* (1996), *Gender Crossing: Feminist Literary Theory and Criticism* (1995), and *Post/modern Woman: Power, Desire and Gender Performance* (1993).

Jianhua Chen is Assistant Professor of the Humanities at the Hong Kong University of Science and Technology. His books in Chinese include *Revolution and Form: Literary Modernity in Mao Dun's Early Fiction* (2007), *Poetry Selections of Chen Jianhua* (2006), *In the Ages of Late Empires and Globalization: Essays on Chinese Literary Culture* (2006), and *Revolution, Discourse and Modernity in China* (2000).

Eileen Cheng-yin Chow is Associate Professor of Chinese Literary and Cultural Studies at Harvard University. She is completing a volume on *Global Chinatowns* and is the co-translator, with Carlos Rojas, of Yu Hua's novel, *Brothers*.

DAI Jinhua is Professor of Chinese Literature and Culture at Peking University. Her books in Chinese include *Scars* (2002), *Misty Scenes: Chinese Cinematic Culture, In the Mirror: 1978–1998* (2000), *Discussions with Dai Jinhua* (1999), *Cartographies of the City of Mirrors* (1999), *Hidden Writings: Studies in 1990s Culture* (1999), *Crossed Gazes: Multiple Identities in Post-1989 Mainland Chinese Art Films* (1998), *City of Mirrors: Woman,*

Film, and Literature (1995), and *Voices Emerging into the Foreground of History: A Study of Contemporary Women's Literature* (with Meng Yue) (1989). English translations of her work appear in Jing Wang and Tani Barlow, eds., *Cinema and Desire: Feminist Marxism and Cultural Politics in the Work of Dai Jinhua* (2002).

Alexander Des Forges is Associate Professor of Chinese at the University of Massachusetts, Boston. He is the author of *Mediasphere Shanghai: The Aesthetics of Cultural Production* (2007).

John Christopher Hamm is Associate Professor of Chinese Literature in the Department of Asian Languages and Literature at the University of Washington. He is the author of *Paper Swordsmen: Jin Yong and the Modern Chinese Martial Arts Novel* (2006).

Michel Hockx is Professor of Chinese at the School of Oriental and African Studies, University of London. He is the author of *Questions of Style: Literary Societies and Literary Journals in Modern China, 1911–1937* (2003) and *A Snowy Morning: Eight Chinese Poets on the Road to Modernity* (1994), and is the editor of several volumes, including *The Literary Field of Twentieth-Century China* (1999).

Ping-hui Liao is Professor of General Literature at National Tsing-Hua University in Taiwan. He is the co-editor, with David Der-wei Wang, of *Taiwan under Japanese Colonial Rule, 1895–1945: History, Culture, Memory* (2006). His books in Chinese include *Another Kind of Modernity* (2001), *Modernity in Revision: Reading Postmodern/Postcolonial Theories* (1996), *Paul Ricoeur* (1993), *Forms and Ideology* (1990), and *On Deconstruction* (1985).

Carlos Rojas is Assistant Professor of Chinese Cultural Studies at Duke University. He the author of *The Naked Gaze: Reflections on Chinese Modernity* (2008) and *The Great Wall: A Cultural History* (2010), and is the co-editor, with David Der-wei Wang, of *Writing Taiwan: A New Literary History* (2007).

Weijie Song is Assistant Professor of Chinese Literature at Rutgers University. He is the author in Chinese of *From Entertainment Activity to Utopian Impulse: Rereading of Jin Yong's Fiction* (1999).

David Der-wei Wang is the Edward C. Henderson Professor of Modern Chinese Literature at Harvard University. His books in English include *The Monster That Is History: History, Violence, and Fictional Writing in Twentieth Century China* (2004); *Fin-de-Siècle Splendor: Repressed Modernities of Late Qing Fiction 1849–1911* (1997), and *Fictional Realism in Twentieth-Century China: Mao Dun, Lao She, Shen Congwen* (1992). His books in Chinese include *Narrating China: Chinese Fiction from the Late Qing to the Contemporary Era* (1992), *Heteroglossia: Chinese Fiction of the*

1930s and 1980s (1988), and *From Liu E to Wang Zhenhe: Essays on Modern Chinese Realism* (1986).

Xiaojue Wang is Assistant Professor of Chinese and Culture at the University of Pennsylvania, and is working on a project on the politics of memory in post-socialist China.

Introduction

The disease of canonicity

Carlos Rojas

In a 1925 essay, Lu Xun, commonly regarded as the father of modern Chinese literature, satirized a recent call for establishing a reading canon for contemporary China, arguing that the classical texts to be included in such a canon were already so ideologically tainted that, "If we want China to improve, it would perhaps be best if everyone simply remained illiterate; because once people learn to read, it is as though they are automatically contaminated by this disease of canonicity (*dujing de binggen* 讀經的病根)."[1]

Needless to say, Lu Xun did not *really* believe that literacy per se was synonymous with ideological contagion. In fact, by the time he wrote this essay, he was already actively involved with the reformist May Fourth movement's attempts to increase literacy by promoting the use of vernacular Chinese for literature and other purposes. Similarly, his critique of a disease of canonicity presumably did not extend to all literary canons tout court, given that he was himself one of the central figures of the May Fourth movement's efforts, during the 1920s, to establish *itself* as the new literary orthodoxy for modern China.

In his critique of the Confucian classics, therefore, Lu Xun was not criticizing the very possibility of a cultural canon, but rather was implicitly trying to rethink what it meant to be canonical in the first place. Before the twentieth century, *all* narrative fiction in China was regarded as essentially popular, particularly in contrast to Confucian texts and other more socially validated literary genres such as poetry. Recognizing the broad appeal of narrative fiction, however, early twentieth century reformers attempted to appropriate it for their own purposes as a didactic tool, even as they found it necessary to contrast their own ostensibly progressive literature with a pre-existing and concurrent body of fiction that they disparaged as being merely "popular." These self-identified reformers dubbed this latter body of literature *Mandarin Ducks and Butterfly fiction* (abbreviated throughout this volume to *Butterfly fiction*)—borrowing metonymically from two metaphors for marital bliss that appear frequently in the genre. Originally used to designate specifically traditional-style romances, the term *Butterfly fiction* has subsequently come to refer more generally to all genres of early twentieth century popular fiction (including martial arts fiction, detective fiction, exposé fiction, etc.) outside of the self-defined May Fourth pantheon, together with the stylistic and thematic tendencies frequently associated with those genres. In this way, Butterfly fiction came to represent the radical Other of the emerging May Fourth canon, defined in oppositional terms by that against which it was being contrasted.

Although the early twentieth century internecine debates between May Fourth and Butterfly authors had profound ramifications for subsequent understandings of the relationship between popular and elite literature, these debates were ultimately characterized by what Freud calls the narcissism of small differences. In other words, part of the reason for the hyperbolic vitriol and animosity between the rival camps was due to the fact that, at the end of the day, they were actually remarkably similar—not only in terms of the class backgrounds of their respective members, but even with respect to the content and style of the fiction they each produced. The resulting stark contrasts between canonical and popular culture derived, therefore, in large part from the considerable *overlap* between the two.

One of the reasons why Lu Xun's notion of a disease of canonicity is so suggestive is precisely because the metaphor, even as it attempts to pathologize the classical canon, simultaneously acknowledges the underlying *power* of that same canon—suggesting that, just as a disease stems from a pathogen lodged deep within the body, the Confucian canon is embedded so deeply within the Chinese body politic that the mere ability to read necessarily leaves one contaminated by its conservative ideology. Similarly, the urgency of the May Fourth movement's rhetorical attacks on contemporary Butterfly literature reflects a desire to quell the disruptive power represented by that literature, and simultaneously to harness and reappropriate that same power for the May Fourth movement's own purposes.

An important precedent for the May Fourth movement's conflicted views on the relationship between canonical and popular literature can be found in Liang Qichao's famous contention, in 1902, that "if one intends to renovate the people of a nation, one must first renovate its fiction."[2] The May Fourth movement built on Liang's suggestion that literature be used as a tool for ideological transformation, yet at the same time remained haunted by the fear that that tool might exceed, and potentially undermine, the purposes to which it was being applied. As a result, even as they were promoting the use of literature to "heal"—as Lu Xun famously put it[3]—the national spirit, the May Fourth reformers were simultaneously disparaging as merely "popular" the literature written by other contemporary figures outside their movement.

Forty years after Liang Qichao helped provide the theoretical basis for the May Fourth movement's use of popular literature as a vehicle for social reform, Mao Zedong advanced a similar argument in his "Talks at the Yan'an Forum on Literature and Art," in which he called for art and literature to be made into "a powerful weapon for uniting and educating the people, for attacking and annihilating the enemy, and to help the people to fight the enemy with a united heart and mind."[4] In this context, Mao praised Lu Xun for having used "burning satire and freezing irony cast in essay form" to fight the "dark forces" of society, though he was nevertheless careful to stress that the "contemporary era requires a very different set of cultural tools in order to accomplish its goals."[5] In other words, even as Mao was using Lu Xun as a model for the socially progressive literature he himself was advocating, he was implicitly trying to quarantine himself from the critical force that Lu Xun represented.

During the third quarter of the twentieth century, Maoist socialist realism became not only synonymous with cultural orthodoxy but also the default popular culture of the period. Following Mao's death in 1976, however, socialist realism's double hegemony as both paradigmatically orthodox and quintessentially popular began to fracture, as a loosening of politico-ideological fetters together with a growing influence of market forces led to a remarkable proliferation of new cultural styles and subject matter. As I discuss in the final essay in this volume, for instance, during the late 1980s and early 1990s the self-proclaimed "hooligan writer" Wang Shuo trumpeted his defiance of existing literary orthodoxies through his iconoclastic attitude of "playing literature." After a long and suggestive public silence on the question of Wang Shuo's significance, in 1993 the former Minister of Culture, Wang Meng, published an influential short essay in which he argued that Wang Shuo's famously iconoclastic style might actually be *beneficial* to the social order, on the grounds that it functioned as an antidote to the hypercanonical tendencies that had developed, for instance, during China's Cultural Revolution (1966–1976). Wang Meng's belated approbation of Wang Shuo's works *as popular fiction*, therefore, illustrates the orthodoxy's attempts to rhetorically appropriate the potentially disruptive power of popular literature to further its own agenda, even as it asserts its own authority to categorize that literature as inherently "popular." This double process of mutual borrowing and counter-identification, therefore, means that these emerging canons remained haunted by the circumstances of their formation, and specifically by their attempts to appropriate the cultural power of the same popular traditions against which they were simultaneously trying to contrast themselves.

Lu Xun's metaphor of canonical disease underscores the degree to which cultural formations (be they canonical, popular, or otherwise) are never unitary, fixed entities, but rather must be seen as inherently relational, inevitably inflected (and infected) by their attempts to differentiate themselves from one another. One of the standards to which the canon frequently appeals in its critique of its popular obverse, for instance, is that of aesthetic value (or lack thereof). Given the fact that the same institutional forces that help construct and maintain the canon are also complicit in defining the standards of aesthetic valuation on which that canon is ostensibly grounded, however, aesthetic appraisals cannot be used as criteria for determinations of canonicity and popularity themselves. Our goal here, therefore, is not to reaffirm the aesthetic valuations on which understandings of canonical and popular culture have traditionally been predicated, but rather to rethink the very question of what it means to speak of popular culture in the first place.

Once the equation of canonical culture with aesthetic value is brought into question, it similarly becomes necessary to reassess the hermeneutic tendencies that that emphasis on aesthetic values has inspired—wherein canonical works are often approached primarily through a close reading of privileged texts, while more popular works tend to be viewed as mere symptoms of the socio-cultural contexts within which they are embedded. Our goal here is to delink these hermeneutic tendencies from the kinds of texts to which they have traditionally been applied, and instead place roughly equal emphasis on textual and contextual considerations in reading *all* texts, be they popular, canonical, or otherwise. Our primary focus is on literature, but we also include detailed and innovative analyses of a variety of other media, including cinema, photography, installation art, and web culture, and many of the conclusions we draw are relevant to popular culture in general.

We begin by looking at the process of producing popularity, and specifically the way in which a variety of twentieth-century literary schools and genres have been defined, and define themselves, in opposition to a constantly shifting array of cultural orthodoxies. The first four essays in the volume each take an author or a literary "school" that has come to be perceived as in some way marginal to established or emerging cultural orthodoxies, and examine the ways in which that sense of marginality was itself discursively constructed and contested.

We open this discussion of the dialectical relationship between centers and margins by turning to a frequently overlooked cluster of popular texts and writers positioned at the figurative margins of the (itself ostensibly marginal) body of Butterfly literature: a cluster of texts and writers known—in a play on the name of the better-known *Saturday School* of Butterfly literature—as the *Friday School*. Challenging the common assumption that, by the 1930s, popular literary traditions like the Friday School were already effectively subordinated by a May Fourth literary orthodoxy, Michel Hockx argues that the Friday School actually more than held its own during this period, noting that the very urgency of the May Fourth's critiques of Friday School literature suggests the degree to which the former was still attempting to establish its legitimacy. Conversely, Hockx emphasizes that the literary styles associated with the Friday School were actually "part and parcel of an elite culture," though these styles "pertain not so much to literary texts as such but rather to the aesthetic function" of those same texts.

One of the implications of Hockx's argument is that the significance of these early twentieth century literary works lay not so much in the texts themselves, but rather in how they were used to affirm (and disavow) social connections between the authors. Alexander Des Forges, meanwhile, examines this issue of authorship from a somewhat different perspective, concluding that at the turn of the century a new category of professional writer began to emerge in China, as inconsistencies in copyright law allowed authors to retain a greater degree of control over their writings, as well as their own subsequent literary fame. Taking as his starting point Liu Shi'e's depiction of a *fictional* professional author in his 1909 novel *New Shanghai*, Des Forges argues that this text anticipates a process wherein authors began to differentiate themselves from journalists in their ability to organize and package their literary creations, even as they themselves were simultaneously being packaged as profitable brand names in their own right.

Part of the reason why some fictional authors were struggling to differentiate themselves from journalists during this early twentieth century period was precisely because the two professions remained, in many ways, closely intertwined with one another. This mutual imbrication is nowhere more evident than in the figure of Zhang Henshui—one of *the* most popular authors of the period, and one who maintained close ties with the journalism industry throughout his career. Like Des Forges, Eileen Cheng-yin Chow begins her essay with a depiction of a fictional figure who dramatizes the author's own status as a professional writer. The work is the author, journalist, and newspaper supplement editor Zhang Henshui's 1920s serialized novel *Unofficial History of the Old Capital*, whose protagonist also happens to be a reporter in his own right. Chow points to the way in which the early twentieth century genre of the novel was itself inextricably bound up with contemporary journalistic concerns with news and novelty, arguing that journalistic and literary concerns coincided in "the aesthetic as well as material connection between the search for novelties in this period, and the new technologies, industries, and forms of expression in which this interest in the 'new' is expressed."

A more contemporary figure whose literary success was closely bound up with his association with journalism is the super-popular Hong Kong martial-arts novelist Jin Yong. Between 1955 and 1972, Jin Yong serialized 14 novels and novellas in Hong Kong newspapers—particularly in *Mingbao*, a newspaper he himself founded in 1959. Even as he was serializing these works, Jin Yong was simultaneously using his editorial voice and the authority of his newspaper to help consecrate the legitimacy of his novels, and more generally of the martial-arts genre itself. John Christopher Hamm notes Jin Yong's comparatively unique (by Hong Kong standards) status of combining the roles of "producer of a fictional product and manager of the print media through which it was distributed," thereby underscoring the significance of cultural brokers in promoting specific texts while at the same time implicitly reaffirming the brokers' own authority to make those consecrations in the first place. In Jin Yong's case, furthermore, this process of cultural consecration did not end with the initial serialization of his novels, but rather entered an entirely new stage when he proceeded to spend another decade systematically revising all of his works and preparing them for republication. Among his goals in undertaking these revisions was to occlude the structural traces of the novels' own serialized origins, while at the same time appropriating the symbolic capital of elite culture and a transcendent Chinese cultural tradition.

Jin Yong's attempts to retrospectively "canonize" his own serialized works underscore the principle that popular culture cannot be understood independently of the elite or orthodox culture against which it is contrasted. In the following three essays, we develop a series of canonical reflections— reflections on the nature of the canon and also, more specifically, on the canon's status as an inverse "reflection" of the popular culture against which it struggles to contrast itself.

This interrelationship between popular and canonical literature can be seen particularly clearly in a 1922 essay in which leading May Fourth author Mao Dun delivered a scathing critique of prominent Butterfly author Zhou Shoujuan's tragic love story "A Gramophone Record," from the preceding year. While post-1949 literary critics frequently cited Mao Dun's essay as they strove to implement Mao Zedong's model of socialist realism, Jianhua Chen notes that these critics nevertheless rarely evinced "any curiosity regarding the subject matter, author, or origin" of the actual story Mao Dun was critiquing. Chen, by contrast, is deeply curious about Zhou's original story, together with the historical context within which it was produced and received. In particular, he brings Zhou's text into dialogue with one of Mao Dun's own subsequent explorations of tragic love in the short story "Creation" (1928), and considers both texts in the context of the 1920s literary polemics wherein Mao Dun and Zhou Shoujuan staked out their respective positions, concluding that Zhou's and Mao Dun's significance as representatives of so-called old and new literature were in fact symbiotically dependent on one another.

While Jianhua Chen looks at the movement of popular and elite themes between texts from the same period, Michael Berry examines the movement of similar themes from the early twentieth century to the contemporary period. Considering two late twentieth century novels both set in 1937, Berry details how the works not only borrowed from popular early twentieth century romance and martial-arts genres, but also incorporated a wealth of detailed allusions to more "elite" literature as well. The resulting allusive patchwork might be seen as a form of self-legitimization, or as a popularization of elite culture itself, wherein fragments of elite culture are stripped from their original cultural moorings and incorporated into a self-consciously hybrid genre.

Like Berry, Ping-hui Liao examines the ways in which Butterfly thematics and narrative structures have been appropriated and redeployed in contemporary works from Taiwan. Although Wang Wenxing and Shi Shuqing are both conventionally regarded as elite authors, Liao nevertheless demonstrates how they each systematically reappropriate romantic conventions commonly associated with early twentieth century Butterfly fiction, transforming those conventions to suit the needs and concerns of contemporary society. In particular, Liao argues that both authors transfigure the trademark Butterfly thematics of romantic affection into something "perverse, grotesque, and uncanny." Romantic attachments in these works typically result in "pathological situations in which the protagonists are forced to act out traumas in a mode of neurotic repetition compulsion or state fetishism," projecting their desires first onto the figure of the ethnic Other, and eventually onto the abstract figure of Capital itself. Liao concludes by detailing how similar permutations of Butterfly romance formulas can also be found in modern advertising culture, arguing that many contemporary Taipei subway ads present shopping as a process of withdrawal from the politicized public sphere into a variety of intimate spheres—spheres, however, that are not really intimate at all, but rather are thoroughly colonized by transnational capital.

Although the canon—seen as the product of a gradual accretion of institutional, aesthetic, and political preferences—is frequently associated with tradition and antiquity, in early twentieth century China there was also an inverse tendency for emerging canons to align themselves with modernity and reform. During the contemporary period, meanwhile, popular culture has come to be associated with nostalgia and amnesia—nostalgia for the cultural traditions of the early nineteenth and early twentieth centuries, combined with a selective amnesia toward various facets of that same history. The following three essays examine the ways in which cultural works from the 1990s have not only positioned themselves with respect to their own past, but have also implicitly attempted to theorize the concept of temporality itself.

A wave of amnesiac nostalgia swept through Mainland China in the 1990s—a nostalgia for the cultural traditions of the Maoist and the pre-Maoist period paradoxically combined with an inverse effort to *forget* many of the specific political connotations of that same period. Through a detailed analysis of a variety of literary and visual works from this period, Dai Jinhua argues that this wave of Red nostalgia paradoxically constitutes an "excision of the socialist historical memory of the 1950s to the 1970s, combined with the purging of the bloody revolutionary dimensions of the 1930s Red historical narrative," thereby allowing 1990s China to "safely link up with the imaginary 'history' represented by 1930s Shanghai." What is at stake in this process of nostalgic displacement, furthermore, is not only a desire to elide the historical legacy of the intervening Maoist era, but equally importantly an attempt to recontextualize the Maoist Red Classics that emerged from that same period, tacitly reconciling them with the concerns and ideals of the current era.

The *fin-de-siècle* nostalgia that swept China in the 1990s extended not only to the Maoist and May Fourth eras, but also to the late Qing era that preceded them. Focusing on Tsui Hark's 1990s *Once Upon a Time in China (and America)* film series, Weijie Song examines how the protagonist, the legendary late nineteenth century martial-arts hero Wong Fei-hung, provides an interesting counterpoint to contemporary concerns about the status of

Chinese identity. The historical Wong Fei-hung lived during a period when Western imperialism was challenging China's sovereignty, and Weijie Song suggests that Tsui Hark uses Wong to comment allegorically on China's ongoing attempts to reassess its position and significance within an increasingly globalized world.

Finally, on a more intimate level, Xiaojue Wang takes the highly personal nostalgia found in Eileen Chang's photo-essay *Mutual Reflections: Reading Old Photographs* (1994)—the last work Chang published before her death the following year—as the basis for a broader discussion of Chang's conflicted relationship with her own public persona. While Chang was writing most of her major works during the 1940s and 1950s, she was regarded primarily as a popular author, and it was not until the 1960s and 1970s that she was figuratively brought into the canon—first by literary scholars working abroad, and then eventually by scholars in China as well. Chang's transformation from a quintessentially popular writer to one of the most critically acclaimed Chinese authors of the twentieth century (who, nevertheless, remained exceedingly "popular" among her devoted readers) was complicated by her ambivalent attitude toward her own fame. A central theme in Chang's autobiographical *Mutual Reflections*, accordingly, is precisely this tension between self-presentation and self-occlusion, between Chang's public persona as an author and the private life she continued to protect so possessively. Underlying the issue of the relationship between her public and private identity, furthermore, is the related question of how she remembers her own life, and how she would like to be publicly remembered.

Named after a metaphor for conjugal harmony, Butterfly fiction has, from the very beginning, been explicitly associated with issues of gender and desire. At the same time, however, the figure of the butterfly also functions as a metaphor for self-transformation—underscoring the fluid nature, not only of gender identity, but also of the categories of canonical and popular culture themselves. In the final three essays in this volume, we examine cultural production through this lens of gender—*not* in order to reduce canonical or popular culture to rigid gender stereotypes, but rather precisely to examine how individual works themselves implicitly attempt to theorize gender and desire as structuring paradigms for understanding the dynamics of popularity itself. If one important factor underlying the production of the popular is, as I have suggested above, a fear of popular culture's inherent power, a parallel consideration is precisely the *desire* for that power, and by extension for the specific texts and genres associated with that power.

Taking his inspiration from Lu Xun's well-known critique of China's theatrical tradition of female impersonation, David Der-wei Wang examines the trope of transvestitism in the 1943 novel *Begonia* by prominent Butterfly author Qin Shouou, whom Wang suggests can be seen as "a Butterfly writer assuming a May Fourth discursive posture." Focusing on the figure of a Peking Opera performer who specializes in female roles and his struggles to achieve real "manhood," Qin's novel grapples with issues of gender performance and sexual desire, together with the way in which transvestitism comes to function as an ironic figure for national identity. Wang argues that Qin's protagonist represents the Chinese nation, while at the same time embodying deep-rooted anxieties about the very possibility of that sort of (national) representation itself.

In the following essay, Hsiao-hung Chang returns to the topic of Jin Yong's martial-arts fiction, previously discussed in Chris Hamm's essay in this volume. While Hamm focuses on the shifting institutional status of Jin Yong's works, however, Chang's approach is very explicitly textual. Inspired by Jin Yong's repeated citation of the Yuan dynasty poet Yuan Haowen's rhetorical question, "Asking the world, what sort of thing is sentiment?", Chang examines Jin Yong's use of a series of fetishized objects in two of his novels to explore a dynamics of desire and attachment. Drawing on anthropological theories of gift exchange and psychoanalytic notions of investment and displacement, Chang analyzes the relationship between sentiment, materiality, and exchange in the two works, and concludes that "the history that one carries on one's body, and the memory that one witnesses with one's own eyes, are both transformed into a desire for objects that one can actually touch." Finally, Chang applies these conclusions about the workings of desire and attachment to a consideration of Jin Yong's novels themselves —arguing that the texts function as material displacements of the cultural histories that they invoke.

In the final essay, meanwhile, I consider a cluster of contemporary works that examine, and themselves exemplify, the tensions between the establishment's apparent fear of cultural production that it perceives to be unorthodox, together with the public's desire for these works. This dialectics of fear and desire is developed particularly clearly, for instance, in Mo Yan's 1993 novel *Republic of Wine*, which revolves around an epistolary dialogue between an established author (also named *Mo Yan*) who finds himself increasingly frustrated in his efforts to complete his ongoing novel, and an enthusiastic fan named Li Yidou who keeps sending the fictional *Mo Yan* drafts of short stories in the hope that the senior author will help get them published. In the end, however, the fictional *Mo Yan* ends up abandoning his own work-in-progress, and then effectively steps into the inchoate textual space associated with his enthusiastic fan. The novel's conclusion, therefore, represents a process wherein the literary establishment is figuratively consumed by the same extracanonical cultural forces that it was attempting to regulate in the first place—a cannibalistic gesture that is reinforced by the explicit fascination with the trope of cannibalism that we find in several of the literary works embedded within Mo Yan's novel itself, including both the fictional *Mo Yan*'s work-in-progress as well as several of Li Yidou's short-story drafts. Given this centrality of a thematics of cannibalism within the novel, it is therefore fitting that a crucial figure in the debates over literary value between the fictional *Mo Yan* and his errant acolyte

Li Yidou is none other than Lu Xun—whose 1918 short story "Diary of a Madman" famously established cannibalism as one of the most enduring symbols of imperial China's self-destructive social ideology.

Lu Xun's conceit of an ideological cannibalism that is passed down via canonical Confucian texts, and his subsequent concept of a disease of canonicity that is similarly transmitted through the Confucian canon, figuratively come together at the end of his "Reading Canon" essay, where Lu Xun develops an elaborate metaphor of a malignantly cannibalistic immune system and benign intestinal bacteria. Here, Lu Xun compares the ossifying effects of traditional literary and ideological canons to the accumulation of waste elements in the body as it ages, which is exacerbated by a process wherein the immune system's white blood cells (monocytes) migrate into the body's tissue and differentiate into macrophages that begin cannibalistically "devouring all [of the body's own] tissue" (*tunshi ge zuzhi* 吞食各組織). Lu Xun then concludes that "in order to eliminate these macrophages (literally 'big chewing cells'—*dajue xibao* 大嚼細胞), it is necessary to take a daily dose of acid." In this medical metaphor, Lu Xun describes an immune system that not only fails to protect the body from foreign pathogens, but furthermore threatens to devour the body itself from within.[6] His rather cryptic suggestion that these cannibalistic macrophages may be eliminated through the ingestion of a daily dose of acid, meanwhile, alludes explicitly to Russian microbiologist and Nobel laureate Elie Metchnikoff's recommendation—in his 1908 study *The Prolongation of Life: Optimistic Studies*—that human longevity could be significantly increased though the regular ingestion of lactic acid-producing bacteria (which may then help control the growth of other bacteria in the intestines).[7] The paradox here is that, even as Lu Xun describes how the immune system's white blood cells may stray from the task of attacking foreign microbes and instead consume the body's *own* tissue, he simultaneously recommends that the subject consume more *foreign* bacteria. This double process of consumption—in which the Self is consumed as though it were an Other, even as a foreign Other is consumed and incorporated into the Self–challenges the underlying concepts of identity and alterity upon which the very notion of cannibalism is grounded.

In cultural terms, Lu Xun's immune system metaphor in the "Reading Canon" essay suggests that an antiquated canon has the potential to stray from its presumptive role of protecting the integrity of the body politic against heterodox elements (both internal and external), and instead become a cannibalistic force that can only be addressed through a dose of "foreign" May Fourth reformist literature.[8] Ironically, Lu Xun's solution to this canonical cannibalism—the ingestion of lactic acid-producing bacteria that then reside in the intestine—is itself implicitly cannibalistic in nature, just as Lu Xun's May Fourth literature attempted to *incorporate* the institutional legitimacy associated with the classical canon, as well as the popular appeal of the Butterfly literature against which it was attempting to position itself. We may speak, therefore, of the *cannibalizations of the canon*—both in the sense of the canon's attempts to cannibalistically consume various aspects of the popular and orthodox cultural traditions against which it seeks to contrast itself, as well as in the inverse sense of the canon's own susceptibility to being cannibalistically consumed and reappropriated by rival cultural formations.

Lu Xun's immunological metaphor implies that culture (both popular and elite) may function as a cannibalistic force capable of devouring the body politic from within, or as a figurative antibody facilitating a process of social transformation and reform. The very concept of cannibalism, furthermore, implies an affirmation of shared identity between the entities being consumed and those doing the consuming, though the conceptual violence of the cannibalistic act necessarily brings that structure of identification into question. Applied to the cultural arena, this model suggests that neither popular nor canonical culture are ever the homogeneous categories they might aspire to be, but rather both are continually evolving and feeding off of each other.

In English, *culture* can refer not only to the body of aesthetic and intellectual texts through which a society's values and ideals are cultivated and transmitted, but also to the cultivation of potential harmful microbes in an artificial environment outside the body. Although this latter, microbiological significance of the English term is not explicitly present in the Chinese term for culture, *wenhua* 文化, it does nevertheless capture quite precisely a crucial dimension of the vision of Chinese cultures and canons that we are developing here. During the early twentieth century, both popular and traditional (canonical) culture were viewed as having potentially infectious qualities, and one of the goals of reformers was to isolate the active agents of each and cultivate them—as though in a virtual petri dish—into a new literary and cultural canon that Lu Xun hoped would be capable of "curing" the national spirit. At the same time, however, Lu Xun's own immune-system metaphor unwittingly illustrates the degree to which even this new canon has the potential of becoming a virulent, "cannibalistic" disease in its own right, thereby inviting new gestures of "cultivation" and cannibalistic appropriation. It is precisely the resulting symbiosis of popular and canonical culture's mutual cultivation and consumption that is the focus of *Rethinking Chinese Popular Culture*.

Notes

1 Lu Xun 魯迅, "*Shisi nian de dujing*" 十四年的讀經 (The reading canon of the 14th year [of the Republic]) (1925), in *Huagai ji* 華蓋集 (Unlucky star), 1926. Reprinted in Lu Xun, *Lu Xun quanji* 魯迅全集 (Lu Xun's collected works) (Beijing: Renmin wenxue chubanshe, 1981), vol. 3, 127–132.
2 Liang Qichao 梁啟超, "*Lun xiaoshuo yu qunzhi zhi guanxi*" 論小説與群治之關係 (On the relationship between fiction and the government of the people)," in *Xin xiaoshuo* 新小説 (New fiction), 1902: 1. Translated by Gek Nai Cheng, in Kirk Denton, ed., *Modern Chinese Literary Thought: Writings on Literature, 1893–1945* (Stanford: Stanford University Press, 1996), 74.
3 Lu Xun, "*Zixu*" 自序 (Preface to *Nahan* 吶喊 [A call to arms]), in *Lu Xun quanji*, vol. 1: 417.

4 Mao Zedong 毛澤東, "*Zai Yan'an wenyi zuotan hui shang de jianghua*" 在延安
文藝座談會上的講話 (Talks at the Yan'an forum on literature and art). See
Bonnie McDougall, trans., *Mao Zedong's "Talks at the Yan'an Conference on
Literature and Art": A Translation of the 1943 Text Commentary* (Ann Arbor: Center
for Chinese Studies, University of Michigan, 1980), 58. Translation adapted.
5 Mao Zedong, "Talks," 80–81.
6 Metchnikoff's discovery of the role of phagocytosis in the immune system was
described in detail by Chen Duxiu in a 1916 essay in the flagship May Fourth journal *Xin qingnian* 新青年 (New youth), and during that same period was immediately mobilized as a metaphor for society by Hu Shi, Lu Xun, as well as Chen
Duxiu himself. For a discussion, see Carlos Rojas, "Cannibalism and the Chinese
Body Politic: Hermeneutics and Violence in Cross-Cultural Perception," *Postmodern Culture* 12: 3 (May, 2002).
7 Here, Lu Xun is conflating Metchnikoff's recommendation on the elimination of
white blood cell macrophages, with his separate recommendation that lactic acid
bacteria can then help raise the acidity level of the intestinal tract, thereby inhibit-
ing the growth of most other microorganisms, including many human pathogens.
8 Not only were Lu Xun and many other May Fourth authors strongly influenced
by foreign literary traditions from Japan and Europe, but furthermore Lu Xun
himself concludes the "Reading Canon" essay by noting the irony that his immune-
system metaphor is itself borrowed from a "foreign" source (i.e., from the Russian
scientist Elie Metchnikoff).

Part I

Producing popularity

1 Perverse poems and suspicious salons

The Friday School in modern Chinese literature

Michel Hockx

Recent articles and studies have unveiled the variety of literary practices on the cultural scene in the Shanghai of the 1930s.[1] The rediscovery of often forgotten groups and individuals has cast serious doubt on the tenability of existing analytical schemes, which discuss the literary history of this period in terms of a binary opposition between "progressive" and "reactionary" writing, or between the so-called "May Fourth tradition" and its avowed nemesis: popular literature. This essay hopes to show that, although members of the May Fourth generation active as critics in the 1930s continued to express their familiar dissatisfaction with writing they considered in bad taste or unenlightened, there is no reason for scholars nowadays to share these critics' judgments of taste. In short, this essay tries to turn a well-known argument on its head: rather than assuming that the May Fourth generation represented an actively repressive mainstream of serious writing which "suppressed" popular literature, I argue that, even in the 1930s, this generation was using strategies for gaining symbolic capital within the literary field that are more in line with those typically applied by an avant-garde that considers *itself* to be suppressed. As a result, it will emerge that the forgotten writers and practices introduced in the main body of this essay did not have much affinity with popular literature at all, but can rather be seen to continue an indigenous moral-aesthetic disposition. These writings and practices were at some time referred to by the term *Friday School* (*Libaiwu pai* 禮拜五派).

Friday School was a disparaging label, invented by critics writing for the newspaper supplement *Ziyou tan* 自由談 (Free talk) to refer to writers perceived to be operating on the borderline between the New Literature and the so-called Saturday School (*Libailiu pai* 禮拜六派). In other words, their writing and behavior were considered dangerously close to a kind of literary activity that lacked seriousness, propagated outdated moral values, and was aimed predominantly at entertainment.

For many decades, the existence of this "school" has been virtually forgotten or ignored in modern Chinese literary studies. The main reason for this has undoubtedly been a political one: the Friday School had an unfortunate run-in with critics associated with the League of Left-Wing

Writers, including Lu Xun 魯迅 (1881–1936). One of the aims of this essay is to show that the quarrel between these two groups had originally nothing to do with politics, but was eventually given a politicized interpretation by members of both camps. The politicized interpretation being the most straightforward one, it survived and is still surviving in general literary histories and reference works. The real reason why critics like Lu Xun, and also Mao Dun 茅盾 (1896–1981), attacked the Friday School was, I argue, because the styles of the Friday School violated and possibly threatened the legacy of New Culture, in which Lu Xun and Mao Dun had invested so heavily during the previous decade. Their objections to the Friday School at first sight appear to be of a moral, more than of an aesthetic, nature, as their arguments rarely relate to elements of writing, but rather to elements of behavior and personality.

However, I would argue that even this approach relies too much on distinctions created by the writers and critics themselves as part of their agency within the literary field. In order to understand the events more fully, I would like to consider the possibility of interpreting both the moral and political aspects of the debate as part of an ultimately aesthetic distinction, this being a distinction between the New Literature and some of its possible alternatives. In approaching my topic in this manner, I am consciously attempting to circumvent a currently popular line of thinking according to which styles such as those of the Friday School were already "repressed" by the New Literature tradition (in that context usually referred to as the *May Fourth tradition*) even *before* the canonization of that tradition in 1949. As the essay will show, the extremely harsh criticism levied at the Friday School by critics in the early 1930s never amounted to any oppression *at the time*. There is no empirical evidence to suggest that the Friday School was at any time considerably less successful than its opponents—and I use the term "successful" here not only with regard to economic capital, but also with regard to symbolic capital. Moreover, the Friday School was, on occasion, equally capable of silencing New Literature voices. In short, what I intend to provide in this essay is an exercise in literary history which views all practices involved as constituents of modern Chinese literature, without making any *a priori* assumptions about supposed centers or mainstreams.

It is important to state at the outset that, although I am interested in reviving the individuals and writings categorized under the term *Friday School*, it is not my intention to reinstate the label itself, or to claim that there was indeed a coherent group of writers operating under this name. The term *pai* 派 ("school" or "clique") is often used in modern Chinese criticism to express a disparaging opinion. The fact that a *pai*-style label was at some point invented[2] demonstrates that a strategic effort was undertaken by rivaling critics to polarize against the writers involved. As such, this essay is also a case study in strategic behavior, from a vantage point inspired by the late Pierre Bourdieu's analysis of literary fields.

Below, I first look more closely at various critical strategies common to the literary field under investigation here and relevant to my argument. After that, the bulk of the essay will be devoted to an overview of the practices of the Friday School and its clashes with the May Fourth-generation critics.

Republican-era literary thought and the notion of normative form

One of the reasons why the now canonical authors and critics of New Literature have been described as oppressive lies in the remarkable aggressiveness of their critical writings, particularly with respect to their critiques of more entertainment-oriented popular literature and culture. These critiques are often characterized by a total dismissal of the works or writers in question, and a lack of willingness to debate literary details. This *ad hominem* style of literary criticism remained common practice throughout the Republican period. This, in itself, is already sufficient to cast doubt on the dominant status of New Literature in its own time, since this style of criticism is not generally characteristic of any literary *establishment*, but rather of the avant-garde.

In modern European literary history, criticizing the establishment for having squandered its allegiance to purely literary values and *therefore* focusing one's critique of the establishment on non-literary issues and couching it in personal or abusive terms, is a recognized strategy in the quest for symbolic capital. As I have argued elsewhere,[3] the literary field of twentieth-century China was characterized by the fact that pledging allegiance to the symbolic principle meant to polarize oneself not only against the economic principle (writing for money) but also against the political principle (writing for some collective non-literary purpose).[4] Some of the earliest examples of attacks by New Literature critics on popular literature can be described in these terms. For instance, critics belonging to the Literary Association, when writing about the "Mandarin Ducks and Butterflies School" (*yuanyang hudie pai* 鴛鴦蝴蝶派), highlighted the commercial aspect of their practice, by referring to them as *wengai* 文丐 (beggars of letters) or *wenchang* 文娼 (whores of letters), rather than *wenren* 文人 (men of letters). Around the same time, the Creation Society's initial attacks on the Literary Association focused on the opponent's alleged factionalism (*dangtong fayi* 黨同伐異), arguing that the Association valued allegiance to its collective more than allegiance to literature. In both cases, the attacking side placed itself in the avant-garde position, claiming superior knowledge of and devotion to literature, while the opponent was regarded as the establishment that monopolized the means of literary production and distribution. However, whereas the debates between the Literary Association and the Creation Society eventually abated as the New Literature sphere developed and grew, the abusive criticism of entertainment fiction, or indeed any kind of literature deemed to cater too explicitly to a large readership, remained a constant element of modern Chinese literary criticism throughout the Republican period.

Apart from the commercial dimension, there was also a moral dimension to New Literature's differences with entertainment writing. After all, reaching a large readership as such was an ideal cherished by many groups within the New Literature community as well. Commercialism only became a serious problem, and a target for attack, if it was considered to be spreading moral values at odds with something I would call—for lack of a better word— modernity. Moreover, critics were convinced that there was a direct connection between writing and personality, very much in line with the critical ideals of traditional Chinese literature, as described by Stephen Owen:

> Throughout the Chinese literary tradition, as in certain phases of Western literature, readers identified the style or manner of the text with the personality of its author. Although current literary opinion considers such an identification misguided, the truth or falsity of the identification is less important than the fact that both readers and writer took it to be true. The powerful intuition of personality in style was a historical fact and a deeply held value.[5]

The New Literature critics, like their traditional predecessors, believed that the moral fiber of an author could be recognized in "the style or manner of the text." As a result, critical boundaries were drawn that precluded, *both on aesthetic and on moral grounds*, the continuity of, for instance, classical language and classical literary forms in modern writing. In poetry, to name but one example, there was to be no free verse in *wenyan* 文言 (literary Chinese), and no continued employment of classical Chinese prosodies in the way in which Western poets have always continued to use the sonnet. Within this critical mindset, New Literature is not synonymous with "modern literature," i.e., it is not an indicator of any and all literature of the modern period. Instead, New Literature of the Republican period is best described as a *ti* 體 or "normative form," i.e., one particular type of writing amongst other, rivaling types, and a type of writing that says something about the author's commitment to modernity as a whole (i.e., not merely aesthetic modernity). The boundaries of the normative form that is Republican-era New Literature are not easy to define. They do not just include aspects of vernacular (*baihua* 白話) language and Europeanized grammar, but also other textual aspects, such as punctuation, and even contextual aspects such as the style of the illustrations or advertisements printed around the text, and in some cases even the price of the publication. They also contain non-textual aspects—aspects of *habitus*—which are even harder to define, but will surface at various stages in this essay.

One way to help define the boundaries of the normative form is to study the reactions of adherents to that form when confronted with styles that were disrespectful of those boundaries, crossing borders between Old and New, elite and popular, and producing "incorrect" combinations of those various styles.[6] However, this does not mean that my study of the Friday School is ultimately only aimed at a better understanding of New Literature (although that is the overall perspective of my current research). Instead, I hope to demonstrate that the reverse perspective is equally applicable, and that Friday School writers and critics responded with similar outrage to what they considered to be the transgressions of their own norms. As will emerge in the conclusion of this essay, I consider the Friday School, despite all its similarities to popular literature and entertainment writing, to represent a coherent aesthetic alternative to New Literature, an alternative which valued personal rather than textual qualities and which, exactly for that reason, remains difficult for scholars and critics to accept.

Now, however, it is time to take a closer look at the writers, publications, and activities that I believe were associated with the Friday School.

The Friday School: journals and activities

Truth, Beauty and Goodness

Perhaps the earliest publication that has been associated with the Friday School is the journal *Zhen mei shan* 真美善 (Truth, beauty and goodness), edited by father and son Zeng Pu 曾樸 (1872–1935) and Zeng Xubai 曾虛白 (1895–1994) from 1927–1931. Starting out as a two-man publication, featuring in each issue an installment of the sequel to Zeng Pu's *Nie hai hua* 孽海花 (Flowers in a sea of sin), the journal gradually developed into a well-filled, semi-commercial magazine, with separate issues often running more than 200 pages. Mainly through the efforts of Zeng Xubai, the journal became more and more oriented toward writing (and translation) in the modern vernacular. The literary orientation of the group around the Zeng family has been described by Leo Ou-fan Lee as "Francophile," with most of its contributors having lived in France or being fascinated by French literature and art.[7] Despite their interest in aestheticism, decadence, and other cultural propensities that would seem to be limited to small cultural elites, the journal itself looks aimed at a much wider audience. The editors' interest in reader participation is demonstrated, for instance, by their establishment of a "readers' forum," and eventually even a "readers' club." Another important connection of the journal to more popular styles, and to the Friday School, is through their regular contributor Zhang Ruogu 張若谷 (1903?–1960?), who edited for the journal a hotly debated special issue on women writers, about which I will say more below.[8]

Tea Talk

A year or so after the folding of *Truth, Beauty and Goodness*, a somewhat similar group, also including a number of returned students from France, began holding meetings in Shanghai every Sunday under the name "Literature and Art Tea Talk Meeting" (*wenyi chahua hui* 文藝茶話會). After the seventh meeting, the group came out with its own journal, entitled *Wenyi chahua* 文藝茶話 (Literature and art tea talk; hereafter *Tea Talk*). The first editor of the journal was Zhang Yiping 章衣萍 (1902–1946), but his involvement with the group was relatively short-lived. From all accounts it appears that the three main motivators of the group, which continued to meet weekly and publish its journal monthly from 1932 to 1934, were Xu Zhongnian 徐仲年 (1904–1981), Hua Lin 華林 (1889–1980), and Sun Fuxi 孫福熙 (1898–1962). All three of them had studied in France, Hua and Sun specializing in art, whereas Xu obtained a Ph.D. in literature from the University of Lyon. Perhaps the most respected and revered member of the group, however, was the famous Liu Yazi 柳亞子 (1887–1958).

The Tea Talk meetings appear to have been relatively informal gatherings, where members could read or show new work to each other, engage in discussion, or give humorous speeches. Their critical statements about other members' work would be predominantly concerned with the personality and personal life of the author or artist. Although difficult to ascertain, it is likely that part of the content of the journal *Tea Talk* consisted of texts and reproductions of paintings produced during or for the meetings. In a few cases, records of meetings, illustrated with pictures, were also published in the journal.

Attendance to the meetings would vary, with one of the largest meetings probably being the 73rd tea talk of November 12, 1933, which was commemorated with an official group picture of the 34 participants, published in the December 1933 issue of the journal. A relatively large number of women would usually be present at the meetings, and the female membership of the Tea Talk group was certainly larger than that of any other literary group at the time.

The male members of the Tea Talks considered female presence part of the necessary atmosphere for their gatherings, and in their writings they often referred to the pleasure of having ladies (in most cases their partners)[9] present. The female presence was far from merely cosmetic, however, as many of the female participants were themselves active as writers and/or artists, and the contributions by female authors and artists to the journal *Tea Talk* were numerous and varied. Nevertheless, male members tended to emphasize gender issues in the context of the meetings, and their attitude towards the female members was one of lingering superiority, mixed with romantic-style gallantry and defiance of gender-related social conventions. As Wu Fuhui perceptively observes, however, the social critique was often a mere veneer for the urge to write about sex.[10]

Writing poetry was a favorite activity of many members of the group. The content of their journal features poetry in a wide variety of styles, ranging from traditional lyrics (*ci* 詞) to vernacular free verse. The April 1934 issue was devoted in full to the memory of the poet Liu Dabai 劉大白, who had died two years earlier and whose posthumous writings had been collected by another active member of the Tea Talk group, Zhong Jingwen 鍾敬文 (1903–2002). A number of the contributions to that issue point out Liu Dabai's interest in poetic form, and his ability to write in every possible style, including the new style, making his work in some sense exemplary for the aspirations of many of the members of the Tea Talk group.[11]

The group's prose writing, as found in the pages of its journal, is difficult to categorize under any single normative form, but appears relatively less indebted to tradition. Although the genre of *xiaopinwen* 小品文, favored by many contributors to the journal, was a genre with traditional roots, it was theorized in an article by Xu Zhongnian in relation to the modern genre of prose poetry.[12] Similarly, when Liu Yazi published a short autobiography in the journal, he pointed out that he had originally written something in the classical *xingshu* 行書 style, but had changed it into something more modern (in the vernacular) on the advice of his son. The journal also contained short fiction (mainly but not exclusively love stories), essays, and criticism, and some articles introducing members of the group to the readership. Apart from *Tea Talk*, another journal related to this group is *Yifeng* 藝風 (Art style) (1933–1936), which is very similar in appearance to *Tea Talk* and features many of the same contributors, but is almost exclusively devoted to art. Another related publication, which I have not consulted so far, is the *China Daily News* supplement, *Miluo zhoukan* 彌羅周刊 (Miluo weekly), edited by Hua Lin, Xu Zhongnian, Li Baoquan 李寶泉 and Tianlu 天盧 (ps. Huang Tianpeng 黃天鵬). The establishment of this supplement was advertised in the first issue of *Tea Talk*, under the slogan: "Elevate love through literature and art, beautify life through love" (*Yi wenyi tigao aiqing, yi aiqing meihua rensheng* 以文藝提高愛情, 以愛情美化人生). Finally, I have found scattered references to a newspaper supplement or journal entitled *Xiao gongxian* 小貢獻 (Little contribution), edited by Sun Fuxi, which may have contained further reports of Tea Talk meetings. The journal *Tea Talk* folded after two *juan* of ten issues each, in the early summer of 1934. In the final issue, Xu Zhongnian promised that something new and "big" would come in its place, but it is not clear what that was, and whether it ever materialized. Whether or not the Tea Talk meetings continued in Shanghai after the folding of the journal is also unclear.

The Chinese branch of the International PEN

Perhaps the most revealing example of how post-1949 canonization processes have completely reversed the original distribution of symbolic capital in the modern Chinese literary field, is the fact that the Chinese branch of the highly prestigious International PEN has sunk almost totally into academic oblivion. Fortunately, there now exists a superbly researched article by Chen Zishan 陳子善, which minutely details all the activities of the branch, and on which the cursory overview below is based.[13]

The first Chinese member of the International PEN was Liang Qichao 梁啟超, who was awarded an honorary membership in 1923. On November 16, 1930, however, an official Chinese PEN branch was established and henceforth represented at International PEN meetings in Europe. The first president of the branch was Cai Yuanpei 蔡元培, who was supported by Ge Gongzhen 戈公振 as secretary, and the famous poet Shao Xunmei 邵洵美 as treasurer.[14] The membership of the branch consisted by and large of literary figures associated with four better-known collectives, some of which were no longer in existence at the time. They were: the Literary Association (*Wenxue yanjiu hui* 文學研究會), represented by its former key members Zheng Zhenduo 鄭振鐸, Zhao Jingshen 趙景深, and Luyin 盧隱; the Crescent Moon society, represented by Xu Zhimo 徐志摩 and Hu Shi 胡適; the group around the journal *Lunyu* 論語 (The analects), most notably Lin Yutang 林語堂 himself; and the *Truth, Beauty and Goodness* group, including Zeng Pu and Zeng Xubai. The branch meetings were also attended by members of the Tea Talk group and others associated with the Friday School, including Wang Lixi 王禮錫, Zhang Kebiao, Zhang Ruogu, Zhang Yiping, Zeng Jinke 曾今可, and Yu Xiuyun 虞岫雲.

Before his untimely death in 1931, Xu Zhimo was the main motivator of the branch, and was even planning to publish a branch magazine. In accordance with its constitution, the branch held monthly dinner parties in Shanghai, and pledged not to discuss politics, an attitude that it maintained even after the Japanese invasion of Manchuria. Both its political stance and its practice of gathering at dinner parties were scorned by members of the League of Left-Wing Writers, which was founded in the same year and considered the branch a "bourgeois organization." When the branch entertained fellow PEN member George Bernard Shaw at dinner in February 1933, however, the chairman of the Left League, Lu Xun, did make an appearance, although his report of the event is highly satirical.[15] Between 1930–1933, the branch was relatively active in terms of social gatherings and entertaining foreign visitors. After 1933 it led a dormant existence until 1935, when it was briefly revived, again under the leadership of Cai Yuanpei, until the outbreak of the War of Resistance.

One of the most regular attendants of the Chinese PEN meetings in the early 1930s was Zeng Jinke,[16] whose career as a writer apparently took off as a direct result of his involvement with the branch, as is explained by Zeng himself in the preface to his first collection of short stories:

> Because members of the PEN must have published works, I cannot but force myself to print these few short stories. It's really a funny thing: the members of the PEN in all countries of the world have all joined after they had published works, but I have had no option but to publish this collection of short stories exactly because I have joined the PEN as a member.[17]

Apart from attending the meetings, Zeng also regularly reported on them in his journal *Xin shidai* 新時代 (The new era), the main journal associated with the Friday School.

Zeng Jinke and The New Era

It is somewhat of a mystery how precisely Zeng Jinke arrived on the literary scene in Shanghai, since biographical materials for the earlier part of his life are relatively scarce. In the late 1920s, he emerged in Shanghai as the manager of a short-lived publishing house called the Malaya Bookstore (*Malai shudian* 馬來書店). In the summer of 1931, he founded *The New Era Monthly*, published by the newly established New Era Bookstore.

The almost immediate success of *The New Era* on the Shanghai literary market was, in my view, due to Zeng Jinke's excellent ability to find the right "market niche" for his new publication. Zeng Jinke's introduction to the first issue announces contributions by two of the most popular New Literature authors of the time: Ba Jin 巴金 and Zhang Ziping 張資平. These two authors are now commonly seen as representing two very different, almost opposed, literary styles. However, Zeng appears to have been on good terms with both of them. He frequently quotes from correspondence with Ba Jin, or recounts meetings with him, in later issues of *The New Era*.[18] Zeng himself was a regular contributor to the journals associated with Zhang Ziping. Before long, *The New Era* published works by the majority of well-known authors on the Shanghai scene. *The New Era* also attracted authors associated with the "Beijing School," including Shen Congwen 沈從文, as well as rising stars like the poets Zang Kejia 臧克家, He Qifang 何其芳 and Bian Zhilin 卞之琳.

The core contributors to the journal, however, were the same figures from literature and art circles who also frequented the Tea Talk and PEN meetings. *The New Era* contributed significantly to establishing the public image of these writers, and of writers in general, not only by keeping its readers informed of their recent works, but also by providing extensive information on their personal lives in a monthly section in the back of each issue called "*Wentan xiaoxi*" 文壇消息 (News from the literary scene). This section of *The New Era* was usually some ten pages long and would contain a few dozen items. Such sections give a good indication of the extent to which literary figures had become objects of interest for a much wider audience than merely the intellectual elite. On the other hand, they also indicate that knowledge of writers' lives was considered necessary background knowledge for appreciating their works. After all, "Writers' news" sections were common in many New Literature journals: Mao Dun (then still using the name Shen Yanbing 沈雁冰) ran one in *The Short Story Monthly* in the 1920s, Shi Zhecun 施蟄存 had his *Yiwen qingbao* 藝文情報 (Art and literature intelligence) in *Xiandai* 現代 (*Les Contemporains*), and even a specialized publishing journal like *Zhongguo xin shu yuebao* 中國新書月報 (China new books monthly)

(1930–1932) devoted much space to news about writers. Although self-styled high-profile journals like *The Short Story Monthly* and *Les Contemporains* tended to limit their news to foreign literary scenes (copying, no doubt, from similar gossip columns in Western journals), in all journals the news reported is often of a personal nature and has little to do with the work of the author in question.

The personality-based view of literature, though rooted in traditional Chinese cultural dispositions, found a specifically modern and popular corollary in 1930s Shanghai, in the form of media interest in authors' private lives, tabloid journalism, and self-promotion. Although Zeng Jinke was skillful in dealing with these aspects of literary practice, it is important to emphasize that he and others in his group had more in common with the New Literature community than with any other literary communities. They certainly perceived themselves as practitioners of New Literature, and were initially perceived as such by others in the field. They had no interest in or associations with, and were at times critical of, the people and publications of the "Saturday School." The way in which Zeng Jinke criticized one such publication, the then recently founded journal *Hongye* 紅葉 (Red leaves), edited by Xu Xiaotian 許嘯天,[19] is not very dissimilar from the typical criticism of popular literature that we find in all New Literature journals:

> What kind of journal is *Red Leaves*? The facts will tell us. *The Saturday* and *Red Rose* were silly journals, so *Red Leaves* will surely be even sillier. The reason why it can exist and why it sells is that there are still many silly people in society: some businessmen, old wives and concubines, as well as some young gentlemen and misses, hoodlums and prostitutes. Those people are rooted in a certain era, so they love to read journals that are rooted in the same era. It is not surprising that they call *The New Era* a silly thing. So who is silly and who isn't? Justice will prevail in the end.[20]

There were other ways in which Zeng Jinke's style of running *The New Era* conformed with the seriousness that characterized the New Literature working style. Perhaps the strongest point of the whole enterprise was his very professional attitude towards the running of the journal. Already in the first issue, he issued a promise that *The New Era* would come out on the first of each month without any delays. This was the kind of promise made by countless new journals at the time, but one which very few indeed were able to keep. Zeng, however, did keep his promise, turning *The New Era* into one of the most consistently appearing, and one of the longest-lived journals of the early 1930s.[21] Zeng cleverly kept reminding his readers of this considerable achievement in various editorials throughout the period.

Zeng also seems to have had an excellent sense of the balance between literary and political forces needed to gain recognition within the New Literature community, i.e., he took care not to associate himself with any

political party or institution, but he did express concern for pressing political matters. For instance, he stated quite clearly in the opening editorial
of the first issue that *The New Era* had no political background and would
not serve the purposes of any "ism." However, in the fourth issue
(November 1931) he opened with a short comment on the Japanese invasion of Manchuria, blaming the Chinese government for its policy of
non-resistance, calling upon all Chinese citizens to unite and fight back. He
immediately added an apology to his readers for breaking with his principle of "not talking politics," expressing the hope that they would understand
and agree, which I am sure many of them did.

In short, Zeng Jinke was a very skillful editor, who turned *The New Era*,
with its attractive mix of serious and slightly less serious content, into a leading literary journal. As we have seen, however, Zeng was himself also a writer,
and he used his journal for relentless promotion of his own work, which he
was churning out at an incredible speed. After his first collection of short
stories, mentioned above, Zeng published five more collections of fiction, two
collections of new poetry, one collection of *ci* 詞 lyrics, and two volumes of
essays, within the space of exactly two years. His most successful work (both
in terms of sales figures and audience response) was probably the sentimental
poetry collection *Ai de sanbuqu* 愛的三部曲 (Love trilogy), which he claimed
to be based on a real, sad love affair. Zeng himself, however, appeared most
proud of his essay collection *Jinke suibi* 今可隨筆 (Jinke's random jottings),
because it was published by the prestigious Beixin bookstore and came out
almost simultaneously with new collections by Lu Xun and Bing Xin 冰心.
Not only did Zeng publish most of this work in his own journal, he was also
in the habit of printing rave reviews of his own collections, sent in by sym-
pathetic friends and readers, to which he would then respond with great
modesty. A typical example is his statement in the May 1933 issue of *The
New Era* that he will no longer publish any reviews of his own work—a
statement that comes appended as a postscript to *five* positive reviews of his
lyrics collection *Luohua* 落花 (Fallen flowers).[22]

Both Zeng's fondness of lyrics and his attempts at self-promotion eventually made him an object of criticism. The underlying reasons for the
attacks on Zeng in 1933 will be analyzed more closely in the next part of
this essay. First, however, there is one more journal left to introduce.

Literature and Art Forum

The journal *Wenyi zuotan* 文藝作談 (Literature and art forum) was founded
by Zeng Jinke in the summer of 1933, in the wake of a number of attacks
by various critics on his writings, but especially on his person. He also founded
a society by the same name, which was to meet fortnightly for dinner. In
the first issue of the journal, Zeng commented on the fact that the PEN
branch meetings had stopped, and described his new society as being of
a similar nature.[23] He listed the founders of the society, which included,

apart from familiar Friday School names, also Zhang Ziping, and even the famous Saturday School writer Hu Huaichen 胡懷琛 (1886–1938).[24]

Each issue of *Literature and Art Forum* numbered only sixteen pages, and the editing and printing do not come across as particularly professional. Part of the content of the journal is devoted to attacks on the League of Left-Wing Writers, especially on Lu Xun, about which more below. At the same time, however, the journal also contains a few relatively objective discussions of socialist literary theory and even of Soviet literature, written perhaps with the aim of challenging the Left League's monopoly on these topics. Of the four issues that appeared,[25] the most substantial is the third, a special issue on authors' lives, with contributions by, among others, Zhao Jingshen, Zang Kejia, and Luyin. The last appears to have been a member of the group, as she appears in a picture of a meeting of the society printed in the February 1934 issue of *The New Era*.[26]

It was the debate between the *Literature and Art Forum* writers and the Left League that served to identify the Friday School (or the "lyricists" [*ciren* 詞人] as they were also derisively called) as a group that could be collectively labeled. So far in this essay, I have also used that label, for the sake of convenience, in the same way in which scholars have in recent years continued to use the term *Mandarin Ducks and Butterflies fiction*, in full knowledge of the fact that it represents much more variety than the label can represent. Moreover, the label *Friday School*, if freed of its negative connotations, does capture nicely what I consider to be the main characteristic of the cultural figures and activities introduced in this section: the fact that they do not fit into any of the binary oppositions established by New Literature critics since the late 1910s. They belong neither completely to New Literature nor to any of its two main opposites—old literature and popular literature, which, in the minds of many New Literature critics, often amounted to the same thing. What the above overview also makes clear, however, is that the Friday School played a much more prominent role in modern Chinese cultural life than is nowadays assumed. When the Friday School clashed with the Left League, therefore, this was not a straightforward case of holders of symbolic power (like Lu Xun) putting some powerless marginal figures (like Zeng Jinke) in their place. Instead, it was an even-handed confrontation between two equally viable aesthetic alternatives, from which no clear "winner" could emerge at the time. In the next part of this essay, I will describe in some detail some of Zeng Jinke's activities, and the various criticisms thereof, in an attempt to further define the constitutive elements of the aesthetics that he represented, and that were later labeled as "Friday School."

Making (Girl-)Friends through Literature

Throughout the first two decades of New Literature, the normal strategy employed by new groups entering the literary field was that of polarization against the establishment, as it would be in most other literary fields. However, it is remarkable that throughout the 1920s and 1930s, this strategy is very consistently employed by numerous groups by invoking one particular concept, that of the Unknown Author (*wuming zuojia* 無名作家, literally "un-famous author" or "nameless author"). In countless manifestos, the Unknown Author is portrayed as an aspiring writer with much talent but few connections, whose eager attempts to get published are constantly frustrated by journal editors who are only interested in buying manuscripts from famous authors. Because of this unfair state of affairs within the publishing world, groups of unknown authors would eventually feel forced to start their own journal or even their own publishing house. They would call upon other victims of the system to join, leading to the establishment of special organizations and publications solely for unknown authors, such as, for instance, the Society of Unknown Authors (*wuming zuojia she* 無名作家社) and its journal *Wuming zuojia* 無名作家 (Unknown authors, founded 1923), together with the United Front of Unknown Authors (*wuming zuojia lianhe zhanxian* 無名作家聯合戰線), announced by the Progress Society (*Jin she* 進社) in its organ *Bailu* 白露 (White dew) throughout 1926 and 1927.

By the early 1930s, the plight of the Unknown Author had become an issue of debate in literary circles in Shanghai, taking the term beyond its initial strategic usefulness. There was widespread concern about the fact that the quality of the work of established authors was suffering under the pressures put on them by journal editors wanting to buy their manuscripts. There was also widespread acknowledgment of the fact that such editorial behavior violated principles of quality and made it difficult for newcomers without connections to publish work of potentially high quality. Many journals began to include specific statements in their colophons that they welcomed contributions by Unknown Authors. Zhang Ziping's journal *Jieqian* 潔茜 even went so far as to publish a special issue in which all contributions were published anonymously, challenging the reader to see if s/he could tell the difference between the works of Known and Unknown Authors.[27]

Zeng Jinke's way of dealing with these forces was perhaps even more inventive. In the same opening editorial for the first issue of *The New Era* in which he proudly announced contributions by many leading authors of the time, he emphasized that his journal would always welcome work sent in by Unknown Authors. A number of letters to the editor published in the next issue demonstrate how grateful many of his readers were for this acknowledgment. Zeng soon made good on this promise by announcing an "Unknown Authors Special Issue," which appeared as vol. 2, no. 1 in February 1932. He also promised prizes for the best contributions sent in for this issue. When the issue came out, a considerable number of Unknown Authors were published, but the "first prize" was not awarded, a clear indication that Zeng intended to be serious about the aspect of literary quality so central to the whole debate. The special issue also contained a dozen or so articles by well-known writers commenting on the problem. Interestingly, quite a few of these commentators, including Zeng himself, applied the label *Unknown Author* to *themselves*, which is a good illustration of its symbolic potential. In his opening comments to the special issue, Zeng Jinke wrote:

> I am not a famous person, nor have I ever wanted to possess fame, although I certainly do not lack ways of "becoming famous" and have also had opportunities to "become famous." I published quite a few works, but my works are as unknown as I am. Naturally I am still an Unknown Author, if I am allowed to call myself an Author at all.[28]

In the same piece, Zeng mentions that his works and the journals he published had been frequently criticized, but that those who abused (*ma* 罵) him in the past, much to his surprise, never pointed out what exactly was wrong with his works. To complicate matters even further, one of the journals in which he was scolded was a publication called *Wuming zuojia zhoukan* 無名作家週刊 (Unknown authors weekly).[29] All this creates the impression that, by the 1930s, the epithet *Unknown Author* had come to represent much more than just the newcomers in the literary field but was instead a coveted and contended source of power and recognition. Being unknown was one of the best ways to get known.[30]

Women writers

It is of course possible to regard all these attempts to discover new talent as nothing but a commercial ploy, aimed at creating the illusion that anyone could be a writer, with the ultimate goal of selling more magazines. However, invitations to Unknown Authors to contribute can be seen in so many magazines of the time that I tend to believe that there was a serious concern about the lack of successors to the famous May Fourth generation, as well as about the prolificacy of writers like Ba Jin and Shen Congwen (and the resulting uneven quality of their writing). Finally, I also detect a certain anti-elitism (for lack of a better word) among some members of the Shanghai literary community. As we have seen, many literary figures (especially, but not exclusively, in Zeng Jinke's circle) found great pleasure and satisfaction in getting involved in literature with a group of good friends, encouraging those who did not previously write to make their debuts as authors. Similarly, Unknown Authors contributing to their journals or salons were all seen as potential friends.

Older New Literature writers such as Lu Xun and Mao Dun, who had founded their careers on the opposition to "writing for money" and "writing as pastime," were suspicious of these ideals, and in their later attacks on Zeng Jinke they would often ridicule Zeng's style by preceding every personal name with the phrase *wo de pengyou* 我的朋友 (my friend). They were similarly suspicious of attempts by the Friday School to involve large numbers of women in their activities.[31] This had already become clear in the debate over the "Women Writers Issue" (*Nü zuojia hao* 女作家號) of the journal *Truth, Beauty and Goodness*. This special issue, which was edited by Zhang Ruogu, came out in February 1929 and sold 3,000 copies in one month, and another 10,000 in the following two years.[32] The special issue included works in various genres (mainly modern but also including classical poetry) by more than twenty women writers, including famous ones such as Bing Xin, Luyin, Wu Shutian 吳暑天, and Bai Wei 白薇. Every contribution was accompanied by a picture of the author in question, and it was this slightly frivolous touch that, among other things, sparked criticism from New Literature puritans. As Zhang Ruogu pointed out, most of the criticism was aimed at him personally, accusing him of selling sex for commercial gains, or, according to some, for personal favors from the women involved.[33] Most critics apparently claimed not to have bothered to read the contents of the special issues, a strategy which we will come across again below.[34]

Zeng Jinke from time to time ran into similar accusations. He, too, gave ample space in his journals to works by women writers. As was the case with the male members of the Tea Talk group discussed above, Zeng was inclined to draw attention to the gender of these writers, in sometimes ambiguous manners. For instance, Zeng was renowned for the way in which he promoted (*peng* 捧) the poetess Yu Xiuyun, the granddaughter of the rich comprador Yu Qiaqing (the owner of the Xiandai publishing house), whose name often appeared in his "writers' news" columns, always preceded by the honorific *nü shiren* 女詩人 ("The Poetess"). Her work also takes up the opening section of a collection entitled *Nü pengyoumen de shi* (Poems by my lady friends), edited and published by Zeng in 1932.[35] The kind of activities described above were frowned upon by the older generation of critics, but they did not launch into full-scale attack until Zeng violated perhaps the greatest taboo of the May Fourth period: attempting to establish a formal continuity between traditional and modern literature.

The liberation of the lyric

In February 1933, *The New Era* published a special issue devoted to the "liberation" of the time-honored poetic genre of the lyric. The genre had been making something of a comeback, especially among the participants in the Tea Talk meetings. The "movement for the liberation of the lyric" (*ci de jiefang yundong* 詞的解放運動), proudly announced and openly led by Zeng, was an attempt to breathe new life into the genre, by employing modern language and subject matter, while still writing according to the traditional prosodies. Whatever the merits of these ideas may have been, they soon became irrelevant to the critical debate, which came to center exclusively on the following New Lyric by Zeng Jinke:[36]

New Year Lyrics
[...]
(To the tune "Spring in the Ornate Chamber"[37])

A new year is beginning, the days are getting longer.
Guests arrive to comfort me in my despondency.
There is nothing wrong with having some diversion for a change.
We play some mah-jong.
We all drink up the wine in our glass.
Affairs of the state, who gives a damn?
In front of the wine-vessel there are red dresses, what great fortune!
But we must not lose our heads.

(To the tune "Song of Divination")

Winter is harsh in the Northeast.
Not warmer than here in the South.
Even the puppet state is at peace.
So why are the "Central Plains" in chaos?
"Parliament" has already convened.
Saving the nation has become an unsettled question.
The lords in session all get official titles.
Nobody cares about the national crisis![38]

The topic of the poem is clearly the political situation that had arisen after the Japanese invasion of Manchuria. If both poems are read together (as they should be in the *ci* tradition, which often works with contrasting pairs of poems), the correct patriotic stance of the author is, in my view, obvious.[39] The first attack on the poem, and on Zeng, that appeared in *Free Talk* only a few days later, was indeed unrelated to any political stance and clearly targeted aspects that can be subsumed under the notion of "normative form."

This first critic was Mao Dun, writing under the pseudonym Yangqiu 陽秋.[40] His review of the special issue of *The New Era*, in which Zeng's poems had appeared, was written as a mixture of satire and abuse. The critic pretended to be in total awe of the special issue, which had been lent to him by "my friend" Li Liewen 黎烈文 (the then-editor of *Free Talk*). He claimed to have read it from cover to cover—whilst burning incense and drinking tea—in the presence of his wife. This description, I presume, is a satirical reference to the entertainment practices and themes that were traditionally linked with the origins of the *ci* genre, about which more below. Emphasizing the unseemliness of a modern journal publishing classical poetry, Mao Dun added a sarcastic "(!)" to the title *The New Era*. He pretended especially to admire the above-mentioned poem by Zeng Jinke (referred to as "Mr Zeng XX"). Unable to maintain the satire near the end of his review, Mao Dun switched to direct abuse, closing his piece with a doggerel poem in which he addressed Zeng directly, in lines such as the following:

> The "era" is new but you hold on to the old,
> Who gives a damn, who gives a damn!
> 「時代」新了你守舊, 管他娘呢管他娘!

The review illustrates well, I think, the idea of normative form and how it links text and author. For Mao Dun, certain formal aspects of the style and language of Zeng's poem were sufficient to trigger associations with an entire lifestyle that fell outside the boundaries of modernity, was both conservative and immoral at the same time, and therefore did not deserve serious textual criticism, but only satire and abuse.

Zeng Jinke's rejoinder, published in the March 1933 issue of *The New Era*, is written in an equally ambivalent critical style. He, too, used an unfamiliar pseudonym,[41] Yangchun 陽春, based on Mao Dun's pen-name above. The opening pages of the four-page rejoinder, an open letter to Li Liewen, refrain from abusive arguments, as "Yangchun" points out that anyone would welcome serious criticism of the "liberated lyrics" and the underlying ideas, but that he fails to understand why *Free Talk* would publish such a malicious review. Closer to the end, however, he, too, loses control and inserts the following highly abusive passage:

> Mr Liewen! Perhaps it was because your beloved wife recently died of an illness, so that you were in low spirits, failed to pay proper attention, and published the manuscript of "your friend" just like that. However, this is going to harm your publication. Your beloved wife's soul up in heaven surely also hopes that you do a good job in editing *Free Talk* [...].[42]

Zeng, in his rejoinder, also referred to the fact that *Free Talk* had previously been an entertainment literature organ, therefore still had a "bad reputation" (*yichou* 遺臭; literally "lingering bad smell"), and that it was up to Li Liewen to change that. He ended with another reference to Li's deceased wife, stating that he hoped she would "bless and protect" him and help him to edit his supplement a bit better.

It is not surprising that the *Free Talk* critics were provoked by this rejoinder. Throughout March 1933, six more reviews of Zeng's liberation of the lyric movement appeared in *Free Talk*, some of them with added postscripts by "Yangqiu." There also appeared one amusing reaction by Lu Xun, a short piece entitled "*Qu de jiefang*" 曲的解放 (The liberation of the ballad), being a satirical imitation of Zeng's poem which, however, did not attack Zeng, but rather, like Zeng's poem, commented on the Manchuria crisis. Half of the reviews contained statements to the effect that the reviewer had not read the special issue, but only the poems cited by Mao Dun in his original review. One of the reviewers making such a statement was in fact Mao Dun himself, this time using his well-known pseudonym Xuan 玄,[43] even though in his previous review he had stated that he had read the issue from cover to cover.

Not all of these six reviews employed the kind of abusive rhetoric seen in the first exchange. Some of the critics took up "the issues" with Zeng as he had requested, pointing out plagiarism of traditional poetry in his lyrics and those of Zhang Yiping, who had recently published a collection of lyrics.[44] The most perceptive and serious review of all, also the last one in the series, was written by Cao Juren 曹聚仁, who did not use a pseudonym. Cao pointed out that Zeng's statement that his liberation of the *ci* was a necessary follow-up on Hu Shi's 1917 liberation of the *shi* 詩 (poetry) was critically untenable, because the lyric, as a genre of poetry (*shi*), was part of what Hu Shi had already liberated. Instead, Cao argued, by writing lyrics containing vulgar language like Zeng had done, he was taking the genre back to its folk-song origins, thereby restricting, rather than enlarging, its literary potential. Cao's conclusion, however, made it clear that he considered any revival of the lyric, in whatever form, to be in conflict with the demands of modern times: the genre had had its moment of glory, and there was no reason to unearth its already buried remains.[45]

The attacks of the *Free Talk* critics on Zeng Jinke's special issue on the liberation of the lyric were, in my view, not related to any particular political conflict, even though most *Free Talk* writers were leaning towards the left while Zeng may have had some ties with the Guomindang authorities. There are certainly no references whatsoever to politics in any of the reviews. Instead, I believe that the style of criticism and the issues raised prove that the attacks were occasioned by what was perceived as the conservative and vulgar nature of Zeng's poems, i.e., by moral-aesthetic issues triggered by the form and language of his infamous "New Year Lyrics," especially by the line "Affairs of the state, who gives a damn?" and by the reference to "playing mah-jong." Paradoxically, though, the perceived transgression of the boundaries of decency reverberates strongly with age-old prejudices against the genre of the lyric and its practitioners.[46] This observation only serves to emphasize the ambiguities inherent in these reviewers' responses. They were clearly thrown into confusion when confronted with writers or texts that could not be fitted easily into existing categories and flaunted the boundaries between New and Old, between elite and popular, and between text and author. As a result, their response was a mixture of facile dismissal and attempts at serious criticism.

Aftermath: a turn to the political

Most orthodox histories of modern Chinese literature, if they mention Zeng Jinke at all, tell us that his reputation was irreparably damaged as a result of the *Free Talk* reviews of his lyrics. This is simply not true, and can be refuted by reading the most orthodox source of all: the collected works of Lu Xun.

The postscript to Lu Xun's essay collection *Wei ziyou shu* 偽自由書 (Writings of false freedom), published in October 1933, contains a very long (re)construction of public literary events from that year, including many long quotations from various Shanghai papers.[47] Lu Xun asserts that Zeng Jinke's launch of the journal *Literature and Art Forum* in July 1933 was an attempt to engage in a collective counterattack on the *Free Talk* writers. Lu Xun singles out the article "*Neishan shudian xiaozuo ji*" 內山書店小作記 (Record of a short visit to the Uchiyama Bookstore) by a certain Bai Yuxia 白羽遐 (possibly another pen-name of Zeng Jinke), in which the owner of the Uchiyama Bookstore, a close friend of Lu Xun's, was accused of being a Japanese spy, implicating Lu Xun by association. The next piece Lu Xun quoted was a reaction to Bai Yuxia's article, by a certain Gu Chunfan 谷春帆 (possibly another pen-name of Mao Dun), published in *Free Talk*. Gu severely scolded Zeng Jinke for "threatening and hurting people," "creating harmful gossip," and "betraying his friends." This was, perhaps, the first time that a political aspect entered the discussion, though not an ideological one: by associating Lu Xun with the illegal activity of spying for the Japanese, for which one could well be arrested by the authorities, the author of the offending article was introducing an element of terror into the literary debate.

Gu also referred to Zeng Jinke's quarrel with another Shanghai writer, Cui Wanqiu 崔萬秋.[48] Lu Xun explained that there were two reasons for this quarrel: first, Zeng Jinke had published parts of a letter from Cui as a preface to his own collection of poems; second, Zeng had apparently published a "writers' news" item in a small Shanghai paper in which he mentioned Cui's address and his political affiliation, which, according to Lu Xun, could have gotten Cui arrested and was done deliberately to terrorize him.

Gu Chunfan's article further criticized Zhang Ziping, who had also been a target of attack by the *Free Talk* group, and called for "banning" (*quzhu* 驅逐) both Zhang and Zeng from the literary scene, claiming that they were ill-behaved men of letters (*wenren wuxing* 文人無行). Lu Xun, in two essays commenting on the concept of "ill-behaved literati," made it clear that he did not wish to include either Zhang or Zeng under the category "men of letters."[49] Instead, he suggested, they belonged to a category of former men of letters who had already changed careers (*wenren gaihang* 文人改行). The second of the two pieces contains a particularly vicious attack on the two, lacking much of Lu Xun's usual satire, indicating that the "grand old man" had truly been angered. He wrote that Zhang and Zeng had reverted to racketeering, having realized that their "masturbation fiction" (*shouyin xiaoshuo* 手淫小說) and "who gives a damn lyrics" (*guantaniang ci* 管他娘詞) were eventually not going to take them much further in their quest for fame and money.

Both *Literature and Art Forum* and *The New Era* responded with a number of articles abusing Lu Xun and calling him "a mad old dog." Lu Xun published at least two more essays in which he ridiculed Zeng Jinke. In the first of the two pieces he even linked him (without evidence) to the Guomindang and to political assassinations. Around the same time (summer 1933) Zeng Jinke, attacked from all sides and apparently no longer interested in fighting back, published a statement announcing his retreat from the literary scene,[50] although he continued to edit *The New Era* until February 1934, revived the journal briefly in 1937, and edited a number of other journals after 1945 in Taiwan.[51]

Instead of drawing the seemingly obvious conclusion that Zeng Jinke, despite putting up a brave fight, was eventually bullied into silence by the literary establishment of the May Fourth generation, I would like to put forward two details that might shed a different light on the whole debate.

First, judging by Zeng Jinke's various articles about the debate, including some of his contributions to *Literature and Art Forum*, and his final public statement, his decision to leave the literary scene was more likely a result of his quarrel with Cui Wanqiu. Zeng had considered Cui a friend, and felt betrayed when Cui started attacking him. This took place shortly after the first issue of *Literature and Art Forum*, in which Cui is still listed as co-founder, had been published. Only days later, Zeng published his first announcement that he was planning to leave the literary scene.[52]

Second, months before Zeng Jinke silenced himself, the *Free Talk* critics had also silenced themselves, as the supplement, in May 1933, openly abandoned its provocative stance (which is why Lu Xun spoke of "false freedom"), and announced a return to "talking about wind and moon" (*tan fengyue* 談風月). As a result, Lu Xun's first attack on Zeng Jinke was actually never published, leaving only three published attacks, all from around the time that Zeng was already considering throwing in the towel. In other words, the politicized aftermath of the debate was but a short-lived excess, remembered mainly because of Lu Xun's writings and their impact on later historiography. The main substance of the debate over the liberation of the lyric revolved around moral-aesthetic, not political issues. Moreover, the debate did not lead to the downfall of Zeng Jinke, which was brought about mainly by a simultaneously occurring personal conflict. The debate did certainly not do any damage to the Friday School and the aesthetic values it represented, for those values, as we have seen, were extremely widespread. But is the observation that they were widespread and that they were opposed by members of what we now believe to be the cultural elite of the 1930s sufficient to conclude that the Friday School was historically part of "popular culture"?

Conclusion

It seems to me that the fervor and downright nastiness with which both sides entered into the debate over the liberated lyrics was the result of a shared, rather than a differing, opinion. For Mao Dun, Zeng Jinke's lyrics are reminiscent of traditional literary practices with a bad moral reputation; for Zeng Jinke, Mao Dun's review is reminiscent of the "lingering bad smell" of the old *Free Talk*. Both critics crossed the boundaries of common decency because the opposing party was not considered to deserve a decent critical treatment. Both critics reacted in this way because they adhered to the notion of normative form, according to which *ad hominem* criticism can never be ruled out. Mao Dun's normative form revolved around a virtually total rejection of formal continuity within literary modernity, Zeng Jinke's around the exact opposite. Both considered themselves to represent the values of the literary establishment, while suspecting the other side of being politically motivated. Later canonization has pushed Zeng Jinke and his style to the margins of modern Chinese literature, to a space that vaguely represents the opposite of "serious" culture—popular culture, perhaps—and that we are now beginning to unveil.

Viewed from a historical perspective, however, it is not entirely accurate to say that the styles I have been discussing in this essay were part and parcel of popular culture. On the contrary, I believe to have demonstrated that they were part and parcel of an elite culture, with activities involving literary figures and groups often considered to be entirely unrelated, ranging from Zhang Ziping to Xu Zhimo, from Hu Huaichen to Hu Shi, and from Tea Talk meetings to the International PEN. These styles pertain not so much to literary texts as such but rather to the aesthetic function of literary texts, incorporating elements of *enjoyment* and *sociability* that are incommensurate with both the socialist and the modernist view of literature, and have therefore seldom been recognized in scholarship applying theories based on those views. And even in current scholarship, employing theories that do allow us to recognize these styles, it is not easy to take them beyond the opposition between elite and popular.

What these styles represent is an aesthetic that treasures literature for its ability to create intimacy or stimulate friendship, in line with classical ideals, while simultaneously reveling in the opportunities for self-expression or self-exposure offered by the phenomenon of modern print culture, as well as in the modern erosion of some (certainly not all) restrictions on contact between members of the opposite sex. The combination is an awkward one for anyone used to finding the value of writing predominantly in texts and can easily lead to a wholesale dismissal of this aesthetic as either "outdated" or "insipid," again pushing the subject into the popular sphere. In doing so, however, one would ignore the challenge that this aesthetic poses to the familiar values of New Literature, which have made it so difficult, especially in poetry, to entertain the thought of formal continuity within modernity. The New Literature normative form was built, after all, on a set of assumptions and oppositions that made it possible to relegate anything that was "old" in form either to the realm of the academic, where it could be studied, or to the realm of popular entertainment, where it could be abused. But in the actual practice of the Republican period, the New Literature normative form was not nearly so dominant, or so straightforward. New Literature certainly never reached a status that enabled it to simply *ignore* people like Zeng Jinke. Not even Lu Xun reached such a status. People like Zeng Jinke, and styles like those of the Friday School, were in fact much less outdated or insipid than they appear now. They represented an alternative aesthetic disposition with high symbolic value, available to anyone willing to read not only the text, but also the context.

Notes

Various parts of this essay appear in Chapters 3 and 7 of Michel Hockx, *Questions of Style: Literary Societies and Literary Journals in Modern China: 1911–1937* (Leiden: Brill Academic Publishers, 2003), and I am grateful to Brill Academic Publishers for granting permission to include the present essay in this volume. I would also like to thank the editors of the present volume for providing me with very helpful comments to show the relevance of the materials presented here to the study of popular literature.

1 See Heinrich Fruehauf, "Urban Exoticism in Modern and Contemporary Chinese Literature," in Ellen Widmer and David Der-wei Wang, eds., *From May Fourth to June Fourth: Fiction and Film in Twentieth-Century China* (Cambridge: Harvard University Press, 1993), 133–165; Leo Ou-fan Lee, *Shanghai Modern: The Flowering of a New Urban Culture in China, 1930–1945* (Cambridge: Harvard University Press, 1999); Jonathan Hutt, "*La Maison d'Or*—the Sumptuous World of Shao Xunmei," *East Asian History* 21 (June 2001), 111–142.

2 I am not certain when and where the term was first used, but it appears in Lu Xun's and others' writing for *Free Talk* around the time the debates discussed below were taking place.

3 Michel Hockx, "Introduction," in Michel Hockx, ed., *The Literary Field of Twentieth-Century China* (Honolulu: University of Hawaii Press, 1999), 1–20.

4 The relevance of this analytical model for describing the underlying forces at work in twentieth-century Chinese literary practice was recently confirmed by Nobel Prize winner Gao Xingjian 高行健, who, in an interview with the German daily *Die Welt*, when asked what the Prize meant to him, replied: "With this prize it is recognized that I write neither to make money nor to serve a political power" (*Die Welt* online, October 14, 2000).

5 Stephen Owen, *Readings in Chinese Literary Thought* (Cambridge: Harvard University Press, 1992), 63.

6 In an article from 2000, I examined the case of Liu Bannong 劉半農, a border-crossing literary figure from an earlier decade. See Michel Hockx, "Liu Bannong and the Forms of New Poetry," *Journal of Modern Literature in Chinese* 3: 2 (2000), 83–117.

7 Lee, *Shanghai Modern*, 20.

8 For more on Zhang Ruogu, see Lee, *Shanghai Modern*, 20–23. For an elaborate treatment of the whole coterie around Zeng Pu, see Fruehauf, "Urban Exoticism." The debate around the women writers special issue and Zhang Ruogu and Zeng Pu's views on women's writing are treated at length in a Ph.D. dissertation by Maria af Sandeberg (SOAS).

9 For a more detailed study of "literary couples" of this period, see Raoul Findeisen, "From Literature to Love: Glory and Decline of the Love-Letter Genre," in Hockx, *The Literary Field of Twentieth-Century China*, 79–112.

10 Wu Fuhui 吳福輝, *Dushi xuanliu zhong de haipai xiaoshuo* 都市旋流中的海派小説 (Shanghai school fiction in the maelstrom of the metropolis) (Changsha: Hunan jiaoyu chubanshe, 1995), 72.

11 Similarly, the group's interest in art was not restricted to traditional landscape painting but included modern art and foreign art. There was also some direct exchange with foreign art circles. The 87th Tea Talk meeting, held on February 18, 1934 and recorded in the March 1934 issue of *Tea Talk*, was devoted to a visit by the Italian artist Carlo Zanon.

12 Xu Zhongnian 徐仲年, "*Lun xiaopinwen* 論小品文" (About *xiaopinwen*), *Wenyi chahua* 文藝茶話 (Literature and art tea talk), j. 2, no. 3 (October 1933): 20.

13 Chen Zishan 陈子善, *Wenren shi* 文人事 (Literati affairs) (Hangzhou: Zhejiang wenyi chubanshe, 1998), 404–451.

14 For more on Shao Xunmei, see Lee, *Shanghai Modern*, 241–257; and Hutt, "*La Maison d'Or.*"

15 Lu Xun 鲁迅, *Lu Xun quanji* 鲁迅全集 (Lu Xun's collected works) vol. 4, (Beijing: Renmin wenxue chubanshe, 1981), 494–499.

16 For more on Zeng Jinke, see Chapter 6 in Hockx, *Questions of Style*.

17 Zeng Jinke, *Xiaoniao ji* 小鳥集 (A small bird) (Shanghai: Xin shidai shuju, 1933), 161.

18 In a picture in *Xin shidai* 新時代 (The new era) 2: 5/6 (December 1932) of Ba Jin is shown participating in one of the Tea Talk meetings, seated next to Zeng Jinke.

19 Xu Xiaotian (Xu Zehua 許澤華, 1886–1946?) was an active contributor to and editor of literary and political journals during the early Republican period (i.e., before the May Fourth), including the well-known pre-May Fourth women's literature magazine *Meiyu* 眉語 (Eyebrow talk), of which his partner Gao Jianhua 高剑華 was the main editor.

20 See the editor's postscript in *Xin shidai yuekan* 新時代月刊 (The new era monthly) 1: 5 (December 1931), 165.

21 Five *juan* of six issues each were published between August 1931 and December 1933. Two more issues appeared in January–February 1934. The journal was revived briefly in 1937. Each issue was over 150 pages, some special issues even over 300 pages. As far as I know, of the 1930s literary journals only *Les Contemporains* and *The Analects* had a longer life-span.

22 *Xin shidai yuekan* 4: 4/5 (May 1933), 289.

23 See the "*Wentan xiaoxi*" 文壇消息 (News from the literary scene) section, written by Zeng under his little-known pseudonym Yunshang 雲裳, in *Wenyi zuotan* 1: 1 (July 1933), 15–16. For confirmation that Yunshang is indeed Zeng's pseudonym, see Zeng Jinke, *Xiaoniaoji*, 187–188.

24 The label *Saturday School writer* does not do justice at all to Hu Huaichen, a fascinating traditionalist poet and theorist who consistently argued in favor of continuity of traditional literary forms, and who was something of a nemesis to many New Literature critics. Although his ideas are related to some of the themes addressed in this essay, they deserve more attention than can be given to them in the current context.

25 I have only seen the first three issues, but reference works claim that a fourth issue did appear.

26 If the picture in question was a recent one, it means that the society may have continued to meet long after the journal folded.

27 *Jieqian* 1: 2 (September 1932). This information is based on advertisements in other journals and references in bibliographies. I have not seen this journal, of which only two issues came out.

28 Zeng Jinke, "*Weishenme yao chu wuming zuojia zhuanhao*" 為甚麼要出無名作家專號? (Why publish a special issue on unknown authors), *Xin shidai yuekan* 2: 1 (1932), 1–10, 9.

29 Unfortunately I have been unable to consult this journal.

30 Shortly after he brought out his Unknown Authors special issue, Zeng Jinke announced the establishment of a new journal, *Wenyi zhi you* 文藝之友 (Friends of literature and art), edited by a society he founded, called the Friends of Literature Society (*wenyou she* 文友社). Every issue of that journal contained a special section, called "*Women de quantou*" 我們的拳頭 (Our fists), in which Unknown Authors sought out shortcomings in the works of Known Authors. Zeng Jinke managed to run and publish both journals for a year or so, despite the fact that many of the Known Authors writing for *The New Era* were attacked in *Friends of Literature and Art*.

31 This did not mean, however, that women writers were identified as a special category of Unknown Authors needing extra encouragement. Although there were quite a few women writers among the contributors to Zeng Jinke's special issue for Unknown Authors, the category itself was presented as genderless. I am grateful to Jeesoon Hong for drawing my attention to this distinction.

32 For the sales figure of the special issue, see its colophon. I am indebted to Hanno Lecher of the Library of the Institute of Chinese Studies at Heidelberg for providing me with a copy of this source.

33 For Zhang Ruogu's overview of the debate, which includes a list of some thirty reviews of the special issue, see Zhang Ruogu 張若谷, "*Guanyu 'Nü zuojia hao'*" 關於‘女作家號’ *Zhen mei shan* 真美善 4: 1 (May 1929), 1–24.

34 For a further example and discussion of this phenomenon, see Thomas Bärthlein, "'Mirrors of Transition': Conflicting Images of Society in Change from Popular Chinese Social Novels, 1908 to 1930," *Modern China* 25: 2 (April 1999), 204–228, 220.

35 Information based on Jia Zhifang 賈植芳, et al., eds., *Zhongguo xiandai wenxue zong shumu* 中國現代文學總書目 (Full contents of modern Chinese literature) (Fuzhou: Fujian jiaoyu chubanshe, 1993), 44. I have not seen this collection, which Zeng edited under the pseudonym Yunshang.

36 I should add that most present-day reference works and overview histories of modern Chinese literature also limit their treatment of Zeng Jinke and his journal to this one poem and the ensuing incident. No matter what one thinks of Zeng's own writing, this dismissive treatment by literary historians is deplorable, because it has led to the almost total neglect of his journal *The New Era*, and its important position on the literary scene of the early 1930s.

37 The English translations of the two tune-titles are taken from Appendix A in Kang-i Sun Chang and Haun Saussy, *Women Writers of Traditional China: An Anthology of Poetry and Criticism* (Stanford: Stanford University Press, 1999).

38   新年詞抄
        [...]
        畫堂春
        一年開使日初長，客來慰我凄涼。偶然消遣本無妨，打打麻將。都喝乾杯中酒，國家事管他娘。樽前猶幸有紅妝，但不能狂！
        卜算子
        東北正嚴寒，不比江南暖；偽國居然見太平，何以「中原」亂？「全會」亦曾開，救國成懸案；出席諸公盡得官，國難無人管！
        [...]

39 This, too, has been totally obscured by most later reference works and histories, which tend to quote only the first poem.

40 Yangqiu 陽秋 (Mao Dun 茅盾) "*Du 'ci de jiefang yundong zhuanhao' hou gong gan*" 讀‘詞的解放運動專號’後恭感 (Respectful feelings after reading "The special issue on the liberation of the lyric"), *Ziyou tan*, February 7.

41 So unfamiliar in this case that it has never been positively identified as his pen-name. Comparing the language and style of the piece to other writings by Zeng, however, I am quite positive that he was the author.
42 Yangchun 陽春 [Zeng Jinke?], "Yu Shenbao *Ziyou tan bianzhe Li Liewen xian-sheng shu*" 與申報自由談編者黎烈文先生書 (Open letter to Mr. Li Liewen, the editor of *Shenbao*'s *Free Talk*), *Xin shidai* 4: 3 (1933), 51–54, 53.
43 Xuan 玄 [Mao Dun], "*Hebi 'jiefang'*" 何必解放 (Why bother liberating), *Ziyou tan*, March 10, 1933.
44 The sources seem to indicate that his collection, entitled *Kan yue lou ci* 看月樓詞 (Lyrics of moon-watch mansion), was published in 1932 with the Women's Bookstore (*Nüzi shudian* 女子書店), which was co-managed by Zhang's partner Wu Shutian. However, the collection is not listed in Jia Zhifang 1993.
45 Cao Juren 曹聚仁, "*Ci de jiefang*" 詞的解放 (The liberation of the lyric), *Ziyou tan*, March 16, 1933.
46 I am indebted to Haun Saussy for providing me with this crucial insight. See also Kang-I Sun Chang and Haun Saussy, *Women Writers of Traditional China* (Stanford: Stanford University Press, 2000), 4–5.
47 Lu Xun, *Lu Xun quanji*, vol. 5, 152–188.
48 On Cui Wanqiu, another forgotten writer of this period, see Wu Fuhui, *Dushi xuanliu zhong de haipai xiaoshuo*, 68–69.
49 Lu Xun, *Lu Xun quanji*, vol. 5, 176–178; and vol. 8, 354–356.
50 There are various versions of this Zeng Jinke qishi 曾今可啟事 (Announcement by Zeng Jinke). The longest I have seen was published on the backcover of *Wenyi zuotan* 1: 3 (August 1933).
51 Lu Xun, *Lu Xun quanji*, vol. 5, 219–221 and 274–276.
52 Cf. Lu Xun, *Lu Xun quanji*, vol. 5, 175–176.

2 Professional anxiety, brand names, and wild chickens: from 1909

Alexander Des Forges

How does an author become a professional? Historians of twentieth-century Chinese media and culture have over the last few decades provided detailed studies of the social and institutional contexts within which certain writers began to earn a living from their fiction and journalism: the family backgrounds of these newly professional authors, the schooling that they received, the publishers that they worked for, the newspapers and magazines in which their work was often published, the transformations of publishing practice after the institution of copyright law, and the new groups of readers that consumed their work in the 1920s and 1930s.[1] And as Perry Link has shown, the rhetorics of the "man of letters" (*wenren* 文人) and the "genius of the foreign mall" (*yangchang caizi* 洋場才子), who claimed to be above writing for money, flourished from the 1910s forward, drawing heavily from the romantic tradition of misunderstood *caizi* 才子 (genius, or man of talent) in Chinese literature.[2] There has been rather less attention, however, to the process through which the author is imagined as a *professional*, one who writes regularly and prolifically for compensation. This chapter investigates the formation of the figure of the professional author within the fictional narratives that those authors themselves produced, in order to demonstrate how a social role can be proposed in literary texts and subsequently adapted as a norm according to which social practice can be organized. How does this figure of the professional author relate to the growing significance of the authorial name as a brand name in the early Republican period? What are the reasons for readers' continued interest in the narratives that this kind of author produced? I aim to show, first, the anxieties inherent in the professional author's attempt at self-definition; second, the mediating role that the successful professional author plays between concepts of capital and labor; and, finally, how the particular kind of readerly desire arising from the installment publication format constitutes the necessary foundation without which the professional author would be a far less significant cultural figure.

Novelists and newspapermen

When Li Meibo, one of the central characters in Lu Shi'e's 陸士鄂 (1878–1944) novel, *Xin Shanghai* 新上海 (New Shanghai, 1909), arrives unexpectedly at the narrator's house on the opening page, the narrator is *editing a novel* that he has written.[3] And this is not his only work of fiction; when Li enters the narrator's study, he catches sight of two completed manuscripts, which he leafs through with great interest: *Fengliu daotai* 風流道台 (A stylish circuit intendant) and *Xin Niehai hua* 新孽海花 (New *Flowers in a Sea of Sin*). Manuscripts showing up within novels is nothing new: their mysterious appearance is a technique first used in *Honglou meng* 紅樓夢 (Dream of the red chamber) and elaborated upon in the best-known novels about courtesans through the nineteenth century. These manuscripts within novels play a central role in the imagination of the author as a recognizable fictional character decades before writers of fiction gained widespread social attention.[4] But each of these previous cases subscribed to the ideology of the novel as a masterpiece, a singular outpouring of all the emotions, perceptions, and experiences that one uniquely qualified individual had gained in the course of a lifetime—each author could be expected to have only one book in him (or her). Even as late as Wu Jianren's 吳趼人 *Ershi nian mudu zhi guai xianzhuang* 二十年目睹之怪現狀 (Strange events eyewitnessed over the last two decades, 1903–1910), the narrative is meant to be the complete recollections of one individual, to be shared with those who can respond to it appropriately.

In *New Shanghai*, by contrast, at least four manuscripts make their appearance and we are told of twenty more by the narrator that have been published—it is strongly implied that the narrator derives at least part of his living from writing these works.[5] In the final chapter, he reveals his most recent project to his friends Li Meibo and Shen Yifan; they are the two characters around which he has organized his newest work, *New Shanghai*. Inasmuch as *New Shanghai* shows us novel writing as a routine practice in a specific social context, rather than as a heartfelt life task that aims to transcend the ages, it presents the readers with an image of the *professional* writer of fiction. The parallel with the new dynamic of artistic fame that developed in Shanghai two or three decades earlier is intriguing. Prior to the 1870s, the *huagao* 畫稿 (artist's sketchbooks) were considered a trade secret, meant to be passed on only to his or her students or assistants, a conception of the book as treasure that circulates only among trusted associates that is quite similar to the long vernacular fiction of the Ming and Qing. By the turn of the century, however, lithographic reproductions of artists' sketchbooks were sold openly, staking the painter's claim to fame through publicity rather than through secrecy.[6] In both cases, cultural authority is redefined as a consequence of regular appeals to a wide audience.

This image of the professional writer is not, however, without its stresses and strains. Early in the first chapter of *New Shanghai*, for example, the reader is abruptly introduced to a newspaperman, Jia Minshi (a homonym for "Fake Gentleman of Renown"), who is obnoxiously self-important, ignorant, and always out for himself. Even his table manners are bad: he is not only greedy, but also omnivorous, and the narrator feels called upon to describe his gluttony in excessive and satirical detail. Such a broad caricature so early in the novel is no accident. The earliest writers of installment fiction were also newspapermen, working as columnists, reporters, editors, and in the case of Han Bangqing 韓邦慶 (author of *Haishang hua liezhuan* 海上花列傳 [Lives of Shanghai flowers, 1892–1894]), Li Boyuan 李伯元 (author of *Guanchang xianxing ji* 官場現形記 [The bureaucrats] and probable author of *Haitian hong xueji* 海天鴻雪記 [A Shanghai swan's tracks in the snow, 1899]), and Wu Jianren (author of *Strange Events Eyewitnessed over the Last Two Decades* and probable author of *Haishang mingji sida jin'gang qishu* 海上名妓四大金剛奇書 [The four heavenly kings of Shanghai: a marvelous tale, 1898]), as publishers as well.[7] We can see the importance of this link not only in the publication of fiction in installments alongside or within newspapers edited by authors, but also in the effect that the narrative structure first implemented in Shanghai fiction had on the format of tabloid newspaper gossip columns in the early 1900s.[8]

By the early 1920s, however, the professional writer of fiction (or editor of a literary magazine) was quite distinct from the reporter. The year 1909 represents a key moment in this process of disassociation; at this point, vernacular fiction was still associated primarily with newspapers, even as fiction magazines began to appear as a separate genre.[9] Though authors of vernacular fiction and newspapermen might already have started to think of themselves as members of separate professions, the distinction would most likely have been very unclear to the reading public. As one writer noted in 1925, "the value (*shenjia* 身價) of professional writers [in previous decades] was not as high as today"; the use of *shenjia*, a powerful term that loses much of its force in translation, highlights the importance of self-definition for the early twentieth century author.[10] In *New Shanghai*, newspapermen are repeatedly satirized as pretenders to literati detachment and/or reformist zeal who are in fact concerned only with turning a profit.[11] In his appetite for everything (barely leaving bones on the plate) Jia Minshi represents not only a type of social conduct to be disdained, but also, more significantly, an approach to literary production that must be relegated to a subordinate position.[12] It was of vital importance to writers of fiction in this period to establish themselves not as indiscriminate collectors and recyclers of anecdotes, but rather as producers of texts with aesthetic and moral value; yet at the same time, it is a newspaperman who is assigned to tell us that the narrator should be considered "a great novelist" (*da xiaoshuo jia* 大小說家), a paradoxical "acquiescence" that reminds us of Pierre Bourdieu's analysis of "cultural goodwill" and its role in the maintenance of twentieth-century French status distinctions.[13]

In eighteenth- and nineteenth-century Europe, the novel rose steadily in the hierarchy of literary genres in part due to Romanticist rhetorics of originality and creativity as central components of literary "genius." As late as the 1890s, we find British authors like Walter Besant maintaining that fiction is the nearly inalienable property of its creator, and that the publisher's role is solely to function as a hired agent in service to the author in distributing his or her text and collecting the ensuing profits more efficiently.[14] No matter that this formulation is absolutely contradicted by the material circumstances under which books are produced in turn-of-the-century Britain; the rhetoric remains important as a means of moving fiction up the hierarchy of aesthetic genres during this period and of distinguishing it from other sorts of writing that it was initially held to resemble.

Despite the enormous influence that European literature had in certain circles in early twentieth century China, not to mention the indigenous discourse of the author of fiction that grew up over the course of the nineteenth century, the emphasis on the fundamental tie between a creative author and his or her original work so important in Victorian England was not immediately applicable in the late Qing and early Republican era. The first major wave of fiction publication in 1870s and 1880s Shanghai consisted almost exclusively of two kinds of narratives: reprints of classics like *Dream of the Red Chamber*, and first editions of novels written years, even decades previously, whose authors were no longer around to demand payment (or provide sequels if they should be so inclined).[15] At this point, profits from the publication of a manuscript or the reprint of an earlier edition generally went to the person who happened to have the manuscript or earlier edition in his or her possession. In almost every case, this person would not have been the author him or herself. By the early twentieth century, translation of works from abroad had to a large extent supplanted original fiction, with the interesting result that the first brand-name "author" of fiction—Lin Shu 林紓—was known (and paid) primarily for his translation work.[16] Given these crucial precedents in the late nineteenth century, in which the person doing the original "creative" work is almost never the person receiving payment for that work, it should come as no surprise that the professional author in the early twentieth century moves to distinguish him- or herself from newspapermen and other purveyors of less privileged genres on different grounds entirely.

A hint of what these grounds might be appears in *New Shanghai*'s insistent and unapologetic use of the word "[raw] material" (*ziliao* 資料) to refer to the sources that the writer transforms into a salable product.[17] Those who supply the narrator with these raw materials within the pages of the novel insist on payment: when the narrator treats a scoundrel to drinks and asks what news he has heard recently, the latter refuses, saying, "You're really cheap, taking me out for a drink but not ordering any food; and then you want to hear the latest news! If I tell you, you'll take it and use it as raw material for a novel." The narrator has no choice but to order some dishes in return for the stories. Bao Tianxiao 包天笑 satirizes the straightforward appropriation of such raw material in his 1920s novel *Heimu* 黑幕 (Scandal), having a publisher commission a "scandal novel" (*heimu xiaoshuo* 黑幕小説) with the following words:

> When you read the newspaper, pay attention to the local city news and that sort of minor news, in those items you will find many scandals. [...] In the newspaper there are just a few short lines, but they give the

beginning and ending, and can be lengthened up to ten thousand words
[...]. Don't you dismiss these few short lines in the paper, they are like
the beef stock that one buys from a pharmacy: add just one teaspoon
of it to boiled water, and you can make a whole bowl [...].[18]

This description of the writing process recalls the intensive use of anecdotes
in the construction of novels of the first decade of the century, especially Wu
Jianren's *Strange Events Eyewitnessed over the Last Two Decades*. In *New
Shanghai*, as discussed above, the indebtedness of the professional writer of
fiction to contemporary newspaper articles and gossip as source material for
individual plots is indicated repeatedly, and leads to the denigration of the
journalist as a figure.

But what Bao Tianxiao criticizes here is not the use of raw material per
se, merely the lazy and careless padding of this raw material by the novelist who adds no value himself or herself. (After all, it is Bao who gives us
the well-known account of Wu Jianren's notebook, in which Wu noted down
stories of interest from the newspapers for use as source material; Bao went
on to make use of this technique himself in writing *Shanghai chunqiu* 上海
春秋 [Shanghai records].)[19] What the fiction writer should add to this raw
material to turn it into an aesthetic product is made clear by Bi Yihong 畢
倚虹, who, writing in the early 1920s, drew a sharp distinction between "non-
fiction writing" (*jishi zhi wenzi* 記事之文字) and "fiction writing" (*xiaoshuo
wenzi* 小說文字): the latter requires artistic manipulation, even if it is based
in part on "real" events. What is of primary importance in a work of fiction
is not the individual plots, but the way in which they are woven together
into a sophisticated self-referential narrative system.[20] Similarly, Wang
Huidun's 王晦鈍 preface to *Xiepu chao* 歇浦潮 (The Huangpu tides,
1916–1921) explains that

> the reader should seek out the places of structural ingenuity; if he or
> she pays attention only to the strange and colorful events, and craving
> more rushes on to the end without reading carefully, using the book as
> material for chatting over tea and wine, this will ill repay the author's
> thoughtful and hard-won organization [of the text].[21]

And indeed, the better works of installment fiction were no mere collections
of anecdotes patched together one after another into an "episodic" structure; the complex interwoven presentation of many narrative lines is a distinguishing characteristic of many of these novels, especially those set in
Shanghai.[22]

The difference between the journalist and the novelist in the Republican
era lies not so much in the latter's creativity, then, but in his or her ability
to take a wide variety of raw narrative material and shape it into a complicated, highly structured text that will involve the reader's capacity for

aesthetic appreciation at multiple levels. This emphasis on structural coherence and organization on the part of professional authors themselves
is seconded by their critics: contemporary intellectuals like Liang Qichao
梁啟超 were quick to attack fiction of this period (especially installment
fiction) as disorganized and incoherent.[23] The merit of these attacks is debat-
able—certain installment fiction of this period is extremely well-organized
despite its multiple narrative lines—but what is most important is that
critics and advocates alike of fiction written for compensation agree that
structure and organization are the criteria according to which fiction should
be judged, not the ability to create something out of nothing.

It is worth noting that this approach to writing fiction has significant
continuities with the processes through which several of the best-known
Chinese novels of the late Ming took shape, despite the appearance in the
intervening centuries of a rather different discourse of authorship as the record
of lived or observed experience.[24] What might have motivated this return to
an earlier aesthetic standard? It seems most likely that the rise of the newspaper as a type of text that observes social goings-on and reports on them
on a regular basis in the last quarter of the nineteenth century called the
discourse of fictional authorship based on observation and experience into
question—why read fiction for an account of things as they are today when
the newspaper is cheaper, more convenient, and always up to date? In
response, the manipulation and reworking of narrative raw material returns
as the significant determinant of fictional quality, and the role of the author
is no longer to observe, but rather to put the unstructured observations of
others into an artistic form.

Should we doubt that the author has begun to take his or her distance
from the job of observation, we might want to look briefly at the professional author's treatment of his two friends in *New Shanghai*. In the final
chapter, these friends demand drinks and dinner from the narrator when they
learn that they have not only provided material for the novel, but also served
as the centers around which the first and second halves of the novel were
organized.[25]

The novel begins with an account of the arrival of the narrator's somewhat old-fashioned friend, Li Meibo, from a nearby town to Shanghai for
a visit. Throughout the novel, Li Meibo remains a tourist: although there is
extensive discussion of Shanghai customs, Shanghai vocabulary, and Shanghai
anecdotes, it's all talk: nothing significant happens to Li or to Shen Yifan
(a friend who appears in the second half of the novel and plays a similar
role); they merely observe events or have anecdotes narrated to them by various interlocutors. A dispute does take place at Zhang's Garden, but Li is
merely an onlooker, and not a participant; a third party tells Shen Yifan at
great length about the exploits of Yang Yuelou, an actor who initiated seduc-
tions of many courtesans and "proper" women merely through appearing
on stage, reminding us of the importance of the theater as a narrative space
in earlier novels, but we never meet Yang himself.[26] Though both Li and Shen

spend long hours in teahouses, they are never defrauded or tempted to misbehave; instead, they quietly listen to stories of what happened to other people in the preceding months and years. Even when the narrative seems to leave one of the two central characters for a chapter or two and focus in on a story, there is invariably a moment at the end of the story in which the presentation is mediated by a reference back to the person who has told it.[27] The job of observation and reporting on what has been observed is delegated to these friends; they are put to work as virtual employees in the narrative enterprise run by the professional author. This author, in turn, appears as a second-order cultural producer—rather like the anthropologist who claims to organize naïve and unformed contributions of a range of "native informants" into a coherent and reflexive system of representation.

"Wild chickens"

The explosive growth in original fiction published in the China of the 1910s and 1920s and the concurrent standardization of payment by the word for fiction manuscripts, is in some senses analogous to the tectonic shifts in the literary and publishing worlds in Victorian England several decades earlier that Norman Feltes explains as a transformation from a "petty-commodity mode of literary production" to a "capitalist mode of literary production."[28] In Britain this transformation consisted in part of ever sharper struggles between authors and publishers to define the terms according to which literary texts were understood as property and commodity, and set the ratio according to which the profits from their manufacture and sale accrued to the two parties. This struggle also had the effect of distinguishing authors and publishers as two separate and mutually exclusive classes of social agents.

There are important differences between literary production in Victorian England and Republican China, however, which relate directly to the figure of the successful professional author. First, the copyright regime was not as thoroughly implemented in Republican China; this meant that authors suffered from unauthorized reprints of and sequels to their work, but it also gave them more flexibility in negotiating with publishers. Zhu Shouju 朱瘦菊, for example, published the first ninety chapters of his novel *The Huangpu Tides* in installments in *Xin Shenbao* 新申報, but retained the copyright to the work as a whole for himself. Towards the end of the serialization, he announced that the final ten chapters of the novel would *not* be serialized in the newspaper, but would be available only to readers who purchased the entire volume edition shortly to appear from *Xinmin tushu guan*, at one stroke converting the previous installments from a simple commodity into a commodity which not only sold as itself, but also in turn generated a powerful desire among its consumers for a specific further purchase that was not available from the original publisher.[29] Second, the importance of certain individual works of installment fiction to the newspapers and magazines that they appeared in meant that publishers often found themselves in the position of supplicants to an author who happened to have a hit on his or her hands. Since installment fiction was an ongoing enterprise, each "natural" ending point of the narrative represented an occasion for the author to renegotiate the terms of his or her compensation, as the publisher would be eager to see a cash cow continue to produce. In the case of *Tingzi jian saosao* 亭子間嫂嫂 (Backroom sister-in-law, serialized 1938–1942), for example, the author first proposed to end the narrative after 50,000 words, but was persuaded to extend it twice, first up to 80,000 words and then to 100,000 words, presumably in exchange for appropriate compensation.[30] Clearly, publishers could get hooked on the installment narratives that authors provided just as easily as their readers could.

These examples suggest to us already that the balance of power between authors and publishers was rather different in Republican China from what it was in late nineteenth and early twentieth century Britain. In addition, the very distinction that is so fundamental to development of the British publishing world—between authors and publishers—is not always so clear in 1920s and 1930s Shanghai and Beijing. Columnists and essayists for newspapers were generally under contract to supply only a given amount of prose daily or weekly to a newspaper publisher; once their quota was filled, they were free to spend the rest of their time—and profit from the name recognition that they had acquired—writing for other publishers or attempting editorial and publishing ventures of their own.[31] As a result, writers as diverse as Zhou Shoujuan 周瘦鵑 and Liu Na'ou 劉吶鷗 functioned simultaneously as salaried employees, freelancers, and entrepreneurs.

In the fifth chapter of *New Shanghai*, one of Li Meibo's new acquaintances makes a brief but revealing comment about the use of the pejorative term *wild chicken* (*yeji* 野雞) in Shanghai:

> In Shanghai, "wild chicken" is not just used to refer to prostitutes. There are wild chicken horse carriages, wild chicken rickshaws, wild chicken porters, and wild chicken translators; whatever goes around looking, without any fixed business, can be referred to generally as a "wild chicken."[32]

In other words, the term *wild chicken* can be translated into English to signify an owner-operator, a freelance worker, or a small independent concern, categories understood as distinct in the early twenty first century American market, but interestingly conjoined in early twentieth century Shanghai.[33] Clearly, small newspapers published, edited, and largely written by a single individual would fall into this category—indeed Jia Minshi disparages one of the competing newspapers by referring to it as a *wild chicken newspaper* (*yeji baoguan* 野雞報館). Similarly, a professional writer of fiction could be understood as a "wild chicken" if he (or she) derived significant profit from the enterprise and was not affiliated with a single larger publisher, or set up shop as an editor of a new magazine or literary periodical.

The term *yeji* is clearly pejorative, and would not have been applied by any writers to themselves. It is useful, however, precisely in the way that it highlights the continuity between freelance work and entrepreneurship, two categories of activity that are often seen as mutually exclusive—the former falling under the sign of Labor and the latter under that of Capital. Over the first few decades of the twentieth century, such author/editor/publishers came to constitute a smaller and smaller proportion of the total number of literary producers as the total number of professional writers continued to rise. Their continued significance, however, comes not so much from their numbers as from their prominence and fame; it was in fact the better-known authors who could leverage their name recognition to ensure an enthusiastic reception for new entrepreneurial projects that they might undertake— projects in which the friends employed as "virtual workers" in fiction such as *New Shanghai* could return as real employees.

Yet even though these "brand-name" authors behave in some senses as capitalists along the lines of late nineteenth and early twentieth century English publishers—retaining copyright to their works, working to manipulate audience demands for more, employing virtual workers in their narrative enterprises and commissioning salaried work from other writers for the magazines and literary supplements that they edited—the rhetoric of labor remains central to their self-definition. Zhou Shoujuan refers to his work as "literary labor" (*wenzi laogong* 文字勞工), and Zhang Henshui 張恨水 remarks "I gain my daily bread by the sweat of my brow" (*liu ziji de han, chi ziji de fan* 流自己的汗，吃自己的飯).[34] Even Zhou Tianlai 周天籟, the highly successful author of *Backroom Sister-in-Law*, creates an alter ego for himself within the text, Zhu Daoming, who writes 8–10,000 words a day for only the smallest compensation.[35]

To what extent can we trust this type of self-representation on the part of professional authors? Or, conversely, to what extent does name recognition by readers function as a kind of capital which authors can invest (with little or no effort) to enhance their own profits (whether by putting together a literary periodical to which they themselves do not contribute substantial amounts of work, or by writing prefaces to fiction by other authors)? Paradoxically, perhaps, the very ease with which a well-known author could exploit weaknesses in the copyright regime to profit from his or her fame at the expense of publishers (or at least, without benefiting other publishers), was closely related to the ease with which unscrupulous publishers could attach a well-known author's name to another person's work. It is hard to imagine a publisher in a more legalistic environment standing for Zhu Shouju's trick of withholding the final few installments of *The Huangpu Tides* in order to increase sales of the volume edition issued through another publisher; at the same time, however, well-known authors such as Zhu Shouju 朱瘦菊, Zhou Shoujuan, and especially Zhang Henshui struggled incessantly against pirated editions of their work, spurious sequels to their fiction, and even novels published under their names that they had no connection with whatsoever. Under these circumstances, a brand name functions as capital in its ease of movement and its ability to add "value" to the ordinary labor of writers, but it is a capital that is available to anyone who is bold and unscrupulous enough to lay claim to it. In light of the relative effortlessness with which one's name-as-capital could be appropriated, even the best-known authors had to work very hard to ensure that they were benefiting as much from the use of their own names as others were.

The brand name

If we are to believe advertising copy, newspaper articles, and stories circulating at the time, early twentieth century Chinese cities (especially Shanghai) swarmed with literary geniuses, each with his or her own distinctive characteristics, habits, and eccentricities.[36] This discourse of "the writer" is less than forthcoming, however, on the question of how these geniuses supported themselves, since the true literary individual was supposed to be above writing for hire. More than two decades previously, Dianshizhai Press had printed a collection of illustrations of Shanghai sights, including an image of the very lithographic presses on which those illustrations were produced.[37] A similar reflexive moment does not appear in Shanghai fiction until *New Shanghai*: in this text we are finally given a picture of the professional writer as a productive figure in the cityscape, whether out on the town collecting useful material, or in his study bent over his desk. If the other figures the professional writer joined in these novels were for the most part rogues, scoundrels, kidnappers, and thieves (rather than the more sedate buildings, gardens, and vistas presented in the earlier illustrated works), it must then have been that much more important to create essential differences between the writer and other "wild chickens" earning a living in the city.

The appearance of this professional writer in 1909 is quite significant, coming as it does in close conjunction with the institution of a copyright regime that defined written narratives, among other products, as intellectual property and the ensuing standardization of payment to authors for their manuscripts.[38] Within a few years, authors like Xu Zhenya 徐枕亞 began to take legal action against unauthorized printings of their works, and by the middle of the 1920s, the professional imagined in this novel of 1909 could command the allegiance of a national audience. *New Shanghai* in this way opens up a space within which the name of the professional writer can be understood to function as a brand name—a function that publishers, and later authors, could systematize and exploit to sell novel after novel on the basis of the popularity of previous fiction printed under the name of that writer.[39] Indeed, the very eccentricities of behavior that defined the proper *yangchang caizi* would prove most useful as well in distinguishing each brand name from all others and rendering it more attractive to potential readers.

But the very utility of a brand-name author lies in the fact that there are audiences who are convinced (or have been persuaded) that yet another installment of the same thing (or something similar from the same source) is desirable: the professional author depends in large part on a readership that is always ready to buy the next portion of his or her literary production on the basis of those portions that it has already consumed. In declining the author's request that he compose a preface for the volume edition of *Backroom Sister-in-Law*, Zhou Yueran 周越然 remarked that all readers would know the quality of the work from what they had read of it in installments or had heard of from others; this, he goes on to explain, is an "unwritten preface" (*bu chengwen zhi xu* 不成文之序), that is by implication more powerful than any written endorsement that another author or editor could provide.[40] Publication in installments not only constituted a kind of platform from which the virtues of a narrative or an author could be advertised; this format also structured readers' desire in terms of brief gratification of the drive to read on that is invariably cut short, eventually giving rise to a reader who is virtually addicted to a text that has no necessary ending point.[41]

Here we can profitably return to the term *wild chicken*. The suitability of this term, associated primarily with prostitutes, to a certain mode of literary production is particularly striking for two reasons: first, the centuries-old heritage of comparisons between courtesans and literary individuals (*wenren*), of which the relations between Shanghai writers and prostitutes might be understood as a debased remnant of a once vital tradition.[42] Second, and more significant, is the similarity between prostitutes and courtesans on the one hand, and writers of installment fiction on the other as cultural producers who manipulate and exploit the consumer's interest in their products with tactics of delay and partial satisfaction. In *Haishang fanhua meng* 海上繁華夢 (Dreams of Shanghai splendor), a serial novel that began to appear in 1898, one courtesan alludes specifically to this identity between seducing by promising sex and seducing by promising narrative closure; worrying that a man who has seen through the falsity of her world will not spend the night with her, she offers to tell him the story of what has happened to another courtesan he knew—but only if he stops by later that evening.[43] In this sense, the term *wild chicken* refers us simultaneously to the position that the early twentieth century successful professional author takes between Labor and Capital *and* to the tactics employed to generate and manage readers' desire for that author's products.

From its earliest moments, installment fiction in Edo Japan and in late Qing and Republican-era Shanghai is preternaturally obsessed with brand-name products and establishments. This is no coincidence, just as it is no accident that the figure of the professional author of fiction appears in China only after the turn-of-the-century efflorescence of installment fiction. Even if this author does not explicitly undertake to publish in installments, his or her continued success as a professional grows out of a particular mode of literary consumption that has everything to do with the endless quest for more, and very little to do with the drive to finish a text once and for all.

Notes

A shorter version of part of this essay appeared in Chapter 5 of my book *Mediasphere Shanghai: The Aesthetics of Cultural Production* (Honolulu, 2007). I am grateful to the University of Hawai'i Press for granting permission to include the present essay in this volume.

1 Perry Link, *Mandarin Ducks and Butterflies: Popular Fiction in Early Twentieth Century Chinese Cities* (Berkeley: University of California Press, 1981); Catherine Yeh, "The Life-style of Four *Wenren* in Late Qing Shanghai," *Harvard Journal of Asiatic Studies* 57.2 (1997): 419–470; Leo Lee and Andrew Nathan, "The Beginnings of Mass Culture: Fiction and Journalism in the Late Ch'ing and Beyond," in *Popular Culture in Late Imperial China*, edited by David Johnson et al. (Berkeley: University of California Press, 1985), 360–395; Haiyan Lee, "All the Feelings That Are Fit to Print: The Community of Sentiment and the Literary Public Sphere in China, 1900–1918," *Modern China* 27.3 (2001): 291–327; Christopher Reed, *Gutenberg in Shanghai: Chinese Print Capitalism, 1876–1937* (Vancouver: University of British Columbia Press, 2004); Roswell Britton, *The Chinese Periodical Press: 1800–1912* (Shanghai: 1933); Yuan Jin 袁進 and Chen Bohai 陳伯海, *Shanghai jindai wenxue shi* 上海近代文學史 (Early modern Shanghai literary history) (Shanghai: Renmin chuban she, 1993); Fan Boqun 范伯群, ed., *Zhongguo jinxiandai tongsu wenxue shi* 中國近現代通俗文學史 (Early modern and modern popular Chinese literary history) (Nanjing: Jiangsu jiaoyu chuban she, 1999); and Michel Hockx, "Playing the Field: Aspects of Chinese Literary Life in the 1920s," in *The Literary Field of Twentieth Century China*, edited by Michel Hockx (Honolulu: University of Hawai'i Press, 1999), 61–78.
2 Link, *Mandarin Ducks and Butterflies*, 161–163.
3 This novel was popular enough at the time to be reprinted at least twice. Lu Shi'e 陸士鄂, *Xin Shanghai* 新上海 (New Shanghai) (Shanghai: Guji chuban she, 1997 reprint), "Introduction," 3.
4 Alexander Des Forges, "From Source Texts to 'Reality Observed': The Creation of the 'Author' in Nineteenth-Century Chinese Vernacular Fiction," *CLEAR* 22 (2000): 67–84.
5 Lu, *Xin Shanghai*, 4.
6 Jonathan Hay, "Painters and Publishing in Late Nineteenth Century Shanghai," in *Art at the Close of China's Empire*, edited by Chou Ju-hsi (Tempe: Arizona State University Phoebus Occasional Papers in Art History, 1998), 173–175.
7 Han Bangqing 韓邦慶 published the literary periodical *Haishang qishu* 海上奇書 (Marvelous Shanghai writings); Li Boyuan 李伯元 published *Youxi bao* 遊戲報 (Entertainment daily) and then *Shijie fanhua bao* 世界繁華報 (World splendor daily); Wu Jianren 吳趼人 was one of the founders of *Caifeng bao* 采風報 (Selected rumors daily). For a discussion of the attribution of certain Shanghai novels to Li Boyuan and Wu Jianren, see Guo Changhai 郭長海, "*Wu Jianren xieguo naxie changpian xiaoshuo?*" 吳趼人寫過哪些長篇小説？ (Which long novels were written by Wu Jianren?) *Shinmatsu shôsetsu* 17 (1994): 24–33; and Alexander Des Forges, "Street Talk and Alley Stories: Tangled Narratives of Shanghai from 'Lives of Shanghai Flowers' (1892) to 'Midnight' (1933)," (Ph.D. dissertation, Princeton University, 1998), 105–111.
8 Alexander Des Forges, "Building Shanghai, One Page at a Time: The Aesthetics of Installment Fiction at the Turn of the Century," *Journal of Asian Studies* 62.3 (2003): 781–810.
9 See the comments of literary critics writing in the first decade of the twentieth century cited in Chen Pingyuan 陳平原, *Zhongguo xiaoshuo xushi moshi de zhuanbian* 中國小説敍事模式的轉變 (The transformation of narrative modes in Chinese fiction) (Shanghai: Renmin chuban she, 1988), 281; Yuan Jin 袁進 notes the difficulties that writers of vernacular fiction encountered in their attempts to publish in literary magazines in the 1900s and early 1910s in *Yuanyang hudie pai* 鴛鴦蝴蝶派 (Mandarin Ducks and Butterflies School) (Shanghai: Shanghai shudian, 1994), 89.

10 Dian Gong 顛公 (pseudonym), writing the "Notes from Lazy Lair" (*Lanwo suibi* 懶窩隨筆) in *Shibao* 時報. Reprinted in Han Bangqing, *Haishang hua liezhuan* 海上花列傳 (Lives of Shanghai flowers) (Beijing: Renmin wenxue chuban she, 1985), 614–616.

11 See Lu, *Xin Shanghai*, 29, 133ff.

12 Note also the figure of Qian Menghua, a newspaperman who has written a new novel (*xin xiaoshuo* 新小説): this transgression of the boundary that the narrator is so eager to have observed leads to Qian Menghua's present reduced circumstances, in which he writes advertising copy for a drug company (Lu Shi'e, *Xin Shanghai*, 75–76).

13 Lu, *Xin Shanghai*, 4; Pierre Bourdieu, *Distinction: A Social Critique of the Judgement of Taste*, translated by Richard Nice (Cambridge: Harvard University Press, 1984), 318–371.

14 Norman Feltes, *Literary Capital and the Late Victorian Novel* (Madison: University of Wisconsin Press, 1993), 13–14, 25.

15 Des Forges, "Street Talk and Alley Stories," 35–39; Rolston, *How to Read the Chinese Novel* (Princeton: Princeton University Press, 1990), 320; Yi Su 一粟, *Honglou meng shulu* 紅樓夢書錄 (Bibliography on *Honglou meng*) (Shanghai: Guji chuban she, revised edition, 1981), 56ff.

16 See Hu Ying, "The Translator Transfigured: Lin Shu and the Late Qing Logic of Writing," *positions* 3.1 (1995): 69–96, for a discussion of Lin's career and reputation.

17 *Xin Shanghai* also makes rather extravagant claims for the beneficial effects that fiction has on the individual reader, and on society as a whole, somewhat along the lines of Liang Qichao's turn-of-the-century advocacy of "political fiction." Such claims are echoed in some later fiction by professional authors, but with notably less enthusiasm and frequency (Lu, *Xin Shanghai*, 37–39, 279).

18 Cited in Fan Boqun's preface to Bao Tianxiao 包天笑, *Shanghai chunqiu* 上海春秋 (Shanghai records), 12–13. No date for *Heimu* is given in this preface, but it is likely that it appeared in the late 1910s, in response to the early Republican period wave of "scandal fiction" (*heimu xiaoshuo*). The exploitative relationship between a publisher and a writer-for-hire can be found in earlier Chinese fiction, most notably in *Rulin waishi* 儒林外史 (The scholars), but in these cases the material produced comprises commentaries to civil service examination essays, not fiction. The production of novels for immediate sale (rather than the reprinting of novels first published years earlier or the production of new commentaries to previously published novels) was a much later phenomenon.

19 Fan, *Zhongguo jinxiandai tongsu wenxue shi*, 342–343.

20 Bi Yihong 畢倚紅, *Renjian diyu* 人間地獄 (Hell on earth), prefaces, 13–14.

21 Zhu Shouju 朱瘦菊, *Xiepu chao* 歇浦潮 (Huangpu tides) (Shanghai guji chuban she, 1991 reprint), prefaces, 5.

22 For analysis of the complexity and coherence of early Chinese installment fiction, see Donald Holoch, "A Novel of Setting: The Bureaucrats," in Milena Doleželová-Velingerová, *The Chinese Novel at the Turn of the Century* (University of Toronto Press, 1980), 76–115; Milena Doleželová-Velingerová, "Typology of Plot Structures in Late Qing Novels," in Doleželová-Velingerová, *The Chinese Novel*, 38–56; Yuan Jin, *Yuanyang hudie pai*, 128; and Des Forges, "Building Shanghai, One Page at a Time."

23 See, among others, Liang Qichao 梁啟超, "*Gao xiaoshuo jia*" 告小説家 (To fiction writers) (1915), and other critics quoted in Chen Pingyuan, *Zhongguo xiaoshuo xushi moshi de zhuanbian*, 280–286; Sima Xiao 司馬嘯, "*Wo de tongshi Zhang Henshui*" 我的同事張恨水 (My colleague Zhang Henshui) *Ta jen* 大人 16 (1971), 60–62; Yuan Jin, *Zhongguo xiaoshuo de jindai biange* 中國小説的近代變革 (The modern transformation of Chinese fiction) (Beijing: Zhongguo shehui kexue chubanshe, 1992), 60.

24 See, for example, the similarity between this use of newspaper stories as "raw material" and the reworking of "popular" sources that was central to the production of *Jinping mei* 金瓶梅 (Plum in the golden vase), *Shuihu zhuan* 水滸傳 (Tales of the water margin), and *Xiyou ji* 西遊記 (Journey to the west) (Andrew Plaks, *The Four Masterworks of the Ming Novel* (Princeton: Princeton University Press, 1987), 71). For the discourse of the fictional author as a recorder of observed reality, see Des Forges, "From Source Texts to 'Reality Observed.'"

25 Lu, *Xin Shanghai*, 194, 278–279.

26 Lu, *Xin Shanghai*, 7–8, 88–92.

27 E.g., the subplot involving Diao Bangzhi, which is drawn to a close at the end of chapter 12. Lu, *Xin Shanghai*, 54.

28 Norman Feltes, *Modes of Production of Victorian Novels* (Chicago: University of Chicago Press, 1986), and *Literary Capital and the Late Victorian Novel*.

29 Zhu, *Xiepu chao*, prefaces, 5.

30 Fan, ed., *Zhongguo jinxiandai tongsu wenxue shi*, vol. 1, p. 86.

31 Link, *Mandarin Ducks and Butterflies*, 154–155.

32 Lu, *Xin Shanghai*, 22.

33 In her analysis of late Qing and Republican-era prostitution in Shanghai, Gail Hershatter translates *yeji* as "pheasant," and stresses the term's related connotations of transience and unscheduled or irregular business (Gail Hershatter, *Dangerous Pleasures: Prostitution and Modernity in Twentieth-Century Shanghai* (Berkeley: University of California Press, 1997), 17).

34 Fan, ed., *Zhongguo jinxiandai tongsu wenxue shi*, vol. 1, introduction, 5.

35 Fan, ed., *Zhongguo jinxiandai tongsu wenxue shi*, vol. 1, 93.

36 Link, *Mandarin Ducks and Butterflies*, 160ff.

37 Des Forges, "Street Talk and Alley Stories," 57–60.

38 Link, *Mandarin Ducks and Butterflies*, 153. For an account of the importance of the new copyright law from the point of view of the publishers, and the subsequent formation of the Shanghai Booksellers' Guild, see Reed, *Gutenberg in Shanghai*.

39 For the use and "abuse" of the names of well-known authors, see Link, *Mandarin Ducks and Butterflies*, 149ff.

40 Other prefaces to the volume edition make similar claims. See Fan, ed. *Zhongguo jinxiandai tongsu wenxue shi*, 1: 86–87.

41 Des Forges, "Building Shanghai, One Page at a Time."

42 Catherine Yeh ("The Life-style of Four *Wenren* in Late Qing Shanghai"), Gail Hershatter (*Dangerous Pleasures*), and Andrew Field ("Selling Souls in Sin City: Shanghai Singing and Dancing Hostesses in Print, Film, and Politics, 1920–1949," in *Cinema and Urban Culture in Shanghai, 1922–1943*, edited by Yingjin Zhang [Stanford: Stanford University Press, 1999]) have demonstrated the close ties between tabloid newspapers (*xiaobao* 小報) and courtesans and prostitutes from the 1890s into the 1930s; it is also worth noting that many of the main characters in installment fiction set in Shanghai during this period are also courtesans or prostitutes.

43 Sun Yusheng 孫玉聲, *Haishang fanhua meng* 海上繁華夢 (Dreams of Shanghai splendor) (Shanghai: Guji chuban she, 1991 reprint), 801–805. It turns out that the courtesan, Liu Xianxian, in fact has nothing to tell him:

> Xianxian chuckled, saying "You fell into my trap! I wanted to trick you into coming to hold a banquet [...]. I was afraid that you would not come, so I said I knew what had happened to her." [...] Shaomu was very disappointed, then laughed at himself for being deceived by Xianxian.

(805)

3   Serial sightings

News, novelties, and an *Unofficial History of the Old Capital*

Eileen Cheng-yin Chow

> To read one's newspaper is to live the universal life, the life of the whole capital, of the entire city, of all France, of all nations [...]. It is the newspaper that establishes this sublime communion of souls across distances.
>
> (1893 editorial in *Le Petit Parisien*)[1]

In Chapter 34 of *Chunming waishi* 春明外史 (Unofficial history of the old capital, Beijing),[2] the journalist Yang Xingyuan heads over to Sanyang Hotel on the west side of town, to meet up with an old friend from the south who has recently arrived. As Yang walks into the door, he sees that his friend Hua Boping is by the window, "carefully poring over a map of Beijing"— but when Hua catches sight of our hero, "he threw down the map and rushed over to shake Yang's hand vigorously, exclaiming all the while" (447). Indeed, not only in this episode but throughout its entire 86 chapters, the novel continually reminds us: why read a map of Beijing when you can have Yang Xingyuan as your guide? In fact, in the very next scene, Yang prevents Hua from being bilked by the hotel attendant, interrupting his offers of expensive services: "That's enough. He may be a newcomer to Beijing, but *I* certainly am not" (448). The original readers of *Unofficial History of the Old Capital* apparently agreed; within a year of the novel's debut in the pages of the literary supplement "*Yeguang*" 夜光 (Moonlight), the newly founded *Shijie wanbao* 世界晚報 (World evening news) became the most sought-after newspaper in town.

Through five years (1924–1929) of daily serialization in the pages of the *World Evening News*, Zhang Henshui's 張恨水 *Unofficial History* takes as its main thread the journalist and poet Yang Xingyuan, and uses him to designate a new social and literary identity—that of the professional eye, the astute, knowing, and expert observer who captures snapshots of the city, its people, and cultural mores for the average reader. "Seeing" now takes place in installments, in quick snapshots and vignettes of the city, and Beijing is mapped by the professional *journaliste-littérateur* who navigates us through the trappings of the modern city, and teaches us what to look for in the dazzling kaleidoscope of a new society. In investigating the rise of the new professional role of "expert eye" journalists now surveying the streets of the city as well as re-creating those streets in the columns of the literary supplement page (*fukan* 副刊), I take as my guide not only the fictional Yang Xingyuan and his various colleagues and friends sojourning in the Beijing of *Unofficial History*, but also Yang's real-life counterparts: the journalist and popular novelist Zhang Henshui, as well as his publisher Cheng Shewo 成舍我, both of whom were writing and working in the streets of the capital in the 1920s.

Serialized fiction becomes a new technology that takes hold in the pages of the daily newspaper: a new technology of narration, of knowledge, and of sight. In what ways is it a "novel" reproduction of a traditional form, a kind of dovetailing of the traditional linked-chapter novel (*zhanghui xiaoshuo* 章回小説) with the new daily serial format? How does the fiction serialized on these pages interact with the newspaper that frames them in every instance? And what is the significance of novelizing news? In addition to serializing *Unofficial History* for *World Evening News*, Zhang Henshui also served as editor of the newspaper's *fukan*, "Moonlight," and penned most of the varied columns and articles that appeared on the *fukan* page every day, under a wide array of nicknames and in a range of voices and registers. In his combined role as journalist, editor, and novelist, Zhang exemplified the manner in which the thinly veiled fiction of contemporary times gets read as news; and news—especially urban news (literally, "society news," or *shehui xinwen* 社會新聞)—is read for its fictional, fantastic subtext. There is a blurring of boundaries between what might be called *news style* (*baozhang ti* 報章體) and *novel style* (*xiaoshuo ti* 小説體), with these two newly defined genres sharing a number of stylistic and thematic conventions.

The collaboration between serialized fiction and the new daily newspapers springing up all over China was immensely profitable—literally so. The serialization of *Unofficial History* provides an instructive example of the new collaboration between news and novels, as well as of that between authors and producers—in this case, Zhang Henshui's longstanding and often fraught relationship with his publisher Cheng Shewo. Cheng provided the initial forum for Zhang's literary career; in turn, Zhang's serialized novels, such as *Unofficial History* and *Jinfenshijia* 金粉世家 (Dynasty of gold and dust), provided the main draw for the newspapers in which they appeared—creating a whole new mass of readership for *World Evening News* and its counterpart, *Shijie ribao* 世界日報 (World daily news). Zhang's interaction with his readers—including letters, responses, editorial decisions—as the editor of "Moonlight" as well as the novelist-poet of those pages, is revealing of a new, public bond between writer and audience. In this instance, then, a reading of Zhang's novels purely for their literary, aesthetic *or* sociological values would not convey the multivalent ways in which his works were conceived, produced, and received.

Just as we should no longer view literature as divorced from the market, we should similarly no longer index historical newspapers as merely news or fact, but rather as a literary genre with its own conventions and tropes, including such concepts as the capturing of objectivity and exclusives in reporting. I therefore also address the larger context of Republican print culture, and the role of *fukan* in fostering Chinese literature in the twentieth century, as well as look at the imbricated relationship between journalism and literature. In this way, I will show the aesthetic as well as material connection between the search for novelties in this period, and the new technologies, industries, and forms of representation in which this interest in the "new" is expressed. How does the "new" become a popular commodity? Newspapers, of course, feed this market for the "new," but there is also the figure of the "newsman," the journalist who records and observes and frames for us what is novel and important to *look* at amidst the bedazzling array of novel scenes. Zhang Henshui becomes the most sensitive register of this "news" culture, which is why it is important to see what kind of story of this period seeing the "world" through his eyes allows us to write.

Newspapers, the novel, and the nation

There is a striking and recurrent series of images in Yuan Muzhi's 袁牧之 classic 1937 film, *Malu tianshi* 馬路天使 (Street angel), which underscores my points about the relationship between print journalism and the popular imagination in twentieth-century Chinese culture. When we first see the rented rooms shared by the young band of friends, led by trumpet player Zhao Dan, we are struck by the fact that the walls of their shabby residence in the crowded Shanghai *longtang* are papered over with layer upon layer of old newspapers: it seems that, in this instance, newspapers provide not only intellectual nourishment but actually offer physical shelter. Of course, this is meant to be ironic: the young protagonists are often victims of social injustice, and their "wallpaper" provides them meager protection indeed against the outside world and even, in one instance, becomes a source of misinformation. Yet, this enveloping visual presence of "news" in the lives of the ordinary city folk of *Street Angel* bespeaks the importance newspapers have come to assume within the popular imagination.

In his now canonical study of modern nationalism, *Imagined Communities*, Benedict Anderson argues that "nation-ness, as well as nationalism, are cultural artifacts of a particular kind" and not *a priori*, timeless givens for any modern nation state.[3] The nation, then, is an "imagined political community" distinguished by the style in which it is imagined, and fostered through education, symbols and rituals and, most significantly for our purposes, through newspapers and the novel. The modern novel draws the broad outlines of society (the nation), whose horizon is clearly bounded, while at the same time assuming that its readers inhabit the same world-space, thus providing an imagined linkage among all those who share this literary world-space. Liang Qichao most famously made this connection in his influential 1902 essay "On the Relationship between Fiction and the Government of the People," in which he begins by asserting: "If one intends to renovate the people of a nation, one must first renovate its fiction."[4] Liang hoped through fiction to create the "imagined community" of which he longed to be a part—yet this performative declaration of the creation of a national community of new citizens (*xinmin* 新民) would need to be substantiated by actual material links with the populace, and he felt that journalism and fiction would be the answer. Liang's call was indeed taken up by many of his generation: in 1895 there were about fifteen newspapers and journals, a number that had quadrupled to sixty-four by 1898, had grown to 487 by 1913, and by the May Fourth period (1919–1928) ranged upwards of 2,000.

Newspapers, Anderson argues, also play a crucial role in cementing the imagined linkage between citizens of an imagined community which derives its power from the idea of simultaneity: "the date at the top of the newspaper, the single most important emblem on it, provides the essential connection—the steady onward clocking of homogeneous, empty time."[5] The pioneering Shanghai paper *Shenbao* 申報 was the first to list both Chinese and Western dates on its masthead, establishing not only the connection between various outlying parts of the Qing empire, but also an equivalence between China and the rest of the world. Liang Qichao describes how, during his journey across the Pacific Ocean on his way to Hawaii, he "could not help but be transformed" from a "provincial" (*xiangren* 鄉人) to a "national citizen" (*guoren* 國人) to a "citizen of the world" (*shijie ren* 世界人).[6] Newspapers played a huge role in introducing the concept of the global, as China finds itself literally as one nation/news item among many, in the pages of a newspaper. Newspapers brought together, on the same page, all the varied events of the nation and the world, the different kinds of commodities available or aspired to by its readers. In fact, the editor Zuo Xiaohong 左笑鴻 called the "*Mingzhu*" 明珠 (Bright pearl) literary supplement (which he took over after Zhang Henshui's departure from *World Daily News*), a "five and dime store" containing all that his readers might want or need—from news on starlets to advertisements of the latest medicines—and allowing them to imagine themselves as part of the national community of readers and consumers.

How might Anderson's insight help us to rethink the relationship between journalism and literature?

First, and most obviously, it makes the link between literature and the outside world, demystifying the notion of *wenxue* 文學 (literature)—in fact, returning literature to a more classical, encompassing notion of *wen* 文 (culture/writing) in Chinese culture. The production of fiction in this period is intimately related to changing print technology—and here we must take into account the social and institutional contexts of cultural production, and how a particular work of art might be created, communicated, and disseminated.

Second, the study of mass culture reminds us that the notion of a single author or a hermetic text is really fictive at best. Roger Chartier, along with other Western cultural historians, has already drawn attention to the materiality of cultural production, stressing the importance of editorial, publishing, institutional processes involved in the creation of any work of art. We might gain from this new interdisciplinarity of our fields by considering, for example, how the study of a pulp novelist like Zhang Henshui (who called himself a "word machine") could be enhanced by reexamining his collaborative relationship with Cheng Shewo. We learn more when we question these shared generic conventions, such as the concern with eyewitness or firsthand accounts as an important marker of authenticity in both fiction and journalism, as well as the recounting of the exotic and foreign alongside the local: a new global sense of "news" and novelties, in the spirit of the pioneering illustrated newspaper popular in late nineteenth century Shanghai, the *Dianshizhai huabao* 點石齊畫報. Moreover, there is a new emphasis on commodification, product placement (even when the results are misleading and fatal, as we see in multiple episodes in *Unofficial History*), and targeted readership.

Finally, Anderson's arguments remind us to think of journalism as a literary genre with its own conventions (including that of objectivity), tropes, and social as well as aesthetic motivations. Cheng Shewo was intensely concerned with the management and promotion of the *fukan* pages for his various newspapers, having learned early that they were the source of a newspaper readership's loyalty. In a critical study of the "newspaper publisher as a young man," Chen Pingyuan 陳平原 has exhorted us to look at journalism and journalists in their larger intellectual environment in order to examine what that might tell us about the imbricated relationship between May Fourth ideals and popular culture.[7] In his examination of the heady intellectual atmosphere of post-May Fourth Peking University in the 1920s, of which the young Cheng Shewo was a part, Chen Pingyuan provides us with insight into much of the editorial direction of Cheng's later journalistic endeavors. Cheng Shewo's early active involvement in translation projects, in promoting new scientific and cultural knowledge from the West, and even in the writing of popular fiction, provides a larger context for his later role as head of a commercial newspaper empire, and also belies the division often drawn between elite and popular print media. Cheng Shewo's famous intention of making his newspapers into "a new form of unstructured space—a mass entertainment center, and a university for the masses," in fact was an innovative melding together of the May Fourth spirit of "enlightening" the people that was shared by so many of Cheng's generation at Peking University, with the commercial imperatives of entertaining them.[8]

A journalist's story: Cheng Shewo and *World News*

My interest here in the figure of Cheng Shewo concerns Cheng's notion of the newspaper as a form of *citizen pedagogy*—the newspaper as both source of useful knowledge and "mass entertainment center"—as well as Cheng's editorial and business policies as they affected the shape and content of the literary supplements for his newspapers, in particular the *World Evening News* in the 1920s.

World Evening News was the first newspaper founded by Cheng Shewo. It began its run on April 16, 1924, in Cheng Shewo's family residence located in "Handkerchief hutong" (*shoujuan hutong* 手帕胡同) in the west-side of Beijing.[9] At its inception, the entire news organization consisted of only three people: Gong Debo 龔德伯, the editor in chief; Zhang Henshui, the editor of the *fukan*; and Cheng Shewo, publisher and investigative news reporter-at-large. Though the paper started out as a very small affair— initially it was only printed on one large sheet, folded into four pages—*World Evening News* from the very first day advertised the "timeliness of its news," making a point of covering that morning's political battles between warlord factions in Beijing by the evening paper's press run. That timeliness of coverage, combined with the popular attraction of Zhang Henshui's serial-ized novel *Unofficial History*, dramatically announced the arrival of a major new player in the crowded journalism business of Beijing in the 1920s.

World Daily News was founded soon after, with a particular emphasis on education news, women's news, and sports news, as well as featuring the fairly recent innovation of "exclusives" (both interviews and news). It hosted a variety of *fukan*, including not only "Bright pearl"—initially edited by Zhang Henshui—but also a more "progressive" literary supplement page edited by Liu Bannong 劉半農, one of the stars of the May Fourth literary movement. At its peak circulation, the circulation of *World Daily News* reached 35,000, marking it as the highest circulation daily in the Beijing area before 1949.[10] The founding of *Shijie huabao* 世界畫報 (World illustrated news), the pictorial supplement to the day and evening papers, on October 1, 1925 completed the "three worlds" of Cheng Shewo, and by the late 1920s Cheng was already nationally recognized for the reach and innovative qual-ity of his "World" publications.

Cheng modeled *World Evening News* on *Qunqiang bao* 群強報 (Strength in masses news), a tabloid (*xiaobao* 小報) that had been highly popular in Beijing in the early 1920s. As Cheng recalled:

> The *Qunqiang bao* did not have any special characteristics [...]. Nor did it look like any of the Shanghai or Hong Kong *xiaobao* with a novel-istic style [...] but this type of small-scale newspaper with no special char-acteristics whatever was Beijing's newspaper for all those who "pulled a cart to buy broth." Rickshawmen, who did not have the time for life and vitality, would sit on the fenders of their vehicles and carefully mull over every word from start to finish. In some detailed research, I asked those rickshawmen why they liked the contents of this poor newspaper. The results I obtained are summed up here. I discovered that: 1) Though all of the news had been cut and pasted from other newspapers, every article had dozens of characters edited out, and the longest piece never

exceeded 200–300 characters. Furthermore, a limited number of characters were used, so [the paper] was relatively easy to understand. 2) At that time the movement for vernacular (*baihua* 白話) writing had just begun, and this paper, from its inception, had run stories like the *Romance of the Three Kingdoms* that were written in the vernacular language. There was also a column called "Talking about the *Liaozhai* [a collection of classical ghost stories]," the stories of which were welcomed by the working class. 3) Other than this, the greatest reason [for its popularity] was that the paper was cheap [the larger papers sold for two or three silver dollars, the *Qunqiang bao* sold for one cash, or less than a penny].[11]

Cheng pretty much copied all the ingredients that he had ascertained were keys to *Qunqiang bao*'s success: his paper was cheap, printed on one large sheet and folded into four; news stories cut and pasted from the morning or big papers (*dabao* 大報) were edited and condensed—though Cheng did have his own reporting, and also published on Sundays when other papers took the day off. Most importantly, he hired his friend Zhang Henshui to edit the literary supplement and serialize his popular fiction, to capitalize on readers' desire for narrative. In nine months the *World Evening News*'s daily circulation reached 10,000 copies.

Publicity slogans for Cheng's papers included "You can afford this paper if you smoke one less cigarette" and "You can understand this paper if you know only a few hundred characters."[12] Certainly the irony here is that Zhang Henshui, whose novels were one of—if not *the*—main draws of the *World* paper series, seemed to assume a fairly literate readership for these papers. Zhang's novels, as well as much of the *fukan* under his editorial direction, were fairly sophisticated in language and literary allusion. Witness the lengthy episode of drinking-game rhymes in classical verse in Chapters 8 and 9 of *Unofficial History*, which ran for almost an entire month in "Moonlight."[13] But was the *fukan* in the *World* papers what we call in contemporary advertising parlance "aspirational?" Readers *hoped to* compose verse like Yang Xingyuan and his friends, and to navigate the city with the confidence of these *journaliste-littérateurs*. In Chapter 72, for instance, Yang is surprised to meet a courtesan who claims to be a fan of his writings and to already "have a good estimate of his character" because she "reads the paper every day" (942). Yang asks her:

"So you read the paper every day? What is your favorite section?"
   Nian Hua smiled and responded, "My daily habit is to first read the serialized novel and the short *xiaopin* 小品 essays, and then the city news."
   Yang Xingyuan queried, "Don't you read the front page news?"
   Nianhua replied, "I'll at least look at the headlines. But I feel that there's not much interest in reading those things."

(943–944)

In the text of *Unofficial History*, we find fictional characters from all walks of life reading Yang Xingyuan's paper, and appreciating Yang for his literary skills—and in this instance, since this passage occurs in a novel that appears on the page that Nianhua claims she reads, it seems to offer us both a pedagogical lesson in the proper way to read the newspaper, and a sly advertisement for the importance of the *fukan* to the popularity of the newspaper.

One of the great secrets to Cheng's success as a newspaper publisher, Fang Hanqi argues, was his firm editorial policy emphasizing wide audience appeal and "inclination toward popularization" (*dazhonghua fangxiang* 大眾 化方向)—a policy that Cheng consciously emulated from the West, based on his understanding of the appeal of broad-based U.S. and European newspapers, in particular the newspaper empire of William Randolph Hearst.[14] Writing in 1923 on "The Natural History of the Newspaper," Robert Park argued that the big breakthrough in the history of newspapers (in the U.S. and Western Europe) was when its creators "discovered that circulation could be greatly increased by making literature out of news."[15] He cites the examples of Joseph Pulitzer and William Randolph Hearst as successful entrepreneurs who had broken away from an earlier model of newspaper as "journals of opinion" (here one is reminded of Liang Qichao's early papers), and points out that the brilliance of Hearst was his realization that "the newspaper was for him first and last a form of entertainment."[16] Both men, but especially Hearst, were explicit models for Cheng Shewo who, though a Peking University graduate involved in the May Fourth movement, felt that Chinese newspapers up to that point were too elitist. Cheng made a conscious effort to "popularize" his papers to reach the largest audience segment possible. He also realized the powerful draw that a well-managed *fukan* had for readers, and therefore deliberately devoted a great deal more attention and energy to the *fukan* sections of his papers than his publishing peers.

Cheng and Zhang met as fellow provincials from the south in early 1920s Beijing, both having gone to the capital in hopes of studying at Peking University. Though only Cheng succeeded in this goal—he managed to enroll in the Chinese Literature Department at Peking University as a protegé of the May Fourth revolutionary Chen Duxiu 陳獨秀—like Zhang he had to support himself through news writing and editorial work. While he was a college student at Peking University, Cheng Shewo served as editor-in-chief at the Christian news daily, the *Yishi bao* 益世報 (Benefit the world news), and achieved a certain amount of notoriety with the sharpness of his editorial pieces. They met, however, very much in the manner of traditional literati: a mutual friend from the Anhui Provincial Association (where they both boarded for a time) introduced Cheng to some of Zhang Henshui's *ci* 詞 (lyric poetry), and Cheng then insisted upon meeting the author. Cheng Shewo recruited Zhang Henshui to work at the *Yishi bao*, and the two young journalist-poets would often match verses and chat through the night. Their poetic habit is then rendered in fictional form in

Chapter 8 of *Unofficial History*, when Yang's friend Shu Jiucheng 舒九成 drops by and the two set off for the amusement park at night, in order to enjoy matching couplets by moonlight.[17]

Novelizing news in *Unofficial History*

No major city in China had experienced the proliferation of newspapers in the way Beijing did in the 1920s—becoming a city adrift in paper, politics, and gossip. Beijing in the mid-1920s was an extremely unstable environment, with warlords competing for turf and political power. Even after the transfer of the national government headquarters to Nanjing in the south, the former capital, as David Strand observes,

> retained a "heavy official atmosphere" [...]. Beijing's hotels, inns, provincial hostels, restaurants, theatres, teahouses, parks, and bathhouses continued to provide a congenial setting for the practice of politics. The city's newspapers mirrored political goings-on with varying degrees of accuracy and distortion.[18]

If the political sphere was turbulent, so was the news sphere—many of the warlords, political factions, and other military powers participated in the news business publishing newspapers and starting wire services, to serve as propaganda devices as well as organs with which to attack one's political enemies. According to *Chen bao*'s 晨報 1925 public accounting of the "publicity fees" given out by the Beiyang warlord regime's six departments (14,500 *yuan* officially accounted for, distributed among 125 news organizations), there were over 100 formally registered wire services. There were around 200 news organizations, in a city that at the time had a population of only a million—an extraordinary phenomenon that was remarked upon by the city's denizens then, and that has led journalism historians to conclude that in the 1920s, "Beijing had a newspaper crisis."[19]

Cheng Shewo himself took advantage of the confusion in Beijing. Right before its initial publication, *World Evening News* ran an advertisement in *Jing bao* 京報 (Capital news), announcing the new paper's five attributes: the accuracy, exclusivity, and timeliness of its local news coverage ("we absolutely do not copy a single word from the morning dailies or the Shanghai papers"); its attention to international news ("in order to promote our citizens' global perspective"); its special focus and columns on education news; the literary supplement page ("Our newspaper has specially created the *"Moonlight"* page, in order to uncover and record all manners of interesting writings—edited and selected by specialists assigned to each item. And *Unofficial History* will give a most incisive and vivid picture of all levels of Beijing society—this is a rare work not to be missed"); and, finally, the paper advertised its objective stance on politics ("when a serious matter arises, we will be sure to invite experts to comment").[20]

Therefore, Zhang Henshui's *Unofficial History* was perceived, from the very beginning, to be a major draw for the newspaper's readers. It was in fact an effective selling point: as Zhang Youluan 張友鸞, a colleague at *World Evening News*, recalled:

> *Unofficial History* described the Beijing of the 1920s, touching upon every level, every sphere of life in the city, its twists and turns corresponded to actual events and characters of the time. Ask any old Beijinger today, and he wouldn't find it difficult to identify the names and dates. When the novel was serialized in *World Evening Daily*, readers treated it as "news" outside the news section, and therefore the attraction was great. Many people spent a dollar to purchase the paper, simply so that they could know how the events in not-in-the-news-section news were unfolding.[21]

How does the consumption of "news" transform people into spectators? While one could argue that any novel interacts with its larger historical frame, in the case of the serialized novel, the novel is *literally* framed by the news events of the day with which it shares space in the pages of the newspaper. Readers consume the fiction alongside the news, and the news events are invariably read and compared to the fiction. As Zuo Xiaohong 左笑鴻, a colleague of Zhang's at the *World* papers, comments in his preface to the 1985 reprint edition of *Unofficial History*, the novel was indeed a *yeshi* 野史 or "unofficial history," of the city:

> *Unofficial History* started to cause quite a stir soon after it began to be serialized in the pages of the *World Evening News*. We witnessed for ourselves the crowds waiting at the doors of newspaper offices every afternoon, waiting to buy the paper. Were they hoping to find out more about affairs of state through reading the news? No! News reporting at that time was heavily censored, and many new items seemed to come from nowhere, hyperbolic and fictive; but the literary supplement pages might from time to time speak for the ordinary people. Especially fiction, with its characters and plots, one might detect some inside information on the current political situation. Oftentimes a scandal from the upper classes would spread throughout society, but would never see the pages of the various newspapers; yet a novel could hint at the shadows and contours of the people and the affairs in which they find themselves involved, giving readers a feeling of instant knowledge. And therefore fiction became the new "unofficial history"—every person can be called out from their fictional counterparts—not only invigorating to read, but even more fascinating under closer scrutiny. Certainly, not every novel in the papers was like this, but Henshui's *Unofficial History* was indeed of just this sort.[22]

To its original readers, *Unofficial History* seemed to both provide useful and timely information on the city and its machinations, but also presented an imaginative re-creation of the world around them, intervening as wish-fulfillment and fantasy.

The content of the novel certainly correlated closely with topical events of the day, as Zuo Xiaohong points out. Indeed, many scholars have painstakingly matched up the actual personages with their fictional counterparts, with lists of names that go on for pages. However, we could even go further and suggest that the very *structure* of *Unofficial History* also conveys Zhang Henshui's vision of Beijing—which is to say, the way characters traverse the city, the people whom they meet, and the "publicness" of life as it is constantly becoming material for the daily newspapers. In Chapter 36, for instance, one of Yang's good friends, the college student Wu Bibo, comments:

> No matter how large or small an item, you should never let it in a news-paper reporter's ears, because he'll holler it all about the place. Take for example this place [an underground high-class brothel for officials]: if a reporter managed to get in, would he publish it as news right away? So when you make new friends, you should take care not to let one of those journalists sneak his way in here.
>
> (478)

Of course, the satisfying irony for readers here is that Yang Xingyuan, going incognito, is the one who has brought Wu Bibo (and us) to this "novel spot." As in an earlier episode, Yang says, "the seedier it is, the more I want to see for myself, at the very least it could give us some material to write about" (54).

In that kind of peculiar environment of a city in which news is constant "white noise," we might ask what the appeal was of a novel that merely recapitulated such an environment. I argue that *Unofficial History* might have spoken a kind of "truth" to its readers within a society inundated with false and questionable news—giving them a sense that what was truly revelatory was to be found in fictional discourse, in gossip and rumors. There is a constant preoccupation with publicity and public exposure among the characters in the novel: what will be published, what will become public "news" as opposed to private gossip. The irony of course, is that all these behind-the-scenes conversations and plots are in fact taking place every day in the public space of *World Evening News*. Might this have given readers of the newspaper a satisfying sense that they were somehow "in on the joke," and hence have been the source of the popularity of the serialization? Gossip becomes in itself a kind of epistemology—but, in this case, face-to-face gossip is replaced with anonymous news items and rumors circulated in the various newspapers, tabloids, journals, and indeed fictions, of the period.

As Richard Stein has said of the Dickensian hero, Zhang Henshui's characters similarly learn "a lesson—not mastering the language of the streets but mastering the streets like a language, and mastering language as part of the education that guarantees increased mobility through and within the city."[23] Urban life seems to demand mediation—Eileen Chang (Zhang Ailing 張愛玲), for instance, has noted with respect to her Republican generation that had grown up in the cities, "our experience of life is often second-hand, aided by human-manufactured drama, and therefore we have a hard time drawing the boundary line between life and the dramatization of life."[24]

Many contemporary critics have designated *Unofficial History of the Old Capital* as a paradigm of a traditional, nostalgic, and romantic mode of novel-writing,[25] but that is a reading which entirely misses the point of what must have struck readers as contemporary and "novel" in Zhang's *Unofficial History*. The city of Beijing, as it exists in Zhang Henshui's novel, is meticulously built up as a lived-in and traversable space. At the same time, however, the novel is also a temporal mapping, insofar as one could think of Zhang Henshui's *Unofficial History* and its years of serialization in the literary supplement, as time-lapse photographs of the city. Therefore, the layering, palimpsestic quality of the narrative becomes important: the sheer repetition of fates, familiar stories gain an accumulative urgency.

How is Beijing mapped out by Zhang Henshui, and Zhang Henshui mapped by Beijing? It is illuminating to see what parts of Beijing exist—and what parts cannot be narrated—according to the imaginative map of Beijing that *Unofficial History* has laid out. What kind of fictional space of Beijing is created through the literary geography of Zhang Henshui's novel? There are rapid shifts of location, with the base always being Yang Xingyuan's home in the *huiguan* 會館 (provincial association). In the first two chapters alone, he dines out with friends at a restaurant, visits the brothel district, goes on an outing with a friend, strolls through a cemetery on the outskirts of town, runs into another friend on the street, meets up with co-workers in the *Yingbao* newsroom, returns to the brothel. What does it mean to gallop around the city so frenetically? Words that recur again and again in *Unofficial History: guancha* 觀察 "observe," *zhentan* 偵探 "detect," *youqu* 有趣 "amusement," *xinxian shi* 新鮮事 "novelty," *xiaoqian* 消遣 "diversion," *canguan* 參觀 "tour," *haowan* 好玩 "fun," *zhang jianshi* 長見識 "gaining knowledge," or calling the whole incident "the makings of a juicy society novel." Locations that recur in the narration of *Unofficial History* include the amusement park, Zhongshan Park, hotels, provincial associations, and *baoguan* 報館 (news offices), brothels, teahouses, opera theaters, movie theaters, and restaurants. Yang is also always "broadening his horizons," insisting upon being taken along to various seedy locations in the city. After the first few chapters, *Unofficial History* also shifts formats from eyewitness accounts by Yang in every instance to, increasingly, almost independent narratives that only use Yang as a thread. The cycle of alternation between narratives told in Yang's presence and those told in his absence are pretty constant, until the last year of serialization (1928–1929) when he disappears for longer and longer stretches. Yang does not always play a significant role in every scene; but I argue that using him—in his capacity as a journalist— as a narrative frame makes this a wholly un-traditional sort of story altogether. There is Yang Xingyuan, classical poet and down-on-his-luck tragic hero of two failed romances; but then there is Yang Xingyuan, intrepid snoop and reporter, who seems to be omnipresent, having sighted scandals and secret goings-on in every possible corner of the city. In fact, in several episodes, Yang "plays" at being Sherlock Holmes, while his friend Wu Bibo is given the role of bumbling Watson. What is interesting to note is how Zhang Henshui does not present the two sides of Yang in any sort of dialectically opposed fashion, but rather that Yang is part and parcel of a new generation of professional writers who might have traditional leanings and classical tastes in poetry and art in their private realms, but who are very much men of the moment and of the city.

However, there are those who also suffer terribly from not being able to read the city (and the proliferation of words in the city) correctly. In one episode, Yang's friend Chen Ruokuang finds himself with a bout of venereal disease, but turns to exactly the wrong source:

> What should he do? This had never happened to him before, and he was too embarrassed to ask anyone about how to cure it. But he seemed to remember that in the unimportant areas of the newspaper, there were always ads for medicine [...] he had never paid careful attention to them before, but now he thought, why not take a look, and flipped through a number of newspapers. After such an investigation, he gained quite a lot of knowledge of the matter [...].
>
> (60)

Chen is bewildered by the array of medicines advertised, since "every advertisement proclaimed that its medicine was the best [...] but who knew that these medicines, no matter how quickly the ads promised to cure you, really weren't of much help" (61). Zhang Henshui here seems to be mocking his own bread and butter—the advertisements that appear in the newspaper. In fact, the hapless protagonist in this mini-drama, Chen Ruokuang, is actually a journalist himself; yet he is fatally misled by advertisements found in "those unimportant parts of the newspaper." The pedagogy of reading the city acquired through the reading of the newspaper now gets turned on its head; and we are told that we *shouldn't* quite trust what is in the papers, either.

The manner in which temporality is marked in this novel constantly shifts: sometimes it is habitual, repeated time (so it seems as if everything has been going on for years), but then in moments like this the marking of elapsed time is very precise, a particular slice of Yang's life in Beijing. How do two separate temporalities denote the two different kinds of storytelling in this novel? *Unofficial History* is often criticized for not being unified in a "novelistic" sense—switching between first- and third-person narrative styles. As Fan Boqun observes,

> Zhang Henshui's intention in structuring his novel is praiseworthy, but yet the effect he achieved was less than ideal. The reason is that he in fact did not make his protagonist the heart of his novel, with the other characters in supporting roles radiating out and traveling along the perimeter of the main story's circle; but rather, the characters are connected only as if through a straight line, seemingly out of the protagonist's reach. Therefore, many of the passages and episodes having to do with Yang Xingyuan seem to be written in a "first person narration"; and then there are many passages that have nothing to do with Yang Xingyuan which seem to be in "third person narration." So *Unofficial History* becomes a mishmash of first and third person narration.[26]

It could be argued that this mishmash is, in fact, the secret to *Unofficial History*'s success; that what readers of the Republican era wanted from Zhang Henshui was a combination of a more traditional "observational" satirical novel combined with a first-person sensibility of a young man of genius; yet at the same time, another mishmash of touristic, pedagogical information on the new city combined with a more familiar sentimentality. In other words, the appeal of the novel lies in its quality of *bricolage* (mishmash, or *jiaocuo* 交錯, to use Fan Boqun's phrase) of genres, styles, temporalities, omniscient and subjective narration.

Not only are Yang Xingyuan and his two good friends, He Jianchen and Wu Bibo, all southerners sojourning in Beijing, but even Yang's two major love interests in the course of the novel, the young courtesan Liyun and the woman poet Li Dongqing, are both also from the south. The number of appearances of "native" Beijingers can be counted literally on one hand, in a novel that has a cast of thousands. Returning to Yang's friend, the tourist Hua Pingbo with whom we began this chapter, we see that he is still trying to figure out the city. Only the next time that Yang and Wu visit him, he is no longer reading a map, and instead they find him with a "big stack of daily newspapers" (463). As Peter Fritzsche has noted: "Strangers found in newspapers indispensable guides to unfamiliar urban territory."[27] Wu Bibo asks where Hua has gone sightseeing in Beijing, and Hua replies:

> "Last night I went to Kaiming Theatre with the express purpose of seeing Mei Lanfang 梅蘭芳 perform. Who knew that when I got there, the theatre had the day off, and I saw that there won't be performances until Saturday." Wu asked, "How come you didn't even rest on your first day here and went straight to the theatre?" Hua replied, "We hear Mei Lanfang's name so often in the south, and I wondered exactly how good does he look? So I wasn't going to be content until I saw him in person. But every time I've been to Shanghai, I've always missed Mei Lanfang;

so this time in Beijing, I was determined to solve this problem." Wu said, "When southerners come to Beijing, they're all the same away. But those in Beijing who like to listen to opera don't particularly welcome Mei." Hua exclaimed, "What? Beijingers don't welcome Mei Lanfang?" Wu Bipo replied, "I know this sounds odd to a southerner/inlander, but if you stay in Beijing for a while, you'll understand. For example, when southerners come to the capital, the wealthy ones will certainly bring home a few leather goods, though Beijing's leather goods are not necessarily cheaper than in the south, and sometimes are even more expensive than in Shanghai. And take for example, those pills that southerners call Beijing 'rat droppings' and treat like they were the miracle cure-alls for any children's ailments—everyone writes letters to Beijing, asking friends to buy some and send it back. Yet, Beijingers call this sort of thing *rat droppings*, and don't think much of it. Furthermore, I thought of something else. Winter in Beijing is extremely cold, and almost every house has a stove. In ordinary households, people burn coal balls in a stove built of white clay. Even lower-class families use these white-clay stoves to cook and boil water on a regular basis, so you can imagine that they aren't very expensive. But the last time I went back south for the winter, I went to a modish person's home, and there in his living room was such a white clay stove, with a white bronze frame constructed especially to hold it up. He was burning some red coals inside, and thought of it as the height of fashion, calling it a 'Tianjin furnace.' I couldn't stop laughing. So when southerners treat Mei Lanfang like a heavenly goddess, perhaps it's the same thing as taking a 'Tianjin stove' for a treasure." Hua Pingbo replied, "I don't believe a word you've said." Wu Bibo responded, "Of course you don't. When you next go to hear Mei Lanfang, pay careful attention to those seated all around you, and see what percentage of the audience speak in Beijing dialect, and you'll sense the truth of my words." But Hua Pingbo was still absolutely not convinced by Wu Bibo, so the two of them argued on without conclusion, all the way until lunchtime.

(464)

This extended passage from *Unofficial History* contains a number of assumptions about the kinds of readers who are reading this novel, and the lessons they might learn from such a reading. Wu Bibo does presents an extended comparison of northerners and southerners, those who are "in the know" about Beijing and those who come from the other provinces (*waidi* 外地). What is "novel" to a southerner like Hua, be it white-clay stoves, rat dropping pills, or Mei Lanfang, is looked upon with indifference by blasé Beijingers. This seems to be reflective of a general sense of urban identification, or a very particular pride in being a Beijinger or Shanghainese—the above episode would indicate the latter, but yet what is interesting is that anyone can *learn* to be a member of the privileged Beijing and Shanghai urbanite community. Wu Bibo, who is giving the grand lecture on "dos and don'ts" in Beijing, is in fact a recently arrived southerner who happens to be studying in the capital; but now he has become the de facto expert on the town.

There is also a more subtle, but equally present, strain of *southern* superiority: after all, it is the outsiders like the young journalists He Jianchen, Wu Bibo, and Yang Xingyuan who have got Beijing all figured out. Life-long Beijingers would be equally blind to the particularities of their city, or how they might be viewed by outsiders. So Zhang Henshui is serving the interests of both his native-born and *waidi* "immigrant" readers; he is also subtly flattering both groups by implying that, either way, by reading his novel and the pages of *World Evening News*, they could never be country rubes.

An unofficial roadmap to Beijing: serial snapshots of the city

As Zhang reminisced in 1941 from wartime Chongqing, "Beijing and I have had the most intimate of relationships."[28] That life-long intimacy with the city of Beijing, in its future, past, and present imaginings, frames the story of Zhang Henshui and the Republican-era spectator. As urban historian Kevin Lynch has noted, "legibility is crucial in the city setting," and with the increasing complexity of China's urban areas, there develops a concurrent need for the skill to "read" texts and spaces. Throughout his writings on Beijing, Zhang Henshui designates himself as expert guide to the city, and demonstrates how "the journalist's eye" with its ability to capture, frame, and narrate a fleeting vision of the city becomes an important metaphor for Zhang's writing. Beyond legibility, a host of attendant issues of "urban spectatorship" also surface regularly in his writings, including questions of visibility, etiquette, pedagogy, manipulation, and control.

Zhang Henshui revisited the actual and imagined spaces of Beijing time and time again in his fiction and journalistic writings. The city is the setting for his best-known works of fiction, including *Unofficial History* as well as *Tixiao yinyuan* 啼笑因緣 (Fate in tears and laughter) and *Dynasty of Gold and Dust*, but also for a host of other novels, from *Siren ji* 斯人記 (Story of thee) to the later *Ye shenchen* 夜深沉 (Deep in the night). Yet unlike famous native-son author Lao She 老舍 (or the late twentieth century writer Wang Shuo 王朔), Zhang Henshui's literary persona vis-à-vis Beijing was always as one who had come from somewhere *else*, and much of the appeal of his knowing observations of Beijing for readers would have been the essentially "outsider" and touristic view of the city that he provided them. Perhaps in light of this, Zhang was in fact asked to serve as the honorary editor of a 1935 edition of *Beiping lüxing zhinan* 北平旅行指南 (Travel guide to Beiping). By writing about journalists writing and reporting—making deadlines and gathering stories around the city—Zhang Henshui transformed the business of reporting into a subject worthy of report and, equally importantly, of fiction.

In 1935, when a fellow southerner and journalist Ma Zhixiang 馬芷庠 asked Zhang Henshui to participate in his project of writing a new "Travel guide to Beiping," Zhang happily agreed. As he wrote in the preface, "I have lived in the former capital for over fifteen years now, and have always keenly felt the lack of such a type of book."[29] Zhang, of course, had been mapping Beijing for at least a decade in the pages of *World Evening News* and *World Daily News*, serving as a figurative Beijing travel guide that was renewed daily. A small and random sampling of news article titles might suggest the sheer range of topics he covered in the pages of "Moonlight": "Let's Talk about Beijing's Theaters," a review of seating, ventilation, and kinds of customers at Beijing's various opera houses; "Let's Go Dancing at the Rain Pavilion," a description of foreign desserts and dancing at the new dance hall in Zhongshan Park; "Going Peony-viewing at Chongxiao Temple," which is actually a taxonomy of the types of spectators one finds among the "crowds" in public places in Beijing; "Elegant and Vulgar Names of *Hutong*"; and "How to Pick a Husband."[30] Similarly, the novel *Unofficial History* is filled with such digressive discussions about the merits of this or that custom or habit, often corresponding with news items and other issues covered in the various editorials and articles in the "Moonlight" page. Indeed, these digressions *constitute the very form of the novel*, just as the pastiche quality of the novel is part and parcel of the experience of reading the *fukan*. You read a little fiction, followed by a few lines of classical verse; then there is the main commentary of the day, usually on contemporary affairs or national politics; then a section on Beijing's theaters, restaurants, popular haunts; usually a comical, anecdotal piece, or letters from readers debating a fashion trend, etc. Finally, there are the occasional pieces on regional dialects or customs, which are also very present in the novel. Essentially all the subgenres that are present in *Unofficial History* are also present in the *fukan*, and so the reading of the novel becomes pedagogically oriented readings of the newspaper, and vice versa.

Readers of "Moonlight"

Who did Zhang Henshui think were the readers of *World Evening News* and "Moonlight"? On July 14, 1926, "Moonlight" was in the midst of running a "discussion series" on its page, and presented "Ten Interesting Questions," subtitled "Part One of the Readers' Club":

1 Who am I?
2 What strange hobbies do you have?
3 If you lost one shoe of a pair, what would you do?
4 If in a letter you've written a friend you suddenly remember something inappropriate but you've already mailed it, how would you remedy the situation?

5   Absentmindedly you go to a restaurant, but midway through the meal you remember that you don't have money—do you eat till you're full? Or drop your bowl?

6   Who spoke first in your initial meeting with your Mrs.? What did you say? (Those who are single can make a prediction. Female readers need not reply.)

7   How do you feel after being robbed?

8   If you were the stone lion outside of Zhenyang Gate, how would you feel?

9   Were you a mischief-maker in elementary school (or in your old-style schoolhouse)?

10   Where do you read "Moonlight" everyday?

We welcome your answers to all ten questions above, though the shorter the answers, the better.

At this point in the fictional world of *Unofficial History*, Yang Xingyuan has been fending off the aggressive submissions of a young student named Bi Poli, who is desperately trying to get published so that he may attract the attention of the object of his infatuation who, he has noted, reads Yang Xingyuan's *fukan* page regularly. Bi Poli therefore composes a short story called "He Has Gone Mad" (*ta fengmo le* 他瘋魔了), and writes Yang daily, hoping to get published.

It is fascinating that, precisely as the fictional Yang Xingyuan is trying to dodge unwanted submissions, "Moonlight" is actively calling for its readers to be interactive—creating a rather random and intimate survey of its readership. The "Ten Question and Answers" are revealing in what they say about "Moonlight's" presumptive readership: mostly male, with some education, including urbanites who have met their wives on their own, who go to restaurants, know the city, and have experienced urban problems such as being robbed. And, of course, the ideal reader reads "Moonlight" every day.

Though, as is apparent from many published letters and exchanges in "Moonlight," Zhang Henshui repeatedly warns his readers not to confuse him with his fictional characters, he simultaneously teases them by encouraging precisely that sort of confusion. Yang Xingyuan's given name, for instance, is a close homophone of Zhang's own, Xinyuan, just as Yang's heartbreak over Liyun's 梨雲 (Pear Cloud) death in *Unofficial History* evokes one of Zhang's own most common pen-names: Ai Li 哀梨 (Mourning pear blossoms).

Just as *Unofficial History* plays with the similarities and differences between the city as geographical place and the city as fictional, narrated form, Zhang repeatedly teases readers with the confusion between his life and his fictional characters. However, near the end of the novel, Zhang Henshui has Yang Xingyuan remind us of the essential difference one last time. In Chapter 83, as Yang is getting sicker and sicker (he will die two episodes later), he still has to go to work in order to make a living. When his friend Jianchen arrives at the news office, he sees Yang in a state of agony:

> His brows furrowed, grimly silent, clasping a dull pencil in his hand [...] with the electric bulb on him, he seemed especially pale. Jianchen then looked at what he was writing, and saw that it was an essay entitled, "Three Types of Hedonism" (*san da kuaihuo zhuyi* 三大快活主義), and couldn't help but laugh, saying, "You're both ill and poor right now, yet you're sitting here writing on how to have a good time—you must really be an optimist." Yang Xingyuan replied: "Since this is my trade, what could I do but give my readers something to amuse them with? According to you, I should be wailing to my readers every day."
>
> (1101)

The sheer proliferation of newspapers in Beijing in the 1920s must have given readers the sensation of having investigative eyes watching their every move, which was probably not far from the truth. The task of Zhang Henshui and the newspapers he worked for, *World Evening* and *Daily News*, certainly had to be a question of distinction: how do you stand out in such a crowded field? Perhaps one way would be to write a fictional work capturing exactly that awareness of being a (potential) public spectacle— a fear and titillation that so many Beijing inhabitants shared; and also let people who felt that they were missing out, have an "in" on the joke and really know what was happening behind the scenes rather than what is being reported in the papers.

Notes

1 Editorial from *Le Petit Parisien*, 1893, cited in Richard Terdiman, *Discourse/ Counter-Discourse* (Ithaca: Cornell University Press, 1985), 131.
2 In Zhang Henshui 張恨水, *Chunming waishi* 春明外史 (Unofficial history of the old capital, Beijing) (Beijing: Qunzhong chubanshe, 1997). *Unofficial History* was originally serialized in the Beijing *Shijie wanbao* 世界晚報 (World evening news) from 4/12/1924 to 1/24/1929. Three single-volume editions were published concurrently by the *World Daily* and *Evening News* press from 1926–1929. Though I have consulted both the original newspaper serialization and the Beijing *World Daily* edition, in this essay I reference the 1997 Beijing edition, which is based on a 1930s Shanghai Shijie shuju reprint edition that had been extensively revised by Zhang Henshui. References to this edition will be cited parenthetically in the text; all translations are my own.
3 Benedict Anderson, *Imagined Communities: Reflections on the Origin and Spread of Nationalism* (London: Routledge, 1991), 4.
4 Liang Qichao 梁啟超, "*Lun xiaoshuo yu qunzhi zhi guanxi*" 論小説與群治之關係 (On the relationship between fiction and the government of the people). Originally appeared in *Xin xiaoshuo* 新小説 (New fiction), 1902. Trans. by Gek Nai Cheng, in Kirk Denton, *Modern Chinese Literary Thought: Writings on Literature, 1893–1945* (Stanford: Stanford University Press, 1996), 74.
5 Anderson, *Imagined Communities*, 33.

6 Liang Qichao, "*Hanman lu*" 汗漫錄 (A record of traveling afar), *Qingyi bao* 清議報 35 (1899), 2275.
7 See Chen Pingyuan 陳平原, "*Yulunjia de taidu yu xiuyang—zuowei daxuesheng de Cheng Shewo*" 與論家的態度與修養—作為大學生的成舍我 (A public intellectual's attitudes and learning—Cheng Shewo's college student days), in *Baohai shengya* 報海生涯 (A life in newspapers) (Beijing: Xinhua chubanshe, 1998), 89–109.
8 Cheng Shewo 成舍我, "*Li Bao xuanyan*" 立報宣言 (Li Bao declaration), *Shanghai Li bao* 上海立報, Sept. 20, 1935.
9 Unfortunately, there are no extant copies of *World Evening News* before 5/1/1926 in the Beijing National Library archival holdings.
10 Fang Hanqi 方漢奇, "*Yidai baoren Cheng Shewo*" 一代報人成舍我 (Cheng Shewo, newspaperman for a generation), paper presented at the "Cheng Shewo Centenary Academic Conference," held at the Academy of Social Sciences, Beijing, August 28, 1998.
11 Cheng Shewo, *Baoxue zazhu* 報學雜著 (Assorted writings on the press) (Taipei: Zhongyang wenwu gongyingshe, 1956), 24.
12 Stephen R. MacKinnon, "Cheng Shewo and the Building of a Newspaper Empire," Paper presented at the Cheng Shewo Centenary Symposium, Shih Hsin University, Taipei (August 31, 1998), 4.
13 See "*Yeguang*" 夜光 (Moonlight) in *World Evening News*, May 1926.
14 Fang Hanqi, "*Yidai baoren Cheng Shewo*."
15 Robert E. Park, "The Natural History of the Newspaper," *American Journal of Sociology* 29 (November 1923), 273–289; the quote is from page 286.
16 Park, "The Natural History of the Newspaper," 288.
17 Zhang Henshui, *Unofficial History*, 104–106.
18 David Strand, *Rickshaw Beijing: City People and Politics in the 1920s* (Berkeley: University of California Press, 1989), 12–14.
19 He Yiwen, Xia Fangya, and Zuo Xiaohong, "*Beiping shijie ribao shigao*" 北平世界日報史稿 (Historical records of Beijing's *World News Daily*). In Zhang Youluan et al., eds. *Shijie ribao xingshuai shi* 世界日報興衰史 (A history of the rise and fall of the World News Daily) (Chongqing: Chongqing chubanshe, 1982), 44–45.
20 He, Xia, and Zuo, "*Beiping shijie ribao*," 51–52.
21 Zhang Youluan 張友鸞, "*Zhanghui xiaoshuo dajia Zhang Henshui*" 章回小説大家張恨水 (Master of the linked-chapter novel Zhang Henshui). Orig. 1981, reprinted in *Chunming waishi—Zhang Henshui zuopin jingdian* 春明外史—張恨水作品經典 (Unofficial history of the old capital—Zhang Henshui's greatest works) (Beijing: Qunzhong chubanshe, 1997), vol. 3, 1164.
22 Zuo Xiaohong, "*Shi yeshi (chongban daixu)*" 是野史（重版代序）. (It is an unofficial history—preface to the new edition). Orig. 1985, reprinted in *Chunming waishi—Zhang Henshui zuopin jingdian*, vol. 1, 2. Zuo and Zhang Youluan were both colleagues of Zhang Henshui at the *World Evening News* and *World Daily News*.
23 Richard Stein, "Street Figures: Victorian Urban Iconography," in Carol T. Christ and John O. Jordan, eds., *Victorian Literature and the Victorian Visual Imagination* (Berkeley: University of California Press, 1995), 233.
24 Zhang Ailing 張愛玲, *Liuyan* 流言 (Written on water) (Taipei: Huangguan wenxue chuban youxian gongsi, 1991), 12.
25 See, for instance, Perry Link, *Mandarin Ducks and Butterflies: Popular Fiction in Early Twentieth Century Chinese Cities* (Berkeley: University of California Press, 1981), and T. M. McClellan, "Change and Continuity in the Fiction of Zhang Henshui (1895–1967): From Oneiric Romanticism to Nightmare Realism," *Modern Chinese Literature*, vol. 10, 1998, 113–134.

26 Fan Boqun 范伯群, *"Lun Zhang Henshui de jibu daibiaozuo—Jianlun Zhang Henshui shifou guishu Yuanyang hudie pai wenti"* 論張恨水的幾部代表作—兼論張恨水是否歸屬鴛鴦蝴蝶派問題 (A discussion of a few of Zhang Henshui's representative works—also, the issue of whether Zhang Henshui belongs in the Mandarin Ducks and Butterflies school), *Wenxue pinglun* 文學評論 Literary Review, no. 1, 1982, 53.

27 Peter Fritzsche, *Reading Berlin 1900* (Cambridge: Harvard University Press, 1998), 8.

28 Zhang Henshui, *"Xiangqi Dongchangan jie"* 想起東長安街 (Remembering East Chang'an Road). Originally written for *"Zuihou guantou"* 最後關頭 (Last stand), the literary supplement that Zhang edited for the Chongqing *Xinmin Bao* 新民報. It ran on 7/8/1941. Reprinted in Xu Yongling 徐永齡, ed., *Zhang Henshui sanwen* 張恨水散文 (Selected prose by Zhang Henshui) (Anhui: Anhui wenyi chubanshe, 1995), vol. 2, 211–212.

29 *Beiping lüxing zhinan* 北平旅行指南 (Guide to Beiping for travelers), edited by Ma Zhixiang 馬芷庠 and "approved and revised" by Zhang Henshui (Beijing: Jingji xinwen she, 1936), 2. As a selling point, Zhang Henshui's name is prominently displayed on the cover, and he is also featured in a photograph in the text itself.

30 *"Tantan Beijing de xiyuan"* 談談北京的戲院 (Let's talk about Beijing's movie theaters), *Wanbao* 5/1–5/5/1926; *"Dao Laijinyuxuan tiaowu qu"* 到來今雨軒跳舞去 (Let's go dancing at the Rain Pavilion), *Wanbao* 4/28/1927; *"Chongxiaosi kan mudan"* 崇效寺看牡丹 (Peony-viewing at Chongxiao temple) 5/7/1926; *"Hutong mingzi yasu yiban"* 胡同名字雅俗一斑 (Elegant and vulgar names of hutong alleys) 4/5/1927; *"Fu de renxuan"* 夫的人選 (How to choose a husband) 5/24/1929.

4 Canonizing the popular

The case of Jin Yong

John Christopher Hamm

It is axiomatic that the literary canon mutates over time. Even at a single moment, moreover, and within a given nation or society, it is perhaps misleading to speak of *the* literary canon; there are rather multiple canons, sometimes coexisting in a peace allowed by mutual disregard and sometimes actively competing for cultural authority. While debates in Europe and America over the last two decades have focused on conflicts motivated by divergent visions of ethnic, religious, and gender identity, even within a relatively homogeneous society struggles over the canon are guaranteed by the structural logic of what Pierre Bourdieu calls the literary field—the network of various actors and interest groups involved in the material and symbolic production of what a given society defines as literature. At any moment in time, a variety of agents are engaged in negotiating both the distribution of cultural capital, one of the fruits of which is canonicity, and the status that confers the right to have a say in the ongoing process of distribution. It is in good measure the synchronic tensions, negotiations, and contestations between the various canon-makers, actual and potential, that generate diachronic shifts in "the" canon.

If the term *canon* designates the body of literary works that a given group sees as articulating its essential values and serving as an instrument for their transmission, we could conceivably speak of each of the agents in the literary field as having its own canon. At the least we might want to recognize several canons—academic, critical, popular—that are the products of broader consensus. Such usage might on the other hand dilute the term to the point of uselessness. We may thus wish to reserve the notion of *canonicity* solely for that body of works (in itself far from uncontested) consecrated by the academy—whether as a matter of definitional fiat, or in recognition of the crucial role that educational institutions customarily play as cultural gatekeepers for society at large. Even in so delimiting our definition, however, we must not lose sight of the larger field within which the academy is embedded, nor of the competing popular and critical claims against which it establishes its body of canonical writings.

Whether we think in terms of competing canons or in terms of an academically consecrated canon distinct from other bodies of writing, the works of Jin Yong 金庸 offer a striking case of mobility across canonical boundaries. Jin Yong is the name under which Zha Liangyong 查良鏞 (Louis Cha, b. 1924) began writing martial-arts adventure tales for serialization in Hong Kong newspaper fiction supplements in 1955. Chinese fiction on martial and chivalric themes traces its roots back at least to the classical tales of the Tang dynasty (618–907), but martial-arts fiction (*wuxia xiaoshuo* 武俠小説) took shape as a genre of mass-distributed entertainment fiction in Shanghai and other urban centers during the 1920s and 1930s. Jin Yong's efforts were instrumental in leading the genre to a new peak of popularity in Hong Kong, Taiwan, and overseas Chinese communities from the mid-1950s on. The fourteen novels and novellas he penned between 1955 and 1972 were quickly canonized, in the loose sense of being recognized by their readership as among the best within their particular genre. The cultural status of that genre as a whole, however, was that suggested by the paradoxical connotations of the English word *popular*: consumed, enjoyed, and in that sense valued by a large and broad-based readership, yet barred by the very breadth of its appeal, and the vulgarity that appeal was assumed to imply, from consideration as a literature of social, aesthetic, or cultural value. Yet in the half-century since his works first began to appear, Jin Yong seems to have made the leap from toiler in a sub-literary ghetto to canonization in the stricter sense of academic recognition as a major figure in twentieth-century Chinese literature. While continuing to attract vast audiences, both in their original form and in film, television, comic-book, and video-game adaptations, his novels have been included in college curricula and addressed in numerous academic articles and conference papers. A 1990s anthology named Jin Yong one of the ten masters of twentieth-century Chinese fiction, ranked among such figures as Lu Xun and Lao She. And the author has received numerous honorary degrees (in part on the strength of his journalistic and political accomplishments, admittedly, and not for his fiction alone), and been appointed Dean of Humanities at Zhejiang University.

An important factor in the recognition of Jin Yong's fiction has been the reconfiguration of the cultural field as a whole during the latter half of the twentieth century, in China as elsewhere—specifically, the erosion of the independence and stature of elite culture, of cultural forms that accumulate value in part through their limited audience and apparent disassociation from the economic marketplace, and the increasing ubiquity and higher valuation of mass-distributed, market-driven forms. Jin Yong's works have obviously enjoyed elevation in part through the rising tide of popular culture, in the academy and in society as a whole; but they have also staked a claim on some of what is left of the high ground of Culture with a capital C. This claim is not undisputed. Every year or two over the past couple of decade has seen a new attack, in the academy or in the popular press, on Jin Yong's work as crass and vulgar. But such attacks only confirm how much ground Jin Yong has already won, and in their way do as much to consecrate his status as does the awarding of a degree by Peking University. It has been remarked that Jin Yong is likely to enjoy the extraordinary good fortune of "seeing the complete canonization (*jingdianhua* 經典化) of his works within his own lifetime."[1] Although claims of full canonization may be premature, it is undeniable that Jin Yong's works have accomplished a remarkable shift in literary status. The good fortune inherent in this shift is therefore shared by literary critics and historians, for whom Jin Yong and his works can serve as a case study, illuminating both general changes in the configuration of the literary field and specific strategies through which its agents seek to negotiate a body of work's cultural position. This essay, part of a larger project, examines one element in the case of Jin Yong: his deployment, at several key stages in his career, of his double role as both author and publisher, in attempts to shape the discursive context of his fiction's reception.

For a sketch of the status of martial-arts fiction in the period when Jin Yong was writing, we can turn to Liu Yichang's 劉以鬯 (b. 1918) modernist classic *Jiutu* 酒徒 (The drunkard), first serialized in 1962–1963 in the literary supplement of *Xingdao wanbao* 星島晚報.[2] The novel's nameless protagonist and first-person narrator is a would-be author, a disciple of Hemingway and fan of the Qing dynasty classic *Honglou meng* 紅樓夢 (The dream of the red chamber), who faces with despair the necessity of penning martial-arts fiction and pornography in order to pay the rent and supply the alcohol into whose embrace his philistine society compels him. For this anguished soul, the demands of art and of the marketplace are incommensurate; the former is in fact recognized and defined by its uncompromising rejection (a rejection which he himself lacks the strength to realize) of the latter. The martial-arts novels he pens in the novel's early scenes and the pornography at which he temporarily succeeds as his degradation progresses are guaranteed both moral turpitude and lack of artistic merit by the very fact that editors and readers are willing to accord it a different order of value in the form of cold hard cash.

The perspective of Liu Yichang's protagonist seems to replicate the model of the cultural economy proposed by the sociologist Pierre Bourdieu. Seeking to account for the mechanisms by which and the ends to which cultural and literary value or "capital" are socially constructed, Bourdieu describes the literary field as existing within the larger networks of society, and yet finding autonomous definition only to the extent that it articulates values unique to itself, distinct from the values and power structures of the society within which it is embedded. Its structure and hierarchies are therefore generated by the continually shifting tension between the autonomous principles proper to itself and the heteronymous principles of political and economic authority in effect throughout society at large.[3] Bourdieu believes the literary and cultural fields to have achieved the above-described configuration in France during the nineteenth century, and to continue to function essentially unaltered through the present day, at least in the society that gave them birth.[4] We might trace this model's reflection in the consciousness of *The Drunkard*'s late twentieth century Hong Kong writer in part to this figure's absorption of the social and aesthetic presumptions of his pantheon of Western modernist literary heroes (Proust, Faulkner, etc.). But at least some of its antecedents are closer to home. The novel's protagonist also sees himself as a (potential) heir to China's May Fourth literary tradition, a movement which was constructed in opposition to and contradistinction from the commercial and popular publications of its day. The leaders of the May Fourth movement (themselves, of course, influenced by Western models) articulated their aims in ideological terms, as rejecting benighted forms of "entertainment"—of which martial-arts fiction and film were perhaps the most regressive—in favor of socially and morally responsible art.[5] But intertwined with these ideological arguments were the Chinese intellectual's traditional disdain for the world of commerce and the prejudice of the academy, based in the north near the seat of political power, against the southern (Shanghai) nexus of the publishing industry.[6]

The Drunkard's linkage of martial-arts fiction with pornography merges a disdain for these genres' contents with an abhorrence for their commercial imperative, and inherits the May Fourth tradition's scorn for "beggars of letters" (*wengai* 文丐) and "whores of letters" (*wenchang* 文娼) who write for the market. In his yearning to realize a literary space unsullied by economic concerns, Liu Yichang's protagonist exemplifies Bourdieu's autonomous principle, the articulation of the artistic domain per se precisely through the "loser wins" logic of spurning the common markers of societal achievement. His attitudes also illustrate the role of journalism (one of the "seemingly most heteronymous forms of cultural production") and the modes of (sub-)literature associated with it (serialized fiction and its thematic subgenres) in defining those reaches of the literary field most barren of symbolic capital.[7] What the novel presents is of course a fictional portrait, and it is possible to read *The Drunkard*'s protagonist ironically, as the self-destructive architect of the system of belief which imprisons him. But the author Liu Yichang clearly seconds his fictional offspring's views. This prominent spokesman for Hong Kong's literary circles has frequently dismissed the bulk of his own writing, produced for newspaper serialization, as "trash,"[8] and in a representative passage reads another author's tale of a woman forced into prostitution as a figure for the plight of the writer in postwar Hong Kong.[9]

Liu Yichang and his protagonist can be taken as speaking for intellectual critics of popular fiction in general and the martial-arts genre in particular, who believed that the commercial imperative fostered formulaicism and an appeal to the readership's baser emotions which consigned such works to the realm of the sub-literary, or even constituted the antithesis which might define pure literature as such. The newspapers themselves did not present the contents of their fiction supplements in quite so harsh a light. What anguished literati viewed as commercialism, they regarded as popularity; and they often presented this popularity, whether of their fiction sections or of their editorial policies more generally, as a form of populism, a solidarity with the social affinities and cultural tastes of their readerships. Jin Yong adopted the populist editorial voice for his own newspaper, *Mingbao* 明報, which he founded in 1959 after working for a decade in Hong Kong's newspaper industry.[10] In its early days the paper's financial existence depended more on sales than on advertising revenue, and sales were made largely on the strength of its fiction supplement, which featured exclusive serialization of Jin Yong's latest martial-arts novels as well as a variety of other fiction—some of it decidedly racy, if not strictly pornographic. And yet from early on we can find in the pages of *Mingbao* a conscious attempt on Jin Yong's part to carve out a specifically literary identity for the fictional genre in which he himself writes. During the first month of publication, for instance, *Mingbao*'s fiction page began running a column entitled "Selections from the Classics of Martial-Arts Fiction" (*Wuxia mingzhu jingxuan* 武俠名著精選), containing excerpts from the work of pre-war authors with introductions signed by Jin Yong himself.[11] The column clearly serves the function of satisfying the appetites of the paper's martial-arts fans, and of doing so with a bit of material for which no manuscript fees were required. In addition, however, by its mere existence the column reifies the notion of martial-arts fiction as a genre with its own identity and tradition. It identifies the classics and model works of this tradition, and through comments on one author's prose style and another's skill in creating convincing characters, makes an implicit case for understanding the genre's features as inhering at least in part in specifically literary qualities. What is more, the series allows Jin Yong to establish his own authority as a connoisseur, arbiter, and spokesman for this tradition of martial-arts literature.

Another example of *Mingbao*'s promotion of the literary qualities of martial-arts fiction and of Jin Yong's work in particular can be found in a film review published the same day as the first installment of the "Selections from the Classics of Martial-Arts Fiction" series—a review of the film adaptation of Jin Yong's *Shediao yingxiong zhuan* 射雕英雄傳 (Eagle-shooting heroes).[12] The paper's film critic, Ye Qin 葉沁, begins by describing her younger brother, a martial-arts fan who reads the fiction far into the night, smuggling a flashlight under the covers to evade his angry mother's interdiction, and whose speech has begun to mimic the bravado and curious locutions of a character from the "rivers and lakes." The writer's assumption that martial-arts fiction is "something for the kids" is shaken when a university professor of her acquaintance shows up for tea with a history of the English novel, a study of the Dumas family, and two volumes of Jin Yong's *Eagle-shooting Heroes*, all tucked under his arm. The critic expresses surprise; the professor paraphrases Zola and urges her to try Jin Yong's work for herself; the kid brother collects the various volumes of *The Eagle-shooting Heroes* lent out to his friends; the critic begins to read, and is utterly entranced; and so it is that she, who has never before bothered with martial-arts films, now finds herself recommending the film version of the novel to her readers.

There are three aspects of this brief review worthy of special notice, in part because they establish the pattern for many future discussions of Jin Yong's work. The first is the fact that what is ostensibly a film review actually serves as an advertisement. The promotional aspect of this and other items appearing in publications owned and operated by Jin Yong is quite evident, yet should not be underestimated as a force in the distribution of his works and the elevation of their status. *Mingbao* was only the first step in what was to become an enormously successful publishing and financial empire. There have been many press barons and financial magnates in Hong Kong, and many popular authors of martial-arts novels or other genre fiction; but Jin Yong is the only figure to have combined the roles of producer of a fictional product and manager of the print media through which it was distributed. In the symbiosis of these two roles can be found at least part of the momentum behind his success in each. And while the symbiosis is on one level financial—the fiction provided the starting capital for the paper and drove its circulation, while the paper and its subsequent affiliates provided the media for the distribution of the fiction—it is also and in a perhaps more important sense discursive. The cultural field is constituted not merely by the artists and writers who produce cultural works but also by the brokers—publishers, critics, gallery owners, etc.—who produce and negotiate the works' value. In the act of consecrating particular works, these brokers also consecrate themselves, that is, affirm that they have the power to perform such consecration.[13] Endorsements of Jin Yong's work in his publications, including such critical interventions as Jin Yong's comments on the "Selections from the Classics of Martial-Arts Fiction," both directly promote the works in question and stake a claim on the cultural capital which alone can give the endorsements force. Jin Yong's publishing empire has thus allowed him to lay claim to the roles not only of author and of financier but of cultural broker as well.

A second striking aspect of the review of *Eagle-shooting Heroes* is the fact that less than half the article is devoted to appraisal of the film itself; the greater part addresses the original novel and the question of its literary value. The early Cantonese film versions of Jin Yong's fiction were only the first step in a process of adaptation into film, television, comic books, and computer role-playing games that continues to the present day. These adaptations have introduced Jin Yong's works to larger and larger audiences, and undoubtedly drawn many new readers to the original novels. In addition, the adaptations have worked to elevate the cultural status of the texts through the logic of differentiation. If we follow Bourdieu in understanding the cultural field as structured in hierarchies of opposition, we can appreciate that the increasing dominance of film and television as media of large-scale production and mass audiences have allowed the novel, "literary" by definition even in popular genre forms, to define itself more credibly as a medium of (relatively) restricted distribution and to ally itself symbolically with the elite arts of the culture. As early as this film review, we can see this dynamic playing itself out in the specific case of the book and film versions of Jin Yong's works.[14]

The third paradigmatic aspect of the review is its deployment of recognizable emblems of high culture to define the position of Jin Yong's fiction. These emblems include representatives of the European fiction tradition, Dumas and Zola; most prominent though is the figure of the university professor as champion of Jin Yong's work. The professor's presence is important in part because it allows us to discern more precisely the status which Jin Yong's work seeks to attain. Jin Yong's novels pride themselves in the same populist stance which was the basis for his newspaper's editorial voice; as such they disavow any claim to the most autonomous heights of the literary field, which are defined precisely by restricted appeal and limited circulation. What they do aspire to is the transmutation of popular appeal into what Bourdieu calls "bourgeois" consecration, "the consecration bestowed by the dominant fractions of the dominant class and by private tribunals, such as *salons*, or public, state-guaranteed ones, such as academies, which sanction the inseparably ethical and aesthetic (and therefore political) taste of the dominant."[15] The university professor in this film review marks the first of many appearances of a figure meant to evoke the authority of the academy, one of the key institutions in the bestowal of such "bourgeois consecration." An evocation of the academy by a film reviewer in a popular daily newspaper is of course something quite different from an endorsement by the academy's own institutions of evaluation. But we see here the first expression of a desideratum.

One of the most influential entries of the academy into the discourse on Jin Yong's fiction was made by Professor Chen Shih-hsiang 陳世驤, a Peking University graduate who taught at Berkeley until his death in 1971. In 1966 and again in 1970, Professor Chen wrote to Jin Yong to share his thoughts on Jin Yong's novel *Tianlong ba bu* 天龍八部 (translated as "The demi-gods and semi-devils"). In his letters Professor Chen describes discussing Jin Yong's novels with his students and colleagues, including another prominent overseas scholar, Hsia Tsi-an 夏濟安 (1916–1965), and states that "what compels my admiration for the accomplishment of Jin Yong's fiction is the way that artistry and talent continually overcome the limitations of form and material."[16] He explains in greater detail that

> readers of martial arts fiction generally develop a habit of casualness; you could say that they read by rote, just as opera fans tend to listen by rote. Once this habit has been formed, what the reader or listener asks for is quite limited and narrow, and so what they get is equally limited or narrow. Ordinary books can be read, and ordinary opera listened to, in this manner; but Jin Yong's novels are not the same. *The Demi-Gods and Semi-Devils* must not be read by rote; if you bear the prologue firmly in mind, you will find the themes of karma and transcendence developed to their fullest throughout the work.[17]

Besides praising the novel's transcendence of genre limitations and the pro-
fundity of its insights on human life, Chen Shih-hsiang lauds its wedding of
form with content and likens Jin Yong's achievement to the sudden flourishing of drama in the Yuan era: "the only difference is that in the present age
there is still only the one [writer] who has appeared."[18]

Although the terms in which Professor Chen chooses to commend Jin Yong's
fiction are not without interest, most significant for our understanding of the
presentation and reception of Jin Yong's work is not the content of these
letters, but their fate. They were penned as a private communication, not
intended for publication, but in 1978 were printed as an appendix to Ming
Ho Publishing's revised edition of *The Demi-Gods and Semi-Devils*. In the
"Afterword" also appended to the new edition, Jin Yong admits that he is
pleased to be able to share this eminent scholar's favorable appraisal of his
own work and his open-minded attitude towards the potentials of martial-
arts fiction as a whole; he feels profoundly embarrassed, however, by the
fulsomeness of Chen's praise. "Given the level of his erudition and his
scholarly status, such accolades are really a bit excessive. They stem perhaps
from his affection for the traditional Chinese novel form, or from certain
similarities in our perspectives on human life."[19] Jin Yong had hoped, he writes,
to have Chen pen a preface for the new edition; but Chen having passed away,
he appends these letters in respectful memory of his friend and dedicates
the novel to his memory.

Within the letters, Chen Shih-hsiang himself brings up the notion of publishing something on Jin Yong's fiction. He mentions that he has considered
writing up his thoughts in a formal article, but has never gotten around to
it; and as far as publishing such an article in Jin Yong's new *Mingbao Monthly*,
that might smack too much of toadying on his part, or of blowing one's
own horn on the part of the magazine.[20] Jin Yong, for all his modesty, was
evidently less hindered by such compunctions. An article in memory of Chen
Shih-hsiang published in *Mingbao Monthly* shortly after his death includes
an extended discussion of his and other overseas scholars' fondness for
martial-arts fiction and respect for Jin Yong's work.[21] His letters were
included as part of the packaging of the revised edition of *The Demi-Gods
and Semi-Devils*. And in the preface to the series of criticism and commentary on Jin Yong's fiction published in 1987 by Yuanliu, Jin Yong's
publisher in Taiwan, chief editor Wang Rongwen 王榮文 cites Chen Shih-
hsiang as one of the path-breaking academics who helped found the new field
of "Jinology" (*Jinxue* 金學).[22]

But what role, exactly, can Chen be said to have played in the founding
of this field? Discussion and appreciation of Jin Yong's fiction within the
culturally influential circles of overseas Chinese scholars of Chen's generation undoubtedly contributed to the validation of Jin Yong's work as literature. Yet none of these scholars published on Jin Yong or made his work
a formal part of their professional lives.[23] We know of their views through
accounts circulated in Jin Yong's own periodicals, in appendices to the
novels themselves, or in appreciative volumes from the author's publisher

in Taiwan.[24] The role Professor Chen Shih-hsiang finds himself playing is thus representative of the early phase of public commentary on Jin Yong's fiction, in which tokens of cultural authority are deployed within a field whose underlying imperative is that of the marketplace—the world of commercial publishing.

Jin Yong's final novel, *Luding ji* 鹿鼎記 (The deer and the cauldron), completed its newspaper serialization in 1972. Throughout the 1970s Jin Yong devoted himself to revising the texts of his novels and issuing them through the publishing company, Ming Ho, established specifically for this purpose. The resulting 36-volume *Collected Works of Jin Yong* was completed in 1982, and the revised editions of the texts have been the standard versions in circulation since that date. Several prominent commentators have criticized the revised texts for their repression of at least some part of the originals' rough vigor and unbridled imagination.[25] An opposing view, however, points out that the continuing popularity of Jin Yong's works rests primarily on the revised versions, which have circulated exclusively for over twenty-years. Li Yijian 李以建, an editor at Ming Ho, provides the most systematic elaboration of this perspective. He reminds us that the project of revision occupied ten years, fully two-fifths of Jin Yong's twenty-five year career as an author of fiction. It is the fruits of this project, Li argues, that have extended Jin Yong's fame beyond the confines of genre fiction, to the point where he now receives consideration as one of the great novelists of twentieth-century China. The revised texts are "better" in the sense of being more literary than the originals; they transcend the formulae and limitations of popular newspaper fiction and hew more closely to the standards and values of "classic" literature.[26]

Without contesting the artistry of the textual revisions, I wish to direct attention here to another way in which the revised versions of the novels undertake to situate Jin Yong's work within a sphere explicitly marked as that of high culture: by the representation and appropriation, both within the texts of the novels and within the physical volumes of the *Collected Works*, of the artifacts and values of the Chinese cultural tradition. The representation of the martial arts as intertwined with other elements of China's artistic and cultural heritages, and citation of these heritages at various levels of the narrative, are recognized characteristics of the "New School" of martial-arts fiction of the 1950s through 1970s. Jin Yong employed such devices even in his first novel, *Shujian enchou lu* 書劍恩仇錄 (The book and the sword), which includes for instance a scene in which the protagonist achieves a breakthrough in his martial abilities through the discovery of an annotated text of the pre-Han philosophical classic, *Zhuangzi* 莊子. It is possible to trace the expansion and elaboration of such "classicizing" narrative elements from the earlier of Jin Yong's novels to the later. It is also easy to discern the increased emphasis given to historical and literary material in the revision of the original serialized texts.[27]

An example occurs in the opening of Jin Yong's second novel, *Bixue jian* 碧血劍 (Sword of loyalty). In its original form, serialized in *Xianggang shangbao* 香港商報(Hong Kong commercial daily) beginning January 1, 1956, the story begins during the reign of the Ming dynasty Chongzhen 崇禎 emperor. The young student Hou Chaozong, son of a retired official from Henan, ignores his parents' warnings about the perilous state of the country and sets out with his servant to see a bit of the world. He witnesses the misery of the peasantry and soon runs afoul of a troop of rapacious Ming soldiers. He is saved from robbery and worse by a chivalrous caravan guard, and he and this hero soon encounter a mysterious group of recluses who are training a young boy in the arts of war. The boy is Yuan Chengzhi, son of a martyred Ming general and the real protagonist of the novel; the rest of the tale recounts his martial training, romances and adventures, and involvement in the struggle between the Ming court, the Manchus, and the rebel Li Zicheng for the throne of China.

The revised text provides an even more circuitous entry to the main characters and events of the story. It tells how the King of Brunei traveled to the court of the Ming Chengzu 成祖 emperor in 1408, noting that "although [Brunei] was separated from the mainland by thousands of leagues of ocean, it had long held China in reverence."[28] The narrative details the gifts presented by the King, and traces the history of Brunei's tributary missions since Song times. The present King of Brunei, entranced by the splendors of the Middle Kingdom, lingers there and passes away. The Ming emperor enfeoffs his son and indites an elegy which is subsequently inscribed on Brunei's sacred mountain. Brunei continues to send tribute to the Ming court, and Chinese travel to Brunei, often serving there as court officials. In later years one of these overseas Chinese, remembering his homeland, names his only son Zhang Chaotang ("facing the Tang," i.e., the Chinese empire), secures for him a classical education from an itinerant scholar, and sends him back to his native land to complete his education and win success through the imperial examinations. The revised text's Zhang Chaotang is the reincarnation of the earlier version's Hou Chaozong. When he arrives on the mainland, only to find it ravaged by bandits and equally rapacious government soldiery, the two versions of the text begin to run parallel.

The revised opening does nothing to alter the adventures of the novel's protagonist, Yuan Chengzhi. Its function is rather to offer a larger frame for his adventures, foregrounding the importance of China as the fountainhead of cultural meaning. Brunei's reverence for Chinese culture, the King's visit and presentation of tribute, and the importance of Chinese officials and merchants in Brunei's government and society, all affirm the pre-eminence and influence of the Chinese cultural tradition. The figure of the King of Brunei rewrites on a more grandiose scale the respect for the Chinese cultural tradition and the desire to drink from its springs that is also present in the transformation of the pleasure-seeking Hou into the earnest scholar Zhang.

But the revised text does not merely narrate the story of two individuals seeking instruction in the Chinese cultural tradition. It also enacts such a process of cultural initiation: it undertakes to provide the reader with instruction in the content and value of the Chinese literary and cultural heritage similar to that undergone by Zhang Chaotang and the King of Brunei. In narrating their stories, it takes pains to offer explanations of geographic and linguistic material likely to be unfamiliar to the modern reader. It reproduces in full the text of the Ming emperor's verses for Brunei's sacred mountain; and in an endnote to the first chapter, it explicates these verses in modern vernacular Chinese.[29] Historical glosses within the text are sometimes enclosed in parentheses or set off by a variant typeface. This typographical practice highlights the authorial voice's departure from simple narrative and engagement in a more schoolmasterly practice of instruction.

Through such apparatus, which appears throughout *Sword of Loyalty* and in many of the volumes of the *Collected Works*, the revised versions of Jin Yong's novels extend the cultural pedagogy represented in the novels' diegetic world into extra-diegetic textual space, a space more plainly oriented towards interaction with the reader. The *Collected Works* further extend this didacticism and cultural appropriation in non-textual directions as well. The front of each volume in the set features a collection of captioned colored plates reproducing works of art, relics, historical documents, maps, portraits, and photographs of famous sites associated with the events of the novels. It is instructive to compare these plates with the black-and-white illustrations at the head of each chapter. The latter, reworkings of the illustrations that accompanied the daily newspaper serializations, simply represent the events and characters of the tale. The former in effect set the novels within a museum of Chinese history and culture. Beyond their explicit pedagogical intent, they make the implicit claim that the *Collected Works of Jin Yong* have a rightful place within such a museum—a claim also inherent in the canonizing gesture of preparing a *Collected Works* in the first place. The significance of Jin Yong's revision of his novels, then, does not lie solely in the refinement of the artistic quality of the texts. It lies also in the advancement, both within the tales and in the publication practice of the *Collected Works*, of arguments for the cultural value of the Chinese tradition and for the novels' own role in honoring and transmitting this inheritance.[30]

My intent here is neither to argue that Jin Yong's work gained cultural consecration purely by voicing a claim, bootstrapping itself as it were into a more elevated status, nor to suggest that Jin Yong intended or was empowered to buy the rights to such a claim through the brute application of his economic resources. Such arguments would render a disservice to the (in my opinion) considerable pleasures and virtues of Jin Yong's fiction. They would also assume a too simplistic view of the processes by which cultural capital is accumulated and cultural consecration bestowed. The crucial question in any act of consecration is that of how the authority to confer such consecration is generated, conferred, and acknowledged; and the answer to this question lies in the complex, mutually sustaining, and continually renegotiated relationships between the various players within the cultural field. Jin

Yong achieved rare success in positioning himself not only as an author but also as a broker with a high degree of control over the distribution of his own fictional products and over a range of associated media channels. The portion of the history of Jin Yong's fiction reviewed here illuminates the extent to which and the strategies by which someone in this position might strive to convert the literal capital of popular success into the literary capital of cultural status. At the same time, however, it also suggests the limitations of such attempts. Even as Jin Yong exercised to the full his control over a certain portion of the cultural field, the very fact of his control constrained his efforts' effectiveness. He was preaching to the choir, to an audience made up primarily of already engaged readers and fans; and to critical or academic groups on the outside, the complicity of producer and broker could not but render suspect the latter's strategies and pronouncements.

Consolidation and wider acceptance of the proposition that Jin Yong's works possess qualities which merit their inclusion in the canon of twentieth-century Chinese literature has required the cooperation of other credentialed and more or less independent agents. The continuation of this study—its chronological extension into the 1980s and 1990s, and its spatial expansion into more of the interlinked spheres of interest that make up the literary field as a whole—would require at the least an analysis of the acts and motivations of various agents in the academic and mass media spheres. Such analysis would have to be attuned to geopolitical variations, for the story of Jin Yong's consecration is inseparable from the story of his works' dissemination from Hong Kong out to Taiwan and overseas Chinese communities, and of their assault on the Chinese mainland in the 1980s. It would also have to consider roles assumed by or imputed to the author beyond those discussed here: his political activities, his emergence as a cultural spokesperson and media celebrity. I believe, nonetheless, that the groundwork for the later stages in the process of consecration—the materials and discursive strategies they employ—was prepared by the elements analyzed in this essay: by the cultural claims made by the texts themselves; by the support lent such claims by Jin Yong's media networks and publication strategies; and by the authority gathered by Jin Yong himself in his multiple, mutually reinforcing roles in the economic and cultural fields.

Notes

Material from this essay has been incorporated into chapters 7 and 9 of my book *Paper Swordsmen: Jin Yong and the Modern Chinese Martial Arts Novel* (Honolulu: University of Hawai'i Press, 2005). Readers interested in an expanded discussion of the issues addressed here are invited to consult that volume. I am grateful to the University of Hawai'i Press for granting permission to include the present essay in this conference volume.

1 Wang Rongwen 王榮文, "*Jin Yong yanjiu de xin qidian*" 金庸研究的新起點 (A new starting point for the study of Jin Yong), in *Zhuzi baijia kan Jin Yong (1)* 諸子百家看金庸 (一) (The hundred schools read Jin Yong (1)) (Taibei: Yuanliu, 1987), 4.

2 The novel was published in book form by Hong Kong's Haibin tushu gongsi in 1963, and has since been republished in several editions, including Taibei: Yuanjing, 1979.

3 Pierre Bourdieu, *The Field of Cultural Production: Essays on Art and Literature* (New York: Columbia University Press, 1993).

4 See the historicized account in Pierre Bourdieu, *The Rules of Art: Genesis and Structure of the Literary Field* (Stanford: Stanford University Press, 1996). For an exploration of the applicability of Bourdieu's theories to twentieth-century China, see Michel Hockx, "Introduction," in Hockx, ed., *The Literary Field of Twentieth-Century China* (Honolulu: University of Hawai'i Press, 1999), 1–20, and other essays collected in this volume.

5 May Fourth critics viewed martial-arts fiction as epitomizing the evils of popular culture, not only because of the violence and "feudal" superstition of its contents but also because of its alleged promotion of a passive fantasy of superhuman saviors which furthered the interests of China's ruling classes. A classic statement of this critique can be found in Shen Yanbing 沈雁冰, "*Fengjian de xiao shimin wenyi*" 封建的小市民文藝 (The feudal art and literature of the petit bourgeoisie), first published in 1933, reprinted in Wei Shaochang 魏紹昌, *Yuanyang hudie pai yanjiu ziliao* 鴛鴦蝴蝶派研究資料 (Materials for the study of the Mandarin Ducks and Butterflies School) (Hong Kong: Joint Publishing, 1980), 25–28.

6 Chen Pingyuan, "Literature High and Low: 'Popular Fiction' in Twentieth-Century China," in *The Literary Field of Twentieth-Century China*, 113–133.

7 Bourdieu, "The Field of Cultural Production, or: The Economic World Reversed," in Bourdieu, *The Field of Cultural Production*, 45, 51.

8 Wendy Larson, "Liu Yichang's *Jiutu*: Literature, Gender, and Fantasy in Contemporary Hong Kong," *Modern Chinese Literature* 7.1 (spring 1993), 89.

9 "Foreword," in *Xianggang duanpian xiaoshuo xuan (wushi niandai)* 香港短篇小説選（五十年代） (Selected Hong Kong short fiction (The 1950s)), ed. Liu Yichang 劉以鬯 (Hong Kong: Tiandi tushu, 1997), 5.

10 On *Mingbao*, see Cheung Kwai-Yeung 張圭陽, *Jin Yong yu baoye* 金庸與報業 (Jin Yong and the press) (Hong Kong: Mingbao chubanshe, 2000).

11 The column began on 6 June 1959.

12 Ye Qin 葉沁, "*You ganqing de wuxia pian*" 有感情的武俠片 (A martial arts film with feeling), *Mingbao*, 6 June 1959. The film reviewed is *Shediao yingxiong zhuan, er ji* 射鵰英雄傳二集 (The eagle-shooting heroes, part II), directed by Hu Peng 胡鵬, Emei Studios, released June 3.

13 Bourdieu, "The Field of Cultural Production," 42; see also "The Production of Belief: Contribution to an Economy of Symbolic Goods," in *The Field of Cultural Production*, 76–77.

14 Huo Jingjue 霍驚覺, *Jinxue da chendian* 金學大沉澱 (Sifting out "Jinology") (Hong Kong: Yuelin tushu gongsi, 1990), 50, makes the simpler but equally cogent point that the poor scripting and production values of many of the television and film adaptations may encourage readers to perceive the more polished novels as "higher quality" works of art.

15 Bourdieu, "The Field of Cultural Production," 51.

16 Letter of 12 November 1970, reprinted in Jin Yong, *Tianlong babu* 天龍八部 (The demi-gods and semi-devils), revised edition (Hong Kong: Ming Ho, 1978), 2129.

17 Letter of 22 April 1966, in *Tianlong babu*, 2127.

18 Letter of 12 November 1970, in *Tianlong babu*, 2129.

19 Jin Yong, *Tianlong babu*, 2125.

20 Letter of 22 April 1966, in *Tianlong babu*, 2128.

21 Shi Chengzhi 史誠之, "*Taoli chengxi nanshan hao: dao Chen Shixiang jiaoshou*" 桃李成蹊南山皓—悼陳世驤教授 (Peaches and plums throng the paths, whitening the southern mountains: in memory of Professor Chen Shixiang), *Mingbao yuekan* 明報月刊 68 (August 1971), 14–22. An article in memory of Chen in the

literary journal *Chun wenxue* also mentions his fondness for Jin Yong's fiction, but only in passing: Ye Shan 葉珊, "*Bokelai: huainian Chen Shixiang xiansheng*" 柏克萊—懷念陳世驤先生 (Berkeley: in memory of Professor Chen Shih-hsiang), *Chun wenxue* 純文學 10.2 (August 1971), 77.

22 Wang Rongwen 王榮文, "*Jin Yong yanjiu de xin qidian*" 金庸研究的新起點 (A new starting point for the study of Jin Yong), in San Mao 三毛 et al., *Zhuzi baijia kan Jin Yong (1)* 諸子百家看金庸 (一) (The Hundred Schools read Jin Yong (1)) (Taibei: Yuanliu, 1987), 2. Yuanliu's 1987 *Jinxue yanjiu ji* 金學研究集 (Collected studies in Jinology) was a reissue and extension of the *Jinxue yanjiu congshu* 金學研究叢書 (Collectanea of studies in Jinology) published by Yuanjing beginning in 1980. In its latest incarnation, as Yuanliu's *Jin Yong chaguan* 金庸茶館 (Jin Yong teahouse), the series numbers thirty-odd titles. Beijing's Wenhua yishu chubanshe is now publishing the series on the mainland.

23 The minor exceptions include a note appended by Hsia Tsi-an's brother C. T. Hsia to his discussion of the figure of the swordsman in traditional fiction: "Most *aficionados* consider the postwar period to be the golden age of *wu-hsia hsiao-shuo* [*wuxia xiaoshuo*] and the Hong Kong author Chin Yung [Jin Yong] to be the reigning practitioner of the genre. Many readers of cultivated taste compare him seriously to Alexander Dumas, *père*" (C. T. Hsia, *The Classic Chinese Novel* [New York: Columbia University Press, 1968], 331, note 49).

24 Again, with exceptions. Lin I-Liang (b. 1919), for instance, himself associated with the intellectual circles that included Chen and Hsia, mentions these scholars' esteem for Jin Yong in a 1969 interview with the author independently published in 1972. Lin I-Liang 林以亮, ed., *Wuge fangwen* 五個訪問 (Five interviews) (Hong Kong: Wenyi shuwu, 1972), 70.

25 See, e.g., Ni Kuang 倪匡, *Wo kan Jin Yong xiaoshuo* 我看金庸小説 (A reading of Jin Yong's fiction) (Taibei: Yuanjing, 1980), 14–18; and Yang Xing'an 楊興安, *Jin Yong xiaoshuo shi tan* 金庸小説十談 (Ten talks on Jin Yong's fiction) (Hong Kong: Mingchuang, 1989), 88–107.

26 Li Yijian, "'Rewriting' Jin Yong's Novels into the Canon: A Consideration of Jin Yong Novels as Serialized Fiction," in Ann Huss and Jianmei Liu, eds., *The Jin Yong Phenomenon: Chinese Martial Arts Fiction and Modern Chinese Literary History* (New York: Cambria Press, 2007), 73–96.

27 Lin Baochun 林寶淳, *Jiegou Jin Yong* 解構金庸 (Deconstructing Jin Yong) (Taibei: Yuanliu, 2000), 211–234, notes an increased emphasis on historicity as one of the chief characteristics of Jin Yong's revisions. In discussing another characteristic, the polishing of the style, Lin focuses on the effort expended in refining the chapter titles; this topic is also addressed in Wu Hongyi 吳宏一, "*Jin Yong xiaoshuo zhong de jiu shici*" 金庸小説中的舊詩詞 (The old-style verse in Jin Yong's fiction), *Mingbao yuekan* 36.3 (March 2001), 77–83.

28 Jin Yong, *Bixue jian* 碧血劍 (The sword stained with royal blood) (Hong Kong: Ming Ho, 1975), 7.

29 *Bixue jian*, 8 and 40.

30 Huo Jingjue, *Jinxue da chendian*, 27, derides the revised edition's "elevation" of Jin Yong's work through the expenditure of effort on factors (binding, illustrations, poetic chapter headings, historical footnotes, etc.) extrinsic to the texts themselves. Insightful analysis of Jin Yong's deployment of representations of Chinese tradition can be found in Lam Ling Hon (Lin Linghan 林凌翰), "*Wenhua gongye yu wenhua rentong: lun Jin Yong wuxia xiaoshuo chengxian de zhimin chujing*" 文化工業與文化認同：論金庸武俠小説呈現的殖民處境 (Culture industry and cultural identity: on the representation of the colonial situation in Jin Yong's martial arts fiction)," *Wenhua xiangxiang yu yishi xingtai: dangdai Xianggang wenhua zhengzhi lunping* 文化想像與意識形態：當代香港文化政治論評 (Cultural imaginary and ideology: essays in contemporary Hong Kong cultural politics), ed. Chen Qingqiao 陳清僑 (Hong Kong: Oxford University Press, 1997), 229–253.

Part II
Canonical reflections

5 An archaeology of repressed popularity
Zhou Shoujuan, Mao Dun, and their 1920s literary polemics

Jianhua Chen

In 1922, at the height of the debate between the old and new literature, the leading May Fourth movement author Mao Dun (茅盾 1896–1981) published his article "*Ziranzhuyi yu Zhongguo xiandai xiaoshuo*" 自然主義與中國現代小説 (On naturalism and contemporary Chinese fiction) in *Xiaoshuo yuebao* 小説月報 (Short story magazine). Of the various targets of this article, the short story "*Liushengji pian*" 留聲機片 (A gramophone record) was extensively quoted and criticized. While Mao Dun did not mention the author by name, he did point to a certain volume of the popular journal *Libailiu* 禮拜六 (Saturday), in which the reader could find the story as well as its author. The author was Zhou Shoujuan 周瘦鵑 (1894–1968), a key figure in the Mandarin Ducks and Butterflies camp, and Mao Dun apparently had good reason to criticize this particular story. At the time Zhou was known as the "king of the sad love story," and was particularly adored by young people as the "God of Love." "Gramophone" struck a sentimental chord; it was said a married woman was so touched by this love tragedy that she was willing to die without regret because she found someone who knew her better than anyone else in the world.

The omission of Zhou's name from this article could be attributed not only to Mao Dun's politeness or even his deliberate dismissal of a rival, but more importantly it was symptomatic of the collective attempt by the May Fourth movement as a whole to exclude from consideration authors like Zhou, together with the old-style literature that he was perceived as representing. In fact, Zhou's status as an author had already become problematic, as he had been portrayed by other prominent May Fourth figures such as Zheng Zhenduo 鄭振鐸 (1898–1958) and Guo Moruo 郭沫若 (1892–1978) as a commercial writer lacking human concerns, modern narrative techniques, as well as scientific knowledge. Moreover, as a symbolic moment in the process of canon formation, Mao Dun's omission here could be seen as an omen of the Butterflies' subsequent exclusion from the emerging Chinese literary canon. In the mid-1950s, for instance, when younger Marxian academics in mainland China, in their mission to put into practice Mao Zedong's "Talks at the Yan'an Forum on Literature and Art," published new histories of Chinese literature, they accused the Butterfly writers of constituting a "counter-current against May Fourth literature."[1] As a leading Butterfly writer, Zhou was harshly targeted and expunged from these new histories. However, although these later literary scholars frequently cited and discussed Mao Dun's 1922 article, they nevertheless rarely showed any curiosity about its context within the 1920s literature debates,[2] nor did they express any interest in the subject matter, author, or origin of "A Gramophone Record" itself.

The present essay seeks to recuperate Zhou as the repressed Other of the May Fourth canon, and to interrogate this process of canon formation in light of the literary polemics of the 1920s. My inquiry, moreover, is itself located at a moment in China's *fin-de-siècle* period when the long-repressed Butterfly School has begun to return in revanchist splendor, together with a plethora of reprinted works and academic reappraisals within which Zhou stands out as the "Master of Sentimental Fiction" (*aiqing xiaoshuo jüzi* 哀情小説鉅子). An influential articulation of this recent resurgence of interest in Butterfly fiction, which itself can be located within the 1980s and 1990s enthusiasm for "rewriting literary history" (*chongxie wenxueshi* 重寫文學史), is literary scholar Fan Boqun's 范伯群 "two wings" model of modern Chinese literary history.[3] Fan's theory asserts that modern Chinese literature consists of both "pure literature" and "popular literature," with the former denoting May Fourth literature and the latter the Butterfly/Saturday School. While Fan's model constitutes a useful corrective to the May Fourth's systematic exclusion of Butterfly works from consideration altogether, it nevertheless explicitly reaffirms many of the same problematic literary valuations (e.g., of purity and popularity) on which that original exclusion was grounded in the first place. A similar problem can be found in the work of Wei Shaochang 魏紹昌 (1922–2000), a well-known historiographer of Butterfly literature. In his reappraisal of the Mandarin Ducks and Butterflies label, Wei affectionately called this term "a beautiful cap" (*meili de maozi* 美麗的帽子) because, he explains, these little creatures— mandarin ducks and butterflies—are beautiful and lovable, symbolizing their popularity and the pleasure they offer. Yet this metaphor implies a re-justification of the "cap" imposed by May Fourth writers. Wei maintains that even the best Butterflies, despite their contribution to modern Chinese literature, failed to compete with Lu Xun 魯迅 (1881–1936), Mao Dun, and other May Fourth giants in terms of the intellectual and aesthetic qualities of their works.[4]

Rather than following Fan Boqun's "two wings" model, with its assumption of a clear-cut binary between elite and popular literature, I will instead develop what I will call a "double mirror" hermeneutical process, whereby I not only seek to bring critical attention to previously obscure works by the ostensibly popular author, Zhou Shoujuan, but more importantly will seek to read each tradition through the lens of the other, thus creating a dialectical vision of Chinese literary modernity. To this end, I will first examine the 1920s literary polemics wherein Zhou and Mao Dun attempted to stake out some of the differences between the two literary traditions they each represented, but at the same time suggest that these two figures actually shared many commonalities that implicitly challenge a rigid dichotomy between the two traditions they have each come to represent. Finally, in the latter half of the essay, I will present a close reading not only of Zhou's "A Gramophone Record," but also of Mao Dun's own short story "*Chuangzao*" 創造 (Creation), which was published in 1928. Here, again, my intention will be both to identify some of the representative characteristics of each work, but also to point to many of the commonalities that they share. In the conclusion, I stress that neglecting the "old" literature has resulted not only in misreading modern Chinese in general, but also in misreading the "new" literature in particular, and vice versa.

Mao Dun and the *Short Story Magazine*

If the May Fourth fight against the old literature began in the late 1910s, a new campaign was launched after Mao Dun took over the *Short Story Magazine* in the beginning of 1921. In turning this journal into the mouthpiece of the Literary Association (*Wenxue yanjiu hui* 文學研究會), Mao Dun and his allies were vigorously supporting the May Fourth project of creating a new literature. Contemporary literary scholar Wang Xiaoming 王曉明 describes, for instance, how their every action was intended to influence the development of literature as a whole, as if the significance of the Literary Association was not to realize the literary ideals of its own members, but instead to provide a dominant central institution for the literary scene.[5] Indeed, centering on the universalistic concept of *literature* (*wenxue* 文學), literary discourse was systematically constituted by the interrelated fields of creative writing, translation, literary criticism, and the study of literary history. In order to build literature into a "system" (*xitong* 系統) or a "science" (*kexue* 科學), Mao Dun stressed the importance of introducing Western literature "systematically and economically." At the time he favored Naturalism, which, he claimed, embodies the "scientific spirit" against subjective Romanticism, signifying the newest development of European Modernism. Obsessed with a kind of scientific objectivism, he asserted that the creation of a work of art requires three things: observation, art, and philosophy, all of which are based on scientific approaches. First, one must observe life from a scientific perspective; second, one must arrange, plot, and describe by using scientific methods; and third, one must provide the background to the story with scientific principles.[6]

Besides Mao Dun's critical essays, between 1921 and 1922, more than 100 letters exchanged between Mao Dun and his readers were published in the "Correspondence" (*tongxin* 通信) section of the journal, vigorously participating in the debate over the new and old literature. Through the various issues discussed by these letters, one can plot the trajectory of Mao Dun's radical agenda, ranging from his advocacy of using "Europeanized grammar" in language to his espousal of Naturalism. The "Correspondence" section began with a discussion between Mao Dun, Zhou Zuoren 周作人 (1885–1968), and Zheng Zhenduo on the topic of translation. Along with their concerns with how to select and evaluate the proper texts for pedagogical purposes, they also emphasized the question of how to establish translation as a form of professional expertise. They contended that translation plays a crucial role in reforming China, for it not only introduces Western literature and culture, but also changes the grammar and structure of the Chinese language, which in turn changes the Chinese mindset. While insisting on "accuracy" and "standardization," they criticized current practices of translation, and Lin Shu 林紓 (1852–1924) was singled out as their main target. Since he didn't know any English, Lin relied on oral interpreters for his translations, but his "inaccurate" style, in Mao Dun's view, was more directly related to his reliance on classical language. These discussions and criticisms embodied the Literary Association's agenda to standardize translation as a rational and scientific activity, and their critiques of Lin Shu signified a move towards repudiating the old literature.

Mao Dun's "Naturalism" article consists of two interrelated parts, with the first part explicating the theory of European Naturalism, and the second criticizing contemporary fiction from this Naturalistic standpoint. Mao Dun claims that his critical targets include both the new and the old schools of the current literature, yet obviously his analysis and critique of the latter are more heavy-handed. While vaguely characterizing Naturalism as embodying the idea of historical progress, he holds that most Naturalist writers are interested in Darwinism and social problems, and that their writings focus on the themes of evolution, psychology, morality, and gender issues. In this article, fictional technique is presented as being no less important than Darwinism. The Naturalist technique, Mao Dun believed, is charged with the most advanced scientific spirit, namely the *Zeitgeist*, or "spirit of the times" (*shidai jingshen* 時代精神). In contrast, not only is the old fiction immune to the idea of progress, it also lacks scientific techniques or advanced artistry, which are critical for the legitimacy of modern literature. In terms of fictional techniques, the old writers all share two kinds of defects. First, they have no idea how to "describe," so their narratives read like dry bookkeeping. Second, they don't know how to observe life objectively, and by plotting at will their works fail to reflect reality. Mao Dun concluded that the old literature exposes its defects in content and form, because its "literary conceptions are linked to pleasure, leisure, and the worship of money."

Mao Dun's critique of Zhou's "Gramophone" story is methodically presented. The story is classified as belonging to the third category of old fiction, the artistic quality of which is higher than that of the first two types. The first type, according to Mao Dun, is the novel in the traditional "chapter form" (*zhanghui ti* 章回體), while the second type is the novel that poorly imitates Western techniques. The third type is the short story, the genre that was best positioned to learn from Western fictional techniques. Having quoted "the most crucial passage" from Zhou's "Gramophone"—which refers to the young hero seeking to end his life because of his tragic love— Mao Dun adds snidely, "here we cannot help admire the author's descriptive method like bookkeeping, perfectly to the point here." Then he asks, "No matter whether the description is good or bad, if a story does not contain any description, can it be counted as fiction?" Mao Dun concludes that the author has neither insight nor objectivity in his observation of life because he lacks sincerity and conscience as a writer.

Mao Dun and other May Fourth theorists attacked Zhou, not only because of his significance within the old camp, but also, ironically, because of his association with the "new." At that time, Zhou was a famous writer, translator, and editor; it was even said that female students collected his photographs as fashionable keepsakes.[7] Zhou's nickname, the "God of Love," was largely due to his passionate introductions of love stories about Western Romantics such as Napoleon, Hugo, and Byron. In 1914, he translated from the Russian the symbolist Leonid Andreyev's "The Red Laugh" (紅笑 *Hongxiao*), which was a groundbreaking initiative in China at the time. In fact, when *Short Story Magazine* announced a reform, Zhou was even invited to serve as co-editor—along with Mao Dun himself!—of the "New Tide" section of the magazine.

Zhou Shoujuan and "Free Talk"

From the outset, the old camp was no less provocative. No sooner had Mao Dun started to turn *Short Story Magazine* into a stronghold of the New Literature, than Zhou Shoujuan created a forum called *Xiaoshuo tekan* 小説特刊 (Special fiction page) for the Sunday "Free Talk" (*Ziyou tan* 自由談) section of the prominent newspaper *Shenbao* 申報. This forum lasted from January to August 1921, through thirty issues. Through this special forum he introduced more than twenty foreign writers, including Balzac, Zola, Conrad, Poe, and Gorky. Zhou himself wrote some of their short biographies, as many of these authors were virtually unknown in China at the time. Evidently, in pursuit of the "New Tide," Zhou intended to take the lead of the literary current, but was soon drawn into the literary polemics with prominent May Fourth figures.

"Free Talk" published many essays on fiction theory, fiction criticism, and fiction history, but presented a strikingly different perspective as compared with the parallel literary essays appearing in *Short Story Magazine*. Rather than asking literature to save the nation, as did Mao Dun and his May Fourth colleagues, the "Free Talk" essays instead insisted on fiction's status as pleasurable diversion. Devoted to the theory of revolutionary emancipation, Mao Dun tried to build a humanist discourse by focusing more on the conception of *wenxue* 文學 (literature), rather than that of *xiaoshuo* 小説 (fiction). Zhou, on the other hand, still cherished the notion of *xiaoshuo* rooted in the traditional meaning of "small talk." It is no wonder, therefore, that the term *wenxue* was splashed across Mao Dun's magazine, yet rarely appeared in Zhou's fiction page.[8]

As *Short Story Magazine* aggressively unfolded its revolutionary agenda, Zhou and his fellow writers grew increasingly alarmed, and differences between the May Fourth and Butterfly camps continued to widen. Mao Dun aimed to reform the national literature and personality after European models, based on his conviction that Chinese culture was totally corrupt and should be eradicated. At the same time, in order to build a revolutionary readership, he placed particular emphasis on the introduction from the West of new theories, new concepts, and a new grammar. By contrast, Zhou's pursuit of the new was primarily rooted in his concerns with daily urban life and the readers' interests and tastes. His commercial priority to amuse this "petty bourgeois" readership was associated with his respect for cultural conventions as well as Western material culture.

Watching *Short Story Magazine* anxiously, Zhou and his followers became increasingly critical of Mao Dun's "New Tide." They suggested that the distinction between the new and the old is determined not by form, but rather by content, and contended that using new theory and terms from the West was not necessarily equivalent with "newness," arguing instead that using the classical language could also express modern feelings. In opposition to Mao Dun's advocacy of European grammar in translation, for instance, Zhou praised Lin Shu for the beauty of his language in translation. In one essay, Zhou's critique was directed at the New Literature:

> Whether fiction is new or old does not depend on its form but on its spirit. If the fiction has a new spirit without using any new punctuation marks or the word *ta* 她 [the new *baihua* pronoun for the feminine pronoun "*she*"], it is not old; if you use many new punctuation marks, it is not necessarily new.[9]

In another essay, he wrote:

> Nowadays there are two ways to write fiction. Some writers like the new type, some like the old. Which type is more authentic? So far there is no conclusion. In my opinion, it is best to let the new writer pursue the new, and the old pursue the old. Each may do as he likes, and let the reader choose. If suspicion grows out of jealousy, or attacks are actually launched in the name of criticism, it shows small-mindedness.[10]

In contrast to Zhou's apparent respect for his readers, Mao Dun's attitude came across as elitist, didactic, and moralistic, as exemplified by his theory of the "mass literature" (*minzhong de wenxue* 民眾的文學), which should serve not to entertain readers but to improve them:

> We should be aware that people's tastes are low, and therefore beautiful literary works are needed to elevate their tastes. Similarly, people are

originally rough and ignorant, and therefore the force of education is required to cultivate them toward the good.[11]

Although in our retrospective look at the polemic it is necessary to recuperate Zhou's voice that had subsequently been silenced by canonical history, it is also necessary to recognize that, at the time, the debates were only implicit, with there scarcely having been any direct confrontation between Zhou and Mao Dun. While accusing the new writers of their "suspicion out of jealousy," Zhou and his fellow writers were complacent enough for their commercial success and yet fearfully regarded the New Literature as a threat to the literary market under their domination. These debates became increasingly heated, and gradually other popular journals joined in, including *Xingqi* 星期 (Sunday) edited by Bao Tianxiao (包天笑 1876–1973), *Jingbao* 晶報 (Crystal) edited by Yu Daxiong 余大雄, and *Zuixiao* 最小 (The smallest), edited by Zhang Zhenlü 張枕綠. The new camp was further supported by Zheng Zhenduo's *Wenxue xunkan* 文學旬刊 (The literary thrice-monthly) and Cheng Fangwu's *Chuangzao zhoubao* 創造週報 (Creation weekly).[12] Moral charges from the Literary Association escalated, especially from Zheng Zhenduo, an ardent advocate of "literature of blood and tears" (*xie yu lei de wenxue* 血與淚的文學), asserting that literature should speak for the oppressed and exploited people in defiance of dark societal forces. In condemning the old literature as aspiring merely to amuse the petty bourgeois for the sake of money and lacking humanist compassion, he even called the old writers "beggars of letters" (*wengai* 文丐) or "whores of letters" (*wenchang* 文娼). In June 1921, when Huang Housheng, a freelance writer, tried to propose a reconciliation between both new and old writers, Zheng responded with a defiant "No."

In July of the same year, meanwhile, Zhou Shoujuan published his essay "*Shuo xiaoxian zhi xiaoshuo zazhi*" 說消閒之小說雜誌 (On fiction magazines for leisure) as a "low-profile" response to Zheng's condemnation. As Zhou argued, there is no reason to despise popular magazines that aim at leisure, as they offered city dwellers a diversion in their spare time. In favor of the interests of consumers, commercialism, and urban life, he hinted that Zheng's concept of literature was too high-minded to suit the common people. In praising popular magazines in England such as *The Strand Magazine* and *London Magazine*, Zhou defended literary pleasure as being not alienated from universal humanism. Compromise seemed impossible between Zhou and Zheng, since they had such different visions of what the goals and means of "ideal literature" should be. Nevertheless, Zhou agreed with Zheng's opinion of "literary refinement" (*wenxue yanjiu* 文學研究) and hatched his idea of creating a magazine by combining "pleasure" with the "literary refinement." It meant that he would raise the literary status of his magazine but at the same time preserve its emphasis on diversion. The essay ended with Zhou's cheerful announcement that a new magazine called *Banyue* 半月 (Semi-monthly) would soon be published as an experiment of his ideal popular magazine.[13] Three months later, he brought this special fiction page to a close, with a note of dignity and toleration: "All the contributors displayed rationality in accordance with facts and did not go beyond the rules."[14]

Zhou's withdrawal, however, by no means abated the conflict. Afterwards he did start his new journal *Semi-Monthly* according to his revisionist scheme, but it was of course not innocent in the new writers' eyes and incited their attacks. In August 1922, after the publication of Mao Dun's essay "Naturalism and Contemporary Chinese Fiction," a letter from readers appeared in the "Correspondence" section, signifying an intensified critique:

> When I was in Shanghai, the "black curtain fiction" was popular, but this did not shock me since I was warned that "Shanghai is a vicious place." Recently, however, I took a trip to Tongzhou, Ningpo, Wuxi and Suzhou doing research on the topic of education, and wherever I went, I saw magazines such as *Saturday, Happiness,* and *Semi-Monthly* [...] and other demons that have captivated the youth—especially young students. How horrible these evils are! Now pitfalls are everywhere. How dangerous and harmful they are to those people crawling in the dark![15]

Although this kind of assault helped lead to the perception, in hindsight, that popular literature had been "repressed" by the emerging May Fourth canon, in actuality Zhou's *Semi-Monthly*, far from being repressed, instead developed into a best-selling magazine in the early 1920s. The situation was similar to the May Fourth critique of the "Friday School" in the 1930s, as Michel Hockx argues in his essay in this volume. In the 1920s, in the literary field different types of partisanship, readership, and literary markets contested with one another. Arguments or quarrels arose therein, casually scattered over the print media, with emotional responses rather than sober discussions. In these polemics, the old writers were less theoretical and combative, and yet showed their cultural stance that was neither conservative nor iconoclast. In stressing literary pleasure as their goal of literary production, they endeavored to absorb Western modernity—largely on the level of material culture—through native literary values and poetics. Yet, paradoxically, while identifying themselves with the label of the *old* in defiance of the new, they became, consciously or not, more defensive in facing the May Fourth claim of saving China. Indeed, the old writers were affected by the readers' letters in the "Correspondence" section, which charged them in the name of national interest. For example, in May 1922, the Butterfly magazine *Youxi shijie* 遊戲世界 (Recreation world) undertook a "big reform" by ruling out those entertainment categories associated with classical literature. This reform, according to the editor's explanation, was in response to "readers' suggestions."

"Women's liberation"

One of the specific intellectual arenas in which these debates over society and culture were played out was in relation to the questions of feminism and "women's liberation." Interestingly enough, if Zhou Shoujuan's and Mao Dun's shared concern is visible from the fact that they previously cooperated to renovate the *Short Story Magazine* in late 1920, then such shared concern is even more evident in their devotion to the question of femininity in their early literary careers. In 1911, when Bao Tianxiao founded the magazine *Funü shibao* 婦女時報 (Women's times), Zhou became its contributor. Mostly drawing from Western materials, the magazine developed a discourse of new women and new nation, from which emerged the ideal of a modern housewife—healthy, educated, and responsible—in an urban "little family." Typical of this trend were Zhou's essays about world-famous women, such as George Washington's mother and wife, as role models for Chinese women. His diverse writings on women also included a piece entitled, "The Roaring Tide of the Women's Franchise Movement by the River Thames," a report on British women's suffrage that Zhou had translated from an English magazine,[16] obviously echoing the debates over women's suffrage that were raging in China at the time.[17]

In two of Zhou's earliest works, "The Complaints of a Fallen Flower" (*Luohua yuan* 落花怨) and "The Flower of Love" (*Ai zhi hua* 愛之花), published in 1911, the central theme was women's romantic love entangled with the power of nation-state.[18] In the former, a classical short story, Miss Huang lives in London as a Chinese student as well as a humiliated "nationless slave" (*wangguo nu* 亡國奴). After marrying an Englishman, she lives with curses from her mother-in-law and the people around them. Finally her husband wants to leave her and she commits suicide. Before hanging herself, she cries out, "My countrymen, listen to me! If you do not awake from this nightmare, you will be worse off than a slave without a home country! What happened to Jews and Poles will happen to us!" In contrast, the heroine Manyin in "The Flower of Love," a pseudo-French play, has an extramarital affair and confronts the power of the nation-state. Whereas Miss Huang desperately calls for a powerful nation-state, Manyin furiously curses the state because it goes to war and thus brings death to her lover. When her lover goes to join the army, she shouts: "Damn the ancestors of our France! Why did they go to war with Palestine and send people there to die?" Both works end with the heroine's suicide in the boudoir, indicating the female desire plagued by moral and political forces in modern times.

During the 1920s, the focus of Zhou's love stories shifted from sentimental and patriotic love to romances about everyday urban life, treating all the problems faced by women in the private and public realms. It was no wonder that his works were widely read by women for their espousal of female freedom from social and ethical restraints. The "new women" in his stories articulated the new values around a nuclear family, including monogamy, economic independence, love with mutual understanding, hard work, and the obligations of citizens.

However, more popular was Zhou's fictional lover with the Western-style name of *Violet*, who was pervasive in his love stories and filled with urban aspiration for modernity. The figure of Violet was richly connected to foreign literature such as Shakespeare's plays or Napoleon's legend, as well as to the traditional literati aesthetics of flower, beauty, and poetry. As a literary commodity, Violet was used for commercial purposes to satisfy male desire and voyeurism, best exemplified by the images of beauties on the covers of the magazine *Ziluolan* 紫羅蘭 (Violet). Yet on the other hand, the magazine was accompanied with Zhou's warm support for the social mobility of women. Special sections such as "Women's Garden" or "Women's Club" opened for publishing women writers' works, though to what extent they expressed women's voices is another question. One female writer, however, was aggressively promoted: when Eileen Chang's first story *"Diyi lu xiang"* 第一爐香 (The first brazier) appeared in Zhou's revived *Violet* in 1943, she rose to fame immediately.

When Mao Dun began to write for *Funü zazhi* 婦女雜誌 (Women's magazine) in 1919, he was as enthusiastic and prolific as Zhou had been eight years earlier when writing for *Women's Times*, but his voice was intentionally radical and subversive. After *Women's Times* stopped publication in 1917, *Women's Magazine* became influential as it aimed to promote women's social standing; it followed the line of *Women's Times* in terms of assimilating the notion of a bourgeois nuclear family in which a "new woman" plays an ideal domestic role. In his memoir from the early 1980s, Mao Dun recalled how he was disappointed at the conservative discourse on women in *Women's Magazine* and intended to change it, and how its editor gladly accepted his writings containing radical opinions about women's emancipation.[19]

"I am a wholehearted advocate of women's emancipation," Mao Dun claimed in his essay entitled "The Emancipated Women and Women's Emancipation," which appeared in *Women's Magazine* in 1919. Steeped in May Fourth anti-traditionalism, he was particularly influenced by the anarchist theory of social utopia, and his theory of "new women" obviously opposed the Butterfly ideal of female domesticity. A real "women's emancipation" meant emancipation from having to be a "virtuous wife and good mother"; in order to realize equality between men and women, "[men] should free women from asking them to be perfect wives and mothers. Men should allow them to share the task of reforming society and developing culture, while women should strengthen themselves to undertake this task."[20] In response to a reader's advocacy of the "small family," Mao Dun replied, "I agree with this idea. However, the small family is too narrow. I hold the belief that the form of the family is not an imperative, and I heartily advocate making public kitchens and public institutions to rear children. I hope someday the human race will live together as one family."[21]

In his memoir, Mao Dun was proud of his intervention in the women's movement, remarking, "For years, *Women's Magazine* had stuck to the ideal of the 'virtuous wife and good mother,' but finally they realized that this line should change."[22] Nevertheless, we must read his reflections on women's issues with some caution. It was also in 1919, for instance, that Mao Dun wrote for a newspaper supplement on the issue of women's emancipation, but his voice was disturbingly contradictory to those published in *Women's Magazine*. In discussing women's role in modern society, he criticized women who

> assume a false civilized mien, implement their "lazyism,"—disdain to do housework and disdain to be a *housewife* and remain at home, but rather become suspicious of their husband's relationships with other women! They want to study, in order to achieve a certain qualification, to be better able to attract a good husband; they study this new scholarship in order to use it as a kind of weapon, to use it to resist their husbands' restrictions [...]. And, in the end, they make their husbands their *play-thing*, and not a *co-partner* [...].[23]

By this statement, Mao Dun expressed a highly conservative fear that the women's emancipation movement might exceed men's ability to control it; perhaps embedded in this fear he shared to some degree the ideal of female domesticity championed by most Butterfly writers.

"Gramophone": domestic agony and the irony of literary pleasure

The plot of "A Gramophone Record" is rather simple: after a failed love affair, a young man named Qingjie Sheng flees Shanghai to the "Island of Regret" in the Pacific Ocean, where unhappy lovers from all over the world congregate. But he finds he is unable to forget Lin Qianyu, his childhood lover, who has married a man chosen by her parents. When on his deathbed eight years later, Qingjie Sheng resolves to send a message of love to Qianyu in Shanghai. Helped by the Pathé (*Baidai* 百代) Record Company on the island, he records his message and then dies. After receiving the record, Qianyu listens to it every day until she too dies, beside the spinning gramophone.[24]

Ironically, given its focus on the "modern" technology of the gramophone, the style of Zhou's story is typically associated with the old or traditional. Categorized as a *yanqing xiaoshuo* 言情小説 (love story), this story belongs to the complex system of "old" romance narratives that still flourished in the early 1920s, and to which Zhou had devoted himself. The term *qing* 情 evokes a long tradition of erotic-sentimental literature and love discourse that blossomed in Jiangnan urban centers during the seventeenth century. As a Suzhou native, Zhou is a natural inheritor of that literati culture.[25] As for the protagonists' names, Lin Qianyu is close to Lin Daiyu in the *Dream of the Red Chamber*, while Qingjie Sheng's 情劫生 name suggests that, in Buddhist terms, he is predestined to be cursed for his love.[26]

"Gramophone" is not merely a simple and entertaining story. It opens plainly enough with a commonsensical statement, "A gramophone is a kind of entertainment," but it concludes melodramatically when the heroine falls dead beside the playing gramophone. Just as pleasure is considered to be one of the bases of Butterfly fiction, such subversion challenges its own codes. In fact, as the whole story shows, while playing with literary conventions, Zhou unfolds the tragic love between a separated couple within shifting spaces that suggest interrelated social and symbolic relations. Moving back and forth between literary convention and invention, the author makes formal twists and breaks. With the tragic ending, ghostly questions overshadow the private space and the gramophone, a familiar fixture of daily urban life. Given the complex motifs of women's suffering, domesticity and Western technology, this story figuratively transcends Zhou's practice of writing for pleasure. Moreover, the gramophone record, which is used simultaneously as a prop, an aural medium, and a symbol of modern technology, dramatically intensifies the tragic romance, and in the process revitalizes this familiar narrative convention.

This story was first published during a period of social and ideological transformation. Although Western-style freedom of love and marriage had spread widely among young people, in reality this ideal of free choice of marriage was compromised by the contemporary judicial system and cultural inertia. Couples in love were not legally free from parental arrangement of marriage until 1930.[27] Early in this century, novels such as Fu Lin's 符霖 *Qin hai shi* 禽海石 (Stones in the sea) and Wu Jianren's 吳趼人 (1866–1910) *Hen hai* 恨海 (The sea of regret) began to focus on the tensions between the "familial despotism" of the old generation, and the progressive values of the new.[28] Lin Qianyu and Qingjie Sheng would belong to this new generation, who grew up in an open social atmosphere early in this century and were influenced by Western ideas of individual passion and free choice in marriage. Scholars typically agree that most of Zhou's love stories oppose the convention of arranged marriage,[29] but "Gramophone" goes a step further: while depicting the tragedy caused by familial despotism, it also exposes a flaw in the new ideal of the "small family," a dream for modern urbanites.

From a brief description of Lin Qianyu, we know that she is an educated woman from a good family who is married to a decent man. But afterwards she lives a miserable life, split between soul and body: outwardly she obeys her fate, yet inwardly she remains loyal to her true love. Female roles in Zhou's love stories usually follow the conventional "virtuous wife and good mother" (*xianqi liangmu* 賢妻良母) model, in accordance with Zhou's ideal of modern urban life based on a harmonious nuclear family. From his praise of "Washington's wife" and "Washington's mother" in the 1910s, to his devotion to the ideal of the "new family" in the early 1930s, Zhou constantly and enthusiastically endorsed the bourgeois vision of the "small family" and domestic femininity.[30] In 1932, he began to edit the journal *Xin jiating* 新家庭 (New family), which was modeled after Western magazines such as *Ladies Homes Journal, Women's Home Companion,* and *Modern Home.* Given that Butterfly literature's emphasis on pleasure effectively articulates the Republican ideology of nationalism and individual consumerism, it is therefore not surprising that in "A Manifesto for the *New Family* Magazine" Zhou stresses the importance of having a comfortable home in everyday life.[31] The idea of the "pleasure of home" is a historically specific concept rooted in bourgeois consciousness.[32] Zhou's advocacy of family values, however, was self-contradictory. In the case of Lin Qianyu, for instance, he notes that

> she married another man, but did not want to betray her true lover. Forced by her parents, she compromised for a better reason, and yet drifted along in her unhappy life. She made a decision to split herself up: giving her worthless body to her lawful husband but keeping the heart and soul for her lover.

At the time this story appeared, the gossip about Zhou's own unsatisfactory marriage began to circulate. His failed first love with a girl known as Violet was similar to Qingjie Sheng's, and as a married man he confessed his undying passion for Violet. Zhou endeavored to construct a literary universe of love and happiness but, instead, as his despair and disillusionment with contemporary reality deepened, his world of love shattered. When his sad romance was made public, it helped to increase his works' value as literary commodities, though it at the same time complicated his identity, placing his passion and ethics in conflict with one another, and presenting a dilemma for his bourgeois ideology. When "Gramophone" ends with Qianyu's madness and death, it brings into question the conservative norm of "virtuous wife and good mother" and the ideal of the "small family." Domestic agony as the central subject in this story implies Zhou's paradoxical gender politics: on one hand female domesticity is encoded by the bourgeois ideology of private and public spaces, yet on the other hand such domesticity is accompanied by permanent pain and subversive force.

A similar paradox can also be found in the figure of Qingjie Sheng, who as a self-exiled lover mirrors Zhou's notion of the world of love as separated from the nation-state. Here a radical change in the exiled hero indicates Zhou's own fading patriotism. In 1915, as a furious response to the announcement of the Twenty-One Treaties between China and Japan, Zhou wrote his famous novella *Wangguonu zhi riji* 亡國奴之日記 (Diary of a slave who lost his country) in which the tragic hero flees to an island in the Pacific Ocean after his country falls into the enemy's hands.[33] Qingjie Sheng's escape from his homeland, therefore, holds a deeper personal significance for Zhou, and could be linked to his disappointment with Republican politics. In the early 1920s, while editing the literary page "Free Talk" in *Shenbao*, Zhou wrote numerous short essays criticizing or satirizing the Republican presidents or the warlords for their actions.

Parallel to his alienation from the nation-state, Qingjie Sheng also implies a satire of the civilized order in a larger context of transnational capitalism. From the late nineteenth to early twentieth century, the knowledge of "islands" presented by newspapers, periodicals, or literary translations was always associated with the exotic imagining of foreign lands and the anxiety of local identity. Similarly, the image of the sea in fiction at the time, such as in Zeng Pu's 曾樸 (1872–1935) *Niehai hua* 孽海花 (Flowers in a sea of sin), conjures up the popular imagination of global and regional geopolitics. In using the figure of the "Island of Regret" inscribed with the implications of regret and retribution, Zhou ingeniously turns the whole world into a "field of love" (*qingchang* 情場), a bittersweet paradise for the lovelorn. In a sense, the indigenous discourse of *qing* is universalized, while at the same time the figure of the exile becomes a focal point within this new microcosm. As the author notes, "Of the hundred thousand islanders, I talk only about the failed lover from the field of love in the Republic of China who is called Qingjie Sheng." The story relates how his cursed love is transmitted and reproduced by modern technology and global capitalism, and when this cultural product returns to the homeland, it intensifies local tragedy and his lover's heartbroken regret.

While describing the despairing lovers on the Island of Regret, the narrator cynically turns the island into a caricature of a gigantic "club," and the reader is ushered into the spheres of a world economy and the diaspora:

> This Island of Regret is simply a huge club. Years ago a few great philanthropists came here with considerable capital and created many places for entertainment. Having invented all means of seeking pleasure, they tried to entice these disappointed lovers there and make them happy. They knew that it is agonizing for those who have lost in love, and that this loss is often unforgettable, but that it is not a sin to give them some solace and let them forget their pain for a while. The island had all the public services as complete as any civilized society. Simply put, this is a new London, a new New York, for stricken lovers.[34]

The detail that his record is made by the Pathé Record Company is inspired by the fact that the company actually had a branch in Shanghai. Among the 100,000 people on the island from China, the United States, England, France, Germany, and the various African countries, 70 percent are described as ailing lovers, and the rest are family members, servants, and coolies. Referring to this fantasy land as the "land of the Peach Blossom Spring" seems a rather conventional gesture, but when it is sarcastically turned into a "new London" or a "new New York" for these lovers, it creates a kind of uncanny unfamiliarity. The picture is gloomy, as it dawns on us that this imagined world is none other than a "civilized state" in the real world.

The story attains its tragic climax when the record reaches Qianyu, exposing complex conflicts while shifting focus from the hero to the heroine, who dies in agony beside the gramophone playing in her chamber. A striking detail is that in the first and last paragraphs of the text, there is an identical metaphor comparing Qianyu's heart and the gramophone. While she listens to her lover's dying words, her broken heart is literally rent: the record ruthlessly turning on the machine is like a grinder that finally crushes her heart to pieces. This ending gives new meaning, both syntactically and practically, to the relation of the female body to pleasure and technology.

Qianyu expresses regret that she has betrayed Qingjie Sheng, but it is not difficult for readers to see that her broken heart is as fragile as the record, thus raising questions about her security and vulnerability in the inner domestic space. The cause of her broken heart is psychological, and yet it is also attributed to outer forces that are social and political. In this typical "small family," there are no overt domestic conflicts. Zhou depicts her as enjoying her leisure, privacy, and secrecy, and her shadow-like husband does not appear until she has gone mad. Here, the causes of her broken heart are ambiguously attributed to the gramophone and the record: as symbols of everyday modernity, the gramophone and record play a decisive role in intensifying the romantic drama and lead to its tragic climax, and they by no means only offer pleasure. Together with her broken heart, Qianyu's entire world is also torn apart: all its internal problems are exposed, and everyday toys now become uncanny instruments. The image of the spinning record as a grinding machine thereby becomes especially eerie.

Analogy and contrast are interwoven throughout the story. The image of Qianyu's heart being as fragile as the gramophone record suggests an intricate web of internal and external relations in terms of space and culture. While ending the story in this boudoir space and revealing her internal anxiety and turbulence, the author provides us with a view of the outside world, from a perspective "inside"—her broken heart. The metaphor of the gramophone as a grinding device leads readers to see its external relationships in making the hero's record, which involves global capital and the power of modern technology. The representation of the heroine's fragility under the pressure of modern technology is overtly ambiguous: on the one hand, her female body alludes to the politics of locality, which are associated with domestic space, internal fear, and outside threat; on the other hand, her romantic desire, which is stronger than death, denies the possibility of abstraction or sublimation.

Zhou's fiction constitutes a way of mobilizing Western values as a form of literary intervention into China's social reality. As the power of the "modern" is introduced to serve local interests, however, that same power is itself presented as the cause of suffering. Contrary to popular perception, the entertainment machine related to the world economy of pleasure is satirically transformed into the grotesque.

"Creation": consuming the female body and utopian space

In the late 1920s, at a time when Zhou had almost stopped writing love stories entirely, Mao Dun embarked on a romantic literary journey of his own with the trilogy *Shi* 蝕 (Eclipse), exploring a new literary trend consisting of "revolution plus love" (*geming jia lian'ai* 革命加戀愛). In a sense, Mao Dun, at this point in his career, could be seen as a mirror image of Zhou, insofar as he, like Zhou, displayed a distinct interest in feminine and feminist issues.[35] For instance, unusual among May Fourth writers, Mao Dun used feminine pseudonyms, such as *Ms Fengxu* (*Fengxu nüshi* 馮虛女士), *Orchid* (*Lan* 蘭, or *Hui* 蕙) and *Fragrance* (*Fen* 芬).[36] In the early 1920s, he was a devoted and prolific contributor to *Women's Magazine*, just as Zhou had contributed to *Women's Times* in the early teens.[37] The Commercial Press asked Mao Dun to reform *Short Story Magazine*, not only because of his association with the "new," but also precisely because of his ties to the "old."

In 1927, after the failure of the "Great Revolution," Mao Dun withdrew from the front, sequestered himself in Shanghai, and immersed himself in writing. His *Eclipse* trilogy drew harsh criticisms from the Leftists, who accused him of catering to the urban petty bourgeoisie by spreading decadence and pessimism instead of a revolutionary spirit. In response Mao Dun wrote his famous essay "From Guling to Tokyo" (*Cong Guling dao Dongjing* 從牯嶺到東京), on the one hand apologizing for his low spirits, and on the other hand arguing that revolutionary writers should seriously consider the urbanites as their readers and learn how to provide them with proper spiritual sustenance. Ignoring the tastes of urban readers, Mao Dun noted, would fail to win them over from the literary market currently dominated by the "old" popular fiction. So, he explained, he had intended to experiment with a new form of revolutionary romance so as to appeal to this petty bourgeois audience.[38]

In "Creation," the heroine Xianxian resembles Nora in Ibsen's *A Doll's House*, who influenced the May Fourth generation as a role model of liberating the self. Mao Dun's treatment of the ending seems milder than in Ibsen's version: unlike Nora, who slams the door while leaving home, Xianxian silently sneaks out of her house. Later, however, she goes on to join the revolutionary movement, and in this way a revolutionary dimension is added to the outside space, from which the new collective call to fight may be heard.

"Creation" was one of Mao Dun's favorite works, for as his first short story it succeeded in representing the contemporary Leftist ideology. As he acknowledged, Xianxian's creation helped him recover his faith in "revolution," insofar as the figure of the new Nora satisfied his needs after the abortive cooperation between the KMT and the CCP. The modern women's search for emancipation was set against the backdrop of the shift, according to Mao Dun, from "individualism" to "collectivism" during the period from the May Fourth to the May Thirtieth movements. When Xianxian was objectified by revolution, Mao Dun himself and his realist fiction were subject to the "mystical frame of History."[39] In the following discussion, I will analyze "Creation" in the context of the 1920s debates about the new and the old. Through the Butterfly's mirror, we can see how Xianxian is charged with the task of subverting the domestic type of "virtuous wife and good mother," and what kind of narrative strategy Mao Dun deployed in order to win over the popular literary market. In "Creation," the Butterfly codes of gender, sexuality, and urban culture are manipulated and displaced.

The whole story takes place early one morning in the bedroom of a middle-class family in Shanghai. When it starts with the author's camera-like eye in the bedroom, we see things looming in the twilight, including the couple in the bed and a pretty woman, her exposed flesh provoking voyeuristic curiosity. The heroine's healthy body and her modern appearance are imbued with urban cultural codes. With these opening shots, an interior setting of urban lifestyle is plausibly created, yet when we look more closely, a conjugal conflict is revealed.

The intellectual gap between Junshi and Xianxian gradually develops in spatial terms. Junshi's patriotism and parochialism are inherited from his father, who is allegedly a reformer in the last days of the Qing. According to his father's plan for his education, Junshi should first learn the new knowledge, then find an ideal woman as a lifetime companion, travel around the world, perfect his personality, give birth to a couple of children—one boy and one girl—and finally in his forties begin serving his country. In this blueprint, the wife's role is ambivalently presented: as a model housewife she should be content to stay home to fulfill her domestic routine, yet intellectually she is expected to keep abreast of the progressive social trends. When Junshi "creates" Xianxian—a "pure jade"—into a new woman, her spirit escapes from the domestic cage, and she becomes increasingly excited. Finally, influenced by Marxism, she goes on to join the revolutionary movement.

Mao Dun's narrative is characterized by a kind of psychological realism that reads Junshi's mind: his first-person voice mixed with the third-person narration unfolds his reflections and the reasoning of his "creation" process. At the same time, the author gives Xianxian limited sequences of description, dialogue, and close-up shots; as the story reaches its climax, the roles of the hero and heroine become inverted, as readers identify with Xianxian in revolt and share her revolutionary values. She becomes closer to readers while Junshi remains unattractive in his self-denial. Ironically, however, the readers' identification with Xianxian is attributed more to the rhetoric of her body language than to the descriptions of her intellectual attraction and persuasion.

In his early novels on love and revolution Mao Dun tries hard to naturalize revolution through love or the female body. In *Eclipse*, those "modern women," including the figures of Sun Wuyang and Zhang Qiuliu, attract readers mostly with their revolutionary passion, their model-like bodies and their sexual freedom. Mao Dun endeavors to impose on them a frame of time-consciousness linked to the dynamic revolution or progressive history, but once they are subject to a "philosophy of the present," their revolutionary consciousness falls into chaos, as their desire triumphs over the historical will. "Creation" comes after a series of experiments and signals success in terms of identifying female desire with revolution, but this success relies largely on the author's rhetorical manipulation of Xianxian's desire.[40]

The narrative mechanism reveals that the plausibility of Xianxian's personality, which entices readers' identification, owes much to the rhetoric of displacement between gender roles, private and public spaces, and sexual and political messages. Devoid of descriptions of her interiority, the narrative instead focuses on her outward appearance. While losing sympathy for Junshi's self-reproaches for his own failed creation, readers accept hints from the narrator that he is far inferior to Xianxian in the "battle of thought" within the private realm. A series of spatial metaphors imply that Junshi has lost his domination in the domestic space and that the only space available to him is the writing desk under the southern window. The role of creator is ironically inverted when Xianxian instructs Junshi: "Let the past be past and never look back. Don't idly dream of the future; we can only know it when it comes. We should grasp the present moment and do what we understand."[41] This *carpe diem* philosophy, imbued with her blind passion and messianic promise of revolution, sounds prophetic yet less convincing. The imposing voice is tinged with the author's utopian fantasy alienated from the heroine as an urban career woman.

While realizing that the boudoir has become "Xianxian's world," Junshi feels that she has jumped out of his "spiritual embrace":

> The difference in their thoughts gradually became apparent. Indeed this was a silent and painful fight. Junshi tried his best to restore his authority [literally, his autocracy] within her heart, but all his efforts were in vain. In Xianxian's heart, there was already a strong fortress, which firmly resisted his attacks; and this new force inside her expanded day by day, driving the old force out. In the past month, time and again Junshi felt his failure. He acknowledged that his control over her would soon be overthrown.[42]

In this family comedy, these combative metaphors carry a sarcastic tone and serve a crucial function in the story. Xianxian's body, represented as a "battlefield," is invested with the author's political fantasy: the bourgeois private realm is taken over by utopian revolutionary space.

Mao Dun's frequent use of the figure of the female heart (*xin* 心) is reminiscent of the female heart in Zhou's "Gramophone." Qianyu's heart is depicted as sensual and fragile, a sign of domesticity under the threat of external forces. While Xianxian wins her independence from her husband's ideological domination, her heart nevertheless becomes as hard as iron as a result of her exposure to new Western social theories. More abstractly, her heart is treated as a cultural battleground on which the old force is driven out by the newcomer—Marxism. So, with this new force she succeeds in breaking her domestic shackles and devotes herself to the revolutionary space outside.

In the last section of "Creation," after the reader is led to adore Xianxian's body and soul, and becomes convinced that Junshi deserves to suffer on account of his male chauvinism and conservatism, the story reaches its climax. From spatial hints and metaphors the reader already knows that Xianxian has subverted the hierarchical order and turned the domestic space into her own world; now the author gives decisive touches to reveal her revolutionary subjectivity. The title "Creation" suggests an ironic reversal of the roles of creator and the created: Xianxian becomes the educator and the creator, while Junshi in effect becomes her creation. Reading Junshi's thoughts, Xianxian says, teasing and yet seriously,

> Hey, silly boy, don't be so wild! You've already succeeded I haven't gone against you. Isn't it true that you have always led me in the right direction? Maybe I really am a step ahead of you, but we are going in the same direction.[43]

In these words, the inner space melts into the air and Xianxian's voice seems enchanted by some external spell. In the following sequence she returns to herself, becoming again more like a mischievous housewife. Oddly, the body politics continues as we read, "Xianxian once again presses her body on Junshi's. Her soft and healthy body rubs his chest, and laughter issues from her mouth and spreads through the room." By deploying these themes of female eroticism, Mao Dun smuggles his utopian vision into the reader's sexual fantasies.

Against the backdrop of the debate of the new and old, we may see how "Creation" functions as a parody of family values, which is encoded with the urban literary culture and yet purports to subvert the middle-class ideal of female domesticity in favor of a revolutionary ideology. Nevertheless, we cannot be certain to what extent this implied revolutionary message was actually received by urban readers in the late 1920s, as many of them probably read this as merely an amusing domestic comedy, containing such familiar elements as sexual provocation, gender problems, and the middle-class lifestyle.

Double mirror: contextualizing the new and the old

Zhou Shoujuan and Mao Dun share an interest in women's bodies and minds in modern society, yet they differ in their use of language, representation, and cultural politics. They both use the female body as a site onto which to provocatively project the male fantasy and anxiety deeply embedded in their perception of, and cultural solution to, reality. While the daily fun-making gramophone is turned into, not only a witness, but also a creator of this love tragedy and nightmarish "small family," Zhou's popular text questions itself as well as the presumption of Butterfly fiction as merely entertaining.

Similarly, through Zhou's lens, we can see how Mao Dun crosses the borderline of bourgeois urbanism and leftist utopianism, ultimately questioning his own "revolutionary" status. A comparative examination of their respective fictional and nonfictional writings suggests the underlying continuities and interconnections between the ostensibly opposed May Fourth and Butterfly literary traditions that they ostensibly represented, and in the process allows us to gain a more complete perspective on the historical conditions of literary modernity out of which these two literary categories emerged in the first place. In fact, even though Zhou and Mao Dun are often regarded as exemplars of these two movements, they themselves at various points attempted to distance themselves from these same categories.[44]

In this regard, I would point out that a major interpretive method widely accepted by literary historians is both inadequate and problematic, i.e., the method of reading May Fourth literature exclusively within a May Fourth context. For example, Marston Anderson asserts: "As its title announces, 'Creation' is a reply to members of the Creation Society, who at the time of its composition were rigorously pursuing a campaign against 'naturalists' like Mao Dun."[45] Anderson correctly relates "Creation" to Mao Dun's mass politics, but he misses the rich signifiers tied to the politics of gender and body, signifiers that articulate the urban reality, charged with the authorial desire to subvert the bourgeois private sphere.

Conversely, many current studies of Butterfly literature similarly overlook the May Fourth element in Butterfly literature. Fan Boqun, in his remarkable edited collection *History of Modern Chinese Popular Literature* (*Zhongguo jinxiandai tongsu wenxue shi* 中國近現代通俗文學史), which deals with Butterfly literature from the late nineteenth century to 1949, apologizes for this oversight in his work, and calls for a new "complete" literary history that should emphasize the relationship between pure and popular literature.

This lack of attention to the May Fourth elements in popular Butterfly literature is inevitably related to the nostalgic ethos of "embracing the old" (*huaijiu* 懷舊) prevailing in 1990s China. With this nostalgia, Butterfly literature returns as a dramatic surprise. The appearance of innumerable reprinted works and academic reevaluations reflect a revival of popular print culture, reading pleasure and generic pluralism, together with a nostalgia for the bygone splendor of urban life and freedom from Communist ideology. In the field of literary criticism, such a resurgence suggests nothing less than an ironic turn after its repression and neglect for more than half a century. However, there is a growing tendency to create a halo above the *huaijiu* nostalgia as a new teleological discourse, and to reposition its May Fourth opponent as the new Other.

History tells a story of repression. Literary historians have long concluded that Butterfly literature was simply defeated by the New Literature in the early 1920s. In a sense, the early 1920s witnessed a crucial moment for Chinese linguistic and literary modernization; with the speedy transition from the use of *wenyan* 文言 (literary Chinese) to the *baihua* 白話 (vernacular), the New Literature decisively triumphed over the old. As a result, the new and old debate at the time proved open to a long process in which the Butterfly writers were labeled by the word *old* (*jiu* 舊) and thereby identified with decadent, feudalistic, and poisonous. The word *old* came to be demonized as a canonical category before the Leftists would brandish it with a total concept of Mandarin Ducks and Butterflies literature in the 1930s.

But, still, what did the Old Literature signify? How should we read it? On the one hand, it is imperative to make the repressed speak, for it is clear that there is more literary modernity in the old literature of the 1920s than contemporary scholarship would suggest. On the other, it is necessary to overcome the logic of repression so as to avoid repeating that same logic. As a way out of the vicious circle, this essay examines Zhou Shoujuan and Mao Dun within their historical context; as a "double mirror" they shed light on each other and question the categories—"old" and "new," "Butterfly" and "May Fourth"—by which they had each long been defined.

Notes

1 In Wei Shaochang's 魏紹昌 *Yuanyang hudie pai yanjiu ziliao* 鴛鴦蝴蝶派研究資料 (Research materials on the Mandarin Ducks and Butterflies school), the texts were selected from *Zhongguo wenxue shi* 中國文學史 (A history of Chinese literature), separately written by the students of Beijing University and Fudan University in Shanghai. Both histories were published in 1960. Others included *Zhongguo xiandai wenyi sixiang douzheng shi* 中國現代文藝思想鬥爭史 (A history of debates on modern Chinese literary thought), *Zhongguo jindai wenxue shigao* 中國近代文學史稿 (A draft history of modern Chinese literature), *Zhongguo xiaoshuo shigao* 中國小説史稿 (A draft history of modern Chinese fiction). These new literary histories were largely identical in terms of analytical mode and critical language, freshly imprinted with the ideology of the anti-Rightist and the Big Leap Forward movements. See Wei, *Yuanyang hudie pai yanjiu ziliao* (Shanghai: Shanghai wenyi chubanshe, 1962), 86–119. In "The Institutionalization of Modern Literary History in China, 1922–1980," Zhang Yingjin succinctly described the development of the historiography of modern Chinese literature in modern China, including the areas of Hong Kong and Taiwan, yet he did not pay enough attention to the period of the 1950s and 1960s in the PRC, in which the above-mentioned works were produced. See *Modern China*, vol. 20, no. 3 (July 1994): 347–377.
2 For example, Marián Gálik, *Mao Tun and Modern Chinese Literary Criticism* (Wiesbaden: Franz Steiner Verlag GMBH, 1969), 75; C. T. Hsia, *A History of Modern Chinese Fiction* (New Haven: Yale University Press, 1971), 161; Rey Chow, *Woman and Chinese Modernity: The Politics of Reading between West and East* (Minnesota: University of Minnesota Press, 1991), 40–42; Wei Shaochang, *Wo kan yuanyang hudie pai* 我看鴛鴦蝴蝶派 (My view of the Mandarin Ducks and Butterflies school) (Taipei: The Commercial Press, 1992), 7.
3 Fan Boqun 范伯群, "*Xulun*" 序論 (Introduction), in *Zhongguo jin xiandai tongsu wenxue shi* 中國近現代通俗文學史 (A history of modern Chinese popular literature) (Nanjing: Jiangsu jiaoyu chubanshe, 1999), 1–36.
4 Wei, *Wo kan yuanyang hudie pai*, 10.

5 Wang Xiaoming, "A Journal and a 'Society': On the 'May Fourth' Literary Tradition," *Modern Chinese Literature and Culture*, vol. 11, no. 2 (fall, 1999): 28.

6 Mao Dun 茅盾, *Mao Dun wenyi lunwen xuan* 茅盾文藝論文選 (Selected essays on literature and art of Mao Dun) (Shanghai: Shanghai wenyi chubanshe, 1981), 16–17.

7 Wang Dungen 王鈍根, "*Zhou Shoujuan xiaoshi*" 周瘦鵑小史 (A brief biography of Zhou Shoujuan), in Wang Zhiyi 王智毅, ed., *Zhou Shoujuan yanjiu ziliao* 周瘦鵑研究資料 (Research materials on Zhou Shoujuan) (Tianjin: Tianjin renmin chubanshe, 1993), 170.

8 In the "*Correspondence*" section, Mao Dun once complained that he could not pursue his reforms as he wished; he was restrained from above. More than once while praising his readers' suggestion to change the name *Xiaoshuo yuebao* to *Wenxue yuekan* (Literature monthly), Mao Dun expressed his frustration that this was beyond his ability, for the matter of naming involved the nature of the magazine and the policy of the publishing house.

9 *Shenbao* 申報 (May 22, 1921): 14.

10 *Shenbao* (March 27, 1921): 14.

11 *Xiaoshuo yuebao* 小說月報 (Short story magazine), vol. 13, no. 8 (August 1922).

12 Wei Shaochang's 1962 *Yuanyang hudie pai yanjiu ziliao* only included the May Fourth critiques by Lu Xun, Guo Moruo, Mao Dun, and Zheng Zhenduo. This canonical compilation seems to provide an incomplete view that in the 1920s there were only the May Fourth criticisms or attacks of Butterfly literature. In his expanded version of the book in 1984, Wei added two Butterfly essays referring to their responses to the May Fourth's attacks in the 1920s. Also in 1984, however, a significant change was made by a new bibliographic book on Butterfly literature compiled by Rui Heshi, Fan Boqun, and others. The book included almost twenty essays by Butterfly writers showing their participation in the 1920s literary debate. See Rui Heshi 芮和師, et al., eds., *Yuanyang hudie pai wenxue ziliao* 鴛鴦蝴蝶派文學資料 (Research materials on Mandarin Ducks and Butterflies literature) (Fuzhou: Fujian renmin chubanshe, 1984). Recently, in *Yuanyang hudie pai sanwen daxi, 1909–1949* 鴛鴦蝴蝶派散文大系, 1909–1949 (Collection of essays on Mandarin Ducks and Butterfly fiction, 1909–1949) edited by Yuan Jin 袁進, the volume *Yihai tanyou* 藝海探幽 (Exploration in the sea of art) contains the firsthand sources of literary criticism by Butterfly writers, many of which are related to the early 1920s debate.

13 Zhou Shoujuan, "*Shuo xiaoxian zhi xiaoshuo zazhi*" 說消閒之小說雜誌 (On fiction magazines for leisure), *Shenbao* (July 17, 1921): 18.

14 *Shenbao* (August 7, 1921): 18.

15 *Xiaoshuo yuebao*, vol. 13, no. 8 (August 1922).

16 Zhou Shoujuan, "*Taiwushi hepan funü yaoqiu canzheng zhi nuchao*" 泰晤士河畔婦女要求參政之怒潮 (The roaring tide of the women's franchise movement by the river Thames), *Funü shibao* 婦女時報 (Women's times) 7 (July 1912).

17 Dai Wei 戴偉, *Zhongguo hunyin xing'ai shigao* 中國婚姻性愛史稿 (A history of marriage and sexuality in China) (Beijing: Dongfang chubanshe, 1992), 357.

18 Zhou Shoujuan, "*Luohua yuan*" 落花怨, *Funü shibao* 1 (May 1911); Qi Hong 泣紅, "*Ai zhi hua*" 愛之花 (Flower of love), *Xiaoshuo yuebao*, vol. 2, no. 9–12 (Sept.–Dec. 1911).

19 Tang Jinhai 唐金海, et al., *Mao Dun zhuanji* 茅盾專集 (Research materials on Mao Dun), (Fuzhou: Fujiang renmin chubanshe, 1983), vol. 1, 438.

20 Pei Wei 佩韋, "*Jiefang de funü yu funü de jiefang*" 解放的婦女與婦女的解放 (Emancipated women and women's emancipation), *Funü zazhi* 婦女雜誌 (Women's magazine), vol. 5, no. 11 (November, 1919).

21 Yan Bing 雁冰, "*Du Shaonian Zhongguo funü hao*" 讀少年中國婦女號 (Reading the special issue on women in the *Young China* magazine), *Funü zazhi*, vol. 6, no. 1 (Jan. 1920).

22 Mao Dun, "*Huiyi lu* 4" 回憶錄（四）(Reminiscences 4), in *Mao Dun zhuanji* 茅盾專集 (Research materials on Mao Dun), 438.

23 See Bing 冰, "*Duiyu Huang Ai nüshi taolun xiaozuzhi wenti yiwen de yijian*" 對於黃藹女士討論小組織問題一文的意見 (Some opinions on Miss Huang's essay on small organizations) in *Mao Dun quanji* 茅盾全集 (Mao Dun's complete works) Beijing: Renmin wenxue chubanshe, 1987), vol. 14, 45–50.

24 Zhou Shoujuan, "*Liushengji pian*" 留聲機片 (A gramophone record). *Libailiu* 禮拜六 (Saturday) 108 (May 1921), 1–10.

25 Patrick Hanan, *The Chinese Vernacular Story* (Cambridge: Harvard University Press, 1981), 79–80. C. T. Hsia, "Hsu Chen-ya's *Yu-li hun*: An Essay in Literary History and Criticism," in Liu Ts'un-yan, ed., *Chinese Middlebrow Fiction: From Ch'ing and Early Republican Eras* (Hong Kong: Chinese University Press, 1984), 201–202.

26 In the eyes of the new writers, this kind of deployment of convention or cliché is unbearable for it manifests the lack of creativity. It might be a coincidence that by the time Zhou's story appeared, Lu Xun had written a short essay entitled "Names" (名字 *Mingzi*), satirizing those authors playing the name game. He said that as soon as he saw a text with this kind of name he would throw it aside. Obviously, Zhou was this type of author. See Wei Shaochang, *Yuanyang hudie pai yanjiu ziliao*, 8–9.

27 Dai Wei 戴偉, *Zhongguo hunyin xing'ai shigao* 中國婚姻性愛史稿 (A history of marriage and sexuality in China) (Beijing: Dongfang chubanshe, 1992), 384; Chang, So-an 張壽安, "*Shiba shiji yijiang chuantong hunyin guannian de xiandai zhuanhua—cong 'Zhongguo benwei' guancha*" 十八世紀以降傳統婚姻觀念的現代轉化─從中國本位觀察 (The modern transformation of the concept of marriage since the eighteenth century: from the Chinese perspective), conference paper for "*Modern Interpretations of Chinese Philosophy and Culture*," at Harvard University, 1999, 3.

28 Patrick Hanan, "Introduction," in *The Sea of Regret* (Honolulu: University of Hawai'i Press, 1995), 1–17.

29 See Wei Shaochang, "*Zhou Shoujuan*" 周瘦鵑, in *Wo kan yuanyang hudie pai*, 83; Fan Boqun 范伯群, "*Zhou Shoujuan he Libailiu*" 周瘦鵑和禮拜六 (Zhou Shoujuan and *Saturday*), in *Minguo tongsu xiaoshuo—yuanyang hudie pai* 民國通俗小說─鴛鴦蝴蝶派 (Popular fiction from the Republican period: Mandarin Duck and Butterfly school) (Taipei: Guowen tiandi zazhishe, 1990), 156–159; Liu Yangti 劉揚體, *Yuanyang hudie pai xin lun* 鴛鴦蝴蝶派新論 (A new theory on the mandarin duck and butterfly school) (Taipei: Zhongguo wenlian chubanshe, 1997), 118–121.

30 Zhou Shoujuan, "*Huashengdun zhi qi*" 華盛頓之妻 (Washington's wife) and "*Huashengdun zhi mu*" 華盛頓之母 (Washington's mother), *Funü shibao* 11 (October 1913).

31 Zhou Shoujuan, "*Xin jiating chuban xuanyan*" 新家庭出版宣言 (A manifesto for the *New Family Magazine*), *Xin jiating* 新家庭 (New family), vol. 1, no. 1 (1932).

32 Witold Rybczynski, *Home: A Short History of an Idea* (New York: Penguin Books, 1986).

33 Zhou Shoujuan, *Wangguonu zhi riji* 亡國奴之日記 (Diary of a slave who has lost his country), in *Shoujuan duanpian xiaoshuo*, vol. 1 (Shanghai: Zhonghua shuju, 1918), 59–62.

34 Zhou, "*Liushengji pian*." *Libailiu*, 108 (May 1921).

35 In his discussion of Mao Dun's early fiction, C. T. Hsia praised Mao Dun as being "distinguished for his gallery of heroines," and pointed out that his fictional style is reminiscent of the "more feminine South, romantic, sensuous, melancholic." Hsia also noted that Mao Dun "records the passive feminine response to the chaotic events of contemporary Chinese history." See C. T. Hsia, *A History of Modern Chinese Fiction* (Bloomington and Indianapolis: Indiana University Press, 1999), 165.

36 Sun Zhongtian 孫中田 and Zha Guohua 查國華, eds., *Mao Dun yanjiu ziliao* 茅盾研究資料 (Research materials on Mao Dun) (Beijing: Zhongguo shehui kexue chubanshe, 1983), 279–281.

37 Ibid., 6–12. For the articles Zhou Shoujuan contributed to *Funü shibao* from 1911 to 1912, see Wang Zhiyi, ed., *Zhou Shoujuan yanjiu ziliao*, 351–354.

38 Mao Dun, *"Cong Guling dao Dongjing"* 從牯嶺到東京 (From Guling to Tokyo), in Tang Jinhai, et al., eds., *Mao Dun zhuanji*, vol. 1, 342, 345.

39 In his analysis of Mao Dun's historical novels, David Wang enunciates how the "mystical frame of History" functions as an omnipotent agent in literary discourse and narrative structure. See *Fictional Realism in 20th-Century China: Mao Dun, Lao She, and Shen Congwen* (New York: Columbia University, 1992), 30–35.

40 On the relationship of the female body and the modern frame of time-consciousness, see Jianhua Chen, *"Geming de nüxinghua he nüxing de geminghua"* 革命的女性化和女性的革命化 (The feminization of revolution, and the revolutionization of femininity) in *"Geming" de xiandaixing: Zhongguo geming huayu kaolun* "革命"的現代性——中國革命話語考論 (Revolution discourse and modernity in China) (Shanghai: Shanghai Guji chubanshe, 2000), 286–333.

41 Mao Dun, *"Chuangzao"* 創造 (Creation), in *Mao Dun quanji*, vol. 8, 23.

42 Ibid., 7.

43 Ibid., 22.

44 In the early 1930s Mao Dun criticized the May Fourth movement as a bourgeois movement. See Mao Dun, *"Wusi yundong de jiantao: Makesi zhuyi wenyi lilun yanjiuhui baogao"* "五四"運動的檢討——馬克思主義文藝理論研究會報告 (Reevaluation of the May Fourth movement: A report to the association of Marxist theory on literature and art), *Wenxue daobao*, vol. 1, no. 2 (Aug. 1931). In Zhou Shoujuan's case, when in the 1960s he was labeled as one of the Butterflies, he only admitted to being a member of the Saturday School. For Zhou's denial of being a Butterfly, see Wei Shaochang, ed., *Yuanyang hudie pai yanjiu ziliao*, 130; and Fan Boqun, *Minguo tongsu xiaoshuo—yuanyang hudie pai*, 5.

45 Marston Anderson, *The Limits of Realism: Chinese Fiction in the Revolutionary Period* (Berkeley: University of California Press, 1990), 180–182.

6 A tale of two cities

Romance, revenge, and nostalgia in two *fin-de-siècle* novels by Ye Zhaoyan and Zhang Beihai

Michael Berry

> In the modern metropolis [of Nanjing], all are helpless to stop development —melancholic sentimentality has never been anything more than a luxury item.
>
> (Ye Zhaoyan 葉兆言)

> As far as comparing Beiping during this era [the glory days of the Republic, 1926–1937] to the Beijing of other historical periods, all I can say is that the earlier period isn't worth mentioning and the later period [the Communist era] isn't worth a breath.
>
> (Zhang Beihai 張北海)

As the end of the last century approached, two writers situated on opposite sides of the Atlantic began, almost simultaneously, to undertake a pair of unrelated literary projects that would directly engage a single, all-but-forgotten historical milieu. The year that captured their literary imagination was 1937, the pinnacle of the Republican era as well as the year of the infamous Nanjing Massacre. Born in 1936, the very year his novel begins, Zhang Beihai (pen-name of Chang Wen-yi 張文藝) is too young to remember the events portrayed in his work. Ye Zhaoyan, who was born twenty-one years later, is even further removed from the historical era in question. Nevertheless, in 1996, the Nanjing-based Ye Zhaoyan published the novel *Yijiusanqi nian de aiqing* 一九三七年的愛情 (Nanjing 1937: a love story) (1996), an encyclopedic reconstruction and chronicle of the final days of the Republican capital. In that same year, in his TriBeCa condo in Manhattan, Zhang Beihai began the research which would ultimately culminate in the publication, four years later, of his own novel *Xiayin* 俠隱 (Hidden knight-errant; translated as *Swallow*) (2000), a nostalgic re-creation of the historical, literary, and topological configurations of Republican-era Beiping [Beijing]. In their respective narrative constructions, literary modes, and strategies of urban representation, both *Swallow* and *Nanjing 1937: A Love Story* function as sentimental, nostalgic gestures to the past. However, in both cases we not only are presented with a reconstructed literary portrait of two 1930s Chinese cities and a contemporary reinvention of popular Republican-era literary genres, but also are offered new possible trajectories for these modes of literary and historical representation.

Through a reading of Zhang Beihai's *Swallow* and Ye Zhaoyan's *Nanjing 1937*, I will compare the ways in which these two contemporary writers represent the historical Chinese capitals of Beijing and Nanjing during a single tumultuous historical period. I will also examine how both Zhang and Ye appropriate, and ultimately transgress, traditional narrative forms. Through a discussion of Ye Zhaoyan's encyclopedic vision and Zhang Beihai's topological desire, I will explore the different, and at times startlingly similar, ways in which a dual nostalgia for both earlier literary conventions as well as for historical cities has manifested itself in the *fin-de-siècle* popular novel.

Butterfly love in a fortress besieged

Starting with its title, *Nanjing 1937: A Love Story* is essentially grounded on an oxymoron. On the eve of the 1937 Rape of Nanjing, one of the most chilling moments in modern Chinese history, how could there be such a thing as love or romance? In Ye Zhaoyan's contemporary take on the Mandarin Duck and Butterfly tradition, conventional dichotomies of love and war are provocatively juxtaposed (and sometimes blurred), creating a unique literary vision where history is romanticized and love is militarized.

Beyond Ye's rich juxtaposition of themes of love and war lies a sweeping vision of Republican China immediately prior to the outbreak of the Sino-Japanese War (1937–1945). The novel functions, simultaneously, as a chronological history of Nanjing's final pre-war year as national capital, as a virtual "who's who" of Republican China, as well as a mini-encyclopedia of modern (and, to a lesser extent, pre-modern) Chinese literary references. The underlying complexity of this often overlooked novel demonstrates how the historical, cultural, and literary burdens of a bygone era merge together, creating a new form of popular literature for the 1990s.

Nanjing 1937 spins a multi-layered narrative in which the epic fall of Nanjing to the Japanese in December 1937 is juxtaposed with the romantic endeavors and misadventures of Ding Wenyu. While still a teenager, Ding Wenyu, the only son of a powerful Shanghai banker, falls head over heels in love with a young married woman, Ren Yuchan, and is sent abroad by his father in an attempt to cure his lovesickness. Seventeen years later, Ding returns to China, only to fall even harder for Yuchan's younger sister, the stunning Yuyuan, on her wedding day.

The novel begins on January 1, 1937, the day of Yuyuan's wedding to the star fighter pilot, Yu Kerun. Taken with the beauty of the bride, Ding Wenyu, now an unhappily married college professor, begins a preposterous letter-writing campaign to win Yuyuan's heart, thus putting the major plot line in motion. Gradually, through a series of uncanny, almost inconceivable, events, true feelings of love actually do begin to develop between Ding and Yuyuan—but only as the Japanese forces are about to enter the capital to commence one of the most brutal bloodbaths in twentieth-century military history. At this moment, national history and personal history, love and war, sacrifice and redemption, are all tragically brought together.

The subplot of the novel, as opposed to the "love story" outlined above, is the "war story"—an extensive series of passages describing the socio-political state of the capital, which serves as a prelude to the massacre. As the novel progresses, these two stories are playfully juxtaposed. Descriptions of the turbulent and complex social and political changes in the capital take on epic proportions as Ye romanticizes the pre-war splendor of the capital through descriptive passages chronicling the pre-war economic development (such as booms in real estate and construction) and the rapidly changing topography of the city.

Ye Zhaoyan's topological imagination captures not only the lightning-quick development of the city, but also underscores the splendor and "Wild West" sense of opportunity in the budding capital at a time when virtually anything seemed possible.[1] At the same time, however, the attention given to this rampant expansion and development also creates a pervading sense of melancholy. All the while, Ye's construction of his imagined hometown, a city of memory, is conditioned by the reader's knowledge that the contemporary progress and expansion are haunted by the impending massacre that will begin before year's end. The author's romantic vision of the thriving capital city paved with opportunities is matched with playful passages where militaristic terminology is appropriated to describe romantic passages from the "love story":

He [Ding Wenyu] continuously sought out different types of women, and once he *achieved his target*, he would immediately *initiate his next campaign*. He was like a *general* who endured a *hundred battles*, *charging forward* amid a sea of women, time after time facing setbacks, time after time losing face for all to see. Even though he usually came off as *the glorious victor in his battles*, his soul had already long been covered with scars.

(32; my emphases here and below)

By running from the *battlefield defeated*, it was as if she [Yuyuan] was guilty of some wrongdoing.

(114)

Neither of them was willing to give an inch—they could go on arguing all day over the meaning of a single word. They adopted a *tactical method of attack* that allowed them to alternate; *while one party took the defensive, the other* would *ferociously charge ahead*. By the time the first party had had about all they could take and rose up to *counterattack*, the other would quickly put up their guard. Since day one, *the battle* between them had been carried out like a *campaign of protracted warfare*; neither wanted to admit defeat—thus neither could ever be the victor.

(143)

Qu Manli's *first offensive* against Yu Kerun was pressing him to divorce his wife [...].

(265)

She [Qu Manli] began her little talk as if she were *launching an attack* [...].

(266)

Ding Wenyu decided to *strengthen his romantic offensive* on Yuyuan [...].

(307)

Militaristic descriptions of romance and interpersonal relationships, as in the preceding passages, pervade the novel. This technique parallels the romanticization of history discussed earlier, while at the same time drawing an uncanny, and at times highly ironic, narrative link between personal history and national history. As a figure seemingly impregnable to the grand narrative of History, the novel's protagonist Ding Wenyu lives in a romantic world of his own creation. It is only through the third-person narrator's martial metaphors in describing Ding's romantic pursuits that a direct parallelism is drawn between the advancing Japanese army and Ding Wenyu's romantic advances on Ren Yuyuan (who ironically is half-Japanese).[2]

The irony of Ding Wenyu's relative imperviousness to the historical events that are unfolding around him is further highlighted by the novel's aforementioned encyclopedic scope. The encyclopedic vision that *Nanjing 1937* reveals can be divided into four subcategories: chronology, historical personalities, literary styles and forms, and literary references.

To begin with, in chronological terms the narrative begins on January 1, 1937 and, progressing along a linear trajectory, culminates on December 13 of the same year, the very day the Japanese army enters the capital and the infamous Rape of Nanjing commences.[3] As the story develops, Ye Zhaoyan goes to great lengths to detail virtually every major political and military development that transpires during the year, including the 1937 Lushan Conference, the New Life Movement, the fall of Shanghai, and the Nationalist retreat to Chongqing. At the same time, he does not overlook "unofficial" history and includes popular cultural events, and even petty tabloid gossip in his historical chronology. Examples of this unofficial history include descriptions of a Children's Day Speech Contest, popular controversy over Spring Festival stage performances, and the "enlisted man marathon." By placing key events in the official history of the era side by side with unofficial history, and giving equal attention to both, Ye Zhaoyan presents an unconventional synthesis of cultural and historical time.

Within both the chronological historical timeline (official and unofficial) *and* the primary "love story" narrative, the reader is introduced to scores of cultural, military, and political superstars of the era. These cameo appearances make up the novel's second encyclopedic function, as a virtual who's who of Republican-era celebrities. All told, there are over seventy-five of these cameos, and although the majority of these appearances are "off screen," there are a significant number of cases in which these historical celebrities enter into the main line of narrative and/or actually interact with Ding Wenyu. The protagonist, for instance, alternately has drinks with Zhu De 朱德, is offered a job by Soong Meiling 宋美齡, and translates for Tang Shengzhi 唐生智. Besides the political arena, the novel also features a host of cultural, literary, and intellectual stars such as the author Eileen Chang 張愛玲, playwright Tian Han 田漢, opera star Mei Lanfang 梅蘭芳, actress Lan Ping 藍蘋 (a.k.a. Jiang Qing 江青), and intellectual Dr. Hu Shi 胡適. This cast of cultural players also works to strengthen the novel's vision as a document of (pop) cultural history as much as official military/political history mentioned earlier.

Textually, the novel also functions as an encyclopedic compendium of styles and forms. Besides the two main respective narrative lines discussed earlier (the "love story" and "war story") that make up the body of the novel, Ye Zhaoyan injects the narrative with a veritable heteroglossia of literary styles. Inserted into the novel are letters, diary entries, newspaper headlines, tabloid reports, song lyrics, newspaper advertisements, playbills of coming attractions, divorce announcements, and so on. This postmodernist construction also bears a resemblance to the Ming literary tradition as embodied in such novels as *Jinping mei* 金瓶梅 (Plum in the golden vase, also translated as Golden Lotus) where an array of literary forms such as poetry, prose, lyric song, and even woodcut images combine to create a new form of popular narrative.

The reference to *Plum in the Golden Vase* brings us to the final, and perhaps most intriguing, dimension of the novel's encyclopedic construction—that of being a sweeping, multi-level compendium of Chinese literary references. Ye Zhaoyan takes as one of his models Mandarin Ducks and Butterflies romantic fiction. As a work of popular romantic fiction (originally published in a popular literature magazine, as were many of the original Butterfly works), *Nanjing 1937* constitutes a conscious effort on the part of Ye Zhaoyan to carry on this popular literary genre. These earlier Butterfly romances can be divided into the two subcategories of *yanqing xiaoshuo* 言情小說, romance novels that generally had happy endings, and *aiqing xiaoshuo* 哀情小說, melancholic love novels that often ended in tragedy.[4] One stock aspect of the former *yanqing xiaoshuo* strain is the standard conclusion that "always ended in marital harmony symbolized by paired ducks or butterflies."[5] While Ye Zhaoyan does follow this obligatory standard with his surprise, rapid-fire union between Ding Wenyu and Ren Yuyuan, the novel's final page nevertheless reminds us that, living in the postmodern age, Ye not only has a very different set of literary and aesthetic strategies as compared with his romantic predecessors, but also a new conception of historical tragedy.

While Ye Zhaoyan's novel is formulated very much in the *yanqing* mode, the line between it and the melancholic *aiqing* tradition is not entirely clear-cut, making the work somewhat of a hybrid of the two styles. At the same time, Ye remains unrestrained by an anxiety of influence, and freely appropriates themes from four of the century's most influential Chinese literary works, Eileen Chang's *Qingcheng zhi lian* 傾城之戀 (Love in a fallen city), Lao She's 老舍 *Luotuo xiangzi* 駱駝祥子 (Camel Xiangzi, also translated as *Rickshaw*), Zhang Henshui's 張恨水 *Ye shen chen* 夜沈沉 (Deep in the night) and, most strikingly, Qian Zhongshu's 錢鍾書 masterpiece, *Weicheng* 圍城 (Fortress besieged). This encyclopedic pastiche, or mini-literary history of pre-liberation literary styles, serves as one of the most intriguing aspects of the novel, and illustrates the "literary historiography" of the work.

Although her fiction was marked by a dark, decadent, and highly personal literary vision which set it apart from other Butterfly works, Eileen Chang actually began her literary career by appropriating popular romantic literary formulas, and published her first series of stories in some of the leading Butterfly magazines of the 1940s.[6] Starting from the title of Chang's 1944 novella, *Love in a Fallen City* (which Ye Zhaoyan might have simply borrowed for his own work), we can immediately see the parallel between the two works. There is a clear influence in the common plot form of a love affair in a city that is in the process of falling to the Japanese, which clearly functions as the narrative hub of both works. The commonalties in terms of plot, however, are arguably secondary to Eileen Chang's decadent aesthetics of romance and semi-detached narrative style. It is this latter pair of aesthetic and stylistic values that have informed Ye Zhaoyan's own *fin-de-siècle* tale of love in a fallen city.

Ye Zhaoyan also owes a debt to Lao She's most famous novel, *Rickshaw*, on which Ye bases one of the secondary figures in his own novel, the rickshaw puller (and keeper of Ding Wenyu's amorous secrets), Monk. Commonalties between Monk and Lao She's protagonist Camel go far beyond their choice of livelihood. Like Camel, who lost both his parents while still a child, Monk is also an orphan, and as a result both characters lack a true identity and are known only by generic nicknames. Regardless of their marginal roles in society, however, both Camel and Monk eventually become the prey of much older women who use deceit to win their affections. For Camel, this older woman is the infamous Huniu, and her counterpart in Ye Zhaoyan's novel is the cunning and flirtatious Mrs. Zhang. Both male characters live in a traditional walled compound with a number of other families, and it is within these walls that both characters meet their eventual true love in the form of a young girl. However, in a curious twist, whereas Camel's love interest is the "good prostitute" Fuzi (who eventually kills herself out of desperation), Monk's love interest is instead Mrs. Zhang's daughter, Little Moon, who dies by Monk's hand in the most violent scene in the novel.[7]

The parallels between Camel (whose incarnations in film, literature, and on the stage have long transformed him into an iconic figure) and Monk are too numerous to be coincidental. Instead, Ye Zhaoyan's novel offers a conscious attempt to conjure up a decadent and postmodern recreation of Lao She's eternal hero in the form of a petty sidekick to accompany the novel's true hero (or anti-hero) Ding Wenyu on his amorous adventures and help him navigate his way through the Nanjing pleasure quarters. Although Monk is a relatively minor character in Ye's work, it should be pointed out that the feverish compulsion and obsession he expresses towards Little Moon serves as a vulgar double to the equally obsessive (but comparatively "cultured") fixation that draws Ding Wenyu to Yuyuan. While Ding expresses overly zealous passion and inappropriate affections through the culturally respected and time-honored tradition of the letter, Monk (who is almost certainly illiterate) resorts to violence to express his own infatuation—however, in both cases the underlying drive is the same abnormally obsessive pent-up desire. Ding and Monk's identities as doubles is further sealed in the final scene when they are reunited in death.

Ye Zhaoyan is not the first writer to have derived literary inspiration from Lao She's classic novel. Decades before, one of the most prolific purveyors and representative authors of Mandarin Duck and Butterfly fiction, Zhang Henshui, offered his own version of Camel's tragic tale in his classic novel *Deep in the Night*. Here, we are presented with not only the same plot parallels mentioned in conjunction with *Rickshaw,* but even the main characters' names, Ding Er*he* and Yang *Yue*rong, each share a common Chinese character with Ye's parallel protagonists *He*shang (Monk) and Xiao *Yue* (Little Moon). At the conclusion of *Deep in the Night*, Ding Erhe is driven by a drunken rage to avenge the injustices done to him. With a butcher's knife concealed under his clothes, he comes close to having his revenge when he suddenly remembers his sick mother in the hospital who needs his care, and therefore abandons his plot. Not until several decades later, when Monk (who, being an orphan, was unrestrained by filial obligations) climbs into Little Moon's attic bedroom with a claw hammer concealed under his jacket, would the deferred act of violence finally be carried out.

Finally we come to Qian Zhongshu's pre-liberation masterpiece *Fortress Besieged*, a novel that has not only had profound influence on Ye Zhaoyan's work,[8] but can be said to be the intertextual skeleton key for entering Ye's conception of 1937 Nanjing. The connection between the two works is so clear that Ye even quotes virtually verbatim a line from *Fortress Besieged*'s famous opening page. Qian's original reads: "Later everyone agreed the unusual heat was a portent of troops and arms, for it was the twenty-sixth year of the Republic (1937),"[9] while Ye Zhaoyan's literary tip of the hat reads: "The summer of 1937 was especially hot. The entire city was like a huge sweltering oven—everyone said that this was a portent of troops and arms; it was going to be a year of crisis."[10] The intertextual similarities, however, go far beyond mere quotations and a common temporal setting. In both works, the protagonist is a Chinese foreign student returning from abroad on the eve of the war with Japan. Neither Fang Hongjian, the hero of *Fortress Besieged*, nor Ding Wenyu is able to attain a foreign diploma (the former purchases a mock diploma from a nonexistent American university, while the latter sees no point in even attaining one). Fang and Ding both hail from Shanghai and both enter academia after their return to China, however while Fang takes a post teaching at a small backwater provincial college, the well-connected Ding heads straight for the capital and one of the country's most prestigious universities.

Although Ding Wenyu is centrally positioned in China's capital, and is surrounded by the grand narrative of History (which comes to him in the form of dinner conversations, loudspeaker announcements, and even direct contact with leading politicians of the day), he, like Fang Hongjian, is seemingly conscious only of his own romantic pursuits. The protagonists' aloofness to the "call of the times" is perhaps best illustrated in the classic lecture scene where Fang Hongjian gives a talk on "the influence of Western civilization on China," which he boils down to the introduction of opium and syphilis. In a dialogic rejoinder written half a decade later, Ye Zhaoyan has his protagonist Ding Wenyu deliver a lecture entitled "A Comparison of Chinese and Western Prostitution Traditions." While Fang Hongjian's lecture succeeds only in embarrassing him, Ding's lecture meets with wild applause and breaks all records for university lecture attendance. The lecture also works to cement the intertextual bond between the two writers, serving as a subtle, tongue-in-cheek display of Ye Zhaoyan's romantic, satiric, and ultimately decadent aesthetics.

Besides the formal and biographical similarities between the two protagonists, Ye Zhaoyan also offers a new interpretation of the allegorical meaning of Qian's work, which is perhaps best described by his wife, the author Yang Jiang:

> Those trapped in a fortress besieged long to escape,
> Those outside want to charge in.
> Such is one's marriage, and one's career,
> Such is the way of most human desires.[11]

This life philosophy is echoed by Ye Zhaoyan when he writes, "Ding Wenyu seemed to realize that there is never a time when man can ever feel truly satisfied—this eternal craving seems to be what makes us human."[12] This principle is developed even more clearly at the end of the novel, when the Japanese army descends on Nanjing. It is at this tragic moment, as the curtain of history falls, that Qian Zhongshu's "besieged city" is lifted from an allegorical to a literal level, and the reader realizes that Ye Zhaoyan has constructed a true "fortress besieged."

It is this encyclopedic tapestry of history (and literature) through which our hero Ding Wenyu navigates, and from which Ye Zhaoyan weaves his city of memory. For Ye Zhaoyan, this nostalgia functions on two separate levels; it constitutes both a longing for the grandeur and decadence of old Nanjing, as well as a gesture of remembering (and re-creating) Republican-era literary texts and traditions. As a Nanjing native long fascinated with both his hometown and the Nationalist era, Ye Zhaoyan has often combined his two passions in such works as *Ye bo Qinhuai* 夜泊秦淮 (Evening moor on the Qinhuai) (1991) and the annotated photo album, *Lao Nanjing* 老南京 (Old Nanjing) (1998). However, it is with *Nanjing 1937* that Ye Zhaoyan most convincingly challenges conventional oppositions between elite and popular literature, from Qian Zhongshu's black humor about modern intellectuals to Zhang Henshui's serialized tales of old Beijing. The author's literary tip of the hat towards both pulp fiction and modern highbrow literary classics functions as a means of questioning the boundaries within which both texts and readers' conventions are contained. And it is a dichotomy that is also echoed in the novel's very structure, which alternates between a "highbrow" historical narrative and a "popular" love story.

While *Nanjing 1937* originally began as Ye Zhaoyan's attempt to face the Rape of Nanjing, one of the darkest pages in his hometown's modern history, the result is nevertheless a sweeping elegiac romance that captures this ancient capital's final hour of glory. Ye's decision to end his novel on December 13, the first day of the infamous massacre, speaks not to his inability to face the tragedy of history, but rather to his nostalgic passion for bearing witness to what was lost.

The last swallow of autumn

After concluding his long-running column for the Hong Kong-based magazine, *Qishi niandai* 七十年代 (The seventies),[13] in which he wrote chiefly about New York culture, and retiring from his post at the United Nations, in 2000 Zhang Beihai published *Swallow*, his first full-length work of fiction. Curiously, Zhang selected the genre of *wuxia* or martial-arts fiction for this work, a genre which has arguably suffered a decline in production as compared with the early- and mid-century periods. While it was the "romantic" strain of Butterfly fiction which provided Ye Zhaoyan's main narrative thrust, it is the "knight-errant fiction" strain's emphasis on "chivalric revenge" that spurs Zhang Beihai's own novel.[14] I will also explore how Zhang's novel is not only a nostalgic revival of a popular literary genre in decline, but like Ye Zhaoyan's work, also functions as a literary and historical recreation of Beijing in the mid-1930s.

Swallow opens in late 1936 just before the Xi'an incident, when the protagonist Li Tianran (the alias of Li Dahan) returns to Beijing after having spent five years in America. After having barely survived the assassination of his entire martial-arts clan seven years earlier (at which time his master and fiancée were both slaughtered by a former pupil), Li is saved by Dr. Stuart McKay, an American doctor sent by his mission to China. McKay hides Li by helping him change his name from Dahan to Tianran, and then placing him in the medical ward of an orphanage where he can slowly recover his health. Later sent to America to study with Dr. McKay's daughter, Li returns to China[15] on the eve of the War of Resistance, bent on avenging his master's death.

Unlike the legendary *jianghu* 江湖, or the martial-arts world of "rivers and lakes," where martial-arts societies and codes of conduct could operate openly and autonomously outside of mainstream society, Li Tianran is forced by both personal (he is a potential target for the men who killed his master) and political (it is now the Republic, a society supposedly ruled by law) reasons to hide his true identity and enter society—hence the novel's title *Xia yin*, which could be literally translated as "hidden knight-errant" or "knight-errant in seclusion." Li Tianran is truly a new breed of hero, a Westernized master of *taihang* 太行 martial arts who has an affinity for sunglasses, whisky, and, during his secret night missions, for tying bandanas around his face in imitation of the masked villain in countless American western films. With Dr. McKay's help, Li takes a job at a small tabloid newspaper where he writes essays on American culture (not unlike Zhang Beihai's own moonlighting job as an essayist) as he falls in love with a young seamstress by the name of Guan Qiaohong, and slowly plots his revenge.

Zhang's choice of centering his tale on a story of revenge was dictated by the constraints of the genre. As he noted in a subsequent interview,

> Traditional *wuxia* 武侠 fiction of the twenties and thirties is based around two main themes; the first is revenge, which I have picked up in *Swallow*, and the other is the internal struggle in a martial clan to become number one—both in the clan and in the martial world. [The notion of writing about] fighting to become the head honcho never attracted me much, so I decided to take *revenge* as the central theme of my novel.[16]

Although Zhang's comments position his novel as a conscious attempt to present a bridge to the pre-war golden age of *wuxia* fiction, as mentioned earlier, his character is nevertheless forced to remain confined, "hidden" along the margins of society. This relative invisibility is necessary to facilitate the revenge plot on his master's murderers, but in a larger context, it can be seen as a symptom of the figure of the knight-errant's already having become a historically irrelevant and socially marginalized figure. In the face of increased globalization, technological innovation (including the mass introduction of guns and other advanced weaponry into China), and the rapidly changing political and social terrain of Republican China, the imaginary "wild west" era of the *jianghu* and *xia* 俠 are declared dead. What place do these Robin Hoodesque codes of righteousness and brotherhood have in modern society, and how can fists and feet compete with guns and cannons? Li Tianran's identity as a *xia yin* is as much a response to a social necessity as it is a personal one.

What is interesting is that this new, historically marginalized positioning of the *xia* is shadowed by that of the city of Beijing itself. Zhang's novel follows the contemporary, Republican-era convention of referring to the city of Beijing (literally, "Northern capital") as *Beiping* (literally, "Northern peace"), in recognition of the fact that the city's multi-century status as the capital of all of China had been temporarily displaced by Nanjing (literally, Southern capital). Now taking a back seat to the political center of Nanjing and the economic center of Shanghai, Beiping must reconcile itself with its identity as a comparatively marginal city—a demotion which the city had not experienced for over 600 years. While Ding Wenyu lives a high-profile life (prominently placing personal announcements in major newspapers and attending elite political and cultural functions) in Nanjing, the newly (re)crowned capital, both Li Tianran and Beiping remain in the shadows, obscured by their new marginalized personal and urban identities.

This newly marginalized city of "Northern peace" not only provides the physical setting for the novel, but furthermore the city could even be seen as one of the novel's own protagonists. As Zhang himself has explained:

> Since I set the novel in the Beiping of the nineteen-thirties and placed this *xia* character in the middle of the real world, the everyday life of Beiping in the thirties, therefore, the fashion, food, living conditions, means of travel, customs and habits, politics, economics, society, culture, the appearance of the city, and even the geographic makeup of the roads and lanes became not only a necessity, but, in the end, actually turned into one of the characters in the book.[17]

Here the nostalgia for the *wuxia* literary mode is matched by a nostalgia for the author's place of birth, Beiping. Unlike Ye Zhaoyan's novel, where the love story (of the individual) and the war story (of the city) are divided by two parallel narrative lines, Zhang Beihai's construction of Beiping is intertwined with virtually every aspect of the central narrative. From the culture of food and drink to the local tabloid gossip of the day, Zhang is meticulous in his attention to detail:

> Just how did they hang bells on camels in Beijing? I looked all over the place trying to find an answer but still came up short. In her novel *Cheng nan jiu shi* 城南舊事 (Memories of old Peking), Lin Haiyin 林海音 wrote about camels, but didn't mention anything about their bells. But what I'm concerned with is precisely these kinds of everyday life details. If one hundred years from now someone wants to write about New York

life in the nineties, and the protagonist takes a subway to Central Park, they can't screw up the number of the train that goes there. At first I was really concerned about this, but later I went to Beijing and met with Zhang Henshui's son, whom I asked [about the camels]. He told me that the people who would remember have either died a long time ago or are so old that they don't read novels anymore. It was only then that I felt I could rest assured and continue writing.[18]

So, while Ye Zhaoyan traces his nostalgia through his encyclopedic literary vision, Zhang Beihai's nostalgic reconstruction of Beiping is built on a meticulous attention to the fabric of everyday life.

Furthermore, nowhere is Zhang's detailed urban reconstruction clearer then in the realm of topography. Within the pages of *Swallow* is a painstaking re-creation not just of the details of city life, but also of the geographic details that make up the city. During his two years of historical research prior to writing the novel, Zhang Beihai's attention to topological detail even led him to create an elaborate computer reconstruction of a 1935 Beiping street map. This attention to the topographical terrain of Republican Beiping can be seen as a key entry-point into Zhang's literary and personal nostalgia. This is the world of 1936–1937 Beiping, the historical era of Lao She's *Rickshaw*, and the alleys and streets that Zhang Beihai re-creates are the same lanes and brick-laid boulevards that Camel slowly drudged through, fueled only by his sweat, blood, and need to survive. Li Tianran, however, when not leisurely strolling through this maze or being driven around in automobiles, instead soars over the rooftops of the ancient capital on his midnight adventures of chivalric revenge. Thus we are presented not only with a new form of topological construction, but also with a new means of revisiting and traversing this urban labyrinth. As one of the few fantasy sequences in the novel, these sweeping night flights also lend a dreamlike aura to the author's realistic portrayal of the cityscape Li Tianran flies through. Not only is Li Tianran's fictional world based on the actual streets and alleys of 1930s Beiping, but furthermore the novel itself as a whole can be seen as an homage to the lost world of Zhang Beihai's own childhood, insofar as the novel constitutes an attempt to pay homage to his father's generation (Zhang bases several of the characters in his novel on his father's former acquaintances and family members).

Night flights aside, Zhang's attention to issues of historical accuracy and the fabric of everyday life helps him bring an attention to "realism" to what is perhaps generally thought of as a genre of "fantasy" literature. This apparent contradiction is resolved when we take into account the fact that the novel is loosely modeled after Yanzi Li San 燕子李三 (Swallow), a historical folk hero about whom tales of physical and moral bravery flourished during the early days of the Republican era. In addition, as stated earlier, the literary paradigm to which Zhang Beihai looks for inspiration is not the later fantastic *wuxia* novels of Gu Long 古龍 and others, but rather *wuxia* novels from the early twentieth century period, as exemplified by such writers as Bai Yu 白羽 and especially Zheng Zhengyin 鄭證因, one of Zhang's primary sources of literary inspiration and also a *wuxia* author noted for his tendency towards "realism." This not only establishes a historical precedent for Zhang Beihai's "*wuxia* realism," but also positions his work as an attempt to revive a strain of chivalric fiction lost during the vicissitudes of twentieth-century China's political (and literary) history, during which time *wuxia* fiction increasingly became an attempt to escape from reality rather than confront it.

When Li Tianran's revenge plot is gradually fleshed out, his primary targets are identified as being Hata Jiro (Yutian Cilang), a Japanese secret agent, and the elusive Zhu Qianlong (Hidden dragon). Zhu Qianlong is Li's former clan brother who later becomes a collaborator for the Japanese and the head of the Chinese secret police. The fact that the two major villains in the novel both have direct connections with the Japanese suggests an allegorical reading to the revenge plot. This tendency to read Li Tianran's actions in the larger context of nationalism is heightened by the imminent fall of Beijing and the author's subtle weaving of such incidents as the Marco Polo Bridge Incident into the narrative. However, while there is a certain symbolic level to the narrative, Zhang Beihai does not reduce his novel to a set of straightforward parallels between Li Tianran's revenge and the impending Japanese occupation of China. In fact, it is the villains' close association with Japan that actually complicates and frustrates Li's attempts to avenge his master, rather than adding nationalistic fuel to his burning passion for revenge.

Both Ding Wenyu and Li Tianran are individuals very much consumed by their own respective personal passions and vendettas, so much so that romance and revenge prove to be the propelling forces behind each narrative. However, no matter how impervious to the discourse of History the two protagonists may appear to be, they remain helpless in its wake and both Ding Wenyu and Li Tianran's fates are decided not by the consequences of their romance and chivalric exploits, but by the cold reality of history. In Ding Wenyu's case, his fate is sealed when the "fortress besieged" is transformed from a metaphor to a harsh reality—and Ding is caught on the inside. For Li Tianran, the consequences are slightly understated, but equally devastating, as we shall see from an analysis of the novel's conclusion.

In the final pages of "Swallow" after Li Tianran has finally tracked down his primary target, the elusive Zhu Qianlong, the reader is finally presented with the long awaited dual-to-the-death between Li and his arch nemesis. The scene is also the moment where the reader might expect the hero to finally display his long coveted *taihang* martial-arts skills. In reality, however, the novel actually concludes with a rather different kind of "bang":

> Li Tianran stood beside Qianlong, and used his foot to lift Qianlong's dangling head. Staring coldly at him he said: "The first three shots were

for Master, his wife, Uncle, and my clan brother . . . This shot is for Danqing and me."

"Bang," a bullet entered Qianlong's skull as blood sprayed out.[19]

In this conclusion, Zhang replaces the conventional duel and accompanying display of martial-arts prowess with a modern gangster-style assassination that could have almost come out of a novel by Mario Puzo. Except for hurling a pair of shish-kabob sticks at his attackers, Zhu Qianlong, the mysterious and powerful villain of the story, is unable to fight back or even protect himself. At one level, the details of Li's act of revenge duplicate Zhu's initial murder of Li's master, which was also a surprise attack, carried out with guns. However, Li Tianran's cold copycat-style execution of his master's killer is less an example of the traditional logic of "an eye for an eye, a tooth for a tooth" than it is a result of practical necessity predicated by the changing historical circumstances within which he finds himself situated. In his unorthodox transgression of the generic *wuxia* formula, Zhang Beihai has not only transgressed readers' expectations, but has arguably signaled the end of the genre itself.

The unexpected brevity of Li Tianran's long-awaited act of chivalric retribution has a counterpart in the surprise realization and consummation of the romance between Ding Wenyu and Ren Yuyuan in *Nanjing 1937*. While Li Tianran goes to great lengths to track down the identity and whereabouts of his targets, Ding Wenyu similarly writes countless letters and devises an untold number of plots to win over Yuyuan. However, it isn't until a somewhat farcical scene at the Garrison Headquarters on the eve of a full evacuation of the city that a certain Staff Officer Li brings about the couple's perfunctory union by granting Yuyuan (who is an army secretary) a twenty-four-hour leave. In an ephemeral, almost dreamlike sequence, Ding Wenyu wins Yuyuan (virtually by default), and they run off together to consummate their relationship. The next day, Ding Wenyu sees Yuyuan back to the Garrison Headquarters and they part after a hasty and chaotic farewell—this turns out to be their final goodbye, as Yuyuan soon leaves the city with the rest of her battalion and Ding Wenyu is killed during a final hopeless attempt to find her.

In the surprise conclusions of both *Swallow* and *Nanjing 1937*, the obligatory fulfillment of each author's respective literary models is satisfied. In Ye Zhaoyan's novel the union of the lovers as stipulated by so many Butterfly romances is fulfilled. For Zhang Beihai, who takes martial-arts/chivalric fiction as his model, the hero avenges his murdered master. Ding Wenyu gets the girl and Li Tianran gets his revenge, but at what cost?

Both writers offer a last nostalgic gesture to the past by presenting a final token of romance and a final act of chivalry, in an era when each was becoming a historical impossibility. The perfunctory, unorthodox, and rather anticlimactic characteristics of both novels' conclusions are almost precisely parallel. And although the obligatory completion of the romance and revenge plots are fulfilled, the very *strategies* that each writer utilizes to do so inherently subvert and transgress the respective novelistic genres within which each is writing. The bullets that emerge from the barrel of Li Tianran's Colt forty-five render his mysterious *taihang* martial arts, along with his chivalric code of ethics, superfluous, while Ding Wenyu's twenty-four-hour romance is transformed into a tragic swan-song to a romantic reality rendered impossible by historical circumstances.

The fact that the two novels are set respectively in Beijing and Nanjing is significant to each of the writers' personal relationships with the cities and the ways in which their literary conception of a *chronotopic* coordinate serves as a means of constructing a personal nostalgia. At the same time, the temporal and spatial components of the novels each constitute a kind of "topological melancholy," by tracing out the historical fissure that signaled the decline of two popular literary genres and the fall of two ancient capitals. By 1937 Beijing was already a *feidu* 廢都, an "abandoned capital" that arguably would never again regain its former glory (according to Zhang Beihai, Beijing's post-1949 history "isn't worth a breath"). Furthermore, although the re-crowned capital of Nanjing was at the height of its power, by year's end the city would, once again, lay in ruins—and unlike Beijing, Nanjing would *never* again regain the splendor of 1937. Written at the end of a modern century, both Zhang Beihai and Ye Zhaoyan's works can be read as elegiac gestures to two Republican capitals in the final days of a bygone era. *Nanjing 1937* and *Swallow* are as much tales of two cities as they are tales of Ding Wenyu and Li Tianran's respective quests for romance and revenge.

More than a tale of two cities, this essay has been a tale of two writers, two capitals, two passionate protagonists (both returned foreign students, one consumed by romance, the other with revenge), two popular literary genres, and one tumultuous historical milieu. Astonishingly, by setting the main action in 1937 and fleshing out lost details in the protagonists' lives through extended flashback sequences (which incidentally both occur during the first third of the respective novels), the novels project a temporal trajectory that is virtually identical. Deeply indebted to the popular cultural trademarks of this distinct era, from Japanese advertisements for medicinal breath mints, to the public passion for fighter pilots[20] and tabloid gossip, both novels present a new conception of popular/folk culture which stands outside the discourse of History. Through their respective encyclopedic vision, topographical reconstruction, and other strategies of representation, Ye Zhaoyan and Zhang Beihai have reconstructed two urban centers of Republican China, and in the process created new paradigms for imagining China and re-employing popular literature at the end of a century. As the *fin-de-siècle* approached, we have an uncanny coincidence whereby, unbeknownst to each other, a Nanjing-based writer and a Chinese-American author writing from the diaspora together present a new interpretation of popular Chinese literature from the 1930s, together with its potential for surviving into the new millennium.

Notes

A portion of this paper appears in a different form in my *A History of Pain: Trauma in Modern Chinese Literature and Film*. Copyright © 2008 Columbia University Press. Reprinted with permission of the publisher.

1 Ding Wenyu is unable to navigate this new topography. His disorientation as an outsider from Shanghai is exacerbated by the rapidly changing cityscape resulting from widespread construction and development, leading in turn to his reliance on the rickshaw coolie Monk to navigate for him. This spatial alienation, furthermore, is mirrored by his aloofness to the political reality he lives in, even though he is constantly surrounded by some of the most important political figures of the era.

2 In his landmark study of Mandarin Duck and Butterfly fiction, Perry Link commented on the links between romantic passion and nationalistic passion as a theme often seen in the genre.

> His heroic, or *yingxiong* passion parallels the passion of his romantic, or *ernü* attachments. A young man's patriotic love and his pure love for a young woman are more than just similar. They are, in fact, two forms of what is fundamentally the same pure *qing* which a given individual will possess in one form if and only if he also possesses it in the other.
>
> (Perry Link, *Mandarin Ducks and Butterflies:*
> *Popular Fiction in Early Twentieth Century Chinese Cities*
> [Berkeley: University of California Press, 1981], 77)

In this context, Ye Zhaoyan's juxtaposition of individual romantic passion and militaristic national passion can be seen as a conscious attempt to revisit and reconceptualize this tropic theme of the genre. While both Ding Wenyu and Monk (who I will later argue functions as his double), are ever lost in their *ernü* attachments, both seem exiled from the heroic world. At the same time, however, both characters do explicitly exercise fantasies about "dying for their country"—in the end both do, but only in the most tongue-in-cheek fashion.

3 Although the narrative progresses along a linear trajectory, many of the events in Ding Wenyu's early life, including his affair with Yuyuan's older sister when he was seventeen, are developed in an extended flashback sequence which occurs early on in the novel. This flashback sequence also conveniently provides many key details and events in pre-War of Resistance Sino-Japanese relations.

4 See Link, *Mandarin Ducks and Butterflies*, 62–63; and Rey Chow, *Woman and Chinese Modernity: The Politics of Reading between West and East* (Minneapolis: University of Minnesota Press, 1991), 36.

5 Bonnie S. McDougall and Kam Louie, *The Literature of China in the Twentieth Century* (New York: Columbia University Press, 1997), 83.

6 For more on Chang's early career and her connection with the Mandarin Duck and Butterfly school, see Leo Ou-fan Lee, *Shanghai Modern: The Flowering of a New Urban Culture in China 1930–1945* (Cambridge: Harvard University Press, 1999), 267–269.

7 The murder and rape of Little Moon was inspired by an actual event that Ye Zhaoyan read about in the newspaper and appropriated into his novel. This is reminiscent of Taiwanese writer Li Ang's 李昂 inspiration for her controversial best-selling novel *Sha fu* 殺夫 (The butcher's wife) and the literary experiments of Chang Dachun 張大春, who also freely appropriates actual news stories into his novels, especially in the case of *Da shuohuang jia* 大説謊家 (*The grand liar*).

8 Ye Zhaoyan not only wrote his 1986 M.A. thesis on the novel, but even today continues to be fascinated by Qian Zhongshu's 錢鍾書 portrayal of petty intellectuals

during the War of Resistance. In the 2000.4 issue of *Shouhuo* 收穫 (Harvest) Ye published the essay *"Weicheng li de xiaosheng"* 圍城裡的笑聲 (Laughter in *Fortress Besieged*).

9 Qian Zhongshu (Ch'ien Chung-shu), *Fortress Besieged*, Jeanne Kelly and Nathan K. Mao, trans. (Bloomington: Indiana University Press, 1979), 1.

10 Ye Zhaoyan 葉兆言, *Yijiusanqi nian de aiqing* 一九三七年的愛情 (Nanjing 1937) (Nanjing: Jiangsu wenyi chubanshe, 1996), 256.

11 Zhang Wenjiang 張文江, *Yingzao Babita de zhizhe: Qian Zhongshu zhuan* 營造 巴比塔的智者：錢鍾書傳 (The wise builder of Babel: a biography of Qian Zhongshu) (Shanghai: Shanghai wenyi chubanshe, 1993), 57.

12 Ye Zhaoyan, *Nanjing 1937*, 273.

13 *The Seventies* later changed its name to *The Nineties* (*Jiushi niandai* 九十年代).

14 As mentioned earlier, *wuxia* fiction technically falls under the larger umbrella of Mandarin Duck and Butterfly fiction (in its broader definition). Although I am herein referring to these two genres as separate literary phenomena, it should be stressed that they evolved from the same tradition and elements of romantic and martial fiction were often blurred and combined by such writers as Wang Dulu 王度盧, who excelled at both, and Zhang Henshui 張恨水, who combined the subgenres of romance fiction and *wuxia* in his classic novel *Tixiao yinyuan* 啼笑 因緣 (Fate in tears and laughter).

15 Ironically, like Ding Wenyu and Fang Hongjian, Li Tianran also fails to complete a university degree. But unlike his foreign-student counterparts, whose academic failure is due to lack of ability or interest, Li's education is forcefully interrupted when he is deported for using his martial arts to set straight a bunch of American college boys.

16 Ye Meiyao 葉美瑤, *"Shidai kaoyan wuxia: wuxia chuangzao shidai"* 時代考驗武 俠：武俠創造時代 (An era tests a knight errant, and a knight errant creates an era) in *Renjian* 人間 (Life), October 27, 2000.

17 Zhang Beihai 張北海, *"Xia zhongjie yu lao Beiping de xiaoshi—Xiayin zuozhe Zhang Beihai da kewen"* 俠之終結與老北平的消逝—《俠隱》作者張北海答客問 (The end of a knight errant, and the disappearance of old Beiping—*Swallow* author Zhang Beihai answers questions), *Zhongguo shibao* 中國時報 (China times), Sept. 16–18, 2000.

18 Ibid.

19 Zhang Beihai, *Xiayin* 俠隱 (Swallow) (Taipei: Maitian chubanshe, 2000), 491–492.

20 Both novels feature airforce pilots as prominent secondary characters. In *Nanjing 1937*, Yuyuan's husband Yu Kerun is a star pilot who at one point leads an air show for Chiang Kai-shek while *Swallow* features a character named Lan Tian (who was incidentally loosely modeled after Zhang Beihai's older brother), who also joins the Chinese airforce. The presence of Yu Kerun and Lan Tian also marks the single most fascinating intertextual moment of the two novels; for both Yu Kerun and Lan Tian die in action during the 1937 Battle of Shanghai, the first actual battle involving the newly formed Chinese airforce. (The disastrous outcome of this battle was later commemorated by the KMT by declaring August 14 National Airforce Day, a holiday still recognized today in Taiwan.) Thus it is ironic that it is not Nanjing or Beiping but the third chronotopic juncture of Shanghai where the narratives converge, providing an uncanny link between not only the fates of Yu Kerun and Lan Tian but also the literary imagination of Ye Zhaoyan and Zhang Beihai.

7 From romancing the state to romancing the store

Further elaborations of Butterfly motifs in contemporary Taiwan literature

Ping-hui Liao

> People have every right in/to the store: to love, to hope, to shop.
> (Sunrise Department Store Advertisement 1997)

Many advertisements in Taipei's MRT mall contain striking images of women with consuming passion. Their captions often consist of intimate stories, brief and disjunctive narratives using innovative hybrid languages that draw on themes from the traditional romance novel to address the secret hopes and fears of young female shoppers, and to enhance the flaneuristic pleasure of romancing the stores. It is precisely in this peculiar form of semantic or even semiotic innovation, of redeploying romantic tropes in emergent consumer cultures, that advertising gives new life to the early twentieth century Mandarin Ducks and Butterflies tradition. In response to such innovative discursive practices, spectators, especially those belonging to the "new, new human species" (*xinxin renlei* 新新人類) or the so-called "X" and "E" generations, see something both fascinating and familiar in the images.[1] These publicity-driven images actually produce a politics of recognition in contemporary Taiwan.

In order to contextualize the form and function of such discursive practices, I will first provide an overview of Butterfly literature in contemporary Taiwan, and will focus in particular on two recent literary works in which the tradition is revised and transformed: Wang Wenxing's 王文興 two-part modernist novel, *Beihai de ren* 背海的人 (Backed against the sea) (in particular Part II) and Shi Shuqing's 施叔青 "Hong Kong Trilogy,"[2] together with her subsequent novella, *Weixun caizhuang* 微醺彩妝 (Light drunken makeup).[3] Highlighting issues that constitute Taiwan's "post-colonial" condition, these two works parody the Butterfly tradition and expand its horizon. They render romantic relations between men and women perverse, grotesque, and uncanny. Blending the Chinese Butterfly literary tradition with that of the Western romance novel, both texts portray psychic fascination and subjection in terms of moral contingency and irony.

Acts of passionate attachment inevitably result in pathological situations in which the protagonists are forced to act out traumas in a mode of neurotic repetition compulsion or state fetishism. Money, sex, and human aggression become entangled and exchangeable. In these two novels and some of the advertisements that appear on the Taipei MRT billboards, Butterfly themes are appropriated and put into new discursive contexts, to reveal different facets of love and life situations as men and women find their destinies entangled with those of others until then unknown to them. The tendency to resort to romance in partial response to the emergence of new social imagery is, as we will see, what has rendered the Butterfly tradition vibrant and exciting.

Butterfly in a new dress

In her book *Woman and Chinese Modernity* (1991), Rey Chow interrogates the gendered connotations of the early twentieth century Butterfly tradition. She notes, for instance, that in the Butterfly literature's human dramas, "love" stories "often take place in the consistent absence of the women's beloved, who 'participate' only by being weak, sick, dead, far away, or a foreigner untouched by Confucian culture [...]. The women are left 'to struggle alone' " (51).[4] Paying meticulous attention to feminine details, Chow finds that the Butterfly literature provides "a wonderful instance of the parodic function particularly because of its popular and marginalized status" (54). The staging of female traumas in such a popular, readable form meant "that sentimental emotions, which had hitherto been hushed up in a society that considered public demonstration of strong feelings embarrassing, were now [around the turn of the nineteenth century] released to untried degrees of exuberance" (55). "What used to be unutterable, 'feminine' feelings were," she adds, "now put on a par with the heroic and patriotic, circulated, and made lucidly 'available' for the first time through the mass practices of reading and writing, activities that used to belong exclusively to the highbrow scholarly world" (55–56).

Alternative forms of rewriting Butterfly literature have also emerged since the 1950s in the country I know best—Taiwan. This reinventing of literary traditions to meet local and global challenges occurred in such subgenres as the nostalgic romance novel, sentimental fiction, erotic or queer writing, and multicultural narratives. In an early reaction to the sense of displacement and exile frequently associated with Taiwan, nostalgic romance by such ultimately expatriate authors as Bai Xianyong 白先勇 and Nie Hualing 聶華苓 focuses on themes of diasporic cultural dislocation and emotional malaise. Written in a refined language drawing on Butterfly literature and Yuan dynasty drama, these novels are largely about disillusionment and disenchantment. From the 1970s onward, female romance authors such as Qiongyao 瓊瑤, Sanmao 三毛, Liao Huiying 廖輝英, and Yuan Qiongqiong 袁瓊瓊 helped popularize Butterfly literature among young readers, who were given imaginative opportunities to conjure dream loves and to repress everyday hardships. Seemingly frivolous, sentimental romance was developed in between Nativist and modernist literary expressions, with the focus on intimate stories of men and women rather than on multinational capitalism and exploitation in the Third World.

In the mid-1980s, however, the idea of different lifestyles and sexual orientations gained momentum, especially with the rise of post-feminist and queer consciousness in both the academy and mass media. Queer (or ventroliquistically queer) authors associated with this sort of movement include such figures as Zhu Tianwen 朱天文, Hong Ling 洪淩, Ji Dawei 紀大偉, and Qiu Miaojin 邱妙津. In these variants of the traditional romance genre, it is no longer a handsome male scholar and a pretty lady who fall in love, nor an abandoned woman struggling to win her love. Here the passionate attachment is to the same sex, as in *Eyu shouji* 鱷魚手記 (Crocodile journals) by Qiu Maojin. Since the mid-1990s, however, readers have increasingly been presented with multicultural narratives of trans-ethnic love affairs, of the art of love and survival in terms of minority rights, of family romances and of ambivalent cultural or ethnic identities. Wuhe 舞鶴, Zhu Tianxin 朱天心, Luo Yijun 駱以軍, and many other new authors continue to broaden the horizon of Butterfly literature. These critical accounts have recently been complicated by David Wang's incisive observations on the rise of female ghosts in popular romance fiction in response to an age of chaos and extremity. In Wang's view, phantasmagoric female characters haunt the pan-Chinese-speaking communities and collapse the distinction between revolution and disillusionment, the imaginary and the real, desire and despair. In the new novels of romantic encounters with strange beauties from the world of fantasy, it is those who stay behind—now, primarily young and attractive men—who suffer and become traumatized. Female ghosts, on the other hand, are empowered and rendered unfathomable, if not necessarily fatal.[5]

It is significant that both Rey Chow and David Wang make reference to Eileen Chang 張愛玲. Although Chang, who was born in 1920, was a mere infant during the early debates between the May Fourth and Butterfly traditions, she has nevertheless emerged as a key figure who reworked and subverted many of the original Butterfly narrative conventions: her female protagonists often re-channel their desires and become victims of chance during hard times. In her novella *Qingcheng zhi lian* 傾城之戀 (Love in a fallen city), for instance, the female protagonist Bai Liusu, during her second visit to Hong Kong, chooses to come to terms with the demands of social practicality by becoming Fan Liuyuan's mistress. As Chang observes, "ultimately, it all comes down to economic safety [...]. In a world of turmoil, money, property and vows are all rendered unreliable. What is reliable is that she still lives and there is still someone lying beside her."[6] Luckily, Bai eventually realizes that she really loves Fan. However, in the case of Suxi, the heroine of Chang's novella *Di'er luxiang* 第二爐香 (The second brazier), "there are not that many husband candidates to choose from." Everything boils down to "a rational calculation of the situation." It is as if life in mid twentieth century Shanghai and Hong Kong had changed so much that the female characters of the novels could no longer embrace these "modern" cities imaginatively in all their awesome horror. In Chang's fictional worlds, however, we can still detect the familiar storylines of Butterfly literature: "Boy meets girl; boy and girl fall in love; boy and girl are separated by cruel fate; boy and girl die of broken heart."[7] Chang is particularly relevant to us here; she provides a crucial bridge linking the early twentieth century Butterfly traditions and contemporary Taiwan authors such as Wang Wenxing and Shi Shuqing.

Educated at National Taiwan University, where he became familiar with novels by James Joyce, Franz Kafka, D. H. Lawrence, and Earnest Hemingway, Wang Wenxing is a mainlander Chinese who came to the island with his family in the late 1940s fleeing the Communists. A stylist, Wang developed motifs introduced by Joyce, Philip Roth, and Samuel Beckett, among others, to deal with alienation and exile. His characters are largely dropouts or social outcasts, battling in infantile or futile ways against patriarchal values or general themes of existentialist absurdity—*Jiabian* 家變 (Family crisis) or *Longtianlou* 龍天樓 (Dragon sky building), for example. However, it is in his recent work, *Backed against the Sea* (1981–1999), that Wang blends the Western modernist discourses with the Chinese Butterfly tradition, to offer a "grotesque" view of contemporary Taiwan society and of humanity.[8] The male protagonist is a poor and miserable retired military man who calls himself *Ye* 爺—"uncle" or "master," connoting on the one hand an imposed self-importance and on the other an ironic label given to a useless old man. Ye (whom I will refer to as *Master* Ye, to highlight the parodic effect) is a pathological case, particularly in the prostitution episode toward the end of Volume I, where he engages in a rather ugly scene with a prostitute who at first refuses to take her clothes off. In rather grotesque albeit realistic language, the narrator elaborates all of the ways in which Master Ye eventually succeeds in getting on top of the ugly and wretched woman. Whoring is certainly not the occasion to display sentimental emotions, although Master Ye evidently is so disoriented that he has no difficulty falling in love with a most uncanny sex object. This is more evident in Volume II, completed by the author over the course of 18 years while Taiwan itself was undergoing an intense period of transition. The latter volume opens with another equally comic-serious description of Master Ye falling desperately in love with a prostitute with red hair. In the first volume of the novel, Master Ye literally rapes a prostitute, while in the second volume he is very much under the control of a red-haired "lady" (in fact, a whore), whom he adores—but who at first ignores and then insults him in a most insolent manner. In both incidents, the female prostitutes, uttering at critical moments vernacular and vulgar Taiwanese, are apparently of Minnan origin. These "romantic" affairs serve to displace ethnic tensions and state violence in the form of an erotic or libidinal economy.

Red-haired normally means "wild or hot-tempered," but Wang uses it to connote ethnic or racial exoticism, probably with an implicit reference to Taiwan's colonial history, in particular the period under the Dutch. The Dutch were known in the early seventeenth century as the *Red Haired Barbarians*— a racial label which is also reflected in the "Red Fort" in Tamshui and a few ports on the west coast of the island. The label has since been attached to foreigners, often denigrated as "ghosts" or "monkeys." Here, the prostitute is referred to as *Red Hair* in part on account of her dyed hair, but also perhaps in reference to an uncanny colonial encounter with an ethnic Other, as someone that is both horrible and fascinating. As the narrator makes explicit, Red Hair appears as a grotesque female "ghost" and an ambivalent love object.

As a social outcast, Master Ye is situated at the margin of margins. His romantic encounter with Red Hair metonymically reveals the workings of state violence and ethnic tension. The novel as a whole opens with his exile from metropolitan culture—first from China, then from Taipei, capital of the refugee Nationalist government. A series of misfortunes ensues while Master Ye is in the countryside and is ridiculed by the dominant Minnan ethnic group around him. With his fortunes on the decline, he has his eye on Red Hair, "probably the very source of all misfortunes" (II: 189). In a parody of the "love at first sight" convention found in many Butterfly romances, however, the narrator observes that, in this case, love "might not happen at first sight; it is at the third, fourth, or fifth." Furthermore, the narrative makes clear that she is no beautiful swan, but rather an "**ugly duckling**" (bold in the original), "like a dried up Peking duck," with her dark-brown eyes poking out, and her red hair bound up tight, as if on fire. Even her distinctive red hair becomes, for Master Ye, an awkward point of semiotic aporia, as he admits that he does know "if it is **real**, or **dyed and printed** on" (bold in the original). Finally, in an ironic twist on the romantic convention of the spurned lover who returns as a ghost, Red Hair herself is explicitly given a spectral dimension, as the narrator remarks that "Master Ye falls in love, practically speaking, with a ghost" (II: 189, underlining in the original).

Red Hair's position in the novel reflects an anxiety and fear regarding the ethnic Other. Slavoj Žižek's observation that one is often bothered by the "excess" of the (ethnic) Other, is relevant here. The "strange" manners, together with the "smell" of unorthodox food, noisy songs and dances, and so on, that indicate the distinctive ways the ethnic Other organizes his/her enjoyment, are not only psychologically disturbing but also physically fascinating. For, as Žižek suggests, "the basic paradox is that our Thing is conceived as something inaccessible to the other and at the same time threatened by him."[9] This may partially explain why Red Hair, an unattractive prostitute, is adored, while Cai Suzhen, a more marriageable female professional and probably much prettier, is scorned by Master Ye. Ye himself attempts to explain this apparent paradox by suggesting that Red Hair is only an exception (II: 243). Seen in this way, the "love" story between Master Ye and Red Hair can be read as a textual strategy of romancing the state and displacing its potential violence, while actually relegating the racial unconscious to the background. In an allegorical mode of erotic pursuit, critical issues of ethnicity and history are here downplayed and even repressed to introduce the freedom of irrational choice, of seeking the hand of an Other, a woman of lowest birth. As if to embrace the propaganda that "four ethnic groups form a collective national body," Master Ye, arrogant and ethnocentric though he is, can go to such extremes by desiring to be in love with Red Hair, to be one with his love object.

To impress Red Hair, Master Ye retells his "heroic," albeit traumatic, past, wherein he alone survived the attacks by the Communists in China. Deep down, he imagines himself a *caizi* 才子 (gifted scholar) in distress or in exile. Often he is quite condescending to his Taiwanese peers and friends—including, for instance, his lady friend Cai Suzhen. He insists that his experience on the mainland should entitle him to a college degree (or at least to half a degree), as well as to a more suitable match in marriage (perhaps "a primary school teacher"). And yet, in his repeated attempts to win the heart of Red Hair, Master Ye subjects himself to all sorts of compromises and humiliations. He addresses her as a *jiaren* 佳人 (lovely lady) in the form of courtly love. The love letters and gifts to Red Hair, however, get trashed in public, and his tender words only make the "beloved" more angry and spiteful. "*Kaopei*" ("to hell with you," or literally, "crying for your dead father"), she shouts in insulting Minnan. At one point, Master Ye becomes jealous of Zhang Fawu, who appears to be Red Hair's favorite man, and even suggests that he is willing to share Red Hair with Zhang if she so desires. Red Hair, however, continues to ignore him and, one morning, she suddenly leaves for Taipei and is never seen again. It is not easy to reconcile Master Ye's disparate responses to the two women. The narrator rationalizes this disparity with an aphorism: "Sometimes you love one person, while being loved by another." But why should there be such a "love" between a social outcast and a prostitute, an insignificant mainlander and an ugly Minnan woman?

To make sense of the "love" story, we need to relate it to the latter part of the novel, where Master Ye teams up with his friends to kill a lost military dog. This violent ritual reminds us of activities in the military compounds (*juancun* 眷村) in which Nationalist troops and their families lived for many years following their arrival in Taiwan from the mainland. This linkage between the killing of the dog and life in the military compounds suggests that the segregated status of Chinese mainlanders in Taiwan may be seen as a reversed form of ethnic segregation, which cuts the people of the compounds off from the outside world where they might be corrupted by the native Taiwanese, who were thought to have been contaminated by the Japanese colonial regime. The dog symbolizes in a very gruesome way what Master Ye and his colleagues had themselves undergone on the island: the experience of being framed and pushed to the dead end. The killing of the dog

thus foreshadows the killing of Master Ye himself and, at the conclusion
of the novel, the tossing of his body into the sea. It is hardly surprising,
therefore, that Yvonne Chang should read this scene as being about a social
misfit and an ethnic Other.[10]

The novel therefore deploys a combination of Chinese and Western
romance genres and translingual practices to complicate the primal scene of
encounter with an ethnic Other. The novel uses and abuses Butterfly motifs
to highlight the erotic-grotesque scenes in the linguistic contact zone, to re-
address love as an irrational and fetishistic obsession, to make the pathological observation of the nation-state in terms of romance which is no romance
at all. As Red Hair is shown to be a fatal attraction despite her grotesque
appearance and temperament, the absurd romantic affair between her and
Master Ye functions only to highlight the impossibility of overcoming
ethnic tension and the affects of internal colonization. The erotic pursuit is
perpetuated by an obsession, and is not only a pathetic case of fetishism but
a parody of romancing the state, of the redemptive and regenerative magic
of love in relation to the national fragmentation.

Old wine in new bottles

To pursue the subject of state fetishism further, we may turn to Shi Shuqing's
"Hong Kong Trilogy," as well as her more recent novella *Light Drunken
Makeup*, about red wine fever in Taiwan. Born in Lugang, a historical town
in central Taiwan, Shi began her career as an existentialist or modernist writer
by presenting stories of young women growing up in a small and decaying
community. However, when she moved to Hong Kong in the early 1980s,
postcolonial subjects became her obsession. She produced the Hong Kong
trilogy to probe the city's colonial past and its postcolonial predicaments,
from a changing perspective of both an insider and outsider, of a traveler-
in-dweller. In 1994 she decided to return to Taipei and witnessed the most
puzzling development of a postcolonial Taiwan, where she found KMT
government officials to be indulging in the consumption of expensive red
wines while common people took to drinking the cheaper kinds. The whole
country was wild with passion for state magic, and red wines were becoming cultural icons charged with erotics and politics. In these fictional works,
Shi elaborated on Butterfly motifs to represent the postcolonial conditions
of Hong Kong and of Taiwan.

The trilogy focuses on the figure of Huang Deyun—a prostitute whose fate
becomes entangled with that of a fictional character named Adam Smith when
he accidentally bumps into her bed while looking for a brothel. Smith
appears as a "foreign ghost," but Huang immediately falls passionately in
love with him and even bears him a child who later becomes a successful
entrepreneur. In many ways, therefore, Huang's life story metonymically
represents the figure of Hong Kong within a global economy.

Of course, Adam Smith is much better off than Wang Wenxing's Master Ye. But, even before he leaves Huang for a local British lady and is subsequently indicted for corruption, Smith has already been suffering from an internal split, an inability to face the intimate enemy within himself, to borrow Ashis Nandy's phrase. Smith's stumbling into Huang's bed in fact constitutes the beginning of his own downfall. The bed represents a conjunction of Chinese and Western perversions, and the greedy and grotesque woman lying on it is simultaneously seductive and fascinating: "Her yellow butterfly wings flutter, fragile and yet refreshing." This yellow Butterfly motif reinforces the tragic and pathological character of transnational love and marriage, similar to that of *Miss Saigon*. The colonial encounter between Smith and Huang in the whorehouse vividly captures the cultural dynamics of a colonial city living on borrowed time and space: the relationship is both contingent and temporary. Evidently, the trilogy owes a great deal to earlier Butterfly literature, and particularly to the novels of Eileen Chang, as the female protagonist literally tries to realize her Butterfly dream and fantasy.

To attract her man, Huang Deyun reenacts the arts of seduction that she presumably learned both from reading Butterfly literature and from her experience at the whorehouse. She develops a fetishistic obsession with arranging the atmosphere for lovemaking and, in the long run, this obsession irretrievably attaches to the superfluous detail of things. In Huang, therefore, we see fetishistic magic and an embodiment of perverse obscenity. This can be seen in the Tang flat that Smith rents for her, a flat which is marred by dark and intertwining shadows even though richly decorated with an array of colorful objects such as veils, dragons, lanterns, vases, and so on. The flat represents both her childlike charm and her destructive sexual desire. She tries every means to win Smith's heart, but ultimately fails. Then, as if in revenge, she proceeds to seduce Smith's aide, Qu Yabing, who is a traitor to his own people and a running dog for the British colonial regime in Hong Kong. What starts as an Eileen Chang-like story eventually disintegrates into a vulgar tale of money, sex, and aggression. As a grotesque body, Huang Deyun is able to engage the racial Other while fulfilling her appetite for money and power. That is why she is a "yellow butterfly with pink wings." Like the figure of Red Hair in Wang Wenxing's novel, the yellow butterfly supports a rich array of racial connotations (as in such sayings as "yellow peril" and "yellow cab").[11] Huang's perversity gathers force in the hybrid form of a strange beauty and an uncanny strength or greed which, to paraphrase E. M. Forster, "sometimes comes to flower in Orientals of low birth."[12]

Most notable in Huang's perversion is her power to simulate and fetishize her own desire and passion. She attempts to find compensation in a male actor after failing to get her men—first Smith, and then his underdog and poor substitute Qu. She fantasizes about her "hero," the actor, imagining all sorts of idealized romantic encounters with him. But with the sudden disappearance of her dream love, she seeks solace in materialistic gains and tries to raise her bastard son as a respectable gentleman and businessman who can help realize her desire to build everything around the commodities of Hong Kong, a capitalist society. Out of frustration and despair, that is, Huang turns to Capital, and rechannels her consuming passion by purchasing more real estate and abstract monetary power. In the latter part of the trilogy, she is only concerned with economic success, and suddenly re-emerges as an entrepreneur and a calculating mother, who becomes not only sexless but also bodiless: a symbol of greed and of instrumental rationality. From this point onward, her lust is no longer for men, but rather for money and power. In a way, her transformation from country girl to whore to capitalist entrepreneur metaphorically represents Hong Kong's socio-economic history in the transnational finance-scape.

The fetishism of commodities, Capital, and the state is elaborated even more explicitly in Shi's novella *Light Drunken Makeup*. In the novella, six male characters represent various aspects of "state fetishism," or the political economy of simulations—including those of "taste," "label," "price," and, most amazingly, of "makeup that gives the impression of sensual intoxication and passion." The whole state of Taiwan is said to be following its leaders in consuming expensive red wines and, as a result, the detailed study of wine connoisseurship has become increasingly popular. Handsome men and beautiful women are stimulated by simulated signs, perfumes, and makeup. Lu Zixiang, a main contributor to the wine column in a leading magazine, for instance, adopts a name inspired by Lu Mingsu, a baseball star, and goes to sleep at night while wearing a hat with Lu's signature. He picks up the habit of drinking red wines by looking at Wang Hongwen performing a fascinating ritual: "the dramatic scene of that ecstatic and pleasurable expression immediately possesses him, becoming a modality for imitation" (237). Instead of reaching out to find love, characters in the new Butterfly literature are now driven instead by their desire for mirror images, by impulses to be able to feel, to sense, to reiterate what the ideal ego has dictated. Religion, spiritual tradition, and ethics are now displaced by fetishisms or manufactured empty sensations—including nostalgia and melancholia, which lack any concrete referents.

For Tang Ren, a retired diplomat who later becomes involved in the production of cheap, counterfeit red wines, Mia comes in handy as a redemption figure in times of crisis. He has just lost his wife, has become weary of foreign affairs in a small South American country, and grown increasingly uncomfortable with the local political situation in Taiwan. Mia, the seemingly innocent, loving, and caring girlfriend, is repeatedly referred to as having a "green thumb," and is regarded as a soul-keeper for the corrupted wine-maker. Like other male characters in the novella, Tang is interested in the fetishistic nature of his relations to Mia, who is evoked in time of spiritual crisis as if she were a fine bottle of red wine that might refresh his wearied soul. That is partly why Tang constantly associates her with flower and aroma, elements that wine connoisseurs cherish. However, this twisted structure of investment and empowerment only indicate how shallow and hollow these men and women are.

Melancholia, acedia, and a lack of sensation have become prevalent diseases in a state in which people worship fetishes and simulated sensual products. As the characters in Shi's novel search for new ways to shock their sensibility and to tap the well of their deepest passions, they find their rational faculties failing. The narcissistic and desperate care of the self—hence, the popularity of DIY (do-it-yourself) kits and goods—reveals the end of true "love" stories. It is as if with expert wine manuals and good-sex guides romantic relations could be guaranteed, if not fulfilled. Unlike Huang Deyun, the yellow butterfly trading sex for money and power, Lu and Tang engage themselves in endless pursuits of finesse and sensation on the assumption that love, like wine, is composed of commodity fetishism.

In love with commodities

With these new trends in rewriting Butterfly literature in mind, it becomes possible to understand more effectively the emergent transnational discourses of contemporary Taiwan, of advertisements marketing the "care of the self." Advertisements in public spaces often use hybrid linguistic and literary expressions, blending Chinese with Taiwanese or English, and tying Butterfly motifs to the latest patterns of consumer culture, in order to lure shoppers to desire commodities in the name of love and the care of the self. The Butterfly motifs are further elaborated to make desirable the romancing of the stores, the fulfilling of one's love and hope in the act of shopping. The message is that in times of economic and political crisis, in which a general sense of powerlessness prevails, the only *sensible* thing to do is not only to be surrounded by beautiful commodities but also to construct oneself as an adorable commodity waiting to be cherished and loved.

Consider some of the images that appear on the public billboards in the Taipei MRT subway's new underground mall. Images of young women eager to romance the stores currently predominate in these advertisements— replacing such patriarchal figures as Cousin Lee, Descendants of the Dragon, and opposition party leaders who predominated in previous decades. This is true not only for cosmetics, fitness, banking, drinks, soy sauce, food, and household goods, but also in advertisements for notebook computers, cell-phones, e-wap (electronic mail services on handheld PDA), and other advanced technological products. With Taiwan's rising unemployment rate, now at a record high of nearly 7 percent, young women are the only demographic group who can be consistently relied upon to do any real shopping. However, these women are by no means merely passive consumers of commodities and fetishistic signs. They shop smart, with character and glamour; and they construct narrative identities through fascinating stories, largely in the esoteric languages used and understood only by the so-called "X" and "E" generations. These narratives highlight the intimate experience of romance in the malls, of the circulation of ecstatic buying power, of the drama of spirit possession. The messages are often delivered in the name of minority rights, feminism, counter discourse, libidinal economy, social movement, and so on, as if consumers could develop an identity politics through these processes of identification and consumption.

The Taipei MRT station underground mall, which for some peculiar reason is called the "Easy," extends about two miles, and has far too many exits with no clear directions. As a result, it is by no means easy to get around. One advertisement on a wall boasts that the mall is a "new flânerie space," with an atmosphere so artistic that one would "revel in Beethoven's musical thoughts, dance with Duncan, and meet Picasso in a happy encounter"— although this sounds like a daydream or, at best, a utopian wish at the mall's current stage. The mall can hardly compete with some of the most elaborate malls in other parts of Asia—such as that of Kuala Lumpur, for example. The mall has more recently aptly reinvented itself as a "zone of enjoyment," or *xiyou* 嘻遊, punning on the title of the classical Chinese novel, *Xiyouji* 西遊記 (Journey to the West). As a signifying practice, the phrase indicates an interesting moment of semantic innovation and cultural twist that gives new meaning to the "adventures" or "journey" to the stores in Taipei's West Side. While playing on the classical journey or quest motif, the neologism also suggests a different way to play around and to enjoy oneself.

Intriguing instances of linguistic and cultural hybridization abound, as in the case of an underwear ad. The woman is having a great time messing up the hair of her man, who evidently can't do anything about it. To reveal intimate secrets of the human drama, the caption—three lines in parallel structure—reads: "It won't be easy to change the mode of his thoughts. It would be fun to change the style of his hair. It is sexy to change the brand of his underwear." The speaker is apparently a young female, and the way she articulates her desire to change her man indicates a subversive intent to reverse gender roles, to make sure that men accommodate themselves to women's sexual fantasies. To paraphrase Julia Kristeva and Janet Wolff, we may call these "feminine" sentences linguistic instances of revolution in a minor scale. "Minor" is used here in the sense of rewriting the dominant discourse, but also in the sense of weak resistance or even of alternative albeit empty rhetorical gestures, of playing with the idea that women could be empowered or in control, even though in reality such quasi-feminine statements might serve Capital. It is in this sort of playfully subversive way that the women in the ads reveal their sexual desires, secret thoughts, political comments, utopian hopes, and so on, along the traditional lines of Butterfly literature, insofar as these female characters seem to be descendants of those fictional characters introduced by Eileen Chang, now dressed in modern Shanghai fashions. In the late 1990s, Xu Shunying 許舜英, a lesbian activist and director of Taiwan's Ideology Advertising Company, for example, deliberately staged her advertisements to evoke nostalgic memories of the *jiaren* figures, but with the twist that these lovely women could simply indulge in reveries or in the most colorful of fashion shows, out of a desperate narcissistic love. For them, a *luanshi yuanyang* 亂世鴛鴦 (Mandarin Duck lovers in war-tossed times) mentality is no longer appealing; it is more affordable and charming to remain single, noble, and queer—as a solitary Butterfly.

Of course, the semantic innovation of such feminine sentences can be traced back to the discursive practices of activists, cab or truck drivers, and more recently, internet bulletin board surfers, who have since the Japanese colonial period invented a kind of short-hand, hybrid language to avoid political censorship or surveillance. With the rise of local identity politics in the 1980s, such discursive practices went even further in the direction of pidgin, punning, trans-coding, or trans-localization. Soon, the political use of language with its symbolic capital or social distinctions became so obvious that ad people and statesmen started to appropriate the neologisms, in order to hail the "new, new human species" of consumers. And in the late 1990s, the practices took a "feminine" or even "queer" turn, oriented toward intimate relations between sexual partners, so as to ascribe membership and to secure the politics of friendship. All of this is seen in the ads of the Taipei MRT mall.

Feminine sentences supposedly uttered by women of consuming passion are ubiquitous in the mall's advertising culture. In one ad, for instance, a woman reclines in the foreground with piles of gifts and beautiful objects surrounding her. This is the most eye-catching picture one sees as one walks toward the trains. Three big characters along the top read *wuligan* 無利感, a pun on the familiar phrase "powerlessness" but with a twist that suggests that one pays "no interest" when using a certain type of Visa card. The message is quite obvious: any fashionable woman will be helplessly in love with the wonderful experience of shopping, if she is smart enough to use the right type of credit card to buy gifts for herself. Bad consequences will not ensue, but only enchantment and even sensual pleasure (*gan* 感 or "affect"). In the picture there are at least four levels of discursive function at work. First, by indicating that the women cannot resist the temptation to be among beautiful objects, the advertisement urges the fair sex to give vent to consuming passion and to charge it, i.e., to gratify desires immediately with the deferral of payment. With the right card, women can have every reason to be lovers of expenditure, to shop desperately and wholeheartedly, and thus give meaning to such popular punning neologisms as *xiapin* 瞎拚 (shop blindly and recklessly) or *xiepin* 血拚 (shop till one's last drop of blood). Perceived this way, the woman in the billboard hails other women and encourages them to exercise their rights as smart shoppers, to spend their money wisely, and to have fun.

The ads also point to the disenchantment people feel with regard to the new government. Under the presidency of Chen Shuibian 陳水扁, there is little one can do to make a difference in the public sphere; everything remains in the hands of the legislature and bureaucrats, who have refused to change or to accommodate. What can one do except to withdraw and to find comfort in the intimate spheres, by spending an afternoon with friends in the mall, drinking at Starbucks and then shopping together? The advertisement turns the public discourse of powerlessness and indifference against itself, to suggest a more "affective" way out. The substitution of "power" with "interest" is very significant here; it speaks to the self-interest of the spectators. While one cannot transform the world, there are, however, ways to save money. The key word is *gan*, which addresses the spectator as a concrete human agent capable of feeling the *jouissance* of shopping smart, of enjoying the plenitude of things, of transforming a financial transaction into something not only economic but also ecstatic. Indeed, most advertisements for cosmetics, fitness, and religious cults stress the art of self-maintenance, of DIY.

More significant, perhaps, is the symbolic rephrasing of the familiar expression "powerlessness" into "paying no interest," with a meaningful pun on seemingly "a-political" disinterestedness, which in fact ironically captures the universal feeling of frustration in the Chen Shuibian era. In a sort of Derridian *différance*, of "repetition with difference," the sensational idiom of "paying no interest" tacitly suggests to viewers that they too understand the economic and political conditions of the time and, equally, desire to transform the disabling situation into an enabling one. By recognizing the three words and attaching personal meaning or intimate feelings (*gan*) to them, spectators may well regard themselves as members of the initiated, elite class more attuned to the art of socio-economic exchange and survival. The ability to perceive the nuances of semiotic free-play, to sense the ecstatic of economic action, makes smart shoppers feel "empowered" within a general situation of frustration and impotence. The discursive practice of understanding subtle puns or tactful substitutions enables young female shoppers to feel that they really can make a difference. An advertisement with such a rhetorical twist therefore speaks to the "X" and "E" generations who have invented and appropriated a rich body of neologisms to make social distinctions. Here it is reappropriated and rendered into a feminine sentence, an intimate mode of hailing those who want to feel better about their buying power in hard times.

In these ads, the women typically are disproportionately surrounded by Euro-American brands. The way that these commodities are arranged is meant to suggest, however, that the woman has just visited a Japanese department store such as Sunrise, SOGO or Shinkong Mitsukoshi. Behind her there are several bags and packages that evoke the presence of Japanese goods, because Japanese cultural products such as cosmetics, comics, soap operas, music, fashions, toys, games, electronic products, and even noodles are all extremely popular in Taiwan. VCD and DVD stores in the mall advertise that they have the most up-to-date episodes of Japanese video programs, while cell-phone companies display the newest arrivals, which have "just been flown over from Tokyo's Electronic Streets," to Taiwan fans. It is hardly a surprise that TV commercials for Pioneer or Mitsubishi products are increasingly in Japanese, with no captions. The advertising image of a pretty woman who has just visited a Japanese department store obviously appeals to young women shoppers.

The figures in the advertisements are either famous models or representatives of the X and E generations. They all have personal stories to share with the spectators, and they utter feminine sentences, even in the case of an advertisement for chicken extracts with traditional Chinese herbs. The girl in this particular ad *complains* that, as a result of eating cans of chicken extracts, she looks healthy and well taken care of. Her rosy cheeks give the impression that she must be in love or even married. That is apparently why men tend not to approach her. "Hear my confession," she laments. "True, I am well fed and naturally have a pretty face. Is, is, is this my fault? I really, really don't have a boyfriend. Interested in chasing me? Please make your move quickly." The syntactic structure and tone are distinctively "feminine," with an idiomatic *la* in the first line and lots of redundant phrases. By claiming the right to be loved and sought after by a man, the speaker displays her charm and self-confidence without sounding explicitly assertive. Traditionally, *siwu* 四物 (the "four items" of traditional herbs) are associated associated with Minnan folk culture, especially with rural women, who frequently suffer from nutrition deficiencies. The juxtaposition of chicken extracts with the four items thus represents the mutual illumination of Western science and Chinese medicine, of technological imagination and folk beliefs, of the global and the local. In this way, the woman in the advertisement represents a synthesis of "traditional" and "modern" culture, and of Butterfly romantic conventions and assertive self-expression. In resentful and even confessional mode, she utters an intimate truth that she needs to be loved and cared for. Her expression might appear quite Western or even modern, but the content proves her instead to be Chinese or, more specifically, Taiwanese.

The woman's gender and cultural identity are revealed by the way she articulates her feminine sentences: blending Chinese and Taiwanese, renegotiating the modern rhetoric of new women to turn it inside out, to make it clear that she needs to be loved. The feminine sentences, though totally innocent of political intentions, serve not only to construct narrative identities for women shoppers, regarding their desires and hopes, but also to shape the cultural identities of real people who learn to take in fetishistic signs and to recognize them as such in terms of their social signification. In the late 1990s, advertisements by the Ideology Advertising Company asserted for Taiwan's "new, new human species" the right to shop. The images centered on the desire to spend, to transgress the limitations of one's shopping capability in the name of love and hope. A large proportion of the advertisements depict naughty boys or girls being punished with no regrets. In one of the chewing-gum advertisements, the girl asks the Minister of Education, who happens to be visiting the school after the spankings, if he knows of any special brand of hand lotion that will help her quickly recover from her injuries. Evidently receiving no satisfying answer from the Minister, the girl decides to turn to Stimorol to ease the pain. Color, sensuality, and secret desire are the fantastic elements frequently associated with consuming passions. That may partly explain why Chinese minority groups in colorful costumes or with exotic melodies are used to describe metaphorically what certain commodities can taste like. Consumers are encouraged to cultivate desires for the extravagant, unorthodox, unknown, so as to deserve the name of the "new, new human species." They are shown as resourceful and totally unpredictable. Sometimes, with a rhetorical twist, they are related to the mysteries of Being, Nature, and Femininity. "Pick up your femininity at the Women's Clothing department; show off your colorful dress at the bookstores," urges one of the Sunrise advertisements.

The feminine expressions one sees on the Taipei MRT billboards carry on the tradition of "love, hope, and shopping." However, instead of developing the dark and transgressive sides of Bataillesque modernity, most of the ads in the Taipei MRT instead tend to place greater emphasis on positive representations of desire and consuming passion. New and belated as it is— the first of the six currently available subway lines, Muzha, was launched on March 28, 1996—the Taipei MRT plays a role in the metropolitan culture, in order to compete with other members of the global village. The construction of narrative identities becomes an important issue here, with linguistic hybridity and feminine sentences as main features showing that the advertisements are a part of the lifestyles emerging in Taiwan that help distinguish it from other locales. The intimate stories told by young women benefiting from Taiwan's multiethnic social environment are rhetorical devices that enhance in more subtle and sensible ways the formation of cultural identity. Nowadays, the MRT announcements are in four languages— in Chinese, Taiwanese, Hakka, and English, in that order—to indicate that people are on the one hand developing global perspectives, while at the same time recognizing the importance of rearticulating ethnicity and history in a more just or balanced way. It is no small wonder, then, that toward the end of the advertising arcades there should appear two beautiful pictures of the Taiwan landscape. They face each other across the platforms. They are photographs of identifiable sites invested with ideological and iconographic content; they work as symbols of the homeland, as sources of social and personal identity. Such images direct passengers to reflect, while "waiting for the train to arrive," on the relationships among memory, identity, and place, to consolidate their sense of cultural belonging. As a topic, Taiwan identity seems powerlessly underrepresented or unrepresentable in the political arena, but in the Taipei MRT advertisements it is given voice by young women of consuming passion under the guise of having "no interest" in anything else except enjoying life as it is, being able to indulge in their Butterfly dreams: to love, to hope, to shop.

Notes

Earlier drafts of this paper were presented at the "Rewriting Mandarin Ducks and Butterflies conference," Columbia University, April 7–8, 2001, and the "Advertising in Asia" conference, University of Hong Kong, April 25–26, 2001. I would like to thank the conference organizers and participants for their comments and suggestions.

1 Younger generations used X, Y, Z to indicate the fact that they were born late— in the 1970s, 1980s, and 1990s, the last three decades before the millennium. Increasingly, scholars have referred to them as "E" generation, a generation that flourished as e-mail and the internet were introduced. The idea of "romancing the state" (or the store) was inspired by Robert Zemeckis's 1984 film *Romancing the Stone.*

2 Shi Shuqing 施叔青, *Xianggang sanbuqu* 香港三部曲 (Hong Kong trilogy), consisting of *Ta mingzi jiao hudie* 她名字叫蝴蝶 (Her name is butterfly), *Pianshan yangzijing* 遍山洋紫荊 (A hillside full of Hong Kong orchids), and *Jimo yunyuan* 寂寞雲園 (Lonely cloud garden) (Taipei: Yuanliu, 1993, 1995, 1997). An abridged version of the trilogy has been translated into English as *City of the Queen* Howard Goldblatt and Sylvia Li-chun Lin, trans. (New York: Columbia University Press, 2005).

3 Shi Shuqing, *Weixun caizhuang* 微醺彩妝 (Light drunken makeup) (Taipei: Maitian, 1999).

4 Rey Chow, *Woman and Chinese Modernity: The Politics of Reading between West and East* (Minnesota: University of Minnesota Press, 1991), 51.

5 David Der-wei Wang, "Second Hauntings," in David Wang and Wei Shang, eds., *Dynastic Crisis and Cultural Innovation: From the Late Ming to the Late Qing and Beyond* (Cambridge: Harvard University Press, 2005), 549–594.

6 Eileen Chang 張愛玲, *Qingcheng zhi lian* 傾城之戀 (Love in a fallen city), in *Zhang Ailing quanji* 張愛玲全集 (Complete works of Eileen Chang) (Taipei: Yuanliu, 1992), 240, 248.

7 John Berninghausen and Ted Huters, *Revolutionary Literature in China: An Anthology* (New York: E. Sharpe, 1976), 3; quoted in Rey Chow, *Woman in Chinese Modernity* (Minneapolis: University of Minnesota Press, 1991), 51.

8 Wang Wenxing 王文興, *Beihai de ren* 背海的人. Volumes I & II (Taipei: Yuanliu, 1981, 1999).

9 Slavoj Žižek, *The Ticklish Subject* (London: Verso, 1999), 203.

10 Yvonne Sung-sheng Chang 張誦聖, *Wenxue changyu de bianqian: Dangdai Taiwan xiaoshuo lun* 文學場域的變遷：當代台灣小說論 (Transformation of the literary field: a theory of contemporary Taiwan fiction) (Taipei: Unitas, 2001).

11 "Yellow cab" is a derogatory label used to describe Asian women who desire exotic sex experiences in foreign countries, especially in places like Hawaii.

12 E. M. Forster, *A Passage to India* (New York: Penguin Classics, 2005), 217.

Part III
Nostalgia and amnesia

8 Rewriting the Red Classics

DAI Jinhua

In the late 1990s, a tide of "Red" nostalgia emerged on the Chinese cultural market and artistic stage, as if the socio-cultural horizon of *fin-de-siècle* China had suddenly been stained a dark reddish hue. This wave of nostalgia could be seen as the product of various transnational factors, which were then overlaid onto an indigenous cultural iconography derived largely from 1930s Shanghai. In this way, the familiar old movie-star photographs, old advertisements, "beautiful woman" calendar posters, 1930s Shanghai legends, coffeehouses with nostalgic décor, and the "Shanghai nostalgia" restaurants that have sprung up throughout China with names like Nocturnal Shanghai and Shanghai Harbor can therefore all be seen as a displaced realization of the call for "rewriting history" that emerged in 1980s elite culture. Through the excision of the socialist historical memory of the 1950–1970 period, combined with the purging of the bloody revolutionary dimensions from the 1930s Red historical narrative, the reality of 1990s China is therefore able safely to link up with the imaginary "history" represented by 1930s Shanghai.

To the extent that this imaginary figure of 1930s Shanghai functions as an object of global nostalgia, as a bland but not entirely displeasing image of "China" itself, then even as contemporary Chinese popular culture is re-embracing the once-slender waists of old Shanghai's *qipao*-clad beauties, it is at the same time carefully excising the memory of the Cultural Revolution's Red Guards. This combination of nostalgia and amnesia could be compared to the way in which contemporary Chinese fashion has embraced a Russian (or Cuban) military style of dress, while deliberately omitting its signature red shoulder badge. Although this omission of the shoulder badge undoubtedly ruins the stylistic effect of the chromatic juxtaposition of olive-green and revolutionary red, by the mid-1990s it had nevertheless become politically necessary to filter out the 1960s ideological connotations of the red badge.

The starting point for this contemporary rewriting of Red history can be located in the contested field of disparate social forces that characterized China during the *fin-de-siècle* period. At one level, this process can be seen as one of the key means by which official discourse succeeded in reproducing itself, while simultaneously constituting a comparatively *ineffective* and *ambivalent* mode of cultural reproduction. This latter mode of cultural reproduction is *ineffective* insofar as 1980s Chinese culture had used a kind of ideological exorcism to reveal the propagandistic character of Chinese socialism, even as the fissures created by society's contemporary transformation led the younger generation to lose their ability to enter into a similar cultural and historical memory, with the result being that this mode of cultural reproduction became essentially a mere platitude. Similarly, this mode of cultural reproduction is *ambivalent* insofar as it straddles the gap between mere propaganda and actual policy implementation. The situation is further complicated by the fact that the underlying narrative of ideological legitimacy had, by this point, already become fragmentary and self-contradictory as the result of its attempts to negotiate the demands of two competing points of origin. First, the founding of the People's Republic in 1949 is recognized as a watershed moment marking the end of the bitter history of old China and the establishment of the new regime of the Communist Party and the proletariat; and second, Deng Xiaoping's 鄧小平 rise to power in 1978 (following the death of Mao Zedong 毛澤東 in 1976) may be viewed as the critical moment in which the "feudal fascist autocracy" was brought to an end and a new, post-Cultural Revolution China was born.

The narrative, and indeed the very narrative structure, of modern Chinese history therefore needed to undergo a timely process of editing and re-arrangement and, oddly enough, even the Red Classics from time to time became subject to official political censorship and revision. Meanwhile, as the Red Classics have filtered down through popular culture, they have come to symbolize for many readers a sentimental and emotional refusal of the Red history with which they are associated—precisely because they invariably evoke the suffering and burden of the not-entirely-distant "revolutionary" era and the Cultural Revolution period. In my view, however, the Red narrativization and imagination of the Maoist era is one of the key cultural achievements of the 1980s. This kind of fashion, or unfashionable fashion, has once again come to form a mottled and listless tide, once again using transnational cultural representations to reveal the process of remapping the contemporary Chinese cultural cartography.

Rewriting and displacement

This process of rewriting the Red Classics could be seen as a crucial social etiology of *fin-de-siècle* China, suggesting a complicated political and cultural trend and a complex mechanism of cultural production. The rewriting of the Red Classics might initially appear to involve an attempt to link up the reality of the end of the twentieth century with the fragmentary and absent history embodied by the literary and cultural texts of the 1950s and 1970s, thereby bringing those earlier texts into dialogue with contemporary trends, but ultimately it remains only a kind of undercurrent or supplement, over-shadowed in Chinese popular culture by the contemporary resurgence of television adaptations of "Qing palace dramas."[1] These dramas respond to, yet maintain a distance from, the contemporary intensification of social contradictions, together with the gradual popularization of the "shock wave of realism" characterized by the notion of "sharing adversity." However, it is precisely this array of cultural "rewritings" that most effectively articulate the mechanism of this transitional period of post-revolutionary Chinese society and culture. Together, they lay bare a cultural public sphere located at the historical interstices of destruction and reconstruction.

A work that received considerable attention in the 1990s was Ye Daying's 葉大鷹 1995 film *Hong yingtao* 紅櫻桃 (Red cherry). Set in the Soviet Union during World War II and featuring children of Chinese Communist martyrs, the film is full of scenes of old Russia, including desolate steppes, white poplars, horses drinking at the riverside, and Stalin-era music—all of which appear to evoke a magnificent array of Sino-Soviet Red Classics. Many of the films scenes evoked the Soviet literary and artistic texts with which middle-aged Chinese viewers were very familiar, thereby evoking an acute sense of nostalgia. As the contemporary novelist Zhang Kangkang 張抗抗 has observed, authors and artists from the 1950s to the 1970s typically viewed their entire world as being "full of Russian and Soviet palm trees, berries, and potatoes."[2]

If we attempt, in the 1990s, to excise the "revolutionary" or "Red" dimension of 1950s culture, nostalgic fashion thereby becomes what I have described elsewhere as a free-floating "ark of nostalgia." While the history of Soviet socialism was certainly far from perfect and the breakup of the Soviet Union in the 1990s elicited a complicated cluster of emotions for middle-aged Chinese, Soviet atrocities such as those described in Solzhenitsyn's *Gulag Archipelago* nevertheless appear quite distant from contemporary reality, especially when compared with Chinese viewers' more immediate memories of China's own Anti-Rightist Campaign of 1957 and the Cultural Revolution of 1966. Conversely, it was precisely Russo-Soviet aesthetics that provided "a foundation of sublimity and beauty"[3] for several generations of Chinese, thereby becoming a perfect basis for contemporary viewers' "unconventional" youthful memories.

As a result, *Red Cherry* could be seen as a crucial turning point in contemporary representations of Red history and the Red Classics. In reality, what many Chinese viewers failed to realize was that, although many of the scenes in *Red Cherry* might appear to evoke their memories of the Communist era, in reality the film's content and marketing were not rooted in the Red Classics, but rather were located within a specifically *European* cinematic tradition from the 1950s to the 1970s. This latter cinematic tradition is both elegant and depressing, and furthermore contains certain fascist elements—including depictions of helpless individuals in a cruel era and elaborate sado-masochistic scenes. *Red Cherry* borrows these elements and repackages them under a mainstream and normative "Red" cover, and in this way successfully establishes a perfect pop-cultural panacea consisting of violence, sex, and children. In this sense, the film succeeded in combining into a new form the disparate elements of mainstream representation, commercial form, and nostalgic sentiment.

As it turned out, this syncretic "new mainstream" narrative form would prove to be difficult to duplicate. In 1998, Ye Daying released the second film in his so-called "Red series," entitled *Hongse lianren* 紅色戀人 (Red lovers; released in Hong Kong under the title *A Time to Remember*). This time, the work was set in 1930s Shanghai and appears to have had a broader and more "mature" commercial dimension: Hollywood scriptwriters and actors participated in the production process, and this was also the second mainland film featuring the Hong Kong superstar Leslie Cheung 張國榮 following his groundbreaking performance in Chen Kaige's 陳凱歌 1993 film, *Bawang bieji* 霸王別姬 (Farewell my concubine). *Red Lovers* featured the same basic plot scheme as *Red Cherry*, only this time it was a piece of shrapnel lodged in the male protagonist's brain that became the physiological (as opposed to psychological) cause of his delirium and hysteria. At the same time, the film also used the female protagonist's nudity to add a "nonsexual" sexual perspective. Perhaps reflecting the introduction into China of Hollywood films, this *Red Cherry*-style European commercial film is endowed with a Hollywood "B-movie" plotline, in which a young American doctor living in Shanghai is unexpectedly visited in the middle of the night by a beautiful and mysterious young Chinese woman, and as a result becomes embroiled in a vast plot and ultimately comes to a tragic end. Unlike *Red Cherry*, this latter film was produced by the "People-run" Forbidden City film studio that had successfully produced many new mainstream movies, and it was eagerly anticipated by the media before its release. Actual ticket sales, however, were far below expectations, and the film eventually became one of the biggest box-office flops in the studio's history.

In my opinion, the success and failure of Ye Daying's two Red films illustrate China's late twentieth century tension between Red nostalgia, on the one hand, and what we may call a process of "Bidding Farewell to Revolution," on the other. In a sense, *Red Cherry*'s success could be seen as the result of the work's thorough sense of alienation. For instance, the film's use of scenes from the former Soviet Union effectively confirms and embraces the alienating and shattered quality of revolutionary narrative, as seen from the perspective of contemporary Chinese reality. Meanwhile, World War II came to function as a period of "myth-making." With the outbreak of the war in Europe, Nazism came to be viewed as the "enemy of humanity" and provided Chinese viewers, at least temporarily, with an effective mode of recognition and reference, given that after the 1980s the narrative and social structure of modern Chinese history had already become unusually tepid and turbid. Furthermore, the fact that the Soviet Union no longer existed helped mitigate the threat that the film's shallow Redness might otherwise have evoked, and consequently safely relegated it to the nostalgic horizon of "history." In contrast, *Red Lovers* was set in China rather than in the Soviet Union and drew from mutually contradictory Chinese historical discourses—and conse-quently this "Red" film could avoid dissolving into a narrative chaos.

One of the reasons for *Red Lovers'* failure lies in the film's misguided fore-grounding of a tension between Shanghai's actual historicity, and the film's contemporary function as an empty simulacrum of artificial nostalgia. Either intentionally or unintentionally, the film attempted to bring together the mutu-ally contradictory discourses of Shanghai as it exists in the Anglo-European colonial imagination, on the one hand, and of Shanghai as it is perceived within Chinese socialist history, on the other. The involvement of the Holly-wood producer Rick Nathanson combined with the first-person narration by the American doctor, help to overlay the film's sense of nostalgia onto a Western/American concern with reminiscence. Although the work pre-sents a tale of a triangular love, and while the revolution witnessed by the American narrator remains merely an evanescent vision, the actual subject of the film is a pair of "Red lovers" to whom the word *love* does not even apply—which is to say, the film is really a story about a Communist and the Chinese Revolution itself. This revolutionary dimension, furthermore, cannot help but collide with the fragmented ideology and hybrid narratives of modern and contemporary Chinese history. In reality, the film's narrat-ive is still firmly located in a 1980s tradition of historical "rewriting," within which the violent conflict between the Nationalists and the Communists is transformed into utter absurdity. A similar internal logic undoubtedly destroys what the director calls a "romantic revolutionary" style of representation.[4]

Ironically, although *Red Lovers* was a box-office flop in mainland China, it turned out to be quite a hit in Taiwan. This success was due not so much to the film's destructive perspective and dark humor, or its evocation of the mirage of 1930s Shanghai, but rather because it was rooted specifically in Taiwan's contemporary fascination with Shanghai following the Asian finan-cial meltdown that, combined with the growth of Shanghai's industry, has helped fuel a decontextualized Red nostalgia on both sides of the Taiwan Strait. The artificial and contradictory nature of this Red nostalgia is revealed by a diverse range of factors, including the influence of Hollywood, Communist revolutionary historiography, Shanghai nostalgia, as well as the second efflore-scence, following the 1980s interest in "rewriting literary history," of famous early to mid twentieth century authors associated with Shanghai, such as Eileen Chang 張愛玲, Xu Zhimo 徐志摩, and Qian Zhongshu 錢鐘書.

Displaced rewriting

Echoing the success of *Red Cherry*, the first major Chinese cultural specta-cle of the year 2000 was the television series *Gangtie shi zenyang liancheng de* 鋼鐵是怎樣煉成的 (How steel is forged), adapted by Chinese director Han Gang 韓剛 from Nikolai Ostrovsky's famous Soviet novel by the same title. While the popularity of both *Red Cherry* and the *How Steel Is Forged* television series was a result of a similar audience response, *How Steel Is Forged,* unlike *Red Cherry*, could be seen as a sort of "super-Red Classic" located in a specific moment in contemporary Chinese history. As a unique phenomenon created by a system of socialist cultural production, the original *How Steel Is Forged* was far more than a mere novel, and instead came to function as a revolutionary model and textbook of life. In this way, the work came to assume a completely realistic "historical" character, inscribing itself firmly within the cultural history of 1950s–1970s China and occupying a prominent position in the memories of several different generations.

It is also worth noting that, within the continual fracturing of historical memory and cultural pedigree as the result of repeated social change and political violence, *How Steel Is Forged* was among the only texts able to continue to serve, and survive in, history. Not only was it unquestionably a Red Classic and a "Life Road Sign" (*rensheng lubiao* 人生路標) during the period from the 1950s to the 1970s, but furthermore it was one of the few works that did *not* come under criticism and censorship during the Cultural Revolution, and was therefore able to remain on the shelves of the public libraries and private households. During the final two decades of the century, meanwhile, it has continued to reappear in state institutions, especially in the booklists of the departments responsible for ideological control. In 1989, the Central Communist Youth League placed *How Steel Is Forged* at the top of its list of ten books to be labeled "Life Road Sign"; in 1999, starting with *Guangming ribao* 光明日報 (Guangming daily news), a wide array of media placed the novel at the top of their list of "Fifty Works That Have Moved the People's Republic"; and in that same year, the writer Zhang Chengzhi 張誠志 did not hesitate in placing the novel *How Steel Is Forged* at the head of his own "Twentieth Century Literary Classics" series. Remarkably (given that it was not even a Chinese novel to begin with), it was even included at the top of a list of so-called "six nationalist works." The novel was the sixth most printed volume in China during the period preceding the Cultural Revolution, and even as recently as 1998 it remained the fifth best-selling book of the year. If we grant that the market success of *How Steel Is Forged* was due in large part to the official support it received, then the question becomes how it was that the novel managed to become one of the essential works on virtually all lists of Red Classics. In the 1990s, the novel appeared in multiple translations in non-official and Leftist publications, in various editions by different publishing houses, was adapted into films and comics by the former Soviet Union, and also appeared in various abridged versions—all of which influenced each other in a very productive manner.

In the 1990s, another interesting example of this process of rewriting the *How Steel Is Forged* narrative can be found in the sixth-generation director Lu Xuechang's 路學長 film, *Zhangda chengren* 長大成人 (Growing up) (1995),[5] which was initially referred to as *Gangtie shi zheyang liancheng de* 鋼鐵是這樣煉成的 (This is how steel is forged) during the production and filming process. Lu's film adaptation was the first version of the work to foreground the position of the individual, and particularly the maturation of a young boy. While in the original novel the protagonist's maturation was presented in terms of a socialist realist model of the hero's "initiation" and realization, *Growing Up* by contrast emphasizes the post-revolutionary social and cultural realities encountered by the generation born in the 1960s, together with their fractured and shattered ideologies. These elements help create a sense of anxiety, which then reveals the narrative theme, found in many works by other sixth-generation directors, that "growing up does not necessarily amount to becoming a person."

Around this time, the well-known young scholar Liu Xiaofeng 劉小楓 published a short essay entitled *"Jilian Dongniya"* 紀戀冬妮婭 (Remembering and loving Tonia) (1996), which delineates an important new cultural trend in the practice of rewriting the Red Classics.[6] In this essay, Liu Xiaofeng takes his personal memory of *How Steel Is Forged* and locates it within some of the bloodiest and cruelest events from the initial years of the Cultural Revolution. In this way, the story of the revolutionary hero is juxtaposed with the corpses of young and innocent people, and is thus used to reveal the violent characteristics of revolution itself. Lu Xuechang's *Growing Up* uses the figure of the young Pavel, together with his idealistic Communist father, Zhu Helai, as the basis for his rewriting of the original novel. Liu Xiaofeng's essay, by contrast, emphasizes the cross-class love affair between the worker's son, Pavel, and the female cadre in the forestry department, Tonia—thus producing a fanciful and ultimately disillusioned story revolving around the processes of "choosing a path" and the decision to become a revolutionary within the realities of class society. It was actually the latter text, when it appeared on the blank canvas of China's socialist culture, which formed the basis of the emotional memories of several generations of readers. Liu Xiaofeng's essay uses the concepts of individuality, desire, and freedom in order to shift the focus from Pavel to Tonia, and in so doing he explicitly refuses to validate Pavel's choice—the essay, then, became an unambiguous gesture of "Bidding Farewell to Revolution." Indeed, Liu's "Remembering and Loving Tonia" did not express an attitude of romantic attachment and nostalgia so much as it communicated a pragmatic *rejection* of nostalgia (for the Revolution).

The *How Steel Is Forged* television series, meanwhile, functions as a staging of commercial, official, and market behavior,[7] which makes it one of the most representative texts of this phenomenon of rewriting the Red Classics, and at the same time reveals a certain feeling of embarrassment and dislocation inherent in this moment of ideological rupture and reconstruction. During the production and release of the series, along with the infusion of capital and the changes in the people involved in the works' creation and distribution, the official character of *How Steel Is Forged* was gradually established. Therefore, the focus on a "fidelity to the original"—which is to say, fidelity to the canonical ideology of socialist realism and to the reproduction of heroic representation—gradually became the television program's orientation, leading the production to function as more than merely an object of nostalgia for older generations. If we observe that this emphasis on "reality" resembles what we have been calling "official" culture—which is to say, the strengthening of the restrictions and emphasis on conformity that cultural institutions have exercised over the production and marketing of cultural texts—then this emphasis clearly reveals that the new mainstream culture industry in the 1980s and 1990s has already achieved a distinct cultural form. The rich ideological symptoms of the *How Steel Is Forged* television series, meanwhile, are first of all revealed in the various points relevant to this principle of "fidelity."

As the inheritor of the 1980s trend of historical rewriting, this television "adaptation" constitutes a kind of historical caulking—in the sense that it complements the scenes that were censored or self-censored under the former Soviet cultural regime, and in this way it fictionally "fills in the gap" concerning Pavel's limited confrontation, separation, and hesitation when confronted with the violence of the Stalinist government. The program's most important and most interesting innovation (undoubtedly inspired by Liu Xiaofeng's essay) lies in its radical rewriting of the love story between Pavel and Tonia—a love story that runs counter to the work's original socialist ideology, or at the very least counter to a cruel reality of the Great Era, and finally shatters into pieces—and the transformation of that original love story into a timeless romance that effectively transcends class distinctions, temporality, and violent reality. As a result, the current rewriting of this Red Classic that had already survived a period of epochal transition has now become a thoroughly foreign and nostalgic soap opera. As a symptom, or perhaps merely an artifact, of the difficulty of adapting a cinematic work, this television program clearly recognizes and draws on a Liu Xiaofeng-style position and critique (at least with respect to the figure of Tonia). However, the program obviously cannot replicate the criticism of Pavel's path and choices that we find in Liu Xiaofeng's essay. To be more precise, the television series is unable to simultaneously replicate and reject this classical socialist ideology, and consequently it becomes an odd compromise between accommodation and critique. Tonia's "class identity" is transformed from that of an idle daughter of a rich family of government cadres in Czarist Russia, to that of a medical school student in a charitable doctor's family, allowing a kind of timeless humanism to transcend the gulf between class identity and political affiliation. In the television program, not only have Pavel and Tonia not yet been tragically separated, but furthermore Tonia remains thoroughly in love with Pavel and, at the end of the work, brings a child named Pavel to show to his adult namesake. It is in this climactic scene, furthermore, that she utters the phrase that encapsulates the significance of Pavel's character: "Pavel, you are made of steel."

What is perhaps even more interesting than the actual contents of this television series is the critical discussion that the series elicited after it aired. We may regard the series as an excellent example of a "socialist 'main melody' classic text with Chinese characteristics," which draws on the revolutionary discourse and even clichés of official mainstream media from the 1960s. The interesting thing, however, is that there was virtually no official criticism of this adaptation's apparent lack of "fidelity." For the mass media, by contrast, it was precisely this question of fidelity that functioned as their primary entry point into the text. When the broadcast began, the *Beijing qingnian bao* 北京青年報 (Beijing youth daily) solicited essays for a special column on the topic, "How should we recognize Tonia today?" This solicitation elicited a vast outpouring of nostalgia for departed youth, effectively exclaiming, "Tonia, how sweet your life is!"[8] Contrary to the tradition of "adaptations of famous works," in which most plot changes are typically met with strong resistance, this particular adaptation was not only embraced by virtually all middle-aged viewers (who were obviously intimately familiar with the original), but furthermore these viewers appear to have completely forgotten the plot and contextual foundation of the original. Viewers praised the logic of the television program's plot and character development, and warmly applauded Tonia's character and her cross-class love affair. They happily adopted Liu Xiaofeng's attitude to reveal their boundless adoration of Tonia while growing up during the Cultural Revolution. However, to the extent that the adaptation of the primary love story was a necessary compromise for the current trend of rewriting the Red Classics, then the deeply nostalgic narrative that was thereby created unexpectedly reveals the audience's feelings of defeat and bitterness, particularly those who are middle-aged and above, when they confront the increasingly stark class divisions and naked worship of wealth that characterize contemporary Chinese society.

Curiously, after the release of the television adaptation of *How Steel Is Forged*, the popular media began to take the figure of Pavel for granted, even as he was eulogized as a Revolutionary Hero by the old-style official media. As a result, the television series constituted not so much the return of an old-style hero, but rather a reminder of the *disappearance* of the hero, or at least of the socialist or revolutionary hero. This paradox is illustrated by another editorial from the *Beijing Youth Daily* from the same period, one that inspired considerable debate and succeeded in redirecting the ideological tendencies underlying this rewriting of the Red Classics. The title of the editorial, "Pavel or Bill Gates: Who Is the Hero?",[9] articulates the fundamental question of whether contemporary China is actually socialist or capitalist. The very fact that such a patently absurd question could stimulate such an energetic debate[10] reveals the fundamental cultural and ideological conundrum facing turn-of-the-century China—namely, the contradictions and silences located at the transition point between different social systems and cultural structures. Therefore, the ambiguous conclusion of this debate was that the hero of our era should actually be "Pavel Gates":[11] a synthesis of Pavel's selfless devotion and Bill Gates's ambition,[12] on the grounds that neither "historical nihilism nor moral nostalgia are to be emulated."[13] The implication of this is that the rewritten Red Classics cannot easily become a bridge or ark to traverse this historical rupture, and instead come to resemble a difficult and ultimately unsuccessful space docking.

Neither history nor case file

What might initially appear as an absolute anomaly to the "Red Tide" of the late 1990s is the creation and release of the *Shuihu zhuan* 水滸傳 (Water margin) television series. Illustrating the "construction of the socialist spirit and civilization," China's government-run CCTV adapted the so-called "four Ming-Qing masterworks" for television. Of the four, *Water Margin*—a series with a big budget and high production values that was three years in the making—was, in 1998, the last to air.

However, even as the television program was going into production, the work already revealed the degree to which it was bound up with the real symptoms of contemporary China's fractured and complex history. Even as a literary classic, *Water Margin* has been known primarily for its heroic characterization of vigilantes, outlaws, and others who resist authority—linking the work directly to a materialist ideology and a rewriting and reconstruction of history from a socialist perspective. One of the key components of this socialist ideological reconstruction of history is that it emphasizes peasant rebellions rather than a more traditional focus on dynastic conquest. As a result, in the history textbooks read by my generation, this Chinese historical scene was populated by famous rebel leaders such as Chen Sheng 陳勝, Wu Guang 吳廣, Huang Chao 黃巢, and Li Zicheng 李自成, rather than by the founding emperors of the Qin, Han, Tang, and Song dynasties. Because it can be read as supporting this historical emphasis on popular rebellions as opposed to imperial authority, *Water Margin* is therefore frequently cited in these sorts of socialist contexts.

Just as the "discussion" of *Honglou meng* 紅樓夢 (Dream of the red chamber), one of the other four Ming-Qing masterworks, played a crucial role in the establishment of New China's thought and culture, the criticism of *Water Margin* similarly became the final chapter of Maoist political culture.[14] Also, because of the intimate mutual relationship between absurd political campaigns such as those of "Capitalists Roaders Are Still Walking" and "Capitulators Do Exist," on the one hand, and the so-called "Reverse the Verdicts of the Subversive 'Criticize Deng [Xiaoping], Attack Rightists' Campaign," on the other, the television adaptation was able to traverse the historical watershed of 1979. As a result, this late twentieth century staging of the "official" version of *Water Margin*, within the solemn and clamorous setting of the CCTV studios, was able to clearly reveal this "Red" historical period. Out of the surprising numbers of people who watched the television series, 40 percent said that the program reminded them of the Maoist "Criticize *Water Margin*" campaign of 1975. Furthermore, this statistic becomes even more revealing if it is broken down by age group, since 60 percent of the audience members aged 35 and over made this connection, while only 20 percent of those audience members under 35 did.[15]

Of the four CCTV adaptations of Chinese literary classics, it was the adaptation of *Water Margin* that was most deeply steeped in Maoist connotations. This was not only on account of the series' use of the truncated and ideologically whitewashed 100-chapter version of the novel, but also because it suggested a reinterpretation of the conventional historical-materialist perspective on peasant rebellion; because the entire first portion of the television adaptation affirms a (socialist?) realist audio-visual mode; and particularly because the adaptation adopts a narrative perspective premised on a Maoist attitude of "supporting [former rebel leader] Chao Gai, and attacking [the subsequent leader, and perceived capitulator] Song Jiang."[16] In order to more effectively create and realize the television program's "detailed realism," or perhaps in order to preserve its ratings and media market in Southeast Asia, the program hired the famous Hong Kong special-effects specialist Yuen Woo Ping 袁和平 to choreograph the fight scenes, and also brought in a Hong Kong special-effects team to enhance the production's realism. However, due either to some sort of ideological tension or to an unexpected conflict between the popular cultural text and reality, this seemingly respectable adaptation proved to be deeply controversial among its viewers, garnering mixed reviews. *Water Margin* became more than a sum of its parts—orthodox history, literary masterwork, singular popular cultural event—as it seemed to strike a deep and complicated cultural nerve that extended into historical issues as well as the present moment.

The realistic approach adopted by the television series was originally intended to function as a reaffirmation of historical materialism, even as it departed significantly from the heroic and romantic characteristics of the original work. As a result, the work's well-known romantic, comradely spirit of "pulling out a knife to help one another in times of difficulty" was, in this more realistic version, "restored" to lawless banditry. Not long after the program aired, some viewers remarked on the internet that this was first time that they had realized that the Liangshan heroes were merely petty thieves and highway bandits.[17] The television adaptation not only implicitly features a dimension of internal rupture, but furthermore constitutes a distortion of the original work's plot and narrative, even as it unexpectedly reveals structural contradictions within socialist ideology itself (e.g., at the level of the dichotomies of order vs. disorder, and of revolution vs. domination). The internal contradictions of these sorts of texts, when they began to appear in the late 1990s in the context of a turbulent and transformed China, necessarily embody this problematic of realism.

The television series' *fin-de-siècle* ethos is revealed most clearly in its depictions of violence (and not merely martial-arts violence). Surprisingly, this "official" and even "socialist" television adaptation of a classical work turns out to be full of extremely violent scenes. If Yuen Woo Ping and the

Hong Kong special-effects team succeeded, in the first half of the series, in transforming the original work's romantic heroism into something completely believable, then, in the latter half of the series, similar techniques were used to create extremely bloody and disturbing scenes of violence.[18] This is odd, however, given that one of the key tenets of the Chinese television and film censorship system has always been to maintain close control over graphic portrayals of violence. In *Water Margin*, however, the audience sees count- less bloody scenes of decapitations right on the television screen—with tele- vision being the cultural medium that penetrates most directly into the home. Therefore, the vast audience of the series (estimated by *Xinwen lianbo* 新聞聯播 [Media news] to be over 35 percent of total viewers)[19] not only watched, but also undoubtedly responded quite viscerally to this extremely disturbing visual spectacle—presumably experiencing shock, terror, as well as deep stupefaction as a result.[20]

In my opinion, the attempts to assert control over cultural representa- tions of violence constitute an important symptom of late-1990s Chinese cul- ture and society. After 1993, the pace of social transformation increased to the point that it further entrenched existing class disparities, leaving society as a whole more turbulent, unstable, and anxious. However, the need to pre- serve social order, together with intellectuals' attempts to "bid farewell to revolution," contributed to the creation of what I have labeled, in another context, a kind of "invisible writing."[21] As a result, this reality of social hard- ships and frustrations came to constitute an anonymous violent under- current flowing through society's culture and psyche. *Water Margin* may be seen as an unexpected manifestation of this phenomenon, or alternatively the television adaptation's violent elements and spectacular scenes can be seen as an example of how this sort of anonymous violence came to constitute a crucial turning point in the original work's appearance and transmission.

However, the reality was not quite so simple. It is precisely in these vio- lent scenes that the television adaptation of *Water Margin* appears to have successfully brought together and revealed the realistic trends and internal tensions originally present in this pop-cultural text. This same violence, how- ever, is elided, or at least downplayed, in the discussions of the work in the mainstream media. In several interviews that my research team and I con- ducted with instructors from different departments at Peking University, for instance, the vast majority of our respondents noted the violent aspects of *Water Margin*, and felt that those aspects had an "educational" function, though they had widely divergent opinions on how to interpret this osten- sibly "educational" function. Of the respondents aged 50 and over, the major- ity felt that there was a clear tendency in the program's "lingering Maoist" characteristics to stir up social unrest and appeal for societal violence. Meanwhile, a significant proportion of the middle-aged respondents felt that the program's use of the 100-chapter version of the novel, together with its violent content, functioned as a warning and deterrent—in contrast to the official discussions of so-called "historical materialism" and of the tragic living conditions giving rise to peasant rebellions, these viewers felt that the television series was instead being used to reveal the necessary *failure* of these sorts of rebellions.[22]

In my view, the television program's use of a realistic representational style, combined with its graphic violence, constitutes a reversal of Maoist historical goals, and instead articulates a more conservative law-and-order position. Nevertheless, the television adaptation was unable to completely erase the original novel's dimensions of extra-legal heroic romanticism, stories of rebellion, and its emphasis on a principle of social equality. As a result, the entire series is full of gaps and contradictions. For instance, a very interesting detail can be found in the fact that, even though the program's realism required the deletion of most of the heroic-romantic elements of the original work, one of the program's trademark songs is the *"Haohan ge"* 好漢歌 (Hero's Song):

> The great river flows East,
> and the stars in the sky join the Northern dipper.
> If you say leave, we will leave.
> What is mine is yours, and is everyone's. . . .
> When we encounter danger, we all cry out.
> When necessary, we will draw arms.
> Hustling and bustling, we travel the nine continents.

When *Water Margin* first aired, the "Hero's Song" immediately became a hit. As a news report noted, "*Water Margin* is vigorous and dynamic, and 'Hero's Song' is soul-stirring and moving."[23] However, this tune, which was supposed to be the TV series' theme song, was secretly replaced by a sad and mournful one, written expressly for the tragic ending. Nevertheless, studies report that 28 percent of viewers found the "Hero's Song" tune to be their second favorite element of the entire production, second only to the martial-arts scenes. Meanwhile, 76 percent of viewers report that these lyrics were the part of the program that left the deepest impression on them— and the line that these viewers cited most frequently was "when necessary, we will draw arms."[24] Not long after the program aired, a ditty expressing a similar sentiment became popular in China:

> A female worker gets off work but does not feel at all low.
> She goes to some bar or dance hall to do the tango.
> And will leave with whomever shows the dough.

> When workers get off they do not feel at all low
> They merely take up their ax and sickle and walk behind a big honcho.
> And if the situation demands, they will happily draw arms and come to blows.[25]

It is precisely these different layers of realism that are revealed in this pop-cultural adaptation of *Water Margin*. In my view, the *Water Margin* television series can therefore be located within a cultural array of "rewriting the Red Classics," even as the realistic appearance of the work undermines the affectionate feelings associated with nostalgia, and specifically Red nostalgia. Even more realistic and "Red" than *Water Margin*, meanwhile, is the Red "little theater" movement that emerged in China shortly afterwards, and which I will consider in the following section.

A "People's Theater"?

The "little theater" production of Dario Fo's *Accidental Death of an Anarchist*, which debuted in October 1998, could be seen as one of the side-effects of China's long-standing obsession with the Nobel Prize for literature. However, just as the socialist street artist Dario Fo's receipt of the coveted prize helped transform him into a peculiar figure within the unique post-Cold War cultural landscape, the circumstances of the Chinese avant-garde director Meng Jinghui's 孟京輝 adaptation of Fo's *Accidental Death* go far beyond China's obsession with the prize.

Meng Jinghui's adaptation of Fo's work, entitled *Yi ge wuzhengfuzhuyizhe de yiwai siwang* 一個無政府主義者的意外死亡, constituted a unique and historical encounter—between not only the European institution of the Nobel Prize and Chinese avant-garde theater, Italian street art and Chinese little theater, but also, and more importantly, it also marked the first encounter (since 1978) between a European Leftism and Chinese critical realism, not to mention between an avant-garde, experimental art form that has become increasingly marginal in 1990s China and a local commercial movement and popular fashion.

The Beijing and Shanghai little theater movements constitute a very prominent and symptomatic social phenomenon. If it is true that the success and failure of spoken drama (*huaju* 話劇) have, all along, been very closely bound up with China's social transformations, then the creation and performance of spoken drama (starting from the initial period of national mobilization in the 1930s) have not only constituted an effective tool for creating a modern national narrative, but furthermore have come to be endowed with clear Leftist connotations. Since 1949, spoken drama has consistently been perceived as a national art form, and therefore the sudden and continued decline of theater following its momentary resurgence in the late 1970s and early 1980s reveals an inescapable truth.

Contemporary China's first avant-garde theatrical movement emerged in the early and mid-1980s. This movement was centered in Beijing and Shanghai and some of its representative works included, in Shanghai, Sha Yexin's 沙葉新 "*Jiaru wo shi zhende*" 假如我是真的 (The imposter [If I were real]), Wang Peigong's 王培公 "WM" and, in Beijing, Gao Xingjian's 高行健 "*Juedui xinhao*" 絕對信號 (Alarm signal) and "*Chezhan*" 車站 (Bus stop).

These works all had clear modernist and even absurdist characteristics, while at the same time engaging with many of the pressing social issues of the day. As a reaction to, and rebellion against, Konstantin Stanislavsky's drama and performance theory, which had become one of the golden rules of official art during the Maoist era, this avant-garde theater movement instead took as its starting point Brecht's notion of "detachment." At the level of the theatrical ontology, the attempt to break down the "fourth wall" in reality marked the beginning of the experimental little theater movement. It could be said, therefore, that the early 1990s little theater movement actually constituted an extension and distant echo of the 1980s modernist avant-garde drama movement. But, on the basis of their setting, performance space, repertoire, and acting styles, these two avant-garde drama movements represent not so much a continuity between the 1980s and the 1990s, but rather a profound break between these two periods. In a sense, the little theater movement that has flourished since the early 1990s could be seen as the first time in three or four decades that the orientation and contents of spoken drama have been able to separate themselves from nationalism.

Although he used European modernism, and particularly French absurdism, as his early models, Meng Jinghui, unlike many of his other contemporary little theater directors, not only drew on an extremely clear stage consciousness and familiarity with the space and form of little theater, but furthermore he very deliberately used avant-garde European theatrical works as a postmodern object of parody. In this way, the "avant-garde" quality of Meng Jinghui's work lies not so much in his selection of an "avant-garde" repertoire, but rather in the way in which he deliberately appropriates and subverts those original texts.

The unprecedented success of the October 1998 performance of *Accidental Death of an Anarchist* had an unexpected and distinctive social significance. This significance derives, first of all, from the Leftist Dario Fo's "Redness," despite the fact that this "Redness" had already been diluted by virtue of its association with the popular, and virtually sacred, Nobel Prize. At the same time, however, the Chinese adaptation of the drama has also been injected with an anti-mainstream significance as the result of Meng Jinghui's and Huang Jisu's 黃紀蘇 treatment of the material, together with additional changes that were introduced during the actual performance. After theater lights come on, for instance, an actor draws an image of a police officer on the blackboard and then adjusts it a little, labeling it *criminal*—thereby eliciting the first laugh from the audience. With this, Meng Jinghui's little theater production appears to have confronted and challenged for the first time the realities of contemporary China. Furthermore, this distinctive social significance also undoubtedly derives from the fact that it was precisely in his adaptation of Fo's *Accidental Death of an Anarchist* that Meng Jinghui for the first time raised the banner of "People's Theater." The term *people* had become overly familiar during the Maoist era, to the point of having become virtually a lifeless signifier. In fact, by the late 1980s, apart from occasionally appearing in official discourse, the term was essentially rejected or even forgotten by the people themselves. When the term appears in popular cultural texts, it generally carries a playful and parodic connotation, though when the avant-garde and "underground" artist Meng Jinghui uses it and invests it with a sublime tone, it produces a fresh and shocking effect. In the middle of the performance, for instance, Meng Jinghui has the chorus sing the "Song of the People":

> At night I don't feel lonely
> In the darkness on the earth
> I am the People
> Countless People
> And my voice is full of power.[26]

Although Fo's original work is associated with the sacredness of the Nobel Prize, the fact that the Chinese version of *Accidental Death of an Anarchist* carries the label of "People's Theater," combined with Dario Fo's own socialist orientation, has led the work to assume a certain vague but portentous quality of spectral return within the context of contemporary "post-socialist" China (a connotation that was further reinforced when the work was unexpectedly applauded and eulogized by the New Leftism that emerged and gained popularity around 1997).[27] If we ignore the "Nobel Prize fever" that for the past 20 years has gripped not only Chinese literary circles but also Chinese society as a whole, and if we note that the appearance of the Chinese version of *Accidental Death of an Anarchist* actually coincided with the exacerbation of class distinctions in contemporary China, together with the fragmentation of intellectual circles described as the division between new Leftists and the neoliberals, it becomes apparent that Meng Jinghui's performance script of *Accidental Death of an Anarchist*[28] was actually not as straightforward as it might appear. Like Meng's previous works, the Chinese version of *Accidental Death of an Anarchist* has a very clear postmodernist quality. Its self-reflexivity, for instance, is revealed in the performance's allusions to Fo's own theatrical career, including his Nobel Prize acceptance speech.[29] The biggest change that Meng Jinghui introduced to the work, however, concerned the identity of the protagonist. In the original work, the protagonist is a lunatic who breaks into a police station, and who uses his intelligence to deduce that the anarchist's "accidental death" was actually the result of his having been thrown out of a window after being nearly beaten to death by the police. In Meng's version, however, the protagonist is a drama student whom the police take into custody and interrogate, and then use to provide an "acceptable" official explanation for the anarchist's "accidental death." In Meng Jinghui's parodic performance, therefore, the process of providing the police with a "reasonable explanation" comes to assume a very "theatrical" quality.

Another important postmodern element in Meng's drama concerns its use of imitation and parody, primarily visible in the last two of the three different scenarios that the student provides the police (these three scenarios being the violent explanation, the civilized one, and the human one). Of these, the "civilized" explanation constitutes a complete parody of the typical performance style of the People's Art Theater, and furthermore it is a parody of one of the most representative works of People's spoken drama: Lao She's 老舍 *Chaguan* 茶館 (Teahouse). Meanwhile, the "human" explanation undoubtedly constitutes a parody of some of the characteristic qualities of the Chinese Youth Theater (viz., a posture and theatrical language characterized by a Europeanized grammar and sentence construction, standard pronunciation, clear enunciation, and passionate recitation). If we regard Chinese theater during the period between 1949 and the early 1980s as one of the models of Chinese art, and if we take People's and Youth drama, and particularly their performative characteristics, and similarly regard them as an exterior form/system of signifiers of typical national art, then it is not difficult to recognize the iconoclastic and critical dimension of this sort of parody. However, if we consider the way in which a parody of mainstream culture of the Maoist era has, during the current *fin-de-siècle* period, already become a safe, mainstream behavior, as well as one of the techniques used in Meng Jinghui's work, we must then see this as a joke, a postmodern salute to the earlier generations in Chinese theatrical history. One of the work's most symptomatic moments in this regard, for instance, is the scene in which the director parodies the policemen's "American dream" by means of the Cultural Revolution-era children's song "The Train Is Going Toward Shaoshan" (with Shaoshan, the birthplace of Mao Zedong, symbolizing a sort of Maoist Mecca).

This development of avant-garde theater also represents a predicament for contemporary Chinese culture, in the sense that any narrative of the social and cultural situation in contemporary China cannot help but evoke Maoist socialist history, even though this historical legacy has already come to assume a very ambivalent and embarrassing connotation within contemporary political practice and popular narrative. On the one hand, this legacy still occupies a sacred and almost unquestionable position as a transcendental signifier in contemporary Chinese culture, although this same sacred quality has already become extremely decontextualized from the history of the international Communist movement and the Cold War, and has become incorporated into the official nationalist narrative of the People's Republic of China ("The Chinese people will now rise!"). At the same time, however, there is no doubt that the official "cultivation" of this sacredness is precisely in order to continue providing the current "single-party" system with a legitimizing narrative. On the other hand, by the 1980s and 1990s the process of delegitimizing, and even demonizing, Maoist-period socialist history was already virtually complete; and although this process is largely the result of a collaboration between Deng Xiaoping's political power and the intellectuals' critique and resistance, it nevertheless clearly derives its basis and support from the injuries suffered during the Cultural Revolution and the collective trauma associated with the June Fourth crackdown on the Tiananmen Square protesters. In this context, Deng Xiaoping's rise to power in 1978 could be regarded as a crucial point of historical transition, wherein "Socialism with Chinese Characteristics" and "Realizing Modernizations" became key mottos of Chinese society's move toward capitalism and its entry into a global economy. As a result, all sorts of parody of the Red Classics became permissible, transforming them from an actual contestation of authority into mere ironic mockery of that same authority.

In the case of the Chinese production of *Accidental Death of an Anarchist*, however, the situation was considerably more complex. We might say that the work borrows from the deep but ultimately ineffable trauma of the Cultural Revolution and the 1989 June Fourth crackdown in order to promote the rejection of the legacies of the Maoist era and socialist practice (in other words, Bidding Farewell to Revolution), which in the 1980s and early 1990s won popular support. Furthermore, Meng Jinghui's work erects on this common understanding a new representation of mainstream ideology, which covers the entire spectrum from an idolization of a simple capitalist system to a blind faith in economic development. In the late 1990s, however, minute but important fissures began to form in this common understanding. This is undoubtedly related to one of the most important and fundamental realities of *fin-de-siècle* China, which is to say, socialism's transformation to capitalism, together with the sudden and violent reappearance of class stratification.

Echo or prologue?

In a sense, the Red Classics fever that erupted in China at this juncture of national and international culture during the current *fin-de-siècle* era can be related to China's increasing entry into a culture of globalization, as well as to the historical and contemporary discursive field associated with the Cold War and post-Cold War, colonial and postcolonial eras. But, unlike the politico-cultural structure of the early to mid-1990s, the current strategies and behavior of the Euro-American world toward Chinese culture, together with the production of native Chinese culture and its political and ideological trends, have become increasingly intertwined with one another. For the moment, we will set aside the particulars surrounding Cai Guoqiang's 蔡國強 receipt of the 48th Venice Biennale International Award for his installation piece "*Weinisi 'Shouzuyuan'*" 威尼斯 「收租院」 (Venice's *rent collection courtyard*), together with the ensuing lawsuit and controversy in China over issues of copying and copyrights, over authorial and intellectual property rights.[30] What is more interesting in my opinion is the cultural significance of this incident within a national and international perspective, and what it reveals about a strand of history that appeared to have been sealed off and forgotten, but which in reality has remained an important historical undercurrent.

The basic facts of the matter are well known: The original large-scale clay sculpture *Rent Collection Courtyard* was built in 1965, in accordance with the class-education requests of Liu Wencai's 劉文彩 "Landlord Manor Exhibition Hall" (*Dizhu zhuangyuan chenlieguan* 地主莊園陳列館) in Sichuan Province's Dayi Prefecture. The sculpture was built by professors and students in the sculpture department of the Sichuan Art Academy, and was individually exhibited in the appropriate spaces in the exhibition hall. In all, the sculpture consists of 114 figures and 108 props, is about 96 meters long, and is divided into seven sections, entitled "paying rent, examining the rent, drying the grain, struggle, squaring accounts, pressing for rent, and fury."[31] This work may be seen as a "living class-education material" and, from the perspective of a class or materialist analysis, functions as a "reflection of old China in miniature." As an iconic reminder that "one should never forget class struggle," the work constitutes one of the key precursors of the Cultural Revolution period, while at the same time becoming one of the most prominent examples of the Maoist advocacy of socialist realism and of a "worker-peasant-soldier literature and art." The work immediately became a household name, not only as a result of the sculpture itself, but also on account of the frequency with which it was reproduced in a variety of other media, including illustrations, posters, comic strips, and so on.

In the 1970s, Tianjin's Three Stones Museum organized and created a clay sculpture entitled *Three Stones Proletariat History of Blood and Tears* (*Santiaoshi gongren xuelei shi* 三條石工人血淚史)—a work which was comparable to the *Rent Collection Courtyard* in terms of being a model for class education, though it couldn't match the latter work in its scale and achievement. Although the *Rent Collection Courtyard* sculpture dated from around the same period as the Red Classic novel *Hongyan* 紅岩 (Red Crag) (together with other works that the novel inspired, including the film *Liehuo zhong yongsheng* 烈火中永生 [Live through the flames] and the opera *Jiangjie* 江姐 [Sister Jiang]), unlike *Red Crag*, however, *Rent Collection Courtyard* and the predecessors of Cultural Revolution model opera (such as modern Peking Opera and modern dance) were all improved and transformed, and came into full bloom during the Cultural Revolution. As a result, *Rent Collection Courtyard* was not only stained dark red, but furthermore it was branded with the mark of Cultural Revolution aesthetics. When the Cultural Revolution became history, *Rent Collection Courtyard* naturally came to be located on the other side of a historical chasm, thereby becoming an object of collective amnesia or attempted amnesia. Although during the two decades of the "new era" *Rent Collection Courtyard* may seem to have disappeared without a trace, it then unexpectedly reappeared on the stage of the contemporary Chinese cultural scene during the *fin-de-siècle* moment.

The awarding of the Venice Biennale prize to "Venice's *Rent Collection Courtyard*" was foreshadowed by the appearance, in 1999, of a book entitled *Liu Wencai zhenxiang* 劉文彩真相 (The true image of Liu Wencai)—a biography of the figure who was the inspiration of the original *Rent Collection*

Courtyard. The book immediately became a hot topic of discussion, with numerous journals and websites publishing notices or reviews of the work,[32] but the curious thing was that, although this five-section book was about the "true image" of Liu Wencai, "the general model of China's landlord class over the past several thousand years"—a figure whom I would call contemporary "political dinosaur"—what the media and the internet focused on, however, was only the first section of this book: "The rise and fall of the 'Liu Wencai myth.'" The propagandistic distortion of Liu Wencai prevalent during the Cultural Revolution constitutes a significant ideological falsification. The true image of Liu Wencai is much more complicated, negative but also positive, but was repressed and reconfigured during that revolutionary period. The effect of this book was to transform the old society landlord Liu Wencai into an empty symbol, presenting his crimes as a political lie that would necessarily be read as an allegory for contemporary Chinese history and social reality—an allegory which constituted a reversal of the Maoist-period ideology symbolized by this figure. This, of course, was not a social effect created solely by the *True Image* book, but rather it can be seen as an extension of the 1980s process of rewriting history, and furthermore reveals even more clearly the cataclysmic reality underlying that process. Through the social transformations of 1990s China, this sort of book was positioned at a crucial transition point from an old mainstream ideology to a new one—a single domino within a multifaceted contemporary society and culture.[33]

Just as *The True Image of Liu Wencai* was becoming a popular after-dinner conversation topic among Beijing's intelligentsia, it was reported that Cai Guoqiang's "Venice's *Rent Collection Courtyard*" had won the prize in Venice. Initially, this was merely of interest to art circle insiders, but it quickly became a hot topic in the general media. With calls to "Protect *Rent Collection Courtyard*," the original clay sculpture was repeatedly touted as "a milestone in twentieth century political aesthetics," even as its significance reflected a typical process of rewriting the Red Classics. As one critic argued, the work's

> primary significance lies in its reliance on reconstructed aesthetics in order to protest the widespread oppression under feudal politics, to reveal humanity's tragic historical conditions, and to give voice to the fundamental spirit of realistic aesthetics. In this way, the work can spur the communication of people's critical abilities and their long-term sense of shock [...]. When the great "spirit" of realism was simultaneously banished by the optimistic utopianism of Western modernism and Stalinist heroic realism, it was spontaneously reborn in the form of *Rent Collection Courtyard*.[34]

At the crucial juncture of the 2000 Venice Biennale, two seemingly opposed tendencies in the rewriting of the Red Classics were surprisingly brought together. One of the contradictions that became apparent in this encounter was the question of whether *Rent Collection Courtyard* was a scene in a shameless farce, or whether it was an extraordinary milestone. After careful investigation, however, we notice that beneath this apparent contradiction at the level of social practice, there actually exist two complementary realistic lines of reasoning.

While the publication of *The True Image of Liu Wencai* adopted a serious position of "returning" to historical reality, the narrative strategy of the book resembles the process of registering a brand for a product. Meanwhile, the call to "protect *Rent Collection Courtyard*" became a call to defend national cultural rights, which clearly takes as its primary basis the current global debate over intellectual property rights. We recognize that the commodity comes to function as its own ideology, and what it responds to is the structure of social desire, while also implicitly promising the fulfillment of this desire. Nevertheless, the "protect *Rent Collection Courtyard*" incident, which was based on the publication *The True Image of Liu Wencai*, was still attacked by the growing new mainstream culture. In this way, the *Rent Collection Courtyard* sculpture became "a classic example of a human rights violation."[35] Therefore, the social reality this incident has brought to light is precisely the development or realization of socio-structural transformations within the redistribution of property. The introduction of international elements evokes an ethnic or national cultural axis—an axis which, in the structural transformations of contemporary culture since the 1990s, has become an effective path for transferring or translating domestic class topics.

Virtually all of the articles on the question of intellectual property rights in the *Rent Collection Courtyard* controversy acknowledge the crucial role played by the Biennale's curator, Harold Szeemann, in the work's receipt of the coveted prize. Szeemann—who claimed that what all curators, past and present, shared was an interest in anarchism and the sexual revolution—had previously invited "Rent Collection Courtyard" to appear in the "Documenta 5" exhibit he curated in Kassel in 1972. That was during China's Cultural Revolution, and therefore the invitation was naturally declined. This time, when Cai Guoqiang's installation-performance piece "Venice's *Rent Collection Courtyard*" was awarded the prize at the Venice Biennale, Szeemann described it as the "fulfillment of his old dream."[36] We could certainly interpret Szeemann's actions and motives from the perspective of a conscious or unconscious Eurocentrism, the rise and decline of a trend of hyper-realism in Western art, postcolonialism and postmodernism, or even from the perspective of "new artistic possibilities for the twenty-first century," but the fact remains that virtually none of the Chinese commentators of this incident has raised the possibility that the "old dream" Szeemann speaks of might be precisely a dream of Red China and revolutionary art. It is a fact that in 1960s European culture, avant-garde art and unrest on university campuses sprang from the same utopian dream of revolution; and even if it is not this exact dream that persists, it still forms the underpinning for how modern China is represented in the world.

Cai Guoqiang has stated that,

> I deliberately used the "Venice's *Rent Collection Courtyard*" exhibition in order to draw people's attention, at this final biennale of the twentieth century, to the socialist period art which is quickly being forgotten by contemporary culture, including its artistic characteristics and the relationship between art and politics.[37]

Some Chinese commentators have clearly recognized the symbolic significance of the selection of Szeemann as curator of the Biennale, and one notes that

> The fact that the Biennale director was able to select this sort of "rebel," this sort of "old movement leader," to curate what would be both the final Venice Biennale of the twentieth century as well as the inaugural Biennale of the twenty-first, must be very significant. One can imagine that his strong utopianism and his idealistic spirit (both of which have their origins in continental Europe) are still valued by the intelligentsia as precious commodities within an intellectual field.

But the same commentator goes on to acknowledge that,

> Cai Guoqiang's use of materials from the original *Rent Collection Courtyard* sculpture to create a new set of decorative artifacts, and his placement of them in a vast, dilapidated factory, gives viewers a sense of both familiarity and unfamiliarity. Liu Wencai, who was previously unjustly accused, is now used merely as a metaphor for reality. For some Westerners, this work stands as a real proof of a timeless theory, as a mockery of contemporary Chinese reality, as well as a symbol of the difficulty which the contemporary Chinese value system has in justifying itself.[38]

Of course, to the extent that the basis of comparison is the 1960s—either the Chinese 1960s of the original *Rent Courtyard Collection*, or the social tumult of the Euro-American 1960s—Cai Guoqiang's "Venice's *Rent Collection Courtyard*" will necessarily appear as only feeble echo. As Cai himself has observed, "My work can be regarded as a 'mobile installation.' Like *Rent Collection Courtyard*, it is purely a kind of temporal mobility. And, like a memory or illusion, it is non-material. As an artwork, it will cease to exist after the conclusion of the exhibition."[39]

The echoes of the *Rent Collection Courtyard* statue quickly came to resonate not only with recent European art, but also at a more local level. More specifically, the little theater performance of *Che Guevara* (which was described at the time, in 2000, as a "Red Storm"[40]) raised the following question with respect to the realities of contemporary Chinese thought and society: "What route should the people, after having traversed the past four decades, follow now?" Having traversed the past four decades, what route should the people follow? Should the Granma yacht leave port?" Even though the play incorporates biographical details from Che Guevara's life and the insurgency led by Fidel Castro, and specifically invokes the figure of the Granma yacht that first transported Che and the Castro brothers to Cuba in 1956, the question of whether the Granma yacht should leave port clearly functions as a more general metaphor for the question of whether contemporary China should, or is still able to, pose the question of social revolution. Here, in the boisterous auditorium where *Che Guevara* was performed, there repeatedly surface references to both the *Rent Collection Courtyard* and *Three Stones* statues, which are no longer historical comedies or nostalgic scenes but rather have become coordinates and directions for the articulation of contemporary reality itself.

Unlike the *Rent Collection Courtyard* statue, the figure of Che Guevara functions as a globally recognized "Red" icon, albeit one that until now has been strikingly absent from the *Chinese* Red Classics. Although Guevara visited China twice in the 1960s while serving as a special envoy from Cuba, these visits were nevertheless insignificant in view of China's isolationist foreign policy at the time. Later, China's official silence following Che Guevara's death in 1967,[41] combined with its internal criticism of the "leftist adventurism" and "banditry" with which Che was associated, led China (itself already embroiled in a Cultural Revolution of its own) to miss out on the global "Che Guevara fever" that raged during the 1960s and 1970s. In 1971 China published *Qie zai Boliweiya de riji* 切在玻利維亞的日記 (Che's Bolivia diary)[42] in an internal "grey book" translation journal, to serve as an "internal document, to be criticized and consulted;" and furthermore it underwent a very circuitous route to reach the disillusioned and frustrated Chinese Red Guards, some of whom then proceeded to cross the border into Myanmar and Vietnam to join the local guerilla fighters in those countries. This, however, is a dimension of Cultural Revolution history that was considered humiliating and was censored, and consequently has for the most part been stricken from public memory. In the eyes of contemporary China, therefore, Che Guevara is actually only a "returned stranger."[43]

Meanwhile, in the drama *Che Guevara*, Guevara is not even an actual character in the play, but rather appears as an enormous, absent presence—as a portrait projected onto a screen, a modulated off-stage voice, and as a starting point for the ensuing discussion. As the playwright puts it, Che Guevara's position in this drama is merely that of a platform for investigating and analyzing contemporary Chinese reality. It is not so much that the play uses the figure of Guevara to transmit an already faded nostalgia for the 1960s, but rather that it uses him as a mere signifier, an ahistorical revolutionary sign that draws on a blinding Redness to passionately signify

and resist the dramatic realities of class division together with the disparities between rich and poor found in contemporary China. Guevara, meanwhile, represents one of the most striking lacunae in contemporary Chinese
society and culture during the last two decades of the twentieth century.
If we can claim that it is always popular culture that produces the most
important invisible writings relating to class and class realities, then these
invisible writings are not a distorted means of revealing and criticizing the
cruel realities of class stratification in Chinese society, but rather constitute
an effective means of side-stepping the discourses of class opposition and
class struggle prioritized by the mainstream ideology under the Maoist era,
precisely in order to reaffirm the legitimacy of a class-based society.

Conclusion

To the extent that performance of *Che Guevara* in 2000 helped to spark a
Red Storm in China, then this sudden appearance of Redness appears to
have faded quickly in today's complex and multifaceted social reality. This
avant-garde and "anti-popular" performance eventually dissolved into the
popular culture of daily life, referenced in the red-and-black Che Guevara
T-shirts that became fashionable on college campuses, presented as "a
faddish symbol of the Cultural Army" sold in specialty shops;[44] in lists of
"the ten sexiest men of the twentieth century;"[45] in the frivolity of "Revolution and Cigars, Heroes and Idols, Romance and Coolness;"[46] and even becoming a term of affection within "petty bourgeois discourse."[47] If this process
is seen as merely another scene in China's current process of globalization,
albeit a slightly belated one, then behind this "unbearable lightness of
being" there also lies a process of globalization wherein the weightiness and
brutality of Third World reality is filtered through the ideological struggle
and real problems revealed by this play, and continues to deepen outside of
the flourishing urban fashions and appearances.

With the beginning of a new century, the rewriting of the Red Classics
has not diminished on account of having lost its original context of *fin-de-
siècle* nostalgia. Although there undoubtedly continues to be considerable
government interference in this process, the writing and acceptance of the
Red Classics nevertheless ultimately lies outside of the scheme of twentieth-
century historical memory as created through official ideology and the new
mainstream representation, and gradually begins to move in a more complex direction. Perhaps this is only because the history that produced the Red
Classics has already become an increasingly distant, misty, and harmless
memory. Or, perhaps it is on account of the fact that, following the process
of modernization, earlier promises of unqualified salvation have been transformed into a mass of suspicions, under which people have come to have
very different realizations and expectations regarding that earlier sealed-off
historical period. Perhaps, this is only the distant echo of the Great Era,

which is now no more than an echo of an echo. Perhaps, the rewriting of the Red Classics was ultimately merely a prologue to a new era.

Notes

Translated and adapted by Carlos Rojas. All embedded translations are also by Rojas.

1 Of these palace dramas, two of the most outstanding were the Qing dynasty dramas *"Yongzheng wang chao"* 雍正王朝 (The Yongzheng dynasty) and *"Huanzhu gege"* 環珠格格 (Princess Huanzhu), which took China, Hong Kong, and Taiwan by storm in 1998. These were followed by *"Kang Xi weifu sifang"* 康熙微服私訪 (The incognito trips of Emperor Kangxi), *"Tiezui tongya Ji Xiaolan"* 鐵嘴銅牙紀曉嵐 (Master of the gab: Ji Xiaolan), *"Kangxi dadi"* 康熙大帝 (The Great Kangxi emperor), among others.

2 Zhang Kangkang 張抗抗, *"Daxie de 'ren' zi,"* 大寫的「人」字 (The character *ren* [human] written in large letters), in *Zhang Kangkang suibi: Mingyun dui ni shuo, bu!* 張抗抗隨筆。命運對你說：不！ (Zhang Kangkang's essays: when fate tells you, No!) (Shanghai: Zhishi chubanshe, 1994), 86.

3 Ibid., 87.

4 Guang Yue 光悅, *Hongse yanchen, langman qinghuai—Ye Daying tan Hongse lianren* 紅色煙塵，浪漫情懷—葉大鷹談「紅色戀人」 (Red dust and romance: Ye Daying discusses *Red Lovers*), in which Ye Daying states that, "Revolution is inherently romantic," *Dianying gushi* 電影故事 (Cinematic stories), February 1998, 8–9.

5 This film was released in 1998 under the title *How Steel Is Forged*. For simplicity, however, in the following discussion I will refer to it as *Growing Up*.

6 *Dushu* 讀書 (Reader), April 1996.

7 See Cai Fanghua 蔡芳華, *"Shichang shouduan yunzuo geming jingdian—Zhipian ren Zheng Kainan tan dalian Gangtie shimo* 市場手段運作革命經典—製片人鄭凱南大煉「鋼鐵」始末" (Using marketing methods to sell a revolutionary classic: the whole story of how producer Zheng Kainan forged *Steel*), *Beijing qingnian bao*, March 16, 2000. According to this article, it had originally been the Shenzhen Wanke Cultural Broadcast Company's idea to adapt *How Steel Is Forged* into a television miniseries, envisioning it as a nostalgia piece for middle-aged viewers. But even as the Shenzhen's municipal party committee criticized this project, it was simultaneously benefiting the project with added attention and investment.

8 This discussion began on February 28, 2000, and continued through March 20. In total, the newspaper printed 14 articles on the topic.

9 This discussion began on March 11, 2000, when *Beijing qingnian bao* published a letter by a reader signed Xiao Fan. Within two weeks, the paper had published eleven responses.

10 In addition to *Beijing qingnian bao*, which initiated the discussion, many other journals also contributed to this debate, including *Beijing qingnian zhoukan* 北京青年週刊, *Zhongguo qingnian bao* 中國青年報, *Beijing chenbao* 北京晨報, *Tianjin ribao* 天津日報, *Nanfang ribao* 南方日報, *Jingpin gouwu zhinan* 精品購物指南. In addition, the vast majority of other Chinese journals also reported on or summarized this discussion, with some of the most extensive discussions appearing on the E-tang website (www.etang.com) and the BBS of the Chinese portal Sina.com (www.sina.com).

11 Summarized in *"Bao'er Gaici: Yi ge 'zhuanjiyin' yinxiong?"* 保爾·蓋茨：一個「轉基因」英雄？ (Pavel Gates: a "mutant" hero?), *Beijing qingnian bao*, March 23, 2000.

12 *"Butong de yingxiong butong butong de jingjie"* 不同的英雄不同的境界 (Different heroes; different realms), *Beijing qingnian bao*, March 14, 2000.

13 *"Daode huaijiu yu lishi xuwu dou shi bu ke qude"* 道德懷舊與歷史虛無都是不可取的 (Neither moral nostalgia and historical nihilism is to be emulated), *Beijing qingnian bao*, March 18, 2000.

14 For an overview of Mao's 1975 critique of *Water Margin*, see Fan Daren's 范達人 article *"Ping shuihu,"* 評「水滸」 (Critiquing *Water Margin*).

15 Beijing's Shaohai Market polling company used residential telephone numbers to conduct a random survey regarding the *Water Margin* television series. The survey results were published in Song Jianhui 宋建輝 and Wu Fei 吳菲, *"«Shuihu zhuan» xili xiwai shi da jiaodian"* 「水滸傳」戲裡戲外十大焦點 (Ten crucial issues regarding the text and context of *Water Margin*), in *Beijing qingnian bao*, February 11, 1998.

16 Though not officially one of the 108 rebels, Chao Gai was the initial leader of the Liangshan rebels, and during the 1975 "Criticize Water Margin" campaign was perceived as being an early revolutionary and the true protagonist of the work. After Chao Gai's death in the novel, Song Jiang replaced him as the rebel leader but is perceived, under the Maoist reading of the work, as a traitor who ultimately capitulated to imperial authority. See *"Wenge" yubi chenfu lu* 「文革」御筆沉浮錄 (The records of the rise and fall of the imperial pen during the Cultural Revolution) (Hong Kong: Mingbao chuban youxian gongsi, 1995), 89–103.

17 A posting signed *Haoshi zhi tu* 好事之徒 (A busybody), posted on the *wangyi* BBS on January 11, 1998.

18 From an August 11, 1995 interview by the author with Zhou Xiaowen 周曉文, the director of *Qin Song* 秦頌 (distributed in English as *The Emperor's Shadow*).

19 Li Wanbing 黎宛冰, *"Shoushilü da 35%, guanzhu jiu shi chenggong"* 收視率達 35%, 關注就是成功 (With viewership exceeding 35 percent, close attention means success), *Beijing qingnian bao*, February 10, 1998.

20 In a random survey conducted by the Cultural Studies Office that I direct, more than ten informants mentioned having had a similar experience. One middle-aged female worker described having to view the series while standing next to her sofa and tightly gripping its back, because otherwise she found it difficult to control her nervousness. Another older male worker described how sometimes he couldn't even watch the images on screen and would have to leave the room, but that he would quickly return so as not to miss anything.

21 See Dai Jinhua 戴錦華, *Yinxing shuxie* 隱形書寫 (Invisible writings) (Nanjing: Jiangsu renmin chubanshe, 1999), 259–283.

22 Random interviews conducted by the Cultural Studies Office that I direct.

23 Zhang Li 張力, in *Beijing qingnian bao*, February 10, 1998.

24 See Song and Wu, *"«Shuihu zhuan» xilieshidajiaodian,"* *Beijing qingnian bao*, February 11, 1998.

25 I first heard this ditty from a taxi driver, but then found it repeated with minor variations in many other sources.

26 Meng Jinghui subsequently advanced the following definition for his concept of *the people*: "The people are those who possess imagination and creative force in this society and age." See Meng Jinghui 孟京輝 and Chen Shui 沉睡, *Yi ge qianwei yishu jia de siliu zhuiwen* 一個前衛藝術家的思流追問 (An inquiry into the thoughts of an avant-garde artist), *Yuehai feng* 粤海風, vol. 4, 2000.

27 After *Dushu*, an important journal of the so-called new left movement of the late 1990s, published an article by Li Tuo 李陀 entitled *"Yi zhi secai banlan de niumang"* 一隻色彩斑爛的牛蟒 (A multihued gadfly), the same issue's "Editorial Diary" declared, "From this [work], we have experienced a long-proscribed revelry," *Dushu*, vol. 1, 1999.

28 In China, there are at least three separate editions of *Accidental Death of an Anarchist*: Lü Tongliu's 呂同六 Chinese edition, Huang Jisu's 黃紀蘇 adaptation (which completely rewrote the original), and Meng Jinghui's performance script, while each performance contained at least 10 percent impromptu modifications by the actors themselves. For the performance script of the text, see Meng Jinghui, ed., *Xianfeng xiju dang'an* 先鋒戲劇檔案 (Avant-garde theater archives) (Beijing: Zhongguo zuojia chubanshe, 2000), 236–275.

29 The Chinese edition of *Accidental Death of an Anarchist* opens with a chorus-like introduction using Meng Jinghui's characteristic vulgarity and humor to describe the furious reaction of the Vatican and Europe's establishment figures after Dario Fo won the Nobel Prize. In the middle of the play, there appear, projected onto a screen on stage, photographs of Dario Fo in real-life and in performance, accompanied by an emotional narration and some eulogistic music.

30 The newspapers *Beijing qingnian bao*, *Guangming ribao* 光明日報, *Beijing chenbao* 北京晨報, *Nanfang zhoumo* 南方週末, *Zhongguo wenhuabao* 中國文化報, *Zhonghua dushubao* 中華讀書報, *Sichuan ribao* 四川日報, *Chengdu ribao* 成都日報, *Tianfu zaobao* 天府早報, *Keji ribao* 科技日報, and *Fazhi ribao* 法制日報, all published either special issues or summaries of this debate over the international lawsuit over the intellectual property rights of *Rent Collection Courtyard*.

31 During the Cultural Revolution, the titles of these sections were changed to "Pressing for rent, examining the rent, struggle, squaring accounts, persecution, revolt, seizing power." See *Geming xiandai nisu—Shouzu yuan* 革命現代泥塑—收租院 (Revolutionary modern sculpture: *Rent Collection Courtyard*) (Beijing: Renmin meishu chubanshe, 1971).

32 Xiao Shu 笑蜀, *Liu Wencai zhenxiang* 劉文彩真相 (The true image of Liu Wencai) (Xi'an: Shaanxi shifan daxue chubanshe, 1999).

33 In reality, even as early as 1997 it was reported that Liu Wencai's name had been registered as its own brand. See Kong Fanren 孔繁任 and Zhang Xin 張昕, "*Qiye xingxiang xiang shilu*" 企業形象警示錄 (Industrial image revelations), in *Xiaoshou yu shichang* 銷售與市場 (Sales and market), 1997, 8.

34 Daozi 島子, "*Weinisi* Shouzu yuan: *Houxiandai? Houzhimin?—Yishi pipingjia Daozi fangtanlu*" 威尼斯「收租院」：後現代？後殖民？—藝術批評家島子訪談錄 (Venice's *Rent Collection Courtyard*: Postmodern? Postcolonial?—An interview with the art critic Daozi), in *Shenghuo shibao* 生活時報 (Life times), July 17, 2000.

35 Xie Yong 謝泳 discusses this issue in "*Shouzuyuan shi dianxing de qinfan renquan de zhengju*" 「收租院」是典型的侵犯人權的證據 [*Rent Collection Courtyard* is classic evidence of human rights violations] (originally published at the "Boku digest" page of the Boku website, April 4, 2001; reprinted at http://arts.tom.com/Archive/ 2001/4/2-78556.html). In this essay, Xie Yong suggests that the person controlling the rights of *Rent Collection Courtyard* must simultaneously "shoulder the responsibility for the psychological scars suffered by tens of thousands of Chinese youth on account of the pernicious influence of the work."

36 Relevant documents can be found in Daozi, "*Weinisi* Shouzuyuan: *Houxiandai? Houzhimin?*"

37 See Cai Guoqiang 蔡國強, "*Guanyu Weinisi shouzuyuan*" 關於「威尼斯收租院」 (About *Venice's Rent Collection Courtyard*), in *Jinri xianfeng* 今日先鋒 (Avant-garde today), 9 (July 2000).

38 Hong Huo 紅火, "*Weinisi de huatong—guanyu Weinisi shuangnian zhan de guannian*" 威尼斯的話筒—關於威尼斯雙年展的觀感 (The Venice megaphone—thoughts on the Venice Biennale), *Diaosuzaixian* (Diaosunet.com), http://www.dspt.com.cn/dszz/9903a.htm.

39 Cai is referring here to the fact that his sculpture would consist of a wire model of the original work onto which he placed a layer of clay, which would then harden

and flake off shortly after the conclusion of the exhibit. See Wu Hung 吳鴻, "*Wenhua zhijian de yaobai: dui Cai Guoqiang de fangtan*" 文化之間的搖擺─對蔡國強的訪談 (Oscillating between cultures: an interview with Cai Guoqiang), in *Diaosu* 雕塑 (Sculpture), 3, 2000.

40 Ling Hulei 令狐磊, "*Dang geming zaoyu shishang: Jiqing yu fengqing*" 當革命遭遇時尚：激情與風情 (When revolution runs into fashion: Fervor and local conditions), in *Xin zhoukan* 新週刊 [New weekly] (129), May 17, 2002.

41 Sun Mai 孫邁, "*Mingren yi shun—Wo suo zhidao de Qie Gewala*" 名人一瞬─我所知道的切‧格瓦拉 (A famous person at a glance: the Che Guevara I knew), in *Lao zhaopian* 老照片 (Old photographs), vol. 5 (Ji'nan: Shandong huabao chubanshe, 2003).

42 Ainesituo Qie Gewala 埃內斯托‧切‧格瓦拉 (Ernesto Che Guevara), *Qie zai Boliweiya de riji* 切在玻利維亞的日記 (Che's Bolivia diary) (Beijing, Communist Party Central Committee liaison department, 1971).

43 Zha Xiduo 扎西多, *Guilai de moshengren* 歸來的陌生人 (Returned stranger), *Wanxiang* 萬象, 2000, 9.

44 Yinda 尹達 and Hong Qingxin 洪清馨, "*Gexing dian: Qiuji sousuo*" 個性店‧秋季搜索 (Unique boutiques: autumn finds), *Shanghai wang yizhan—wanwanle* 上海網易站─玩玩樂 (Shanghai net—let's play) (January 2001) (no longer accessible).

45 Chen Tong 陳彤, "*20 shiji da xinggan nanren*" ２０世紀十大性感男人 (Sexiest men of the twentieth century), *Shizhuang* 時裝 (Fashion), 2000, 3.

46 "*Elong*" 巳龍 website news topic, "*Qie Gewala*" 切‧瓦格拉 (Che Guevara) (May 2000) (no longer accessible).

47 Hong Jiwei 黃集偉, "*Xiaozi yuwen*" 小資語文 (Petty bourgeoisie lexicon), *Beijing qingnian bao* (Beijing youth daily), August 7, 2001.

9　The reproduction of a popular hero

Weijie Song

> In the *fin-de-siècle*, we find ourselves in the moment of transit where space and time cross to produce complex figures of difference and identity, past and present, inside and outside, inclusion and exclusion.
>
> (Homi Bhabha)[1]

Since its first wave of popularity in 1920s Shanghai, particularly the hits *Burning of the Red Lotus Temple* (*Huoshao honglian si* 火燒紅蓮寺) and *Red Heroine* (*Hong xia* 紅俠),[2] Chinese martial-arts film has become a beloved topic of the masses, a conundrum for critics, as well as a pleasure and pitfall for screen-writers and film directors. In recent decades, thanks to the performances of movie stars such as Bruce Lee 李小龍, Jackie Chan 成龍, Jet Li 李連杰, Donnie Yen 甄子丹, Vincent Zhao 趙文卓, Chow Yun-Fat 周潤發, Michelle Yeoh 楊紫瓊, and Zhang Ziyi 章子怡, together with contributions from directors like King Hu 胡金銓, Chang Cheh 張徹, Tsui Hark 徐克, John Woo 吳宇森, Wong Kar-wai 王家衛, Ang Lee 李安, Zhang Yimou 張藝謀, and Chen Kaige 陳凱歌, martial-arts film has come to assume a transnational, and even global, significance.

The contemporary martial-arts genre can be traced back historically to such texts as the section on assassins in Sima Qian's 司馬遷 *Shiji* 史記 (The historical records), late imperial vernacular fiction about outlaws such as the Ming dynasty classic *Shuihu zhuan* 水滸傳 (The water margin), as well as a broad range of novels published in Hong Kong, Taiwan, and Mainland China in at the end of the early twentieth century.[3] During the latter half of the century, meanwhile, the genre of the martial-arts film has developed in several different directions. In the 1960s, for instance, when martial-arts works were forbidden in mainland China, the expatriate director King Hu (1931–1997) developed a groundbreaking model of martial-arts narratives by combining subtle historical reconstruction (an obsession with Ming history and the politics of identity/loyalty) and splendid sets and costumes in his films *Dragon Gate Inn* 龍門客棧 (1968) and *A Touch of Zen* 俠女 (1971). By contrast, another prominent director, Chang Cheh (1923–2002), developed a different mode featuring the exhibition of bloody masculinity and tragic brotherhood, as in his *The One-Armed Swordsman* 獨臂刀 (1967) and *The Heroic Ones* 十三太保 (1970).

In 1990, however, shortly before King Hu passed away, the cooperation and tension between Hu and the young director Tsui Hark (1950–) marked a turning point in the evolution of the genre. More specifically, Hu's and Tsui's problematic production *The Swordsmen* 笑傲江湖 (1990) highlighted the differences between the two directors, and signaled the decline of King Hu's paradigm and the rise of Tsui Hark's mode of spectacular martial-arts representation. Since then, Tsui Hark has established his reputation as one of the most productive, ambitious, and influential directors in the industry. I will use Tsui Hark's 1990s series featuring Wong Fei-hung (Huang Feihong 黃飛鴻—a popular hero based on a historical figure—to illustrate how Tsui adapts traditional visions of the genre while simultaneously introducing transnational themes that resonate with contemporary geopolitical concerns.

Tsui Hark's Wong Fei-hung films are only the most recent iterations of what has been claimed to be the longest-running series in world cinema. According to a recent edition of *The Guinness World Records*,

> Wong Fei-hung martial arts films are the longest film series: from the first Wong Fei-hung martial arts film, *The True Story of Wong Fei-hung* produced in 1949, to the most recent *Once Upon a Time in China 5* produced in 1995, Wong Fei-hung series have created a miracle in the history of world cinema. A total of 103 films have been made about the 19th-century martial arts hero Wong Fei-hung.[4]

Despite this long tradition, Tsui Hark's version of the Wong Fei-hung tales not only marks an important new development, but also transforms the series from old-fashioned large-scale production in the tradition of Cantonese martial-arts films[5] into innovative works featuring transnationally circulated images, stunts, and plots embedded with historical content and political concerns.

Tsui Hark has contributed (as director, producer, and screenwriter) to six Wong Fei-hung films in the series known in English as *Once Upon a Time in China*,[6] as well as a 22-episode Wong Fei-hung TV drama. The films feature his distinctive "Tsui Hark-style specific effects,"[7] together with amazing choreography, exhilarating fight scenes, melodramatic and humorous stories, local and transnational romances, elaborate historical settings, indigenous Cantonese customs, and even assorted foreign elements including Jesuit missionaries, British soldiers, American brokers, and Russian diplomats. As Lisa Odham Stokes and Michael Hoover point out, Tsui Hark's Wong Fei-hung

> not only celebrates Chinese cultural identity and humanistic ideals (defending the weak, championing justice, and redressing the wrongs

of the oppressed); he also denounces imperialism and considers loaded issues of modernization, progress, and future.[8]

In other words, besides including the entertaining, humorous, and ironic elements typical of popular culture, Tsui Hark's Wong Fei-hung series also confronts serious and thorny turn-of-the-century issues such as the foreign powers' ambition of carving up China "like a melon," China's quest for wealth and power, and the physical and emotional hardships (the history of blood and tears) of Chinese immigrant laborers in the United States.

In the following discussion, I will examine the figure of Wong Fei-hung in history and legend, including the significance of Tsui Hark's remodeling of the character as a young hero from Foshan City. In particular, I consider how Tsui Hark maps Wong Fei-hung's imaginary journey from the local town of Foshan, to the provincial capital of Guangzhou, and then on to Beijing and even San Francisco, the frontier of the Western world. This transnational journey is significant because Tsui Hark consistently portrays Wong Fei-hung as a master of Chinese martial arts and traditional medicine, and it is his association with these indigenous epistemological systems that allows him to resist the colonizing and symbolically castrating power-knowledge structures associated with Western science and technology.

The rebirth of a hero: history, fiction, and cinematic imaginary

Despite the more than 100 films featuring Wong Fei-hung, we know relatively little about his real life. There are hardly any extant descriptions, photos, or drawings of him. We do know, however, that he was born in Guangdong province in 1847, and that his father, Wong Kay Ying 黃麒英, was a famous martial-arts master who studied the Hung Kuen 洪拳 (Hung's fist) style of martial arts and was one of the Ten Tigers of Canton, an elite group of masters. Wong Fei-hung was famous for his expertise in Hung Kuen, Chinese medicine, and the southern Chinese tradition of lion dancing. He died in 1924, at the age of seventy-seven. The Hong Kong film industry has responded to this relative dearth of historical information by portraying Wong Fei-hung in a variety of ways—as a combination of physician, martial artist, and citizen-philosopher.[9] The images of Wong Fei-hung range from Gordon Liu's 劉家輝 serious face in *Martial Club* 武館, to Kwan Tak-hing's 關德興 aged hero in Golden Harvest's *The Skyhawk* 黃飛鴻少林拳, to Jackie Chan's comic portrait in *Drunken Master* 醉拳 (1978) and *Drunken Master II* (1994), as well as the young, proud, and romantic figure played by Jet Li and Vincent Zhao in Tsui Hark's *Once Upon a Time in China* series.[10] On January 14, 2001, Foshan—the third largest city in Guangdong province and the hometown of the prominent late Qing scholar and politician Kang Youwei 康有為, the famous late Qing writer Wu Jianren 吳趼人, and Bruce Lee 李小龍—established a Wong Fei-hung memorial hall, thereby marking a remarkable climax to Wong Fei-hung's process of symbolic legitimization.[11]

Indeed, *Foshan Wong Fei-hung* is currently Wong's best-known nickname, and can therefore be regarded as an abbreviated symbol of Tsui Hark's series as a whole. Yet, Wong Fei-hung's association with Foshan is itself open to question. Ru Shi, a roommate of Wong Fei-hung's disciple Jian Wenying, for instance, has argued that Wong was actually born in Xiqiao, a small village near the Southern Sea; that he subsequently achieved fame in Guangzhou rather than in Foshan; and that at most he only paid several short visits to Foshan.[12] In Tsui Hark's Wong Fei-hung series, it was not until *Once Upon a Time in China II* that *Foshan Wong Fei-hung* began to emerge as a central mark of Wong's identity. This process of geographic legitimization continued in the following films, precisely as the Wong character—beginning, as I will discuss below, in *Once Upon a Time III*— was himself simultaneously moving farther and farther *away* from his home province of Guangdong.

Ackbar Abbas has called attention to Tsui Hark's "reworking of traditional storytelling,"[13] and Bordwell also argues that Tsui Hark "revived the historical kung-fu movie with his nationalistic epic *Once Upon a Time in China* (1991)."[14] For me, another important dimension of Tsui's adaptations lies in the specific actors he selected to play the part of his hero. Cinematic images of Wong Fei-hung have ranged from the middle-aged and elderly character played by Kwan Tak-hing (1905–1996) to the young Wong Fei-hung played by Jet Li and Vincent Zhao. Kwan Tak-hing was a fatherly and grandfatherly master, "a beloved theater performer, [who] portrayed Huang (Wong Fei-hung) as a peace-loving Confucian who used kung-fu as a last resort."[15] Ange Hwang points out,

> The character of Wong Fei-hung represents many of the traditional Confucian virtues: propriety (willingness to stand up for what is right), charitable love (veneration for the old and compassion for the poor), and peace (resolving problems without the use of violence). According to the traditional concept of *wu de* 武德 (morality of martial arts), the true martial arts practices the art for the sake of physical health and self-defense; he declines violence unless it is unavoidable.[16]

Kwan Tak-hing's Wong Fei-hung is no doubt a righteous old man who represents traditional Confucian virtues such as benevolence, forbearance, and forgiveness. The martial arts world *jianghu* 江湖 (region of rivers and lakes) Kwan Tak-hing's Wong Fei-Hung inhabits is imagined as being intact, autonomous, and totally indifferent to the outside influences that began to affect China during the late nineteenth century, and the elderly Wong Fei-hung's confidence and worldview are never significantly challenged. Both the localized Cantonese community and the kung-fu world are presented as being small but remarkably self-sufficient.

Tsui Hark was quite dissatisfied with the previous adaptations of the Wong Fei-hung story, and confessed that, when he was young, whenever the topic of Wong Fei-hung "came up with a whole ton of Chinese philosophy, maybe Confucian philosophy," he and other kids would respond, "I don't want to listen to this, let's have some fun."[17] Therefore, he chose two young stars, Jet Li and Vincent Zhao, both martial arts champions who left China to join the Hong Kong film industry, to play the part of Wong Fei-hung in his films. Tsui Hark's new version of the character is a young hero whose activities reveal not only a traditional confidence but also an increasing perplexity amid turbulent times. Young Wong Fei-hung feels uneasy and confused when confronted with material and cultural novelties ranging from guns and firearms to steam engines, from foreign languages to photography and film. On one hand, Tsui Hark was pushing his Hong Kong audiences to rethink their own identity crisis and formation in the 1990s. As Lisa Odham Stokes and Michael Hoover point out, "With Hong Kong's return to China on the horizon, Tsui Hark, who says his movies must 'reflect what we are thinking at this moment in our time,' serialized Wong Fei-hung in six pictures between 1990 and 1997."[18] On the other hand, Tsui Hark showed the different possibilities of Chinese modernity that existed during this turn-of-the-century period, by interweaving the legendary folk hero's stories, whether real or imaginary, with actual historical incidents. As a result, Tsui Hark's young Wong Fei-hung can be related to the discourse on "Youth China" that Liang Qichao 梁啟超 (1873–1929) and other intellectuals introduced in the late Qing period to replace the image of an old and grand empire. Although Tsui Hark's Wong Fei-hung series was produced in the 1990s, we might say that it adopts and transforms these earlier Youth China discourses from a century earlier.

Tsui Hark's Wong Fei-hung films can therefore be seen as re-creating a late Qing popular hero within the sociocultural context of 1990s Hong Kong. This constructed history and "imagined memory"[19] constitute not only the employment of previous Wong Fei-hung legends but also the interweaving of people and events from modern history and the experiences of modernity. These historical figures include Sun Yat-sen 孫逸仙 (a.k.a. Sun Zhongshan 孫中山), the founder of the Chinese Republic; Lu Haodong 陸皓東 (1868–1895), an important activist and martyr during the 1911 Revolution; Liu Yongfu 劉永福 (1837–1917), a military leader in Guangdong; Li Hongzhang 李鴻章 (1823–1901), the prime minister during the late Qing period; and Zhang Baozai 張保仔 (1786–1822), the notorious head of a pirate brigade who had his own kingdom on the open sea, among many others. Tsui once confessed his motive for producing his own version of Wong Fei-hung:

> In the Wong Fei-hung series we had in the past, the guy had *no background*; we knew he was in the Qing dynasty but we never knew what year it was or what kinds of things happened in that period of time [...]. *I decided that if I had the chance, I would link Wong Fei-hung with every incident in the modern history of China.*[20]

> (Emphasis added)

Tsui's new narrative strategies incorporate "many action sequences and references to history and colonial history."[21] He intentionally focuses on the cultural trends of the late nineteenth century from the perspective of the current *fin-de-siècle* moment. These new imaginary scenes—like Wong's protecting Li Hongzhang, defeating Zhang Baozai, befriending and helping Sun Yat-sen—create fascinating linkages to the shared mental world, or "spiritual situation," of the late Qing era.

A geopolitical journey

Kwan Tak-hing starred in more than eighty Wong Fei-hung films, in which local color is manifested through Cantonese folk arts (such as the Lion Dance), dialects, habits, geographical characteristics, food, music, and other forms of entertainment.[22] Tsui Hark, by contrast, fundamentally transformed the regional settings of Wong's storylines and extended the sphere of the protagonist's activities from Guangdong to a broader national and international setting.

Throughout the entire Tsui Hark series, the young and handsome martial-arts master and herbalist Wong Fei-hung runs Pao Chi Lam, a medical clinic and martial-arts club. Wong's favorite disciples include the heavyweight pork Butcher Lam; Leung Foon, a Chinese Casanova with second-rate martial-art skills; the fictional Master Kicker Club Foot, a rickshaw boy previously based in Beijing; and Buck Tooth Sol, an overseas-educated doctor who is fluent in English but can only stutter in Cantonese, obviously making him a symbol of the cultural dilemma in the British Crown Colony Hong Kong. By rewriting and expanding the plots and subplots of his hero's adventures, Tsui Hark has used his historical imagination and geopolitical esthetics to go far beyond the spatio-temporal scope of previous Wong Fei-hung works.

The geopolitical implications of Tsui Hark's series can be glimpsed, for instance, when, in *Once Upon a Time in China III*, Wong Fei-hung leaves Guangzhou for the first time and travels to Beijing to attend the national Lion-Dance contest—a symbolic competition to see which lion can eat the most sheep (the term for sheep, *yang* 羊, is a homonym in Chinese for "foreign," or *yang* 洋)—hosted by Empress Dowager Cixi 慈禧太后 (1835–1908) and Prime Minister Li Hongzhang. At the end of the competition, Wong saves Li Hongzhang from an assassination attempt by the Russians, thereby teaching him a lesson: a symbolic victory in a Lion-Dance contest doesn't necessarily mean that the Chinese people can subdue the ambitious foreign powers. A similar topic is developed in *Once Upon a Time in China IV*, in which eight countries (including America and Germany) challenge China in an international lion-dance competition, and Wong Fei-hung has to stand up to defend his country's honor. In *Once Upon a Time in China and America* (VI), Wong Fei-hung and his disciples embark on a long journey to America, where Pao Chi Lam's overseas branch in San Francisco encounters racial prejudice and discrimination. Thanks to Wong Fei-hung's efforts, though, Chinatown is ultimately renamed in recognition of Chinese immigrants' contribution through blood and tears. In *Once Upon a Time in China and America*, Tsui Hark transforms the blood and tears into victory, glory, and dignity. From Canton to Beijing and then on to San Francisco, therefore, Tsui Hark's Wong Fei-hung series maps a Chinese hero's local, national, and international conquests.

In Tsui's series, Wong is a young kung-fu master, specializing in the southern Shaolin School style. He is presented as being among the best martial artists of his time, whose skills include "Shadowless Kick," "Iron Wire Fist," "Five from Fist," and "Tiger Vanquishing Fist"—colorful techniques that fans of martial-arts film track with considerable pleasure and interest. Wong's medical skills are no less extraordinary, and in one scene in *Once Upon a Time in China III*, Sun Yat-sen, the future founding father of the Chinese Nationalist Party, describes to foreign audiences how Wong Fei-hung is even able to use acupuncture to stop the knee-jerk reflex. This episode illustrates the effectiveness of Chinese martial arts and medicine, and implies that power and knowledge belong not to the Western colonizers but rather to Wong Fei-hung, the Chinese doctor and martial artist.

Furthermore, the martial-arts world can establish and reinforce the traditional bonds of brotherhood and the ideal master–disciple relationship. For instance, Master Kicker Club Foot, was originally the former rickshaw boy, is arguably Wong Fei-hung's best disciple. He could be compared to Lao She's 老舍 (1899–1966) "Camel Xiangzi," the rickshaw puller who pursues his dream in Beijing. From Lao She's point of view, Beijing becomes a laboratory of modern ideas, such as independence, individualism, illusion, and alienation.[23] While Camel Xiangzi witnesses the impossibility of individualism in semi-feudal and semi-colonial Beijing, Master Kicker Club Foot, by contrast, discovers and reinforces the typical master-disciple affiliation in traditional martial arts narrative after Wong Fei-hung cures him and takes him in, whereupon the former rickshaw puller becomes one of his master's staunchest supporters.

The popular world of martial arts is stable, independent, and self-sufficient, but Wong Fei-hung cannot pretend to be blind to what is happening during those turbulent times. In *Once Upon a Time in China II*, Dr. Sun Yat-sen often checks his watch, a distinctively foreign and modern artifact. The frequency of his action and his new conception of time underscore the arrival of the modern. Old habits, traditional inertia, and outmoded values are being challenged and altered. These modern trajectories can be found everywhere in Tsui Hark's series. At the beginning of *Once Upon a Time in China III*, for instance, the train whistle is shrill and shocking, not only signaling that Wong Fei-hung and his disciples will take this modern mode of transport to Beijing, but also implying that this new technology is changing Beijing's social, political, and cultural situations. As Wolfgang Schivelbusch argues, the railroad during this period "introduced a new system of behavior: not only of travel and communication but of thought, of feeling, of expectation."[24] Wong Fei-hung's railway journey, therefore, is symbolic of the ongoing struggles among traditional and modern materials and knowledge systems.

These competing epistemological systems have their own hierarchy in Tsui Hark's reproduction of the popular hero. In *Once Upon a Time in China III*, Wong's father buys a steam engine in order to improve the quantity and quality of medicine production. After Leung Foon uses the steam from the machine to cook eggs, the steam engine breaks down. Wong Fei-hung's attitude towards the problem is simply to ignore it and "let it be." When Tamansky, the Russian diplomat, is invited by Aunt Yee to come repair the machine and proceeds to expound on the meaning of the Industrial Revolution, Wong Fei-hung loses his patience and protests at what he perceives to be the diplomat's propaganda:

Wong Fei-hung:	Didn't you promise me that you'll never see him again?
Yee (Aunt 13):	I ask him to repair the steam engine for us.
Wong Fei-hung:	Just let it be this way.
Tamansky:	You are so stubborn. Never underestimate the importance of this machine. The steam engine increases the productivity of this factory. It can accomplish the job that manpower can't. The industrial revolution has changed the world. And whoever owns the machine, will be the leader of the world. So powerful that he can even replace the emperor. Russian Empire and Ching Dynasty can't run away from what's fated to happen.
Wong Fei-hung:	We'll face it if that's the case. Since it's the fate, we'll see who will be the winner at last.

(Original English subtitles)

Interestingly, in this sequence, Tsui Hark places Wong Fei-hung in a shadow, while Tamansky is bathed in the light of his torch. Tamansky's explanation of the significance of the steam engine and the Industrial Revolution is appealing and powerful, while Wong Fei-hung's critical response underscores his general skepticism about the value of Western knowledge.

Indeed, the colonizing/castrating power of Western knowledge looms large throughout Tsui Hark's series. Trains, cameras, steam engines, and gunpowder, among other imports, represent the material existence and challenge of Western powers. An example of this threat can be seen in *Once Upon a Time in China I*, when Wong Fei-hung's Westernized lover, Aunt Yee, tries to take a picture of Wong Fei-hung and a local gentleman, whereupon the magnesium powder in the flash explodes and chars a beautiful pet bird to a crisp. Perhaps the most striking moment is when Master Yim, Wong Fei-hung's rival, is dying: he finally confesses that his Iron Robe kung-fu, the symbol of the solidarity and self-sufficiency of Chinese martial arts and culture, cannot resist the power of bullets and guns.

As the late Qing Empire was faced challenges from Western science, technology, and military might, the question of how to subdue the foreigners became one of the most important tasks for Wong Fei-hung. Wei Yuan's 魏源 (1794–1856) solution to this problem was articulated in his famous slogans: "use foreigners' strength to subdue them" (*yi yi zhiyi* 以夷制夷) and "study the strength of the foreigners so as to subdue them" (*shiyi changji yi zhiyi* 師夷長技以製夷), while the contemporary novelist Yu Wanchun 俞萬春 (1794–1849) implicitly presented, in his novel *Dangkou zhi* 荡寇志 (Quell the bandits), an ironic variant on this strategy: subdue the foreigners so as to learn their skills.[25] In Tsui Hark's 1990s series, by contrast, Wong Fei-hung never expresses any desire to study the strength of the foreigners, but rather seeks to use *his own* strength in order to subdue them.

Is there anybody in Tsui's Wong Fei-hung series still willing to study the strength of the foreigners so as to subdue them? Actually, it is Aunt Yee, the heroine located between China and the West, who partly follows Wei Yuan's strategy by studying the strength of the foreigners. She knows how to take pictures, use cameras, and communicate in English, and attempts to teach Wong Fei-hung how to understand and confront the new world. Tsui Hark has pointed out that

> actually Wong Fei-hung is a male chauvinist from a chauvinistic society. This male chauvinist mentality is being threatened by a very strong woman who knows a lot of things about the world that he doesn't know so he really has to struggle to be humble and ask what's going on in the outside world. The woman can tell him what's going on. And that's a fun relationship.[26]

I would argue that Aunt Yee's stories are not just for fun and entertainment but rather imply a subtle change and displacement in the epistemological politics of the period. In *Once Upon a Time in China III*, the most important Western novelty is a movie camera, which was originally given to Aunt Yee by the Russian diplomat. But afterwards, the camera subverts the diplomat's interests when it witnesses and eventually helps defeat the Russian conspiracy to assassinate Li Hongzhang. The camera subplot illustrates precisely Wei Yuan's strategy of studying the strength of the foreigners so as to subdue them.

In Tsui Hark's series, the confrontation between China and the West is sometimes reduced to the spectacles of fighting scenes between Wong Fei-hung and Western forces. In a discussion of Hong Kong cinema, John Charles notes that "the foreign characters are ridiculous caricatures scarcely more believable than the yellowface performers in the Hollywood movies of the '30s and '40s,"[27] and this is no less true of the Westerners in Tsui Hark's films. Meanwhile, Wong Fei-hung is reconfigured as a bayonet- and bullet-proof hero. In *Once Upon a Time in China and America*, the head of the white bank robbers is so frightened by Wong's martial arts that he asks, "Who is this Wong Fei-hung?! The Devil?" This is just one of the many episodes that depict the birth of an omnipotent figure, a popular hero, "a righteous martial artist, traditional healer, and champion lion dancer, who becomes the metonymic figure for China encountering modernity and the West."[28]

Tsui Hark reforms and reshapes the popular genre of martial-arts film and endows it with a consciousness of crisis and modern experiences. From Foshan to Guangzhou, Beijing, and San Francisco; from the local town to the provincial capital, and on to the imperial capital and the Wild West outside China, Tsui Hark's Wong Fei-hung films not only depict a variety of *fin-de-siècle* geographic and cultural spaces, but also help interrogate the meaning of historicity itself. As Tsui Hark has observed, "[T]o look at the past is pretty much to look at ourselves now because so many of the decisions that the people in that period of time had to make are very similar to the decisions that we are making now. *Once Upon a Time in China* can be now, [and] can be the future."[29]

Notes

A longer version of this article, entitled "Cinematic Geography, Martial Arts Fantasy, and Tsui Hark's Wong Fei-hung Series," appeared in the journal *Asian Cinema* 19, no. 1 (2008): 123–142. I am grateful to Professor John A. Lent, publisher/editor-in-chief of *Asian Cinema*, for granting permission to include the present essay in this volume.

1 Homi Bhabha, *The Location of Culture* (New York and London: Routledge, 1995), 1.
2 See Zhen Zhang, "Bodies in the Air: The Magic of Science and the Fate of the Early 'Martial Arts' Film in China," in Sheldon H. Lu and Emilie Yueh-yu Yeh, eds., *Chinese-Language Film: Historiography, Poetics, Politics* (Honolulu: University of Hawai'i Press, 2005), 52–75.
3 For recent critical discussions of Jin Yong and Chinese martial arts culture, see Weijie Song, *Cong yule xingwei dao wutobang chongdong: Jin Yong xiaoshuo zai jiedu* 從娛樂行為到烏托邦衝動：金庸小說再解讀 (From entertainment activity to utopian impulse: rereading Jin Yong's martial arts fiction) (Nanjing: Jiangsu renmin chubanshe, 1999); and John Christopher Hamm, *Paper Swordsmen: Jin Yong and the Modern Chinese Martial Arts Novel* (Honolulu: University of Hawai'i Press, 2005).
4 Tim Footman and Mark C. Young, eds., *The Guinness World Records 2001* (Stamford, Conn., 2001).
5 Yu Mo-wan, "Swords, Chivalry and Palm Power: A Brief Survey of the Cantonese Martial Arts Cinema, 1938–1970," in *A Study of the Hong Kong Swordplay Film (1945–1980): The 5th Hong Kong International Film Festival April 9–24, 1981, City Hall* (Urban Council, 1981, reprint 1996), 87–106; and Sek Kei, "The Development of 'Martial Arts' in Hong Kong Cinema," in *A Study of the Hong Kong Martial Arts Film: The 4th Hong Kong International Film Festival April 3–18, 1980, City Hall* (Urban Council, 1980, reprint 1994), 27–46.
6 Tsui Hark's Wong Fei-hung series includes *Once Upon a Time in China* (1991; Golden Harvest/Film Workshop/Paragon Films) (Tsui Hark was director and, one of the four writers); *Once Upon a Time in China II* (1992; Golden Harvest/Film Workshop/Paragon Films) (Tsui Hark was director, one of the three writers, and producer); *Once Upon a Time in China III* (1993; Golden Harvest/Film

Workshop/Paragon Films) (Tsui Hark was director, one of the two writers, and producer); *Once Upon a Time in China IV* (1993; Golden Harvest/Film Workshop/Paragon Films) (Tsui Hark was one of the two writers and producer); *Once Upon a Time in China V* (1994; Golden Harvest/Film Workshop/Paragon Films) (Tsui Hark was director and one of the three writers, and one of two producers); *Once Upon a Time in China and America* (1997; Win's Entertainment) (Tsui Hark was producer).

7 Ackbar Abbas, *Hong Kong: Culture and the Politics of Disappearance* (Minneapolis: University of Minnesota Press, 1997), 32.

8 Lisa Odham Stokes and Michael Hoover, *City on Fire: Hong Kong Cinema* (London and New York: Verso, 1999), 94.

9 Stokes and Hoover, *City on Fire*, 93.

10 It was the original 1949 black-and-white Wong Fei-hung film that introduced the now famous theme music used in every movie featuring the character. The tune is a Cantonese melody entitled "Under the General's Orders".

11 See http://www.foshanmuseum.com/WFH/MENU.HTM.

12 See Yu Mo-wan, "The Prodigious Cinema of Huang Fei-hung," in *A Study of the Hong Kong Martial Arts Film*, 73, 79.

13 Abbas, *Hong Kong*, 19.

14 David Bordwell, *Planet Hong Kong: Popular Cinema and the Art of Entertainment* (Cambridge, Mass.: Harvard University Press, 2000), 5.

15 Ibid., 204.

16 See Ange Hwang, "The Irresistible: Hong Kong Movie *Once Upon a Time in China* Series—An Extensive Interview with Director/Producer Tsui Hark," in *Asian Cinema*, vol. 10, no. 1, Fall 1998: 11.

17 Ibid., 16 (emphasis added).

18 Stokes and Hoover, *City on Fire*, 93.

19 See Andreas Huyssen, "Present Pasts," *Public Culture*, vol. 12, no. 1 (2000), 27.

20 Hwang, "The Irresistible," 12.

21 Abbas, *Hong Kong*, 31.

22 See Yu, "The Prodigious Cinema of Huang Fei-hong," 73–86.

23 Lao She, *Rickshaw: The Novel of Lo-t'o Hsiang Tzu*, trans. by Jean M. James (Honolulu: University Press of Hawai'i, 1979). For discussions of Xiangzi the rickshaw puller, see David Der-wei Wang, *Fictional Realism in 20th-Century China: Mao Dun, Lao She, Shen Congwen* (New York: Columbia University Press, 1993), chapter 4; and Lydia H. Liu, *Translingual Practice: Literature, National Culture, and Translated Modernity—China, 1900–1937* (Stanford: Stanford University Press, 1995), chapter 4.

24 Wolfgang Schivelbusch, *The Railway Journey: The Industrialization of Time and Space in the 19th Century* (Berkeley and Los Angeles: University of California Press, 1986), 1.

25 David Wang, *Fin-de-siècle Splendor: Repressed Modernities in Late Qing Fiction: 1848–1911* (Stanford: Stanford University Press, 1997), chapter 2.

26 Hwang, "The Irresistible," 17.

27 John Charles, *The Hong Kong Filmography, 1977–1997: A Complete Reference to 1,100 Films Produced by British Hong Kong Studios* (Jefferson, NC: McFarland & Company, 2000), 726.

28 Bhaskar Sarkar, "Hong Kong Hysteria: Martial Arts Tales from a Mutating World," in Esther C. M. Yau, ed., *At Full Speed: Hong Kong Cinema in a Borderless World* (Minneapolis: University of Minnesota Press, 2001), 170.

29 Quoted from Hwang, "The Irresistible," 12.

10 Memory, photographic seduction, and allegorical correspondence

Eileen Chang's *Mutual Reflections*

Xiaojue Wang

In his retrospective essay on Eileen Chang (Zhang Ailing 張愛玲, 1920–1995), Ke Ling 柯靈 insightfully observed that if it had not been for Shanghai under the Japanese occupation between 1942 and 1945, there would have been no other site, spatial or temporal, within which to place Eileen Chang in modern Chinese literature.[1] Indeed, it is the chronotope of this transient ideological vacuum of Shanghai that occasions Eileen Chang as the most talented and legendary female writer in twentieth-century China. Her short novel collection *Chuanqi* 傳奇 (Romances) and essay collection *Liuyan* 流言 (Written on water) are doubtlessly the most brilliant cultural events of the Occupation period.

Although Eileen Chang's current literary significance is based primarily on a body of work that she produced in Shanghai during a relatively narrow three-year period between 1943 and 1945, her reputation has nevertheless undergone many transformations. Chang was virtually erased from Mainland Chinese literary histories even before she left Shanghai for Hong Kong— and eventually for the United States—shortly after the great historical divide in China in 1949. Outside of Mainland China, she tended to be perceived primarily as an essentially popular writer, a latter-day Butterfly. In his influential 1961 study, *A History of Modern Chinese Fiction*, however, C. T. Hsia famously devoted an entire chapter to Eileen Chang, thus, for the first time, endowing her with a canonical position in modern Chinese literature. In fact, Hsia dedicates more attention to Chang than he does to any other author, including even the arch-canonical Lu Xun. More than any other single factor, Hsia's attention to Chang served as a catalyst for a subsequent flurry of academic research on her works in Hong Kong, Taiwan, as well as abroad.[2]

It was not until 1984 that Chang's literary legacy was effectively resurrected in Mainland China, with the republication in one of China's most important literary journals of her novella *Jinsuo ji* 金鎖記 (The golden cangue), which also happened to be the text to which Hsia gave the greatest attention in his earlier study. This process was further reinforced eight years later with the publication of the four-volume *Zhang Ailing wenji* 張愛玲文集 (Selected writings of Eileen Chang) and the *Zhang Ailing sanwen quanbian* 張愛玲

散文全編 (Complete essays of Eileen Chang), both of which became best-sellers that year and further kindled the Eileen Chang fever spreading through the nation. Four biographies of Chang appeared the following year, followed in 1994 by her own figurative autobiography, *Duizhao ji: kan laozhaoxiangbu* 對照記：看老照相簿 (Mutual reflections: reading old photographs),[3] one year before she passed away in 1995. With the emergence of Shanghai as a focal point of "the most intense and ubiquitous nostalgic trend of the 1990s,"[4] Eileen Chang becomes a crucial site within the memory culture in Mainland China—a significance that is particularly evident in *Mutual Reflections*, the last work before her death, a photographic farewell ceremony that both culminates and anticipates the "Eileen Chang legend."

What role does photography, a modern technology of visual reproduction, play in the construction of memory? Is a photograph unavoidably a spatial fixation within the flow of time? Or, might this temporal and spatial fragment also provide an umbilical cord between past and present, an indexical link to lived or imagined memory? These are some of the questions I will consider in my reading of Eileen Chang's *Mutual Reflections*. At the same time, I will reference writings on photography by some of Chang's European contemporaries, particularly Siegfried Kracauer and Walter Benjamin. Similarly, I will offer an intertextual reading of Roland Barthes' influential meditations on the nature of photography in *Camera Lucida*, which, like *Mutual Reflection*, is not only a reflection on loss and death, but also uncannily anticipates the author's own death shortly after the work's completion.

In my analysis of *Mutual Reflections*, I will explore Eileen Chang's understanding of the relationship between photography and memory. My argument is that Chang's final work constitutes an intriguing allegorical correspondence —or, in her own words, a mutual reflection—between language and vision, and thereby provides a unique window into her aesthetics of desolation and politics of representation. For Eileen Chang, photographs are constitutive parts of memory images, while photographs themselves simultaneously also function at a non-representational level as physical artifacts. What she stresses is not only the physical resemblance between the image in a photograph and the object it represents in reality, but also an uneven correspondence between images and words. In such correspondences, history is no longer the grand narrative of modernization and progress, instead, it emerges as a petrified face, a desolate landscape. Herein lies Eileen Chang's very conception of modernity and her unique version of historiography.

In the final decades of the twentieth century, Eileen Chang emerged as one of the most significant literary phenomena in modern China, as articulated by the question posed by the International Eileen Chang Conference in Hong Kong in 2000: "Is Eileen Chang becoming, or, has become, yet another 'legend' after Lu Xun in modern Chinese literature?" Intriguingly, the Chang legend has affected not only the academic world, but also a vast cultural market. From the impressive number of reprints of her old works, to various cinematic adaptations, a plethora of research papers and books, as well as the sudden boom of biographic literature and numerous clubs of Chang fans on the internet, Chang has become one of the most salient scenes of the memory culture in Mainland China after the 1989 Tiananmen incident.

What can be easily overlooked in this conspicuous explosion of Chang's popularity is the narcissistic investment of the author herself who, even at the beginning of her career, was fond of using a variety of visual strategies to stage herself. An examination of *Mutual Reflections* and its relationship to her early works reveals that the work is haunted by a specter of photographic seduction. More importantly, this seduction is particularly evident in the transplantation of this family album from the private to the public sphere, and in its fetishized position within the 1990s Chinese Eileen Chang craze. Via diverse media ranging from print, television, film, CD's and the internet, these photographs have circulated among people obsessed with Eileen Chang and the old Shanghai she represents. What is striking here is not so much the commodification of Chang and her work, but rather her own strategic complicity with the cultural market and her conscious manipulation of the mechanism of culture consumption. On the other hand, however, it was also Chang who constantly argued against the theatricalization of life. How may we come to terms with the apparent paradox between Eileen Chang's agoraphobia and her spectacular self-staging?

Reading *Mutual Reflections*

Mutual Reflections was the last book Eileen Chang published before her death. It was completed in 1993 and published by Taipei's Huangguan (Crown) Press of Taipei in 1994. The following year, Eileen Chang was found dead on the floor of her apartment in Los Angeles, the city where she had lived incognito for the final twenty-three years of her life. Her will specified that there be no funeral rite and that her ashes be cast in a desolate place.[5] In this light, *Mutual Reflections* becomes an anticipatory "visual memorial ceremony,"[6] arranged and performed by Eileen Chang herself.

The volume is Eileen Chang's reading of her own family album. It contains fifty-four photographs, most of which are of her father, mother, aunt, her grandparents, her brother, her best friend Fatima, and herself. Most of the photographs are accompanied by textual captions. Some of these captions consist of just one short sentence, noting when and where the picture was taken, while others are miniature essays, reminiscent of Chang's two famous autobiographical essays *"Tongyan wuji"* 童言無忌 (The guileless words of a child, 1943) and *"Siyu"* 私語 (Intimate words, 1944), and anticipating her unfinished final work, the memoir *Xiaotuanyuan* 小團圓 (Small family reunion).[7]

Eileen Chang once remarked that "photographs are merely the fragmentary shells of one's life. As time goes by, the kernels become eaten up, the taste of which only one oneself knows. All that remains to show others are the black-and-white shells thrown on the floor."[8] However, this "black-and-white shell" of one's life is not what Kracauer calls "a spatial continuum devoid of both time and meaning,"[9] which he contrasts with "the last memory image"[10]—a utopian notion of memory existing either in the redemptive moment or in modernity's prehistory. For Chang, instead, photographs are constitutive components of memory construction, the remainders of an irrecoverable past, through which the process of remembrance begins.

In Chang's view, through the practice of reading life's "shells," which outlive their original moment in time, one is thereby able to recall the past and retain memory images. Walter Benjamin articulates similar considerations on the problematic of individual memory after surviving his suicide impulse in the early 1930s. In his autobiographical essays written after this life crisis, Benjamin describes the act of remembering as listening into an empty conch shell. Regarding the practice of recollection as listening to a remote yet familiar voice, Benjamin compares the nineteenth century to a conch shell, which "remains now an empty shell in front of me. I hold it upon my ear. What do I hear?"[11] In such moments of reconstitutive memory, a bygone time is conjured up on an acoustic level. A similar *déjà entendu* moment can also be found in Chang's own attempt of remembrance in *Mutual Reflections*. "Not knowing the woe of losing a country, the singsong girl is still singing the decadent *Houtinghua* tune from across the river," recites the four-year-old Chang, standing in front of an old man (12). This is the visual and acoustical image Chang achieves as she reads a photograph taken when she was four. The boundaries of sight and sound are blurred in remembrance.

The photograph in question is the fourth one in the album (11). The image depicts the four-year-old Chang and her niece Niu'er, who is more than fourteen years older than she. Niu'er sits on a chair and Chang in her lap, both of them facing the camera. The original photograph was evidently cropped along silhouettes of the figures and then repositioned against a blank background, and as a result the background of the current picture is now utterly black. This is all we can "literally" read from this picture. Ironically, the accompanying text of this minimalist image extends for two whole pages, though only the first sentence, "I like my eyes full of skepticism when I was four" (10), refers directly to the image in question.

It is precisely this skeptical look in little Chang's eyes that connects the text with the image, and the present with the past. The eyes of the little girl, "the delayed rays of a star,"[12] touch the elderly Eileen Chang in the present as she views the photograph. As she looks back, she sees what those skeptical eyes had seen at that earlier time. The text here is not a reading of the picture *per se*, but rather of what "the skeptical eyes" had themselves seen in the past: an old man seen through the eyes of the four-year-old girl. The man is Chang's uncle Zhang Renjun 張人駿, the last governor of the Liangjiang district of the Qing dynasty. Although no single photograph of Zhang Renjun is available in Chang's volume, she nevertheless vividly conveys a prose picture of him by means of a "visual narrative":[13]

Finally, the servant led me to a small room with better lighting. A tall old man sat in the rattan chair. He seemed to have been sitting there forever. Other than him and the chair, there was no other furniture or decorations in the room [...]. Every time he heard me reciting "Not knowing the woe of losing a country, the sing-song girl is still singing the decadent *Houtinghua* tune from across the river," tears would run down his cheeks.

(10)

Thus, the parallel gazes of Chang as a child and as an adult observer of the photograph function as a bridge or, to borrow Roland Barthes' term, as a figurative umbilical cord,[14] between the past and a present moment.

One of the most intriguing parts of *Mutual Reflections* is Chang's remembrances of her grandparents, especially of her grandmother, the daughter of the legendary Qing statesman and general Li Hongzhang 李鴻章. Her grandmother died long before Chang was born, and it is the photograph that shows her what the grandmother looked like. Chang's reflections on the grandmother's photograph here are also reminiscent of a series of very similar reflections on the part of Siegfried Kracauer: "Is this what grandmother looked like? The photograph, more than sixty years old and already a photograph in the modern sense, depicts her as a young girl of twenty-four."[15] Kracauer uses this question as the starting point for a broader exploration of the nature of photography. He argues that photography is incapable of representing the "actual history" of the original object photographed, precisely because the photograph is inevitably a spatial fixation of a past moment. From this point of view, Kracauer maintains that the grandmother disappears from her photograph before the eyes of the grandchildren only with her traditional costume "remain(ing) alone on the battlefield—an external decoration that has become autonomous."[16]

In Roland Barthes' equally influential work on the nature of photography in *Camera Lucida*, meanwhile, he similarly takes an old photograph of a close family member as his starting point. In the place of Kracauer's grandmother, however, Barthes focuses on a photograph of his mother, and more specifically the famous "Winter Garden" photograph depicting his mother as a five-year-old girl, which ironically is not reproduced directly anywhere in Barthes' book. In his discussion of this image, Barthes emphasizes the temporal dimension of the photograph. He contends that the essence or the *noeme* of the photography is a notion of *ça a été*, "that-has-been":

I call "photographic referent" not the *optionally* real thing to which an image or a sign refers but the *necessarily* real thing which has been placed before the lens, without which there would be no photograph [...] in Photography I can never deny that *the thing has been there*.[17]

In this light, Barthes is able to read the essence of her mother, "the assertion of gentleness"[18] in the picture taken in her childhood. While the grandmother/young girl as a spatial fixation disappears in Kracauer's passage, Barthes recognizes his mother/child as *ça a été*.

Chang's own treatment of this photograph of her grandparents can perhaps be seen as a synthesis of Kracauer's and Barthes' respective approaches. Like Barthes, Chang is fascinated by the illusion of lived presence (*ça a été*) conveyed by these images of her grandparents. On the other hand, Chang's attitude towards these images also appears to reflect an attitude similar to Kracauer's notion of retrospective fetishization. More specifically, it is striking that Chang's remembrances of her grandparents are actually completely imagined. To be sure, all memory is to a certain extent imagined and constructed. What I would like to call attention to in this regard is the fact that Chang's memory of her grandparents is neither her lived experience, nor is it a generational memory recounted by her parents or other family members. Instead, Chang achieves this memory through reading the 1905 historical novel *Niehai hua* 孽海花 (Flowers in a sea of sin), which traces the decline of the Qing dynasty and describes the story of the legendary courtesan Sai Jinhua 賽金花, who allegedly saved China by offering herself to Count Waldersee, the commander of the eight foreign armies during the Boxer Rebellion. More importantly for our purposes here, the novel also contains detailed accounts of Zhang Peilun 張佩綸, Chang's grandfather, and of Li Hongzhang, the father of Chang's grandmother, together with a dramatic account of the romance between Zhang Peilun and Li Hongzhang's daughter.[19]

Therefore, it is from this quasi-fictional account that Chang derives her knowledge and memory images of her own grandparents. They are now no longer merely "a photograph of grandmother and an oil portrait of grandfather" hanging on the wall at the memorial ceremonies (34), and instead have gained life within her memory. Chang treasured the memory of her grandparents so much that she was greatly averse to her aunt's suggestion that "grandma was in fact not willing to marry grandpa" (43). Chang's memory of her grandparents can be seen as an example of what Andreas Huyssen would call an "imagined memory."[20] Huyssen introduces this concept in his exploration of the booming memory culture that has emerged in contemporary Western societies, and uses it to describe those memories that have been "pillaged from the archive and mass-marketed for fast consumption," to which he opposes actual "lived memory." While Huyssen locates this imagined memory within the public sphere of "new information technologies, media politics and fast-paced consumption,"[21] Chang's imagined memory is more individual and rooted within an intimate familial space, though nourished by the public memory depicted in the most popular fiction at that time.

Chang's obsession with this imagined memory is also revealed in the extraordinary attention she devotes to the remembrances of her grandparents.

Mutual Reflections has a total of eighty-six pages, and the section describing her grandparents accounts for twenty of those pages (33–52), or about one-fourth of the entire volume. As she herself describes at the conclusion of that discussion, "They lie quietly in my blood, only to die once again when I die. I love them" (53). We might ask, therefore, why precisely is Chang so obsessed with these images of her grandparents? A close examination of Chang's text suggests that part of the reason lies in the way in which this imaginary memory of her grandparents actually serves to displace her own lived experiences during that same early twentieth century period: namely, her school years, which she refers to as her "awkward age" (54). As we know from her autobiographical essays "Guileless Words of a Child" and "Intimate Words," during this period Chang's mother divorced her father because she could no longer bear his opium-smoking and money-squandering, and she subsequently left China for Europe for the second time. Chang's father was remarried to Sun Yongfan 孫用蕃, the daughter of another distinguished family, and who was also addicted to opium and mistreated Chang. After returning from France in 1936, Chang's mother encouraged her to take the examinations for entering London University. Because her father was not supportive of her applying to college, Chang instead went to live with her mother for two days in order to take the examinations. When her stepmother discovered this, she urged Chang's father to beat her and ground her for half a year. Eventually, Chang managed to escape from her father's house and went to her mother, never to return.[22]

While these traumatic experiences are elaborated in Chang's early autobiographical essays, they are nevertheless mentioned only briefly in this family album that she arranges before her death. Instead, here she foregrounds the imagined memory of her grandparents, whose marriage she is convinced "must have been happy" (44). The rosy stories of the grandparents help to screen her from her own gray experiences: "Then follows the adolescence, long and endless. It is a desolate period. Only the romance of my grandparents is bright and colorful, which appeases me to a great extent. This is the reason why it takes up such an inappropriate space in this book" (88). Here, Chang is remembering to forget, or more specifically, she is remembering her grandparents' story in order to help forget or displace her own spiritual wound.

"Reality in the form of the ruin"[23]: Eileen Chang's photographic representation

Writing about the classic Qing novel *Houlong meng* 紅樓夢 (Dream of the red chamber) in the postscript to her Mandarin translation of the late nineteenth century courtesan novel *Haishang hua liezhuan* 海上花列傳 (Lives of Shanghai flowers), Eileen Chang observes, "in the original eighty chapters of *Dream of the Red Chamber*, there is no single important event. [...] All the important events happen in the last forty chapters. . . . What the first eighty chapters provide is the vivid and close texture of life."[24] If we approach Chang's own life allegorically along the lines of her own textual analysis of her favorite novel, *Dream of the Red Chamber*, we might then ask, How should we treat the "first eighty" and "last forty chapters" of her own life, with the dividing point being the early 1950s, when Chang left China for Hong Kong, and eventually for America?

In this regard, her first husband Hu Lancheng's 胡蘭成 reflection on Li Shutong 李叔同 (1880–1942) can be regarded as one of the most revealing indirect portrayals of Eileen Chang herself. In this discussion, Hu Lancheng observes that one can be a Buddhist monk for the second half of one's life, using the splendor and charm of the first half as nourishment. Like "Master Hongyi" (*Hongyi fashi* 弘一法師), as Li Shutong was known later in life, Eileen Chang lived in seclusion during her years in the United States, working primarily on her research on *Dream of the Red Chamber* and her translation of *Lives of Shanghai Flowers* into both English and Mandarin Chinese. She composed her "last forty chapters" through aesthetic self-fulfillment. While Master Hongyi wrote *Beixing jiaoji* 悲欣交集 (Grief and joy mixed together) as his own epitaph, Eileen Chang finished *Mutual Reflections*, in which her aesthetic of desolation is conspicuously crystallized.

The photograph on page 68 of the volume, which was taken in 1944 when Eileen Chang was arguably at the peak of her literary career, is evidently one of her favorite photos—one which she had selected for both the cover page and the cover design of her essay collection *Written on Water*. In this image, Chang appears wearing her distinctive Qing dynasty-style dress and stands with her back to a wall, leaning so close to the wall that her shadow resembles a ghostly presence bearing down on her from behind. An ominous sense of catastrophe and death haunts this wall, echoing the way in which the wall in her earlier novella *Qingcheng zhilian* 傾城之戀 (Love in a fallen city) connoted both the foundation of civilization as well as its inevitable ruin. "The wall," she wrote in that earlier work, "is cold and coarse, and has the color of death. One day, when our whole civilization has been destroyed, when everything is burnt, burst, utterly collapsed and ruined, this wall might still be there."[25]

In the *Mutual Reflections* self-portrait, meanwhile, Chang's face leans to one side and her eyes appear to stare at something far beyond the frame of the photograph. The figurative umbilical cord in her childhood photographs is missing here. In effect, this is characteristic of most of her photographs since adulthood. The sharp contrast of light and shade between her face and her clothes lends her face a gloomy appearance. How should we read the look on her face? Happy, contemplative, or desolate? Or, perhaps, the countenance portrayed as a pure blank in her self-portrait for the cover page of *Written on Water* would evoke more poignant meanings?

With her face turned toward the past, what is Chang gazing at? It seems as if she might be staring at the ruins of civilization itself. Chang's retrospective gesture here is reminiscent of Benjamin's nearly contemporary discussion, in his "Theses on the Philosophy of History (which, like Chang's *Mutual Reflections*, was the final work Benjamin wrote before his death in 1940), of Paul Klee's "Angelus Novus," whose face remains firmly oriented toward the past even as he is inexorably propelled *backward* into the future.[26] In Benjamin's visual narrative of the angel of history, the angel is caught in a momentary hiatus between the past and the future. In this instant of the *Jetztzeit* (the present moment), the angel is expected to make the tiger's leap, a leap into the open air of history, the messianic redemptive moment.

In Chang's image, however, the massive presence of the wall stands at her back, simultaneously signifying both the ruin of civilization as well as the basis of all human civilizations. At the foot of this wall, as Chang remarks, "in the wilderness of the future, amidst the ruins, the heroine of the *bengbengxi* 蹦蹦戲 [a sort of local opera] survives and lives on peacefully."[27] Accordingly, the moment of the present is also essential for Eileen Chang's cultural and historical conceptions. Nevertheless, Chang's notion of the present is by no means the same as Benjamin's "*Jetztzeit*." While Benjamin emphasizes the sacred or messianic dimension of experience, Eileen Chang instead attempts to capture the meaning of life without necessarily discovering the transcendent within the quotidian. Thus, Chang's aesthetic and historical conception is marked by her profound concern with the ethical and the very materialist base of life. This notion is clearly reflected in the caption she wrote for this particular photograph: "One day, our civilization, whether sublime or superficial, will vanish into the past. However, it is autumn now, [with the weather] as clear as water and as bright as a mirror. I should be happy" (68).

From Eileen Chang's standpoint, therefore, the linkage between the image in a photograph and the object it represents lies not merely in their physical resemblance. Instead, she stresses a special mode of correspondence, a correspondence of non-representational similarity between the photograph and the object it represents, as well as between words and images. What Chang seeks to capture in *Mutual Reflections* is what Benjamin refers to at one point as the legibility and recognizability of the photograph. Alternatively, to borrow one of Chang's own trademark critical terms, we might see her creative goal in this work as lying in a kind of "uneven opposition" (*cenci de duizhao* 參差的對照), which is to say, an allegorical way of seeing. In his study of *Trauerspiel*, the German form of tragedy from the Baroque period, Benjamin notes, "Whereas in the symbol destruction is idealized and the transfigured face of nature is fleetingly revealed in the light of redemption, in allegory the observer is confronted with the *facies hippocratica* of history as a petrified, primordial landscape. Everything about history that, from the very beginning, has been untimely, sorrowful, unsuccessful, is expressed in a face—or rather in a death's head . . . This is the heart of the allegorical way of seeing."[28]

Indeed, instead of constructing a harmonic unity between images or words, what Chang strives to convey is the desolate illumination unleashed in such moments of an uneven correspondence with a crumbling civilization looming large in the historical background. Eileen Chang's imagery is compounded with such a petrified face, or the death's head. The thirty-third picture in *Mutual Reflections* serves as a good example. Taken and colored by her close friend Yanying, this photo shows Chang's head with her eyes looking down. The face is colored in a kind of ghostly green. This color together with the obscure background renders the impression that her head has abruptly intruded from a phantom world into the picture frame. This ghostlike, disquieting intrusion also appears on the cover design of the second edition of *Romances*. It depicts the profile of a modern woman leaning into a window of a boudoir, where a Qing-style dressed lady is playing *gupai* 骨牌 (an old Chinese card game). The intruding woman's head is disproportionately large and her countenance is hidden behind a veil or a mask. According to Chang's description, the head should be light green, indicating a ghostly presence. The disturbing feeling also comes from the fact that the lady in the inner chamber doesn't seem to notice this trespass at all.

This theme is presented even more evocatively in another photograph (Figure 51), which was taken in Chang's apartment in San Francisco in 1961. Later that same year, Eileen Chang went to Hong Kong to write film scripts, out of financial considerations. In this picture, we see the contrast between Chang's head and a big Noh mask. The mask is extraordinarily large compared with Chang's face below it. It seems as if the Noh face was intruding into the room from behind the wall. While Chang's eyes look at the right side, the eyes of the Noh mask are gazing somewhere beyond the frame. The nonchalant atmosphere prevailing in this photo only stresses the notion of death, which the Noh play is preoccupied with.

While Eileen Chang creates an allegorical configuration of visual and verbal representations, portraying reality in the form of the ruin, one also discerns her indulgence in photographic images in this elaborately constructed family album. To be sure, Eileen Chang claimed as one of her aesthetic principles the notion that "the theatricalization of life is not healthy."[29] Ironically, however, she was clearly very fond of theatricality in her own life. From her spectacular clothes to her fascination with photographic seduction, she never grew tired of the theatricalization of life. Also, the photographic seduction plays an important role in transplanting Chang's family album into the massive public space of the contemporary Chinese culture market. Examining Chang's work and the Chang legend in regard to the memory discourse of *fin-de-siècle* China, the last section of this essay attempts to come to terms with the paradox between Chang's self-concealment and her spectacular self-performance, and to explore the formation of the distinct "memory mania" for Eileen Chang in contemporary China.

Memory culture: the photo album as a *lieu de mémoire*

How did Eileen Chang arrange and construct her family album? What has been filtered out? And what has been included? Furthermore, how does *Mutual Reflections*, a family album belonging to the private sphere, enter the public realm and become a fetish of millions of Chang fans and, even more, a cipher for the memorial culture that circulates around Chang herself? At the end of the album, Eileen Chang claims that the only criterion in choosing photographs is whether or not they might be easily lost. Nevertheless, it is clear that other criteria also operate in the collecting process. For instance, photographs of Chang's two husbands, Hu Lancheng and Ferdinand Reyher, are conspicuously absent, as many critics have pointed out.[30] Moreover, except for some pictures from her childhood, there are very few of the sort of every-day life snapshots one would typically expect to find in a family album.

My purpose here is not to pry into "the original intention" of the author, but rather to call attention to the strategies Eileen Chang appropriates in her act of self-representation. To begin with, the organization of the volume follows a basically chronological trajectory from Chang's childhood to her latter decades in the United States. However, with varying length of texts and varying numbers of photographs provided for each life stage, there are different temporalities at stake. Compared to the period of her adolescence, which was long but gloomy, her meteoric career as the most popular and successful writer in fallen Shanghai appears short but joyful. "Then time rushes by, faster and faster" (88). There are only three photographs on six pages for the entire decade of the 1950s, during which she experienced the most tremendous transitions both in Chinese politics and her own life. On the final five pages, she only presents four photographs to cover a time span of thirty-two years in the United States. And, strikingly, all four of these photos were taken in the 1960s. There are neither visual nor verbal descriptions from the remaining quarter-century of her life. As she notes, "the paces are getting faster and faster. A series of montages are followed by a fade-out" (88).

Furthermore, corresponding to the varying paces of representation and textual temporalities, Eileen Chang chooses to emphasize certain self-images. Evidently, the central portion of the album with the densest collection of photographs is dedicated to her career years. Whereas the twenty-page adolescent portion contains only five pictures, there are no less than eighteen pictures for the eighteen-page description of her career years. While the few photos from the 1950s and 1960s are mostly passport photos, the photographs from 1943 to 1945 were taken in photography studios and feature Chang in theatrical poses and wearing idiosyncratic costumes she herself designed. As a result, even before she was fetishized by her readers, she had been rendered herself a fetish by self-staging in front of the camera.

Eileen Chang surely knew the seductive power of visual representation, especially of photography. From the very beginning of her writing career, she was good at mobilizing visual strategies to enhance her visibility and popularity. Her photographs were published along with her writings in the most popular journals of the Occupation period, such as *Tiandi* 天地 (Heaven and earth) and *Zazhi* 雜誌 (Magazine). They appeared on the cover pages of the second edition of her work, *Romances*, and the essay collection *Written on Water*. They flooded Shanghai bookstores and newsstands in the form of posters. Among modern Chinese writers, Eileen Chang is virtually the only one who is famous not only for her literary talent, but also for her dazzling fashion. When she went to the printing house for the proofreading of her essay collection, *Written on Water* wearing her famous Qing dynasty coat, her fashion aroused such a sensation that all the workers stopped their work to admire her dress.[31]

Paradoxically, just as the imagined memory of Chang's grandparents serves as a displacement of her traumatic adolescent years, this exquisitely produced family album implicitly distances Eileen Chang further from her adoring audience, even as it presents some of her most intimate photographs. The flipside of the self-indulgence in photographic imagery is Chang's absolute self-concealment in that Chang virtually vanishes from her own family album. What this volume presents is a desolate yet seductive gesture of refusal and disavowal.[32] With this desolate and spectacular autobiographical photo album, Eileen Chang, half a century after her meteoric literary career, once again positions herself as one of the striking phenomena within the Chinese cultural terrain. In this sense, Yang Ze 楊澤 is correct in observing that *Mutual Reflections* constitutes a "visual memorial ceremony"[33] that the author arranged for herself.

Crown Press spared neither labor nor money in producing this splendid family album. Special stocks of paper were used for the printing, and photography experts were hired to repair the already faded, yellowed, and partially destroyed old photographs, and restore them to the greatest possible clarity and visibility.[34] These photographs, in turn, have been repeatedly reprinted in numerous biographical and scholarly books. From books to periodicals, from television to the internet, the photographs continually seduce readers. The publication of the Mainland edition of *Mutual Reflections* by Huangcheng Press of Guangzhou, which appeared the same year that it was published by Crown Press in Taipei, surely represents the culmination of Eileen Chang craze in Mainland China at the turn of the century.

Moreover, the Eileen Chang craze is part of a larger memory discourse that swept the country during the final decade of the twentieth century. As Dai Jinhua discusses in her essay in this volume, the cultural market has been overwhelmed by various series of volumes of old photographs, mass-marketed old nostalgic fashions, as well as reproduced calendar posters from Shanghai in the Republican period, etc. With old Shanghai functioning as the focal point of Chinese mnemonic scene, Chang has become a figurative *lieu de mémoire* (realm of memory) within the landscape of memory culture in *fin-de-siècle* Mainland China.[35] While the ideological vacuum of Shanghai during the Occupation period gave rise to Chang's literary reputation, *fin-de-siècle* Mainland China witnessed a most successful conspiracy accomplished by the author and the cultural market in the mass marketing of Eileen Chang and her legend.

How should we interpret this phenomenon? What drives the Chang craze in Mainland China, where she had been repressed for nearly half a century? Obviously, the Chang phenomenon is part of a prevalent mnemonic discourse on old Shanghai that has sprung up during the last decade of the twentieth century. Accompanying the economic revival of Shanghai and Yangzi delta, there arose a memory mania focused on the "Paris of the Orient"—the old cosmopolitan Shanghai in its golden age.[36] This memory discourse is focused on a particular region and regional culture, to be sure, but the memory practice doubtlessly sweeps the whole country, "display[ing] a nostalgic cultural penchant/tendency that is extraterritorial and trans-regional."[37] Eileen Chang, whose literary career is inseparable from the specific chronotope of 1940s Shanghai, has always been regarded as representing "the original Shanghai." Therefore, it is not surprising that Chang and her works have been rediscovered and become best-sellers.

However, it would be unwise to dismiss the Chang phenomenon as merely another mass-marketed nostalgic fashion. To begin with, as Andreas Huyssen has pointed out, "there is no pure space outside of commodity culture."[38] Furthermore, even if we say that Eileen Chang has been commodified and her *Mutual Reflections* fetishized as a commodity, we might still ask what is it that distinguishes the Eileen Chang craze from other recent nostalgic waves in China—such as the fascinations with old calendar posters, Shanghai cuisine restaurants, *qipao* dresses, and so on? I would posit that there is something more at stake, something that produces the obsession with Eileen Chang and makes people respond so favorably to the memory markets. A close look at the historical, political, and cultural context of contemporary China will help us understand the Chang obsession better.

With the development of a market economy, contemporary Chinese society has witnessed an unprecedented wave of commercialization and urbanization. Ever since the early 1990s, China has been inexorably involved in the process of globalization. With more and more shopping malls and highways, McDonald's and internet cafes, new lifestyles and changing perceptions of time are deeply permeating the everyday life of urban dwellers. Modernization brings progress and hope, but when people notice the tremendous transformations in their life world, they often find themselves gripped by a profound identity crisis. Eileen Chang's works, which are permeated with a deep sense of *moshi gan* 末世感 (*fin-de-siècle* sensibility), capture this uncertainty and anxiety. More precisely, what "*fin-de-siècle* sensibility" refers to here is a mood of "desolation" in any transitional age going through tremendous transformations. Eileen Chang describes her famous "philosophy of desolation" in her essay, "*Ziji de wenzhang*" 自己的文章 (On my own writings):

In this age, old things are crumbling and new things are growing. People feel that things in their daily lives are just not right—even to the point of terror. They live in this age, but this age is sinking like a shadow, and people feel abandoned.[39]

The *fin-de-siècle* ethos Chang describes here does not necessarily carry the apocalyptic connotations that the concept frequently connotes in the West. In any discussion of the memory culture in China at the turn of the century, one must bear in mind that the Western calendar was not used in China until at most 100 years ago. For contemporary China, therefore, the last *fin-de-siècle* period suggests instead a new beginning, a voyage of hope crossing over the threshold of the century. In fact, it suggests progress, modernization, and catching up with the West.

A second reason for the Chang fever relates to the repressed modernity that has emerged since the 1990s. After the failure of the 1989 democracy movement, the master narratives of revolution and enlightenment which dominated the whole 1980s have come to an end, and society finds itself in a state of "asphyxia and aphasia."[40] The tremendous success of the TV series *Yearning* (*Kewang* 渴望, 1990), which brought together individual memory and collective trauma, normal people and everyday life, suggest a transition from the heroic era of the preceding decades dominated by Maoist ideology to the quotidian era of the 1990s.[41] In the final decade of the twentieth century, there has erupted a strong "yearning" for new discourses and narratives to reflect the tremendously transforming social and cultural configurations.

It is no wonder, therefore, that readers are now turning to Eileen Chang, whose works are characterized by minute and ingenious depictions of modern urban sensibilities and spatio-temporal perceptions in the material daily life. Rey Chow considers Chang's literary world as "the world of details," where "details" are understood as "the sensuous, trivial, and superfluous textual presences that exist in an ambiguous relation with some larger vision such as reform and revolution, which seeks to subordinate them but which is displaced by their surprising returns."[42] Whereas Chow relates Chang's politics of details to issues of femininity and domesticity, Leo Lee extends the significance of this theme in Chang's works to the broader urban world of Shanghai. He argues that "with her details Chang forces our attention to those material 'signifiers' that serve not only to tell a different story about Shanghai's urban life but also to reconfigure the spaces of the city—private and public, small and large—in accordance with her own vision."[43]

With the fracturing of earlier discourses of revolution and enlightenment, a previously repressed modernity, which focuses on the urban sensibility, individual perception, and everyday life, springs up from beneath. Eileen Chang conveys best this expression of repressed modernity. If Shanghai under Japanese occupation, which undercut the dominant discourse of nationalism and enlightenment, provided Chang with the opportunity to emerge on the stage of Chinese modern literature, then the historical and political constellation of the 1990s witnesses a triumphal return of Eileen Chang. And herein lies the historical irony: Eileen Chang, the one who shunned monumentality throughout her life, becomes one of the most monumental of the *lieux de mémoire* in China at the turn of the century.

Notes

1 Ke Ling 柯靈, "*Yaoji Zhang Ailing*" 遙寄張愛玲 (In memory of Eileen Chang), in Zheng Shusen 鄭樹森, ed., *Zhang Ailing de shijie* 張愛玲的世界 (The world of Eileen Chang), (Taipei: Yuncheng, 1989), 3–15.
2 See C. T. Hsia, *A History of Modern Chinese Fiction*, third edition (Bloomington: Indiana University Press, 1999), 389–432.
3 Eileen Chang 張愛玲, *Duizhao ji: kan laozhaoxiangbu* 對照記：看老照相簿 (Mutual reflections: reading old photographs], (Taipei: Huangguan, 1994). Below, citations of this edition will be noted parenthetically within the text. In the same year it was published by Crown Press of Taipei, the Mainland edition of *Mutual Reflections* appeared as one of the nine volumes of *Zhang Ailing wenji* 張愛玲 (Zhang Ailing's collected works) published by Huangcheng Press of Guangzhou. In 1999, *Guangming Daily* press published a new photo album entitled *Chongxian de meigui* 重現的玫瑰 (Re-risen rose). This is an extended edition of *Mutual Reflections* and includes many quotations from Eileen Chang's works and more photographs of Eileen Chang, photographs of Shanghai and Hong Kong, where Chang lived and described in her writings and even photographs of her husbands Hu Lancheng and Ferdinand Reyher, who are absent in *Mutual Reflections*. See, for instance, C. T. Hsia, "*Yi duan kuduoleshao de Zhong Mei yinyuan*" 一段苦多樂少的中美姻緣 (A marriage between a Chinese and an American, which has more bitterness than happiness), in *Shijie ribao* 世界日報 (World daily), April 12, 13, 1996.
4 See Dai Jinhua, "Imagined Nostalgia," in *boundary 2*, vol. 24, no. 3 (fall 1997), 143–163, p. 155.
5 See Lin Shitong 林式同, "*Youyuan shide Zhang Ailing*" 有緣識得張愛玲 (The Eileen Chang I knew), in *Huali yu cangliang: Zhang Ailing jinian wenji* 華麗與蒼涼：張愛玲紀念文集 (Splendor and desolation: commemorative anthology on Eileen Chang) (Taipei: Huangguan, 1996), 9–89.
6 Yang Ze 楊澤, "*Shigu de shaonu: Zhang Ailing chuanqi*" 世故的少女：張愛玲傳奇 (A precocious girl: the legend of Eileen Chang), in Yang Ze, ed., *Yuedu Zhang Ailing: guoji yantaohui lunwenji* 閱讀張愛玲：國際研討會論文集 (Reading Eileen Chang: proceedings from an international conference on Eileen Chang) (Taipei: Maitian, 1999), 9.
7 See her letter to Ping Xintao 平鑫濤, chief editor of Huangguan Press. Included in Peng Shujun 彭樹君, "*Guimei de chuanqi, yongheng de tingge: fang Ping Xingtao tan Zhang Ailing zhuzuo de chuban*" 瑰美的傳奇，永恆的停格：訪平鑫濤談張愛玲著作的出版 (Splendid legend, eternal stop: an interview with Ping Xingtao on the publication of Eileen Chang's works), in *Huali yu cangliang*, 175–187.
8 Eileen Chang, *Lianhuantao* 連環套 (Tales in circle) (Taipei: Huangguan, 1984), 68–69.
9 Siegfried Kracauer, "Photography," in Kracauer, *The Mass Ornament: Weimar Essays*, trans. Thomas Y. Levin (Cambridge: Harvard University Press, 1995), 49.
10 Ibid., 51.

11 Walter Benjamin, "*Die Mummerehlen*," in Benjamin, *Berliner Kindheit um neunzehnhundert* (Berlin childhood around the turn of the century), (Frankfurt a/M: Suhrkamp Verlag, 1987), 59.
12 Susan Sontag, *On Photography*, New York: Farrar, Straus and Giroux, 1977. Cited in Roland Barthes, *Camera Lucida: Reflections on Photograph*, trans. Richard Howard (New York: Hill and Wang, 1981), 80–81.
13 I borrow this term from Marianne Hirsch's discussion of Barthes' *Camera Lucida*. See Marianne Hirsch, *Family Frames: Photography, Narrative and Postmemory*, (Cambridge: Harvard University Press, 1997), especially the introductory chapter, "Family Frames," 1–17.
14 Roland Barthes, *Camera Lucida: Reflections on Photograph*, 81.
15 Siegfried Kracauer, *The Mass Ornament*, 48.
16 Ibid., 14.
17 Barthes, *Camera Lucida*, 76.
18 Ibid., 69.
19 Zhang Peilun and Li Hongzhang are two important political figures in Chinese modern history. Zhang Peilun was the chief commander of Qing navy during the Chinese–French War (1863). Li Hongzhang was the last Prime Minister of the Qing dynasty, who signed the Treaty of Shimonoseki after China lost the first Sino-Japanese War (1895).
20 Andreas Huyssen, "Present Pasts: Media, Politics, Amnesia," in *Public Culture*, vol. 12, no. 1 (winter 2000), 21–38.
21 Ibid., 27.
22 See Eileen Chang, "*Siyu*" 私語 (Intimate words), in Chang, *Liuyan* 流言 (Written on water) (Taipei: Huangguan, 1991).
23 See Walter Benjamin *The Origin of German Tragic Drama*, trans. John Osborne (London: Verso, 1977).
24 Eileen Chang, "Postscript," in Chang, trans., *Haishang huakai, haishang hualuo* 海上花開，海上花落 (Shanghai flowers blooming; Shanghai flowers falling) (Taipei: Huangguan, 1983), 639.
25 Eileen Chang, "*Qingcheng zhilian*" 傾城之戀 (Love in a fallen city), in *Qingcheng zhilian* (Taipei: Huangguan, 1991), 226.
26 Walter Benjamin, "Theses on the Philosophy of History," in *Illuminations*, ed. Hannah Arendt (New York: Schocken Books, 1969), 262.
27 Eileen Chang, "Chuanqi *zaiban zixu*" 傳奇再版自序 (Self-preface to the second edition of *Romances*), in *Zhang Ailing duanpian xiaoshuo ji* 張愛玲短篇小説集 (The collected short stories of Eileen Chang) (Taipei: Huangguan, 1980), 3.
28 Benjamin, *The Origin of German Tragic Drama*, 166.
29 Eileen Chang, "*Tongyan wuji*" 童言無忌 (The guileless words of a child), in *Liuyan*, 12.
30 See, for instance, Hsia, "*Yi duan kuduoleshao de Zhong Mei yinyuan*."
31 See Yu Bin 余彬, *Zhang Ailing zhuan* 張愛玲傳 (Biography of Eileen Chang) (Hainan: Hainan chubanshe, 1993), 165.
32 Yang Ze, "*Shigu de shaonu*," 9.
33 Ibid., 9.
34 Peng Shujun, "*Guimei de chuanqi*," 175–187.
35 Pierre Nora uses this term in his seminal seven-volume work *Les Lieux de mémoire*, which is an attempt to rewrite the history of France in symbolic terms, namely, through constructing and interpreting all the sites of collective heritage, French national symbolism and mythology. This work appears in English translation as *Realms of Memory* (New York: Columbia University Press, 1992) in three volumes.
36 On the nostalgia toward Shanghai, see Dai Jinhua, "Imagined Nostalgia," especially the section "The Emergence of the South," 155–161.

37 Ibid., 158.
38 Huyssen, "Present Pasts," 29.
39 Eileen Chang, *"Ziji de wenzhang"* 自己的文章 (On my own writings), in *Liuyan*. English translation taken from Leo Lee, "Eileen Chang: Romances in a Fallen City," in Leo Lee, *Shanghai Modern: The Flowering of a New Urban Culture in China, 1930–1945* (Cambridge: Harvard University Press, 1999), 282.
40 For a discussion of Chinese culture of the 1990s, see Dai Jinhua 戴錦華, *Yinxing shuxie* 隱形書寫 (Invisible writings) (Nanjing: Jiangsu renmin chubanshe, 1999).
41 See *"Zaidu* Kewang" 再讀「渴望」 (Re-reading *Yearning*), in Dai Jinhua, *Youzai jingzhong* 猶在鏡中 (as if in the mirror) (Beijing: Zhishi chubanshe, 1999), 231–236.
42 Rey Chow, *Woman and Chinese Modernity: The Politics of Reading between West and East* (Minneapolis, Minnesota: University of Minnesota Press, 1991), 85.
43 Leo Lee, *Shanghai Modern*, 271.

Part IV
Gender and desire

11 Popular literature and national representation

The gender and genre politics of *Begonia*

David Der-wei Wang

> The greatest, most long-lasting, and most popular art in China is man impersonating woman.[1]
>
> (Lu Xun, "On Photography")

Thus Lu Xun 魯迅 wrote in an essay in 1928. For the master of the May Fourth enlightenment, female impersonation represents the ultimate oddity in the Chinese practice of gender aesthetics:

> Man and woman are meant to attract each other. Eunuchs are not our concerns in this regard because nobody would fall in love with them; they are de-sexed [...]. Female impersonators, however, come across as being most extraordinary because they don't always let us feel at ease. They appear to be the opposite sex from the perspective of either men or women. Men see in them women and women see in them men. They are thus forever on display behind the windows of photo studios, and in the hearts of the Chinese people.[2]

Lu Xun finds in the Chinese craze for theatrical impersonation an example of decadence, something that threatens to prevent the representational system of modernity. For the master, sexual impersonation causes a confusion in gender roles, thereby obstructing the normal circulation of desire. When man appears to be woman and woman, man, a phantom gender is called forth, an image of something that is neither male nor female. As Lu Xun would interpret it, this phantom Chinese gender constitutes a sexual sham in the sense that cannibals masquerade as civilized, and madmen pretend to be rational.

More intriguing is Lu Xun's contrast of female impersonators to eunuchs. Both are deemed as men who have denied or have been denied manhood. But whereas eunuchs, having lost the capacity to desire, are also ruled out as objects of desire, female impersonators titillate and arouse precisely because of the uncertainty in their sexual identities. At a time when the act of physical castration had passed into history, Lu Xun might well have considered female impersonation as spiritual castration, a second ancient practice that continued to maim Chinese humanity. Indeed, his comment shows that he was startled by the fact that female impersonation could coexist with and blend into modernity. Images of celebrated impersonators were on display as often "in the hearts of the Chinese people" as in "the windows of photo studios." They had left their everlasting imprints in both psychological reflection and its technological reproductions.

Lu Xun above all is worrying about the masculinity of the Chinese national character.[3] He shares with contemporary intelligentsia a yearning for a strong, virile Chinese figure, as opposed to China's old emaciated, feminine image. Lu Xun differs from his contemporaries in that he is capable of looking into the corporeal dimension of the national body politic; sexuality always occupies a prominent place in his investigation of Chinese humanity.[4] For Lu Xun, the breeding of strong, modern Chinese people presupposes love and procreation, which must not be distracted by theatrical tricks of any kind.[5] What bothers him, therefore, is that the ghostly chain of make-believe has not lost its grip on the Chinese imagination. Sexuality might end up in a wayward play of erotic games, indefinitely postponing China's serious commitment to modernity.

In female impersonation is hidden the secret of how modern Chinese watch, and listen to, gender performances. Lu Xun would have to conclude that, whereas Chinese audiences enjoyed watching a man being decapitated in actuality as if it were theater, with an equal passion they viewed a man being symbolically transgendered for the stage as if it were real. Worse, thanks to the advent of modernity, the traditional spectacle of impersonation could now be captured, duplicated, and eternalized in a magic of a photographic snapshot. Thus for Lu Xun photos of female impersonators were displayed and disseminated precisely where the slide show of decapitation, which he claimed to have seen in Japan in 1906, could have been mounted.[6] Lu Xun had tried to embody the maiming of Chinese humanity in the photograph of a beheading, only now to find that the Chinese had retouched the image. There are moments in which the image of a missing head could be confused with that of a missing phallus. Now the act of castration has been prettied up, and a female-male image catches the wayward eye. A nightmarish discovery, indeed. But one question remains. Despite his self-privileged status of watching others watching, Lu Xun cannot distance himself from the circulation of spectral reflections. His critique of the decapitation slide show may not prove any more authentic than his discovery of Chinese theater lovers and their fascination with photos of female impersonators.

Female impersonators are made not only to look and behave like women but also to *sound* like women. They win popularity by being able to sing in high and light registers, comparable to women's. The secret is a male larynx which fails to descend after puberty, thereby keeping the vocal cords closer to the cavities of resonance. Just like the boy singers of Medieval and Renaissance Europe,[7] Chinese female impersonators start vocal training in childhood. But during puberty these boys' larynxes usually descend and thus "break" their high, feminine voices. To forestall this natural mishap, there appeared in eighteenth-century Europe, especially Italy, the custom of creating *castrati*.[8] Boys with a talent for singing were castrated so as to ensure the lasting feminine voice quality. Unlike the European *castrati*, Chinese female impersonators, at least since the late imperial era, did not undertake castration to guarantee their vocal femininity. This fact made their training all the more risky because each boy was gambling against tremendous odds. Few were the number of those who survived the voice-change period and could continue their careers; those who lost their voices ended up in minor theatrical roles or simply left the stage forever.

Theoretically, as a simulation of feminine singing, the parts created for female impersonators could equally be taken up by women. But female impersonators, thanks to their male biological attributes, can cultivate their muscular system and physique in such a way as to form a real sounding box in the service of small-sized vocal cords. Thus when they sing, they can demonstrate a "hybrid" power and plasticity that surpass women's. For Lu Xun, as for like-minded advocates of realism in art, the resonant voices of female impersonators were the product of fakery, and therefore suspect. When May Fourth revolutionaries orchestrated the *call to arms*, there was no place on the score for female impersonators. In their high notes and strident *coloratura* Lu Xun seems to have heard lingering echoes of castrated children. Hence female impersonation is another casualty in his campaign to "save the children."

Not unlike the *castrati*, the female impersonators enjoyed tremendous fame and popularity for their exquisite skill at mimicking women. Thanks to their gender ambiguity, they were often pursued by both male and female fans.[9] Honoré de Balzac's "Sarrasine" (1830), made famous by Roland Barthes in *S/Z*, vividly portraits a murderous romance between a sculptor and a castrato resulting from mistaken gender identity. In the Chinese context, Chen Sen's 陳森 *Pinhua baojian* 品花寶鑒 (A mirror for judging flowers, 1849) provides a panorama of the life of female impersonators and their patrons, thereby inaugurating the late Qing fiction of decadence.[10] Compared with their European counterparts, Chinese female impersonators tend to engender more complex sexual and social disturbances. This is due not only to their low social esteem which, up till the turn of the twentieth century, was comparable to that of the prostitutes, but also to their hidden sexual threat: although they may sound and look like women on stage, these female impersonators are "real" men in reality.

Of all the female impersonators of his time, Lu Xun may have found in Mei Lanfang 梅蘭芳 (1894–1961), the most celebrated male/female star of Beijing opera in modern China, his primary target.[11] In an essay entitled "*Lüelun Mei Lanfang ji qita*" 略論梅蘭芳及其他 (On Mei Lanfang and other issues) published on November 5 and 6, 1934, Lu Xun ridicules Mei's recent overseas tours as a sign not of his rising stardom worldwide but of his decreasing popularity in China.[12] He charges that the way in which Mei's elite patrons refined the female impersonator's art had diminished its inherent earthy vitality. But Lu Xun's most vehement attack is directed against Mei's planned performance in the Soviet Union, the holy land of proletarian revolution. He was exasperated by the fact that an aging female impersonator should entertain revolutionary cadres on behalf of China and that the star should bill his art the "purest presentation of symbolism."[13] For someone like Lu Xun who had been converted to socialist realism long before 1934, symbolism meant the worst kind of art form which employs a game of metaphors to camouflage real problems and avoid real solutions. With circuitous logic, Lu Xun links Mei Lanfang's ill-defined symbolism with the symbolism promoted by Shanghai Neo-Sensationalist writers such as Shi Zhecun 施蟄存 and Du Heng 杜衡, and he insinuates that both forms of symbolism are dangerous because they blur one's judgmental faculties and, worse, misrepresent revolution.[14]

Though aimed at Mei Lanfang and female impersonation, Lu Xun's argument boils down to the question of who was more entitled to represent China on the stage of global politics. Lu Xun was not alone in addressing such questions. As will be discussed below, the issues of nation and impersonation, sexuality and political representation, constitute a peculiar subject for Chinese writers of the revolutionary age. And among these contests for leadership positions, traditional theater and its transvestite dramaturgy are continuously called on, as true or false impersonations of China in the theater of the world.[15]

In what follows I will concentrate on the case of Qin Shouou's 秦瘦鷗 (1908–1994) *Qiuhaitang* 秋海棠 (Begonia, 1943), arguably the most popular Mandarin Ducks and Butterflies novel in the Second Sino-Japanese War era. This novel, about a female impersonator's attempt to become a "real" man, his truncated romance with a warlord patron's concubine, and his tragic death, has been regarded by critics as a mere tearjerker. As such it is a far cry from the formula endorsed by the wartime discourse of national literature—in generic preferences, political alliances, social vision, writing skills, or intended readership. But close reading indicates otherwise. Besides telling a highly entertaining story, *Begonia* won its phenomenal popularity, I argue, because it hit home at its wartime readers' quandaries, especially regarding gender identity. More, insofar as it brings the subject of female impersonation to bear on the question of the Chinese national character, it still serves as a rejoinder to Lu Xun's critique of sexual variability.

Impersonating China

Begonia has enjoyed a dubious position ever since its serialization in Shanghai in 1941. When the novel first appeared on the *Chunqiu* 春秋 (Spring and fall) literary page of the newspaper *Shenbao* 申報, in February 1941, Shanghai had entered its fifth year as a wartime "orphaned island" city. As Japanese troops swept through other parts of China, Shanghai was left "bracketed" thanks to her semi-colonial status. This momentary pause in history gave rise to the city's miraculous prosperity, particularly in the culture industries. The phenomenal success of *Begonia* was a case-in-point for such political circumstances. The novel already had drawn thousands of fans during its ten-month newspaper serialization, and it was an immediate best-seller when the bound edition came out the next year. A stage adaptation won equal popularity in 1943, followed by a *tanci* narrative production and a movie, which also were box office hits.[16] Moreover, the next five decades would hold a continuously warm reception for the novel in various media formats, in Taiwan, in Hong Kong, and on Mainland China. A fictional sequel, *Meibao* 梅寶 (Meibao), by Qin Shouou himself, appeared as late as 1984.

Literary history, however, has given this novel little credit. To mainstream critics, a novel like *Begonia* was negligent for having failed to strike clear patriotic postures during the war. Spanning the twenties through the forties, the novel vividly portrays Chinese warlord brutalities but makes only a brief reference to the war. Qin Shouou may have had good reason to be evasive about the war because, when the first edition of *Begonia* was published in 1942, Shanghai had already fallen into Japanese hands and wartime censorship was strictly enforced. But Qin always insisted that, despite appearances, *Begonia* was actually a patriotic novel. As early as 1944, he did try to tell a story that fell more directly under the heading of wartime literature. He never fully exonerated himself, and the dispute about Qin's conformity to the standards of patriotism has continued to this day.[17]

Can a novel be enrolled in the canon of wartime literature even if it barely touches on Japanese aggression and, more, attributes Chinese misery mostly to the evildoing of Chinese warlords? Prominent political issues aside, a more deep-seated reason for *Begonia*'s suspect position may be that it belonged to the Mandarin Ducks and Butterflies school of fiction. Until recently this genre was deemed inferior to the May Fourth tradition in subject matter, rhetorical register, authorship, and readership,[18] and as such it was presumably incapable of being taken seriously.

My reading, however, suggests that *Begonia* is one of the few wartime novels that transcend the limitations of reportage and propaganda. Although barely referring to the war, it offers a unique perspective from which to view a nation in crisis. Instead of foreign invasions, it focuses on the home front, and instead of the battlefield, it describes life-and-death struggles in a theater. Indeed, the novel's theatrical motif is crucial because among other things it fully situates Qin Shouou's patriotic endeavors. He is a Butterfly writer assuming a May Fourth discursive posture, and, being under Japanese rule, he dresses up patriotic agony as harmless romance. In any case, apart from the tactics of wartime publication, Qin Shouou still leads attentive readers toward a rethinking of the issues of performativity and representation, insofar as readers are ready to undertake a radical reconfiguration of their national identities.

The plot of *Begonia* evolves along with the rise and fall of a Beijing opera singer, from early Republican days to the beginning of the Sino-Japanese war. Its protagonist, Wu Yuqin, first appears as a popular Beijing Opera female impersonator. In Beijing and in Tianjin he draws hundreds of female *and* male fans, including the warlord Yuan Baofan, who is particularly eager to make Wu his "friend." Despite his popularity, Wu is discontented with his female stage role, especially when it results in unsolicited homosexual liaisons off the stage. He wants to be a "real" man of the theater, like his two sworn brothers, one of whom specializes in orthodox male roles from generals to scholars, and the other is good at clowning and acrobatics. Wu escapes Warlord Yuan's approach, only to fall in love with Luo Xiangqi, a girl student recently tricked into becoming a concubine of none other than Warlord Yuan! The opera singer and the concubine lead a clandestine life together, and as a result their baby girl, Meibao, is born. Their relationship is finally exposed, and Warlord Yuan punishes Wu not by killing him but by carving a big cross on his face. Wu's career is ruined.

From such a summary of part one of *Begonia*, one can already discern the Mandarin Ducks and Butterflies style. Qin draws his characters from stereotypes of the old society, relies heavily on melodramatic twists, indulges in sentimentalism, and takes a narrative stance suggestive more of an old-time storyteller than of an enlightened representative of the New Literati. Moreover, the novel shows its indebtedness to at least three strains of late Qing popular narrative: it reminds one of the "wayward" romance (*xiaxie xiaoshuo* 狹邪小説) when depicting illicit affairs and dubious sexual games; of the social exposé (*qianze xiaoshuo* 譴責小説) when lashing out at social absurdities and injustice; and of the chivalric romance (*xiayi xiaoshuo* 俠義小説) when featuring the fraternity and gallantry of sworn brothers in a theatrical setting.

But Qin Shouou differentiates himself from his Late Qing and Butterfly predecessors by grafting his novel onto nationalist discourse. Under his pen the triangle between warlord, Chinese opera actor, and concubine, a stale convention of Butterfly fiction is turned into an allegory of national self-renewal. Qiu Haitang's struggle to become a man is presented in parallel with a growing romantic *and* nationalist consciousness. Nationalism, admittedly, had itself become a literary cliché by the early forties, but it had seldom been so ingeniously packaged in a popular formula as in the case of *Begonia*. This is where Qin Shouou broke new ground. By combining an incredible romantic tearjerker with an equally incredible allegory of political emancipation, Qin Shouou blended the crude and predictable discourse of patriotism with the irresistible and vulgar discourse of sentimentalism, reaching a vast audience that could hardly understand, much less imbibe, the new political consciousness. Thus, *Begonia* demonstrates both an eager approximation of mainstream subjects and a shrewd appropriation of "marketable" vulgarity in service of the new national awareness.

All these arguments hinge on the protagonist Wu Yuqin's pursuit of gender identity. In the novel's beginning, Wu appears already beset by *ressentiment*. For all his stardom as a female impersonator, we are told, Wu is unhappy because he has been made into what he is not. Ever since he was trained to become a female impersonator and assumed the feminine professional name of Yuqin, "he feels as if he had become a woman in spirit." Mischievous fellow actors joke about him, and salacious directors and patrons chase after him, so much so that "he develops a strange mindset, suspecting that he must be a woman by nature."[19] "The female role is not to be sung by men!" sighs Wu one night.[20] Wu's repugnance about his stage identity is further intensified as Warlord Yuan repeatedly propositions him. Meanwhile, he learns more and more about China's crises from a conscientious patron, Yuan Shaowen, who happens to be Warlord Yuan's cousin and an army officer in his own right.

This leads to the first climax of the novel when, at the suggestion of Yuan Shaowen, Wu renames himself Qiu Haitang or Begonia—a flowering plant whose leaves resemble the shape of China. "The map of China is shaped like a Begonia leaf. Japan and the other invaders are just bugs eating the leaf [...]. If these bugs can't be driven away now, they'll soon devour the whole leaf."[21] To express his patriotism, Begonia even draws a painting of a begonia leaf being consumed by insects and has it hung on the wall; he titles it *Chumu jingxin* 觸目驚心 or "eyes open in shock."[22]

The renaming of Begonia triggers a cluster of analogies between the young female impersonator and his nation. Just as Begonia suffers from unfulfilled manhood, so China appears to be a country suffering from frustrated sovereignty. For the newly inspired Begonia, singing female parts on stage can no longer be mere routine performances, any more than a dramatized call on the shared fate between a humiliated man and a humiliated nation. Impersonation helps flesh out the gender and national authenticity in distortion. Begonia's painting becomes relevant here, too. Whereas he has to let his face be made up—painted—into a woman's for the entertainment of the public, Begonia's *own* painting presents a different vision of himself and his nation. The caption of his painting, "eyes open in shock," besides indicating Begonia's personal political awakening, takes on an additional dimension. It insinuates the visual *and* epistemological incongruity between what things seem and what things really are, between Begonia's bewitching stage personality and his agonized patriotic self-awareness.

But there will be an irony in Qin Shouou's treatment of Begonia's struggle *after* he has his stage name changed. Instead of pursuing a new social role, as would have been expected of a formulaic May Fourth hero, Begonia settles for fame and fortune as a female impersonator. Meanwhile he directs his desire somewhere else by falling in love with Warlord Yuan's embittered concubine Luo Xiangqi. Whereas Warlord Yuan wants Begonia because he looks like a gorgeous woman on stage, Luo Xiangqi is charmed by him because he is definitely *not* a woman off stage. More complications ensue. Xiangqi encourages Begonia to cultivate his masculinity, to the point where Begonia sings for her a *xiaosheng* 小生 aria, written for a young man's role, thus consummating their love that night. Begonia capitalizes on his being both man and woman. His profession as an effeminate performer becomes good camouflage for his secret, masculine love affair, and it provides him with the extravagant resources to afford such an affair. Left unattended, ironically enough, is the nationalist cause, which presumably gave Begonia the idea of this new, exciting double life.

A critic like Lu Xun would not have approved of Begonia's way of "becoming a man." The actor's romance at best proves Lu Xun's fear of female impersonation: by playing with his gender ambiguity, Begonia personally embodies the ambiguities in Chinese civilization. And so he acts out Lu Xun's curse that female impersonators are like uncastrated eunuchs. Whereas a eunuch, a man-turned-nonman by reason of castration, is prevented from sexual activity, a female impersonator represents a society in sexual chaos because in his feminine guise he hides a male sexual drive and intentions.

The problem entailed by Begonia's sexual adventure also besets the realist project of mainstream literati and to that extent it can be read against Balzac's "Sarrasine." "Sarrasine" relates the mistaken sexual identity that permits a romance between the sculptor Sarrasine and the pretty soprano La Zambinella. As Barthes argues in *S/Z*, Sarrasine's passion is premised on the presumption of female identity, when La Zambinella is in actuality a castrato. Sarrasine's heart breaks when he discovers La Zambinella's real gender. In despair he cries, "Monster! You who can give life to nothing. For me, you have wiped women from the earth [...]. No more love! I am dead to all pleasure, to every human emotion."[23]

As a castrato, La Zambinella is presumably desexed, yet he was capable of arousing his patrons' desires. In Barthes' view this castrato embodies the seductive signifier par excellence, one bringing society's erotic impulses into play while maintaining the enigma of its origin. Like La Zambinella, Begonia is good at inciting both homosexual and heterosexual fantasies about his female stage image. Begonia can appear more womanly than a "real woman" because he embodies femininity carried to its most exquisite; he excels in being a "surface," ever ready to be encoded and decoded in accord with the "essence" of woman. But he is different from the Italian castrato in that he maintains a biologically intact manhood and that he in fact wants to deny theatrical illusion and return to his originary manhood. Whereas La Zambinella plays with sexual "mythology" so well as to thwart hermeneutic analysis, Begonia strives to undo the spell of his gender masquerade, and he so well resumes his essential masculinity as to father a child (a daughter). Shuffling back and forth between womanhood and manhood, Begonia deepens his society's quandaries, and neither Chinese gender totems and taboos nor Chinese sexual logic and semiotics have been resolved by his new life. Little surprise that, in contrast with La Zambinella, who conveniently vanishes after disillusioning and ruining his admirer, Begonia should bring himself to the brink of destruction.

The private trial of Begonia and Luo Xiangqi at Warlord Yuan's residence best symbolizes this new crisis. Warlord Yuan is outraged by Luo Xiangqi less because she betrayed him than because Begonia turns out to be her seducer—the man he once wanted for himself. On the other hand, for all their adulterous behavior, Begonia and Luo Xiangqi win our sympathy because both are people wronged by a society whose claim to justice and morality is questionable. They are nevertheless to be faulted for their inadequate resistance and naiveté in the face of danger. When homosexual and heterosexual desire, familial and social justice mix, Qin Shouou demonstrates a keen awareness of the conflicting ethical/sexual forces of his time, and he is willing to push the conflict even further. At the suggestion of one of his followers, Warlord Yuan decides not to kill Begonia; he instead prolongs the actor's pain and humiliation by cutting the cross on his face.

A scarred face and a severed head

As a physical trace of wound, a *scar* represents the body's way of simultaneously affirming and denying a certain man-made or accidental injury. The scar is a sign of healing, and sealing, of that which has been unnaturally opened and exposed. But so long as the line of laceration remains, it is a reminder of the moment of violence. Implied in the scar is its corporeal testimony, pointing to the infliction upon the body of intrusion, to the passage of time, and to a contested desire to deny, while revisiting, the scene of violence. Upon the examination of one's scars, memories are brought back and an implicit narrative takes shape.[24]

By the early forties descriptions of wounds and scars had become subjects familiar to modern Chinese readers. I have discussed elsewhere how Lu Xun's obsession with decapitation—the fatal wound that never scars—motivated his inscription of Chinese literary modernity. For Lu Xun, the headless body spews out a maimed national imaginary, and the ontological break with the past is manifested as physical mutilation. Hence the (truncated) origin of modern Chinese literature.[25] I argue that the scarring of Begonia's face contains a somatic allegory no less provocative than the one evoked by Lu Xun from a headless body. Given that Begonia was created to embody China, any violence inflicted on the actor takes on a symbolic dimension as a crime perpetrated upon the nation. Therefore, when Warlord Yuan cuts into Begonia's face, he is not merely behaving like a cuckolded patriarch punishing the seducer of one of his concubines; rather he impresses one more as an imperial autocrat abusing an unfaithful slave. The informed reader understands that Yuan's choice of punishment represents something far more than it appears; among others it reminds one of the ancient penal device *qing* 黥 or inscribing/tattooing signs of criminality on the convict's face.[26] With his sword Yuan reinscribes his power over the actor's body; the scar on Begonia's face is meant to be a permanent reminder not only of his sexual misconduct but also of his social and political vulnerability. Begonia's screams of excruciating pain call upon a primitive fear—one that recognizes that the face, the façade of the soul, is the entry point to power in traditional theater, and losing it, in traditional tyranny, marks the onset of humiliation.

The violation of Begonia, however, may warrant a different reading. For critics in the vein of Lu Xun, Begonia may be excused for his sexual misdemeanor, but is still liable on a larger account, since his problem did start from a matter of face. One needs to rethink the meaning of that scar: the scar is left on the face of Begonia *as a female impersonator*. Begonia's face is a male face that, when properly made up, will be taken for a woman's—a face that tantalizes its audience because it replaces depth, biological or social, with charm. In the eyes of the May Fourth hard-liners, Begonia's face could not evoke any (Roland Barthesian) aesthetic simulacrum but a morally ingrained crisis of representation. As if his stage transvestitism were not dubious enough, Begonia causes more ambiguities when he assumes a cluster of new faces off-stage, as patriot, as lover, as husband, as father, and as Chinese Everyman. It is in this realm of "real life" that Begonia is seen as blurring the distinction between performativity and lived experience.

In his essay *"Lüelun Zhongguo ren de lian"* 略論中國人的臉 (A brief discussion of the Chinese face, 1927), Lu Xun observes that, compared with Westerners and Japanese, Chinese appear to lack something in their faces. What Chinese lack, and what Westerners have, is "a bestial nature" or *shouxing* 獸性. For Lu Xun, this shortage of bestial nature in the Chinese face does not mean that Chinese are more human; instead, it points to the docile and tamed character of a domesticated animal. Cultured by the long tradition, the Chinese face has become so malleable and "obscure" that it betrays the deficiency of the Chinese national character. Lu Xun could not tolerate Chinese people's callous yet gratified facial expressions at the beheading of some nameless compatriot. He also abhorred the way in which "Chinese open their mouths and let their jaws drop way down when marveling at a certain strange incident or a pretty woman."[27] Lu Xun no doubt would have extended his attack to the face of "the pretty woman" had he known it belonged to a man. As already made clear in his criticism of their photos on public display, female impersonators signified, for him, the final degradation of the Chinese face.

Extrapolating this Lu Xunesque logic, one sees in Begonia's "face-off" adventure a double betrayal. When identifying himself with China, Begonia destabilizes rather than strengthens his nation's gender identity. And when diverting his newly gained nationalist sentiment to personal, heterosexual desire, this female impersonator insults nationalism, a sentiment which above all demands that one do away with individual, erotic yearnings in deference to love for one's nation. Insofar as he mixes the art of simulation with reality, Begonia is not an innocent victim. Rather he acts out a familiar malaise of bad faith and as such is as culpable as the Chinese spy in the Russo-Japanese war Lu Xun saw in the controversial slide show in Japan. Where the Chinese spy scouts for foreign armies who make China a parade ground for their cruelties, the female impersonator belies his origins in service of perversions which make the theater a showplace of their temptations.

The last twist of the argument could be this: since Begonia's face is the origin of his seductive power, to dissipate its spell, something as drastic as scarring must be regarded as a necessary evil. Without beauty, Begonia no longer enchants; rather he can live life regardless of appearance, as a "real man." For those who sense the cynicism of such logic, Lu Xun might come to its defense. Rethink his comment on the necessity of decapitation: "the people of a weak and backward country, however strong and healthy they may be, can only serve to be made examples of, or to witness futile spectacles; and it does not really matter how many of them die of illness."[28] For Lu Xun, before the Chinese soul is rehabilitated, the Chinese body will be used as the raw material for decapitations and futile suffering. And, until the Chinese national subjectivity is reformed, a pretty male face—or worse, a strong female sword arm, or worst of all, a person who is neither male nor female, nor both female *and* male—it does not really matter how many of then are slashed, or cut in pieces, by brutish Chinese armies. Lu Xunesque logic can lead (did lead) to most sinister conclusions. Thanks to Warlord Yuan's exquisitely Chinese justice, Begonia is at last forced into the manhood he has always yearned for. Warlord Yuan is thus a fiendish persecutor, secret sharer, and *deus ex machina* all in one!

But one must ask whether the kind of manhood imposed on—carved into —Begonia really brings him this ideal masculinity. It will be recalled that, with his decapitation complex, Lu Xun ended up having trapped his nationalist ontology in a "headless condition," the dichotomy of body and soul bringing him nothing but a bifurcation of the terrible Void of Identity that haunted him. When turning to Begonia's rescue by deformation, one discerns a parallel recapitulation of a lack in the unsatisfactory opposition created to hide it. That is, Begonia's scar does not merely make him a man by cutting off his means of continuing his feminine past; it also incises into his face the symbol of his infamous prior achievements. As will be shown, the female impersonator may (accidentally) restore his masculinity as a result of disfiguration but, paradoxically enough, the scar also emasculates him, depriving him of male pride, if any is left. It injects into Begonia's imagination the haunting idea of lack, or spiritual castration.

The making and unmaking of a male mother

As the story resumes, Begonia, upon seeing his scarred face in the mirror, collapses and almost loses his will to live. No longer presentable on stage and the center of a sex scandal, Begonia can no longer carry on his life in Beijing and Tianjin. Meanwhile Warlord Yuan has detained Luo Xiangqi and is looking for new excuses to track him down and humiliate him. To survive, Begonia decides to take his daughter Meibao and leave the city for good. In the following episodes, we see Begonia returning to his home village, reunited with his peasant brothers, hiding away from curious village folks, and sulking continuously about his fate. When his savings are almost gone, he comes to realize that, for his daughter's sake, he must start life anew. He overcomes his embarrassment and joins his brothers as a farmer. He changes his name again, this time from *Begonia* to the rural *Laosan*, becoming just *Wu the Third*.

For Qin Shouou and his contemporaries, Begonia taking up of the vocation as a peasant constitutes the turning point of his life. As Qin puts it in his preface to the novel, "in the most wretched circumstances Begonia returns to the country, engaging in the task that we Chinese should all be proud of and obliged to—farming."[29] Farming represents for Qin the foundation of Chinese civilization. If theater encapsulates the illusory and decadent nature of city life, agriculture brings one back to the congenial, authentic contact with mother earth. Qin takes pains to describe the trials Begonia undergoes in learning to be a good peasant. Working hard under the sun day after day, the ex-female impersonator becomes tanned and coarse, and his erstwhile effete mannerisms change into those of a rustic countryman. As time passes, "nobody can associate this dark, haggard, middle-aged-looking peasant with the star who charmed every city just a few years ago."[30]

Nevertheless, Begonia's metamorphosis is not complete. He has come to the countryside with his daughter Meibao and, as the narrator keeps reminding us, bringing up Meibao becomes the only goal of his life. In the years that follow, we are told, Begonia undergoes all the hardships to ensure Meibao's good life and education. To his consolation, Meibao grows up to become a pretty, intelligent, and filial daughter. The father and daughter form a unique family and their intimate relationship is the envy of the village folks.

Echoing Qin Shouou's idealization of the Chinese earth, critics have discussed the peaceful days Begonia and Meibao lead in the countryside as a return to the roots of "Chinese everyday life," one underlined by its self-sufficient domestic economy and ethics.[31] What they have ignored is the fact that this idyllic episode may project nothing but Qin's own wartime yearning for an earthy utopia. There are cautionary elements about Begonia's "everyday life." Despite his hard work in the field, Begonia is never an integral part of the village. "Because of constant labor, his physique has become much better than when he was earning tens of thousands of dollars on stage. But compared to other peasants, he is still weak."[32] Nor can he truly forget his scar, which always scares people on first encounter. He is nicknamed by Meibao's mischievous classmates as the grotesque, the ghost, and even the monster. Most important of all, although he is a loving father, he cannot make up for the absence of a woman householder in his home. He tells the village folks that his wife Luo Xiangqi is dead.

We thus come to the key issue of the second part of the novel, about the absent mother. As the narrator tells us, given all the circumstances, Begonia actually has several chances to be reunited with Luo Xiangqi, especially so after Warlord Yuan loses power. But he deliberately bypasses these chances, and later on he even rejects his daughter's request for a mother. Along with Qin Shouou one can conclude that, as someone who has "lost his face," Begonia cannot bring himself to see Luo Xiangqi, the person who truly appreciates his male identity. I suspect that the scarred actor may harbor a deeper motivation. Luo Xiangqi is not only Begonia's lover and common-law wife; insofar as she encouraged the female impersonator to recognize his gender, to become a "born-again" man, she played a spiritual mother role too. This fact adds one more psychological dimension to Begonia's resistance to being reunited with her. His inferiority complex resulting from the scar notwithstanding, Begonia shows an increasing tendency toward self-inflicted loneliness and suffering, as if only through pain and separation could he atone for his love for Xiangqi.[33] The scar materializes Begonia's fixation on his pained severance from Luo Xiangqi, as both his romantic lover and spiritual mother. More paradoxically, only by dwelling on his facial disfiguration and self-disavowal can Begonia sustain his (incomplete) manhood as well as his fantasy for the ideal woman in absence.

As critics have argued repeatedly, the call for motherhood constitutes one of the most important features of modern Chinese literature.[34] What concerns me here is how Meibao's repeated invocation of her missing mother calls forth Begonia's longing for his own lost object of desire, and how, in answering Meibao's need, he quietly transforms his life into a theater by assuming a mother-like role. But the most challenging question remains: can a man be a mother nurturing the new generation of Chinese?

While Begonia is *seen* as the dominant figure throughout the middle part of the novel, the reader sees nevertheless that Meibao's yearning for a mother is the clue to understanding his dominance. As the years continue, Begonia takes care of every detail of Meibao's life, listening to her troubles and making sure that she acquires the best possible education. He acts as if he were determined to act out the mother figure as a way to redeem his incomplete womanhood on stage. Before he was a father, he was in the first place a superb impersonator of feminine roles. Now, performing on the stage of ordinary life, he does not even need makeup or costumes to activate the impersonation. Driven by paternal as well as maternal love for Meibao, he "naturally" acts out a semblance of the "Second Mother." In other words, he renders in reality the simulacrum in which male and female, mothering and fathering, pain and pleasure, interplay.

Qin Shouou puts special emphasis on Begonia's effort at making Meibao accept modern-style education. As costly as it is, Begonia is willing to support his daughter's advancement even at the risk of bankruptcy. The one thing he severely forbids his daughter to learn is Chinese opera, which she nevertheless manages to master in private. Begonia's love, self-sacrifice, and endeavor to find the best possible educational environment for Meibao brings back the Male Mencius Mother created by the early Qing writer Li Yu 李漁 (1601–1689) in "*Nan Mengmu jiaohe sanqian*" 男孟母教合三遷 (A male Mencius's mother educates a son and moves house three times). In that story, the Male Mencius Mother outshines his female peers by defying all adversities and making his male lover's son from the previous heterosexual marriage a first-rate scholar.[35] There exist many differences between Li Yu's and Qin Shouou's attitude toward their protagonists, the most salient being that, whereas Li Yu means to satirize the social mores of heterosexuality and the stereotypes of the perfect mother, Qin Shouou sincerely makes Begonia an enthusiastic parent who supports his daughter's acquisition of the new knowledge. More, it is not all coincidence that both writers put their protagonists' manhood on hold so as to fulfill their maternal commitments. Li Yu's Male Mencius Mother castrates himself to insure "his" widowhood and maternal legitimacy. In the name of taking care of Meibao, Begonia abstains from all women, including even Luo Xiangqi, Meibao's "real" mother.

If his is a story about a Chinese man's search for masculinity, Begonia's demonstration of motherly nature must lead one to insinuate the novel's actual premises. When hundreds and thousands of fathers and sons are marching toward the frontlines, Begonia does his best by staying at home, taking care of his daughter like a true mother. The call for motherhood, it will be re-called, originated with the sentimental strain of May Fourth nationalism and it gained increasing currency during wartime. To safeguard Mother China and eventually to return to her tender embrace became as much a moral imperative as the emotional need to survive hard times. To that extent a novel like *Begonia* amplifies the national imaginary of motherhood. Although masculinity is what the formation of the national subjectivity is all about, it presupposes the continued invocation of, and return to, motherhood, the only form of femininity sanctioned by wartime discourse. (The hundreds and thousands of mothers and daughters were encouraged to stay at home and produce more sons for the frontlines, or if necessary, to work at the frontlines in motherly or other peculiarly feminine occupations.) My point, nevertheless, is that as a Butterfly writer, Qin cannot curb his inherent impulse to melodramatize his version of the motherhood story and that, precisely by making a man a mother-like figure, Qin brings to the fore the sexual and gender complex the May Fourth Mother/China myth tries to suppress. What mainstream discourse fetishizes, Butterfly narrative trans-poses. Qin's interpretation uses a peculiar tactic taken from Butterfly fiction to renegotiate its image of Chinese genres/genders.

Halfway through the novel, the Second Sino-Japanese War breaks out. On the eve of the Japanese takeover of their village, Begonia and Meibao flee to the south. By then Begonia's health has deteriorated as a result of years of hard work and unhappiness. After all the ordeals of refugees, father and daughter arrive in Shanghai, only to meet more frustrations in the urban jungle. At the end of his wits, Begonia finds his way back to the stage, signing on as supporting acrobat, the least paid and most exhausting job in the traditional theater. From female impersonator to male impersonator, Begonia thus completes the circle of theatrical roles.

Mau-sang Ng suggests that, in withstanding bruises, wounds, and harassments from leading actors, Begonia wins back fellow actors' and theater managers' admiration, and he has finally "succeeded, albeit, tragically, in his quest to acquire manliness—the singing of female roles is displaced by the masculinity of doing somersaults."[36] This is an overstatement. Impoverishment, disease, and shame have already consumed the man's dignity; he is buying the last bit of his life in exchange for a little "manliness." He finally collapses on the stage, making a public spectacle of himself.

Now it is Meibao's turn to take care of her father, resorting to her secret talents at singing Chinese opera. As a street singer she makes a little money from one restaurant to another, till she comes across a young customer. The two develop a crush on one another and the young man confides in his aunt, who just happens to be Luo Xiangqi!

The process through which Luo Xiangqi left Warlord Yuan and ended up in Shanghai comes as one long string of clichés. At stake here is how her surprise appearance and reunion with Meibao affects the relation between Begonia and Meibao. All along we have been informed of Meibao's dream to be reunited with her real mother, as opposed to Begonia's reluctance to discover her whereabouts. The return of Luo Xiangqi functions like a precondition for the ending of *Begonia*, not only because it serves as a device to consummate the genre's melodramatic expectations but also because it completes an inherent psychological circle. When Meibao finally sees her mother, it is a moment of fulfillment, one that makes each party's waiting and longing all these years seem worthwhile. From the perspective of the "maternalized" national imaginary we have discussed, the return of the missing mother fulfills the popular desire for a restoration of Mother China, the state of primordial plenitude.

But Begonia has not been brought into this scene of reunion, and his absence creates the final suspense of the novel. We are told that, as mother and daughter reunite, Begonia is dying in a dilapidated attic. He has hidden himself from Xiangqi for almost twenty years. Now, bedridden and penniless, will he see his old beloved one last time? Upon learning of his perilous condition, Xiangqi rushes to Begonia's bed in the hope of bringing him to the hospital. It is too late. Just moments before her and her daughter's arrival, Begonia has ended his life by jumping out of his window.

The death of Begonia saddened thousands of contemporary readers who would rather have seen the novel end in a grand, happy finale. Zhou Shoujuan 周瘦鵑, Qin Shouou's friend and editor-in-chief of the *Shenbao*'s literary supplement in which *Begonia* was serialized, even ventured to write a sequel to resurrect the ill-fated actor after Qin rejected his request to do so. Zhou allegedly wrote the sequel for his three daughters, who were among the vociferously protesting fans.[37] Butterfly fiction, of course, had a long tradition of concluding with the death of its protagonist(s); among the best examples are Xu Zhenya's 徐枕亞 *Yu Lihun* 玉梨魂 (Jade-pear spirit, 1911) and Zhang Henshui's 張恨水 (1895–1967) *Tixiao yinyuan* 啼笑因緣 (Fate in tears and laughter, 1930), two all-time bestsellers. For a genre specializing in sentimentalism, death—especially the untimely death of virtuous characters—was frequently invoked as a device to inspire sighs and tears. What then made the death scene of *Begonia* so controversial?

Qin Shouou actually offered three different versions of Begonia's death. In the 1941 *Shenbao* serialization version, Begonia dies at home moments before the arrival of Luo Xiangqi and Meibao. In the 1944 version, on which this discussion is based, he jumps from his window. In the 1957 version, he returns to the theater despite his frail health and, upon seeing the arrival of his wife and daughter, rushes on stage, only to be fatally wounded by fellow actors playing swordsmen roles. Before he dies, he rants against the evils of the old society and entrusts Meibao to Xiangqi.[38] The last version was no doubt inspired by the new party policy; ironically, its arrangement and rhetoric are so hackneyed that they do read like that of a Butterfly novel— the ordinary kind.

Of the three endings Qin Shouou favored the second one. Deplorable as it is, Begonia's suicide reveals an aspect of his personality hitherto unknown to us. Having been through too many ups and downs in his life, he takes charge of ending his life as if he was still determined to take action in defining his own fate. In view of the actor's lifelong pursuit of beauty in both male and female terms, scholars such as Fan Boqun suggest that Begonia's suicide is an artist's decision because it is the only way by which he can maintain his pride and leave Xiangqi, the primal connoisseur of his art, a lasting memory of his beauty. Moreover, seeing that Meibao has inherited his talents and looks and that Xiangqi will find more solace beholding her daughter, Begonia has another reason to bring his own life, which has been stained by too many ugly things, to closure.[39] By contrast, Qin Shouou's comment holds that the abrupt ending reflects nothing but the Buddhist view of the contingencies of life: Begonia's death is only part and parcel of the unexplainable and unending mutations of humanity.[40] The two interpretations form a conventional dialogue, with one stressing the autonomy of art and beauty and the other inculcating the ephemeral nature of human illusions.

I suggest that Begonia the male mother must excuse himself from the world when the "real" mother returns. Despite his determined search for authentic love, gender, politics, and family ethics, he proves to be most at home when he takes up *roles* on behalf of these goals. The return of Luo Xiangqi reminds Begonia of what he has failed to carry out, as a "real" man, and what he is actually good at, as a female impersonator. This is of course the ultimate dilemma for a novel claiming to redefine Chinese manhood. One can argue that, by jumping from the window to end his own life, Begonia manages an ultimate, unrepeatable affirmation of his right to choose his own life. It is a "final performance," one that terminates all previous ones. But if masculinity constitutes the core of the novel, there must be an irony to see only two women weeping over a man's body at the ending. Begonia tries to do away with his label as an emasculated man most of his life, and he dies an emaciated man.

Farewell, My Concubine

The writing and reading of Butterfly fiction peaked in the mid-thirties and its popularity continued in Japanese-occupied cities during the war. This amazing adaptability, however, became for mainstream critics evidence of a sell-out. In fact, ever since the May Fourth era, Butterfly fiction had become the target of progressive literati for various reasons: its dilettantish posture, its attention to human trivia, or its indulgence in sentimentality. Lu Xun criticized the genre as catering to those with a taste for "talented scoundrels" (*caizi jia liumang* 才子加流氓); Mao Dun called it a literature of feudalism written for petit bourgeois mentalities.[41] Zheng Zhenduo classified Butterfly writers as "whores of letters" (*wenchang* 文娼).[42] Even when Butterfly writers endeavored to cater to mainstream critics by writing about social abuses and national crises, their motives were treated with suspicion and their products were dismissed as nothing but vulgar posturing.[43]

In her study of Butterfly fiction, Rey Chow proposes a different tactic, namely reading from a woman's perspective. Despite the fact that its writers were mostly men and that male readership constituted the major component of its circulation, Chow argues, Butterfly fiction sustains a feminine motivation. Not only does the genre concentrate on the fate of women during a time of change, it also evokes a cultural ambiance (domesticity), narrative structure (fragmentation), and affective responses (tears) attributable to a feminine consciousness. Chow holds that instead of fostering reactionism or decadence, these characteristics provide signs of an alternative Chinese modernity, one that fractures the totalizing premises of Chinese reality and realism. Implied in Butterfly discourse, accordingly, is a "politics of detail" which is in contestation with the grand, monolithic narrative of History and Nation.[44] Chow's approach casts a new look at Butterfly fiction but it does not fully examine the flux of gender effects vis à vis the project of reconstructing national sexuality. To tease out the gender implication of Butterfly fiction, the "woman figure" Chow proposes must be reassessed in terms of the mercurial transaction of woman-in-man and man-in-woman, inter-textually and extra-textually.

With female impersonation as my point of reference, I have read *Begonia* as a text that *lays bare* the gender theatrics of Butterfly fiction. The ambiance of Beijing opera is also suggestive here: as a traditional theater still

popular in early modern times, it actualized bygone morals and manners
on- and off-stage, and therefore captured a social stream that had yet to
break away from convention. This theater epitomized the space that best
accommodates the ambivalent cultural forces and emotive registers—neither
new nor old, both new *and* old—of the Butterfly world. Amid new forms
of performing arts—from cinema to radio and from spoken drama (*huaju*
話劇) to Western-style variety show—Beijing opera secured its own position
by adhering to tradition, however ingeniously maintained. It derives its
modernity from its self-conscious preservation and, more importantly,
simulation, of that which was rapidly disappearing from the world of the
Chinese Republic.[45]

Qin Shouou found in the world of Beijing opera a repertoire of virtues—
from teachings of ethical edification to the wisdom of surviving daily life—
that obviously resonated with those endorsed by Butterfly fiction.[46] But
he could not be unaware that the theater, just like the fictional genre he
inhabited, suffered from a tarnished image in the eyes of modernity-minded
critics. Beneath his chronicles of the joy and sadness of theater life, Qin inserts
a subtext, one that adumbrates the charms and limitations of Butterfly
fiction. The subject matter of his novel, female impersonation, invites such
an allegorical reading. Insofar as it is a "feminine" genre perfected in the
hands of male writers, Butterfly fiction features a textual spectacle not
unlike that of theatrical female impersonation. Both enchant us not because
they are womanly arts as such but because they induce a specular sensation
among the audiences making gender attributes appear to be transferable
artifacts.[47] In vocal terms, both depend on falsetto—a voice with such a
high pitch and refined tonality that it surpasses that of ordinary women—
to cultivate the acoustic aspect of feminine similitude.

For mainstream readers and critics, the visual and vocal artificiality in female
impersonation or in Butterfly fiction threatens to undermine the "effect of
the real"—real man, real woman, real life, real modernity, real politics, real
war—a guilty self-indulgence during the national crisis. Indeed, at a time
when the whole nation was reverberating with battle cries, falsetto, whether
textual or theatrical, was bound to grate and irritate the new establishment.

What Qin Shouou tried to accomplish *with* a novel like *Begonia* is not unlike
what Begonia tries to accomplish *in* the novel: a textual as well as a sexual
rehabilitation of masculinity (and reality). By having Begonia scarred, Qin
Shouou enacts a symbolic surgery of his narrative, as a way to cut open the
surface of the genre and reveal the "dark reality" hidden in it. At the violent
laceration of Begonia's face, an old performing art is torn apart. Defaced
at the same time, by corollary, is the simulacrum brought about by the Butterfly
vision of life.

I have argued, however, that the scar does not reveal reality any more
than conceal it. Begonia accomplishes his most intriguing performance, as
the Second Mother, only after he is denied the privilege of impersonating
woman on stage. The reality Qin Shouou and Begonia pursue best reveals

its "effect" not in Begonia's metamorphosis but in the discrepancy between what he hopes to be and what he becomes. Genuine masculinity, just like genuine femininity, remains an object to be desired and named best in fictional terms.

While Begonia may never be able to grapple with the evasive nature of his identity, his wartime readers must have. Traditional critics hold that they enjoyed the novel merely as an escapade. But along the way they must have sensed that the textual break—and physical scar—dramatized their truncated circumstances in imagining and embodying China. For all the national machine mandating heroism and machismo, most wartime Chinese, especially those who lived in occupied areas such as Shanghai, were keenly aware of their incomplete eligibility to total, virile citizenship and their subjection to changing roles so as to survive Chinese reality. It is in this sense that Begonia "embodies the spirit of Chinese people."

One more comment on the "effect of the real" accomplished by *Begonia*. In an uncanny way it prefigured the political choice of selected female impersonators in real life in the forties. The novel makes a clear reference to Cheng Yanqiu 程硯秋, one of the Four Great Female Impersonators in the Republican era. Cheng won plaudits for his melancholy and repressed tonal interpretation; in fact he is cited in the novel as Begonia's rival before the latter's career was ruined by his scar. Cheng too was celebrated for playing roles of delicate, suffering women in traditional society. Off stage, however, Cheng appears to have been a man of tall and robust physique. After the fall of Beijing, Cheng, like most of his colleagues, kept a low profile under the Japanese and their collaborators. He carried on with his performances, till one day in November of 1941, when he is said to have been harassed by several inspectors at the Beijing railway station, so much so that he lost his temper and scuffled with them. As the story goes, Cheng turned out to be good at martial arts and succeeded in knocking out his adversaries in a matter of seconds.[48] Thus the renowned female impersonator became a chivalric superman for the citizens of Beijing, a fine example of life imitating art. Later in 1943, in protest of the continued Japanese oppression, Cheng Yanqiu quit the stage altogether and took shelter in a suburb of Beijing, where he led a life as a farmer.[49] He thus lived out the fate assigned to his fictive rival, Begonia.

Yet more pertinent was the case of Mei Lanfang, the leading modern Chinese female impersonator and the presumed target of Lu Xun's critique. In 1938, one year after the out break of war, Mei Lanfang brought his troupe and family to Hong Kong and took refuge there after his performance was over. In the following three years he continuously turned down Japanese invitations to return to the stage. Hong Kong fell into Japanese hands after Pearl Harbor, and Mei was again under pressures to cooperate. But in early 1942, Mei Lanfang made a public appearance which shocked both his fans and enemies—he had grown a mustache.[50] With this conspicuous flaunting of a male facial trait, Mei Lanfang gestured farewell to his past as female impersonator, a drastic deed indeed. In a way, his mustache brings to mind Begonia's scar, in that both are bodily signs of a return under duress to ordinary manhood, and that both are redundant signs written on an otherwise impeccable (sur)face of theatrical illusion.

But Mei Lanfang's mustache ultimately became the prop of yet another form of his performance, this time on the stage of life. More than Cheng Yanqiu's demonstration of martial skills and seclusion as a farmer, the mustache of Mei Lanfang represents the ultimate token of the Chinese opera's contribution to the *man*-made campaign of patriotism. In response to national crises, the two female impersonators were willing to let go of their makeup and costumes and reveal their true faces as patriotic men. They were hailed as new symbols of heroism. But compared to the millions of lives tortured and destroyed in the war, to what extent do we see a martial kick, a farmer's image, or a mustache represent the rejuvenated, male national subjectivity? Can it be possible that Mei Lanfang's and Cheng Yanqiu's live stunts constitute no more than part of the repertoire of wartime myths, of which the most important is masculinity lost and regained?

Both Cheng Yanqiu and Mei Lanfang resumed their stage lives after the war, but traces of incurable severance, of historical scars, had been left by the war on their theatrical careers. Thanks to his age and rural life during the war period, Cheng Yanqiu had put on enormous weight, so much so that postwar audience's were often stunned by his over-size stage physique.[51] He was able to charm them nevertheless with his unique voice and stylized acting skills. Mei Lanfang shaved off his mustache on August 15, 1945, the day when China declared victory over Japan, as if the newly won nationalist pride would permit him to resume his professional womanhood. And his performances were as popular as ever, despite obvious signs of age. For their fans, neither age nor weight could matter, and gender was not even an issue. But could such art withstand the hostility of the powerful and the indifference of the young?

Cheng Yanqiu and Mei Lanfang continued to perform after the founding of the new China. While they were respected as popular artists, their art of female impersonation had been abolished from the curriculum. In the new China, men were expected to act like men and women were supposed to act like women. Artists like Cheng and Mei had become national treasures, or more exactly, living antiques. Behind such a rectification of gender roles, however, lay an international subjectivity which was committed to gender simplification and national unity. It was not yet obvious that these resolutions would lead not to *men who are men* and *women who are women* but to a new, *unisex* design, in which both men and women dressed alike, worked alike, thought alike, and, viewed from afar, would be seen to function as one mass. In Xueping Zhong's words, China was a culture suffering from a syndrome of "masculinity besieged."[52] This leads one to observe that a great country can turn a sweeping spectacle of *male* impersonations into an even more astounding carnival of *sexless* impersonations.

Cheng Yanqiu and Mei Lanfang were sworn in as Communist Party members in 1957 and 1959 respectively, perhaps a Party recognition of their gender restorations as much as their political conversions. In their new political circumstances, Mei Lanfang's and Cheng Yanqiu's stage transvestitism, as exquisite as it was, could never be what it had been. They were the last masters of a closed tradition of female impersonation; each performance signals a deeper gap between the new masculine China and the old feminine China. Haunting their poses and songs are the invisible existence of a mustache, a slippage of a manly tone, a scar, carrying the national theater and its two sopranos a step closer to the sexless perfection of old age and death. They did not live long enough to experience the ultimate unification of ancient and modern, theater and criticism, in the period of the Model Operas, or *yangbanxi* 樣板戲, and of Jiang Qing 江青, the premier male impersonator of the new age.

Begonia's scar was not to be the last in Chinese literature. The "scar" can be discerned in the case of Qin Shouou and Butterfly school fiction. Under the banner of History and Revolution, PRC literature demonstrated an impulse unmatched even in Republican days, to place the mark of modernity and purity on every Chinese artifact. So, like most of his fellow Butterfly novelists, Qin Shouou gave up writing and became an editor. A revised version of *Begonia* was published in 1957, with a new ending in which Begonia merely dies from exhaustion on the stage. For a writer who had already rewritten his novel to accommodate Japanese censorship and nationalist propaganda, suppression of creative independence may not have seemed too hard.

But the new regime proved to have a far more efficient machinery for the suppression of creativity than either the Japanese or the nationalists. In 1960, Qin Shouou published an essay in which he denounced the Butterfly school *in toto*. He confesses that

> the greatest defect of Butterfly writings is that they are out of tune with reality and suffer from sentimental whining. Their subjects are mostly fictitious, unable to reflect reality [...]. Writers of the school tend to stress circuitous plotting so as to draw readers' attention. They exaggerate romantic clichés, and often end with a tragedy so as to earn readers' tears.[53]

It was not until 1981, at the encouragement of Ba Jin, that he renewed his writing career. A sequel to *Begonia*, *Meibao*, focusing on Begonia's daughter Meibao's adventure, came out in 1984.[54] The novel, on the vicissitudes of Meibao in pursuit of her career as a Beijing opera singer, might sound as melodramatic as the original. But this is a time when millions of Chinese writers and readers were consuming Scar Literature, or *shanghen wenxue* 傷痕文學, which, though allegedly based on reality, in effect derived its power from melodramatic interpretations of the atrocities of the Cultural Revolution. The truly melodramatic *Meibao* could hardly hope to win the popularity that the profoundly innovative *Begonia* enjoyed.

The most powerful "sequel" to *Begonia*, I argue, is not *Meibao* but *Bawang bieji* 霸王別姬 (Farewell, my concubine), the Hong Kong writer Lillian Lee's 李碧華 best-selling novel from 1985. Much has been said about the novel, and about its movie adaptation by Chen Kaige 陳凱歌 (1992).[55] But an inquiry into its depiction of female impersonation in light of theater history has yet to be done. The novel was inspired by the Chinese opera *Farewell, My Concubine*, which was made popular by none other than Mei Lanfang in 1921.[56] Mei's production was loosely based on the Ming *chuanqi* drama *Qianjin ji* 千金記 (A story of a thousand gold taels), by Shen Cai 沈采, which was in turn derived from an ancient story in the *Shiji* 史記 (Historical records). In this original source, the hegemon king of Chu, Xiang Yu was said to offer a deadly farewell to his favorite concubine Yuji after realizing he had lost the war to Liu Bang of Han. Mei Lanfang successfully switched the story's focus from a chronicle of ambition and defeat into an embittered concubine's deadly goodbye to her beloved—a masculine topic readapted to feminine perspective. What Lillian Lee's novel does is to give the old farewell another twist, a woman writer taking a female impersonator's view of embittered love and finding in it once again a male defeated by history.

For our purposes, the protagonist Cheng Dieyi, the female impersonator who performs through all the periods of modern Chinese history, can be read as a reincarnation of Begonia. Just like Begonia, Cheng Dieyi is sold to a Beijing opera troupe to learn the skills of female impersonation, and he eventually becomes a famous star. But Cheng parts ways with Begonia in his relation to his own identity. He never harbors fervent patriotism and he never resists the flow of events. Most important, when he falls in love, his heart goes to a man rather than a woman. Cheng loves his sworn brother *cum* stage partner Duan Xiaolou, who in his turn loves the prostitute Juxian. Lillian Lee is reticent about Cheng's real sexual orientation. His homosexual passion can be interpreted as resulting either from his environment or from his instincts. In any case, his being a female impersonator is ironically justified, as it predicts his choice of sexual preference.

The entangled relations between Cheng Dieyi and Duan Xiaolou proceed in parallel to the ups and downs of modern Chinese history. The two are at last reunited in Hong Kong in the early eighties, when Duan Xiaolou has become a new immigrant in the colony and Cheng Dieyi is visiting as senior member of a Beijing Opera delegation. Duan had lost his wife during the Cultural Revolution due to Cheng's jealousy and betrayal. Duan's revenge, if there is one, takes place only in a most roundabout way, when he learns that Cheng had been directed after the Revolution to marry a woman. Cheng Dieyi seems to have accepted this fate, too, unlike Begonia four decades before him: he has spent the first half of his life impersonating famous women, and the second part of his life impersonating, ironically, ordinary men.

At a time when impromptu death could become a routine of life, the real drama in *Farewell, My Concubine* is that both Cheng Dieyi and Duan

Xiaolou survive the horrible parade of wars and revolutions. They have killed themselves numerous times staging the opera *Farewell, My Concubine*. As survivors of the life-and-death spectacle of the past, they have persisted, repeatedly bidding farewell to evaporating dreams and desires, a life of useless theatrics. Cheng Dieyi and Duan Xiaolou are last seen bathing together in a misty Shanghai-style bathhouse.

By making her novel echo the historical play, Lillian Lee reopens a theatrical circulation between past and present, reality and the stage, elite culture and popular entertainment, and, of course, man and woman. Unlike her predecessors such as Qin Shouou, however, Lee invokes neither a nationalist agenda nor a Butterfly dream. Instead, she titillates her readers with the changeable identities of her narration, in such a way that she assumes radical posture when depicting a post-Mao politics on the verge of nihilism while she appears no less nonchalant when packaging modern Chinese history as a queer romance.

And most interestingly, in her idiosyncratic retelling of *Farewell, My Concubine*, Lillian Lee bids farewell to Lu Xun, the "hegemon" of modern Chinese literature, and the politics of representation he initiated. "The greatest, most long-lasting, and most popular art in China is man impersonating woman," was the master's bitter condemnation. Where the master pontificated, Lillian Lee invites us to reconsider. Thus, after a century-long search for China's authentic representational gender/genre by predominately male writers, that the story might have another side had to be revealed by a Hong Kong woman writer. In this view, the fate of modern Chinese men and women had never been so powerfully represented as in the universal art of man impersonating woman.

Notes

An earlier version of this essay appeared in *Chinese Literature: Essays, Articles, and Reviews*, Vol. 25 (December 2003), 133–163. I am grateful to CLEAR for granting permission to include the present essay in this volume.

1 Lu Xun, *"Lun zhaoxiang zhilei"* 論照相之類 (On photography), in *Fen* 墳 (Graves), *Lu Xun quanji* 魯迅全集 (Complete works of Lu Xun) (Beijing: Renmin wenxue chubanshe, 1981), 181–190.
2 Ibid.
3 For Lu Xun's contemplation on a new national character, see, for example, Lydia Liu's discussion, *Translingual Practice: Literature, National Culture, and Translated Modernity—China 1900–1937* (Stanford: Stanford University Press, 1995), chapters 2–3.
4 See, for example, Lu Xun's critique of widowhood, in *"Guafu zhuyi"* 寡婦主義 (Widowhood), in *Fen*, reprinted in *Lu Xun quanji*, 1, 262–269. Also see Wang Xiaoming 王曉明, *Wufa zhimian de rensheng: Lu Xun zhuan* 無法直面的人生：魯迅傳 (A life that cannot be faced up to: a biography of Lu Xun) (Taipei: Yeqiang chubanshe, 1992), chapter 6.
5 Lu Xun's own sexual life comes to mind. For more discussion of Lu Xun's critique on Chinese sexuality, see, for example, Wang Xiaoming, *Wufa zhimian de rensheng.*

6 See my essay, "Lu Xun, Shen Congwen, and Decapitation," in Liu Kang and Xiaobing Tang, eds., *Politics, Ideology, and Chinese Literature: Theoretical Interventions and Cultural Critique* (Durham: Duke University Press, 1993), 174–187.

7 For cross-dressing and the "transvestite stage" in Elizabethan theater, see Jonathan Goldberg, *Sodometries: Renaissance Texts, Modern Sexualities* (Stanford: Stanford University Press, 1992), chapter 4. Also see Vern L. Bullough and Bonnie Bulough, *Cross-dressing, Sex, and Gender* (Philadelphia: University of Pennsylvania Press, 1993).

8 For a detailed discussion of the rise and fall of castrati, see, for example, Angus Heriot, *The Castrati in Opera* (New York: Da Capo, 1974); Patrick Barbier, *The World of the Castrati*, trans. Margaret Crosland (London: Souvenir Press, 1996).

9 Barbier, *The World of the Castrati*, 148–158.

10 See my discussion in *Fin-de-siècle Splendor: Repressed Modernities of Late Qing Fiction, 1849–1911* (Stanford: Stanford University Press, 1997), chapter 2.

11 For more information on Mei Lanfang, see, for example, *Yidai zongshi Mei Lanfang* 一代宗師梅蘭芳 (The master of Beijing opera, Mei Lanfang), ed. Mei Shaowu 梅紹武 (Beijing: Beijing chubanshe, 1997); Xu Jichuan 許姬傳 et al., *Zhongguo sida mingdan* 中國四大名旦 (The four great female impersonators in Chinese opera) (Shijiazhuang: Hebei renmin chubanshe, 1990), 1–132.

12 Lu Xun, "*Lüelun Mei Lanfang ji qita*" 略論梅蘭芳及其他 (On Mei Lanfang and other issues), *Lu Xun quanji*, 5, 579–584.

13 Mei Lanfang made the statement on September 8, 1934; quoted from Lu Xun, "*Lüelun Mei Lanfang*," 583.

14 Ibid.

15 Gender, performativity, and sexual politics have been among the issues that concern contemporary Western gender critics. My study may be inspired, by but is not limited to, their dialogues. See, for example, Judith Butler, *Gender Trouble* (New York: Routledge, 1992); Marjorie Garber, *Vested Interest: Cross-Dressing and Cultural Anxiety* (New York: Routledge, 1992); Lesley Ferris, *Crossing the Stage: Controversies on the Stage* (New York: Routledge, 1993); and Sabrina Petra Ramet, ed., *Gender Reversals and Gender Cultures* (New York: Routledge, 1996).

16 *Begonia* was published first in July 1942; its movie copyright was obtained by the famous director Maxu Weibang 馬徐維邦 in August 1942 and the movie was premiered in late December 1943. A stage production based on the novel ran from December 1942 to May 1943, with more than 150 performances. It was followed by other forms of performing arts such as the *tanci* 彈詞 narrative. For the serialization, publication, and reception of *Begonia* see, for example, Fan Boqun 范伯群, *Minguo tongsu xiaoshuo yuanyang hudie pai* 民國通俗小說鴛鴦蝴蝶派 (Mandarin Ducks and Butterfly school: the popular fiction in the Republican China) (Taipei: Guanwen tiandi zazhishe, 1989), 251–168; Fan Boqun, ed., *Zhongguo jinxiandai tongsu wenxueshi* 中國近現代通俗文學史 (A history of popular literature in late Qing and modern China) (Nanjing: Jiangsu jiaoyu chubanshe, 2000), vol. 1, 305–312; Wei Shaochang 魏紹昌, *Wokan yuanyang hudie pai* 我看鴛鴦蝴蝶派 (My view of Mandarin Ducks and Butterflies fiction) (Taipei: Shangwu yinshu guan, 1992), 148–155.

17 See, for example, Fan Boqun's edited book, *Zhongguo jinxiandai tongsu wenxueshi*.

18 For a general survey of the Butterfly school fiction in English, see Perry Link, *Mandarin Ducks and Butterflies: Popular Fiction in Early Twentieth Century Chinese Cities* (Berkeley: University of California Press, 1981). Also see Thomas Bärthelein, "'Mirrors of Transition': Conflicting Images of Society in Change from Popular Chinese Social Novels, 1908 to 1930," *Modern China*, 25, 2 (1999): 204–227.

19 Qin Shouou 秦瘦鷗, *Qiuhaitang* 秋海堂 (Begonia) (Chengdu: Baixin shudian 1945), 2. I wish to thank Dr. Jianhua Chen for locating this precious edition of *Begonia* for my study.

20 Ibid., 4.
21 Ibid., 19.
22 Ibid.
23 Honoré de Balzac, "Sarrasine," Appendix, Roland Barthes, *S/Z* (New York: Hill and Wang, 1973), 252.
24 Odysseus' scar, therefore, is treated as that which motivated the mimetic discourse of Western realist narrative in Auerbach's classic study. See Erich Auerbach, *Mimesis*, trans. Willard R. Trask (Princeton: Princeton University Press, 1953), chapter 1.
25 See my discussion in "Lu Xu, Shen Congwen, and Decapitation."
26 See, for example, Wang Yongkuan's 王永寬 discussion in *Zhongguo gudai kuxing* 中國古代酷刑 (Brutal forms of punishment in ancient China) (Taipei: Yunlong chubanshe, 1991), 93–103.
27 Lu Xun, *"Lüelun Zhongguo ren de lian"* 略論中國人的臉 (A brief discussion of the Chinese face), *Lu Xun quanji*, 3, 413.
28 Lu Xun, preface to *Nahan* 吶喊 (A Call to Arms), in *Selected Stories of Lu Hsun*, trans. Hsien-yi and Gladys Yang, (Beijing: Foreign Language Press, 1981), 3.
29 Qin Shouou, Preface to *Begonia*, 3.
30 Ibid., 176.
31 Mau-sang Ng, "Popular Fiction and the Culture of Everyday Life: A Cultural Analysis of Qin Shouou's *Qiuhaitang*," *Modern China*, 20, 2 (1994): 131–156.
32 I am using Ng's translation, 137.
33 In a way his is already a case verging on masochism, a psychological mechanism which fashions the subjectivity through its self-deprecation and even self-negation. Freudian critics suggest that the masochistic impulse compels the subjectivity to reenact a "theatrics" of loss, above all the deprival of the desired origin, Mother. See Gilles Deleuze, *Coldness and Cruelty*, in "Masochism: Coldness and Cruelty" by Gilles Deleuze and "Venus in Furs" by Leopold von Sacher-Masoch, trans. Jean McNeil (New York: Zone Books, 1989). For a recent application of masochism to modern Chinese literary texts, see, for example, Rey Chow, *Woman and Chinese Modernity*, 123–127; and Xiaobing Tang, *Chinese Modern* (Durham: Duke University Press, 2000), 143–156.
34 Lung-Kee Sun 孫隆基, *Zhongguo wenhua de shenceng jiegou* 中國文化的深層結構 (The deep structure of Chinese culture) (Taipei: Jiegouqun, 1989), and Sun, *Wei duannai de minzu* 未斷奶的民族 (China: a people yet to be weaned) (Taipei: Jiuliu tushu gongsi, 1995), chapters 1–3; Rey Chow, *Woman and Chinese Modernity: The Politics of Reading between West and East* (Minneapolis: University of Minnesota Press, 1990), chapter 4.
35 See Patrick Hanan, *The Chinese Vernacular Story* (Cambridge: Harvard University Press, 1981), 175; Hanan, *The Invention of Li Yu* (Cambridge: Harvard University, 1988), 97–98; and Sophie Volpp, "The Discourse of Male Mother: Li Yu's 'A Male Mencius Mother,'" *positions*, 2, 1 (1994): 113–132.
36 Ng, "Popular Fiction," 139.
37 See Zhou Shoujuan 周瘦鵑, preface to *Xin Qiuhaitang* (Shanghai: Zhengqi shuju, 1949), 1–4.
38 See Fan Boqun, ed., *Zhongguo jinxiandai tongsu wenxueshi*, 310–311; Ng, "Popular Fiction," 152.
39 Fan Boqun, *Minguo tongsu xiaoshuo yuanyang hudie pai*, 255.
40 Qin Shouou, preface to *Qiuhaitang*, 3.
41 Lu Xun, *"Shanghai wenyi zhi yipie"* 上海文藝之一瞥 (A glance at Shanghai literature), in Wei Shaochang, ed., *Yuanyang hudie pai yanjiu ziliao* 鴛鴦蝴蝶派研究資料 (Research materials on Mandarin Ducks and Butterflies fiction) (Hong Kong: Sanlian shudian, 1980), 3; Mao Dun 茅盾, *"Fengjian de xiaoshimin wenyi"* 封建的小市民文藝 (Feudal literature for the petite bourgeoisie), in Wei, *Yuanyang hudie pai yanjiu ziliao*, 25–28.

42 Zheng Zhenduo 鄭振鐸, "*Wenchang*" 文娼 (Whores of letters), in Wei, ed., *Yuanyang hudie pai*, 40.

43 See Qian Xingcun's 錢杏屯 critique of Zhang Henshui's fiction on national crisis, "*Shanghai shibian yu yuanyang hudie pai wenyi*" 上海事變與鴛鴦蝴蝶派 文藝 (The Shanghai Incident and Mandarin Ducks and Butterflies literature), in Wei, *Yuanyang hudie pai yanjiu ziliao*, 53.

44 Chow, *Woman and Chinese Modernity*, chapter 2.

45 Ibid., 85–88.

46 See Ng's discussion, "Popular Fiction," 139–141.

47 Roland Barthes, *Empire of Signs*, Richard Howard, trans. (New York: Hill and Wang, 1983).

48 Xu Jichuan et al., *Zhongguo sida mingdan*, 176–177; Hu Jinzhao 胡金兆, *Cheng Yanqiu* 程硯秋 (Changsha: Hunan wenyi chubanshe, 1987), 124–128.

49 178–179; Hu Jinzhao, 129–134; see also, Ding Bingsui 丁秉鐩, *Qingyi, hualian, xiaochou* 青衣·花臉·小丑 (Gentle women, masculine figures, and clowns) (Taipei: published by the author, 1979), 61.

50 Xu Jichuan et al., *Zhongguo sida mingdan*, 105. Mei Shaowu, ed., *Yidai zongshi Mei Lanfang*, 216.

51 Ding Bingsui, *Qingyi, hualian, xiaochou*, 52.

52 Xueping Zhong, *Masculinity Besieged: Issues of Modernity and Male Subjectivity in Chinese Literature of the Late Twentieth Century* (Durham: Duke University Press, 2000).

53 Ningyuan 寧遠 (Qin Shouou), "*Guanyu yuanyang hudie pai*" 關於鴛鴦蝴蝶派 (On Mandarin Ducks and Butterflies school), *Dagongbao*, Hong Kong, July 20, 1960; quoted from Fan Boqun, *Minguo tongsu xiaoshuo yuanyang hudie pai*, 265.

54 See Qin's afterword to *Meibao* 梅寶 (Meibao) (Shanghai: Shanghai wenhua chubanshe, 1984), 260–261.

55 See, for example, Liao Ping-hui, 廖炳惠 "'*Bawang bieji': xiju yu dianying yishu de jiehe*" 霸王別姬：戲劇與電影藝術的結和 (*Farewell, My Concubine*: a mixture of dramatic and cinematic arts); Cheng Pei-kai 鄭培凱, "'*Bawang bieji' de lishi suixiang*" 霸王別姬的歷史隨想 (Random historical thoughts on *Farewell, My Concubine*), *Dangdai* 當代 (Contemporary), 95 (1994): 70–87; Deborah Tze-lan Sang 桑梓蘭, "*Cheng Dieyi: yige quanshi de qidian*" 程蝶衣：一個詮釋的起點 (Cheng Dieyi: a starting point of an interpretation), *Dangdai*, 96 (1994): 54–73.

56 Xu Jichuan et al., *Zhongguo sida mingdan*, 64.

12 "What sort of thing is sentiment?"

Gifts, love tokens, and material evidence in Jin Yong's novels

Hsiao-hung Chang

Fans of Jin Yong's fiction all know that his novels' addictive appeal lies not only in their depiction of the marvels of the martial-arts world, but also, and even more importantly, in their treatment of romantic attachment. In other words, Jin Yong's skill in writing about romance lies precisely in his insertion of these affairs of the heart into the violent fury of swords and daggers, with the result being that martial arts and romance become equally perilous and soul-stirring narrative paradigms, which mutually reinforce each other in his work.[1]

A central question in Jin Yong's fictional world of martial arts and romance becomes, to borrow a line from a poem by the Yuan dynasty poet Yuan Haowen 元好問, one of "Asking the world, what sort of thing is sentiment, that which is so powerful as to make the lovers promise to be true till death do them part" (問世間，情是何物、直教生死相許). Jin Yong himself quoted and popularized this line in his novels *Shediao yingxiong zhuan* 射雕英雄傳 (Eagle-shooting heroes) and *Shendiao xialü* 神雕俠侶 (Giant eagle and its companion) and I, in turn, will take it as my starting point for rereading these two works.[2] Although easily posed, this question, however, remains difficult to answer. Even though it is merely a rhetorical question, it has nevertheless succeeded in attracting the interest of many critics, who have drawn from fields ranging from folk culture to sexual psychology in their attempts to come to terms with it, earnestly debating the socio-cultural and psychological premises of desire and obsession. In this essay, by contrast, I will return again in a frivolous if not too provoking manner to the original question, "What sort of thing is sentiment?" and use this as an entry point for a "literal" reconsideration of the relationship between "sentiment" and "thing." Rather than embarking on a meta-physical and metaphorical discussion of amorous obsession and infatuation, I propose instead to take the sub-physical material infrastructure of amorous gifts, love tokens, and material evidence, as a point of departure to explore the intertwined relationship of love, fetishism, and martial arts.

This essay's theoretical basis is derived in part from Marcel Mauss' discussion of the logic of the gift in cultural anthropology and Jacques Lacan's psychoanalytical discussion of the "gift of love." Under this structure of "gift theory," I will use Jin Yong's novels *Eagle-shooting Heroes* and *Giant*

Eagle and Its Companion as my primary texts, to pursue a series of theoretical considerations, including: If the term *object* can be used both to refer to a person as well as to a material artifact, then what are the cultural and psychological implications of a process of displacement from a loved one onto a love object? In the alternately intimate and distant relations between subject and object within a love relation, what then is the dialectics of Kristeva's notion of the "abject" (an ejected or purged fragment of the Self) and Lacan's notion of the *objet (petit) a* (an externalized fragment of the Self, or partial object, which comes to function as an object of desire)? Finally, if the "nothingness" of love is really a kind of "no-*thing*ness," then how is the material basis of memory mutually implicated with the exchange of actual objects?

In this essay, I develop these considerations of "sentiment" and "thing" specifically through an examination of six key objects that circulate through those two works: a pair of short swords, an iron spear, a handkerchief embroidered with a pair of mandarin ducks, another handkerchief embroidered with a red flower, a pair of tiny jadeite slippers, and a shirt made out of tree bark. The materiality of the question "What sort of thing is sentiment" effectively traverses the boundaries between life and death, between love and hate, and between history and legend. From martial weapons to embroidered slippers, from spear-fighting techniques to styles of clothing, these various artifacts are precisely the material evidence of gift exchange and social alliances and, even more importantly, they constitute the foundation of both love and fetishistic investment, on the one hand, and of martial-arts narratives, on the other. National enmity and familial hatred, together with the amorous development of young men and women, are all contained within this symbolic economy of the gift.

The *Jingkang* short swords: liminal fetishism and martial-arts narrative

Eagle-Shooting Heroes and its sequel, *Giant Eagle and Its Companion*, are two of Jin Yong's best-known works, and they have provided the inspiration for numerous television series and movies (including Wong Kar-wai's 王家衛 critically acclaimed 1994 film *Ashes of Time* 東邪西毒). The works are set in the late Song dynasty (eleventh to twelfth century), as China was being threatened by the Mongols in the north. While each multi-volume novel is a complex network of intersecting plotlines, in general they revolve around the figures of Guo Jing and Yang Kang, who are the sons of the sworn brothers Guo Xiaotian and Yang Tiexin. Guo Jing figures particularly prominently in *Eagle-shooting Heroes*, and is described as a Han who grew up with the Mongols, but who subsequently declared his support for the Song emperor in resisting the Mongol invasion. The narrative also gives considerable attention to Guo's romance with Huang Rong, the daughter of a powerful martial artist. *Giant Eagle*, meanwhile, takes place about twenty years following the events of *Heroes*, and foregrounds the figure of Yang Guo, together with his romance with his martial-arts instructor, Little Dragon Girl. (There is also a third volume in the trilogy, *The Heavenly Sword and the Dragon Saber* [*Yitian tulong ji* 倚天屠龍記], which is set roughly a century later, but which I do not address in this essay.)

The narratives of these two novels revolve around a pair of short swords and the parallel cycles of revenge and retribution that they each occasion. These swords are both a product of the martial-arts narratives in which they appear, while at the same time being a force that propels those same narratives forward—and in this way they constitute a typical example of the mutual creation and destruction of a "material object" and a "narrative object." As Susan Stewart has noted, narrative can be seen as "a structure of desire, a structure that both invents and distances its object and thereby inscribes again and again the gap between signifier and signified that is the place of generation for the symbolic."[3] These gaps exist between signifier and signified, as well as between narrative and material/objects. The inability of the linguistic signifier to unite directly with the signified or referent is similar to the narrative's own inability to unite with an external material-object. The sense of lack and loss brought upon by this semiotic gap is precisely the power of desire that nostalgia continually inspires linguistic narrative to try to fill this gap.

As for the origins of this particular pair of short swords that provide the impetus for the narrative as a whole, this must be determined from a consideration of the narrative itself. The novel describes how, in the Song dynasty, in the Niujia village in Lin'an prefecture, there lived a pair of sworn brothers, Guo Xiaotian and Yang Tiexin. One snowy night, their respective fates happened to intersect with that of the Taoist Master Qiu Chuji of the Quanzhen sect. Because Guo's wife Li Ping and Yang's wife Bao Xirou were both pregnant at the time, the two families asked Qiu Chuji to come and select names for their unborn children:

> Qiu Chuji sighed softly and decreed, "Brother Guo's child will be called Guo Jing, and Brother Yang's child will be called Yang Kang. Regardless of whether their children turn out to be boys or girls, these names will still be usable." Guo Xiaotian replied, "Good. The Taoist Master's implication is that they not forget the humiliation of the *jingkang* year [i.e., 1126, the first year of the reign of Emperor Qin of the Song Dynasty, and the year in which both Emperor Hui and Emperor Qin were captured by the Jin Army], and they must remember the experience of having our two emperors captured and humiliated by Jin People."
>
> Qiu Chuji replied, "Precisely!" and reached into his coat to pull out two short swords, placing them on the table. The length and shape of these two swords were precisely identical, both being short swords with green leather scabbards, made of black wood with gold inlays. Qiu picked up Yang Tiexin's dagger, and on the handle of one of the swords

he inscribed the name "Guo Jing," and on the other carved the name "Yang Kang."

(Eagle-shooting Heroes, 29)

After Qiu Chuji left, Guo Xiaotian and Yang Tiexin took the inscribed swords and exchanged them, vowing that if they both had sons then they would be brothers, if they both had daughters they would be sisters, and in the event that they should have one son and one daughter, then the two swords would function as a wedding present when the two eventually married.

In this way, Qiu Chuji's pair of short swords entered into a double-layered process of exchange. At one level, the swords are given by Qiu Chuji to Guo and Yang, serving not only as a birth present for their unborn children, but also specifying the children's future identity as students of the martial-arts technique which the swords represent. At the same time, the same swords are also exchanged between the two sworn brothers (who hope to die on the same day of the same month of the same year), thus affirming that their as-yet unborn children would later become brothers, sisters, or spouses. These swords, therefore, are used not only to affirm a bond of sworn brotherhood between Yang Tiexin and Guo Xiaotian, but also to consecrate a marriage. In the case of these short swords, their potential status as a wedding gift does not end when Guo's and Yang's families give birth to the two boys, but rather, after Yang Tiexin's death, his sword (now inscribed with Guo Jing's name) is bequeathed to Yang's adoptive daughter, Mu Nianci. Mu Nianci comes to regard this sword as having a special significance, since it continually reminds her of her adoptive father's arrangements before his death that she be married to Guo Jing.

This use of gifts to reaffirm social bonds inevitably brings to mind Marcel Mauss' discussion of gift exchange in his classic cultural-anthropological study, *The Gift*. In that work, Mauss describes several "pre-capitalist" societies that still use ritualistic exchanges of "gifts" and "countergifts" to reinforce the social ties between giver and receiver. In this way, Mauss suggests, the social identity of the tribe as a whole is grounded on this reciprocity of exchange.[4] The importance of this system of gift exchange lies not only in the fact that it functions as an economic and cultural activity that constitutes an alternative to commodity exchange,[5] but more importantly it lies in the way this exchange of gifts illustrates a fundamental interdependence between objects and people. As Mauss points out, the objects being exchanged each have their own "names, identity, and history," just like people, and they bear witness to the pacts or oaths taken between people. This anthropomorphism of the gift object stands in stark contrast to the way in which capitalist society would postulate an absolute, binary opposition between people and objects. In this way, the practice of gift exchange emphasizes both social reciprocity as well as solidarity, inserting objects into the relationships between people, with the effect being that the circulation of objects becomes coterminous with the circulation of social relations.[6]

These short swords function not only to advance the plot and serve as archetypal gifts in these two novels, but even more importantly they come to function as a kind of "border fetish." I borrow this concept from Patricia Spyer, who describes a border fetish as that which is "neither here nor there, past or future, fully absent or unambiguously present. [T]he notion of a border fetish is meant precisely to foreground the unresolvable oscillations, the restless toing-and-froing, and the cultural, commercial, and political crossings that distinguish fetish formations."[7] Spyer's discussion of this thread of cultural history is inspired in part by her analysis of the circulation of people and objects between Africa and the West, but the concept can also be applied more broadly to the thread linking different cultural histories. Here, I primarily wish to emphasize the way in which the concept of "border fetish" can not only foreground the psychic dynamics of acknowledgment and disavowal, presence and absence, but also point to a different delineation of ambiguous boundaries and flexible subjectivity (obscuring the distinctive boundaries and reducing the sharp opposition between subject and object).

Considered from this perspective, the Jing and Kang swords function as a kind of border fetish, located not only at the actual boundaries between the opposing Song and Jin dynasty troops, but also at the figurative boundaries between history and legend, secular and martial-arts society, as well as between narratives of national royalty and narratives of sentiment. A pair of short swords introduces Master Qiu Chuji, one of the Taoist Masters of the Quanzhen sect (who are historically identifiable), who once visited Genghis Khan of the Western Regions. The same pair, meanwhile, also introduces the legendary seven eccentrics of the Wulin school of Jiangnan (who are purely fictional creations within the textual space of Jin Yong's novel). Both Qiu Chuji and the seven eccentrics agree to give the swords to their apprentices Yang Kang and Guo Jing respectively, in order respectively to have them compete on their behalf. In other words, a single pair of swords penetrates both history as well as legend, representing both the "historical figures" recorded on ancient stele and in historical documents, while at the same time representing the purely fictional seven eccentrics of Jiangnan. In these interstices of history and fiction, there is a mythification of history, but also a historicization of myth and legend. The name *Jing Kang* constitutes an inscription of national hatred onto interpersonal relations, a mutual swaying of ethnic and personal consciousness, in a continual interpenetration of public and private spheres.

From the seven masters of Quanzhen to the seven eccentrics of Jiangnan; from the historical "*jingkang* year" humiliation, to the fictional figures of the characters Guo Jing and Yang Kang—history in these two novels no longer functions merely as the background of knight-errant fiction, and knight-errant fiction is no longer merely an escape from the disorder of worldly history. The border-crossing between history and legend in *Eagle-shooting Heroes* and *Giant Eagle* is materialized in the form of a pair of swords which, when exchanged as gifts, link together the oaths of brotherhood and matrimony, as well as using a border-fetish method to inspire a narrative desire.

The Yang family iron spear: family genealogies and love tokens

To the extent that the Jing and Kang short swords have a fetish-like ability to traverse individual identity, historical periods, as well as relations of vengeance and retribution, then this function is revealed most clearly at the beginning of *Eagle-shooting Heroes*, where the two swords are juxtaposed with the figure of an iron spear. From here, there opens up a circulation of fetish objects functioning as mortuary relics, while at the same time destroying the patriarchal genealogy and serving as the convergence point of affective fetishes.

In *Heroes*, the iron spear comes to function as evidence of one's identity within a patrilinear genealogy of a particular martial-arts sect. This is not because of the spear's actual appearance or value, but rather it is on account of its relation to a specific tradition of spear-fighting techniques. These Yang family techniques (which are passed down only to their sons and not to their daughters, as were family surnames at the time) demonstrate that Yang Tiexin is actually a descendant of the Yang family. One of the distinguishing characteristics of martial-arts novels lies in their thematization of a variety of different kinds of "genealogies"—including both actual family genealogies, as well as figurative "genealogies" of different martial-arts schools or sects. However, there are important differences between the former family genealogies, and the latter sectarian genealogies. In the case of family genealogies, the primary prerequisite for inclusion is simply having or assuming the appropriate surname, and in this way the family surname comes to function as a synecdoche for the entire patrilinear line. However, the fact that Yang Tiexin is surnamed *Yang* is not in itself sufficient evidence that he belongs to the Yang clan. As a result, the family's spear techniques come to assume a synecdochic significance and genealogical status comparable to that of the family surname itself. In addition, aside from their parallel synecdochic status in relationship to the family genealogies, the family surname and the martial-arts techniques nevertheless use quite disparate means to denote the sanguine relationships that underlie them. The surname is, in effect, a metaphor for a blood relation, while martial-arts practice can be seen as a transformation of these blood bonds onto a more abstract notion of a martial-arts school, which is then recoporealized to make it one of the rules and practices of flesh-and-blood existence. This flesh-and-blood existence, in turn, foregrounds martial arts' own proximity to the human body, and in this way becomes a metonymy for an actual blood relationship.

Although the iron spear and short swords in Jin Yong's novels possess characteristics of a "border fetish," their status can also be related to the preceding discussions of the relation between hereditary and sectarian genealogies. However, the initial, sudden appearance of the iron spear in *Eagle-shooting Heroes* also represents the beginning of a new process whereby a material object becomes transformed into bodily memory, and desire itself comes to assume a material form. The novel describes how, after the "striking casualty" incident on a windy and snowy day, Yang Tiexin's wife Bao Xiruo was married to Wanyan Honglie, the sixth Jurchen prince, and this change in her social status from being a mere village wife to being a royal consort, is paralleled by her geographic move from the Niujia village to the royal palace. The "striking casualty" lies not only in the fact that husband and wife are separated and each sent to distant provinces, but more importantly it lies in the attendant splintering of a social system, and the ensuing confusion of interpersonal relations. Bao Xirou's attitude of "not being surprised by casualty," is incarnated in her strategy of the "spatial replication and temporal fixation" function of the fetish, which simultaneously accepts and disavows the attendant separation, fracturing, and transformation.

Bao Xirou commanded the personal guards of the Jurchen palace to travel thousands of miles to her former home in Niujia village. They were to make this special trip in order to bring back all of the personal property from the old residence, including old lamps and worn-out chairs, as well as the iron spear and the ploughshare. During the period of separation following the "striking casualty," these materials were transformed from being objects of collection, to being objects of *re*collection. This reconstruction of sensory perception and sensuous memory is grounded on a displacement of the old home onto the space of the royal harem, but at the same time it also constitutes a juxtaposition of the home and the harem: a simultaneous recognition and negation of a redoubled fetishistic consciousness.

Because of the long eighteen-year separation that was supposed to last forever due to the alleged death of the husband, the scene of Yang Tiexin and Bao Xiruo's reunion is therefore characterized by a distinct sense of Freudian uncanniness—a sense that everything remains frozen in time:

> Yang Tiexin stood in the middle of the room and looked around, and saw a table, stool, counter and bed. It turned out that there was not a single object that was not as he remembered it, and he suddenly felt heart-broken. His eyes reddened, and he couldn't help crying. Wiping his tears with his sleeves, he walked over to the wall and pulled down a rusty iron spear that was hanging there. When he brought it close to take a look, he was able to see that, on the six-inch tip, there were inscribed the characters "Mr. Tiexin Yang." He gently stroked the shaft of the spear, and exclaimed, "The iron spear has rusted. It has been a long time since anyone used it." [...] Yang hung the spear back up on the wall. He then examined a broken plough next to the spear, and remarked, "This ploughshare is broken. Tomorrow I will ask Zhang Mu'er from the Eastern village to come over with some molten iron to fix it." [...]

The consort's legs suddenly became weak, and she fell into a chair, saying, "Who [...] who are you? How [...] how do you know what my husband said the night that he died?"

(*Eagle-shooting Heroes*, 369–370)

When the old couple finally found each other among their old household objects, all temporal memory seemed to have frozen in that ordinary conversation which had taken place on the eve of Yang Tiexin's "death." Bao Xiruo had already given up the palace pavilion with its carved beams and painted rafters, but remained fetishistically attached to assorted pieces of furniture, such as tables, chairs, each of which had the power to call up memories of the past, leading her to reminisce tearfully about years gone by. In their reunion, the broken plough share still had not been fixed, though the iron spear inscribed with the characters *Mr. Tiexin Yang* had already rusted over. Temporality finally invaded this frozen instant; even Yang Tiexin's own body had already suffered the ravages of time.

In *Eagle-shooting Heroes* there is another incident that develops this theme of the fetishization of the iron spear even more explicitly, wherein it is presented in terms of the materialization of the sensory perception and sensuous memory of abandoned objects. The incident in question involves Bao Xiruo's relationship with the iron spear, as seen through the eyes of Qiu Chuji:

Last night I went to visit the palace. I wanted to see with my own eyes what was the use of all of these old artifacts that [Wanyan Honglie] had brought in from far away. After my visit, I could not help but feel angry and upset, because it turned out that brother Yang's wife, Mrs. Bao, had already been promoted to the position of high-ranking royal consort. I was furious, and attempted to kill her with a thrust of my sword. But when I saw her standing there in the middle of the room, caressing brother Yang's iron spear, and crying deep into the night, I realized that she had actually not forgotten her deceased husband, and therefore was not entirely lacking in feelings of lamentation. For this reason, I decided to spare her life.

(441)

The reason why Bao Xiruo was able to avoid being killed was precisely on account of her deep feelings, and her refusal to love the Jurchen prince, Wanyan Honglie, instead remaining devoted to her "former" husband Yang Tiexin. As evidence of this devotion, she is described as continually "caressing Brother Yang's iron spear, and crying deep into the night." This act of "caressing" an old object belonging to the deceased also appears in the description of Wanyan Honglie after the death of Bao Xiruo. This time, it was through Huang Rong's eyes that Wanyan Honglie appeared in Bao Xiruo's chamber recalling his beloved:

Huang Rong saw the light come in through the small crack, and when she looked more carefully, she only saw a moth flying around a candle, soon plunging into the flame. Its wings were immediately scorched, causing it to fall to the table. Wanyan Honglie picked up the moth, and could not help thinking, "If my wife Bao were here, she could surely find some way to heal you." From his chest pocket he pulled out a small silver knife and a small medicinal vial, and gently fondled them.

(954–955)

The silver knife and the medicine vial were both objects belonging to Bao Xiruo, and more importantly they are objects that she used to save Wanyan Honglie's life when they first met nineteen years earlier. These forms of intimate contact between people and objects, including Bao Xiruo's "fondling" of the iron spear and Wanyan Honglie's "fondling" of the silver knife and medicinal vial, can be contrasted with Qiu Chuji's and Huang Rong's own acts of visually observing these respective scenes from a distance, and in this way illustrate the differences between distance and proximity, between tactile and visual perception. Furthermore, this contrast also foregrounds the degree to which the material basis of the act of remembering fetishized and vestigial objects necessarily lies outside of visual representation, together with the way in which this act of tactile caressing comes to constitute its own form of sensory perception.

Just as Marx famously described fetishism as "the religion of sensuous desire," similarly human sensibility is also located within a material dialectic between sensuous perception and external objects: the senses make it possible for people to feel pain and suffering, and therefore to be controlled by Others and other objects. Meanwhile, the mutual interpenetration of materiality and reality, of memory and desire, is also at the heart of Henri Bergson's argument, in *Matter and Memory*, that if memory is a kind of a "nexus of mind and matter," then this so-called "matter" is located ambivalently between the material object and its representation.[8] As Judith Butler has observed, the English word "matter" carries connotations of both "materiality" as well as of "significance," and therefore can function as both the fantastic superstructure of reality, and as the material infrastructure of fantasy.[9]

The mandarin-ducks handkerchief: tokens of love and evidence of revenge

In the preceding discussions of the spear and swords, we moved from a consideration of the social bonds of gift exchange, to one of relics of the dead and of mortuary edicts. Although this may illustrate the fetishization of weaponry within martial-arts novels, it is perhaps less directly relevant to the libidinal fetishism of our original question of "What sort of thing is sentiment?" Therefore, the following discussion will switch from lethal weapon to the secrecy and intimacy associated with the circulation of various love tokens associated with the physical body, including brocade handkerchiefs and embroidered slippers. In this way, we will consider the multiple interactions between loves and love objects.

One of the key tokens of affection permeating both *Eagle-shooting Heroes* and *Giant Eagle and Its Companion* is a handkerchief embroidered with a pair of mandarin ducks. The novel describes how, at one point, the entire Wang Chongyang sect went to the kingdom of Dali to study martial arts, while the junior fellow apprentice Zhou Botong and Consort Liu stayed in the rear palace practicing a form of martial arts involving the touching of vital points on the body. In this way, they repeatedly came into close physical contact, and gradually began to develop feelings for each other, which in turn precipitated a major calamity. When their love affair came to light, Wang Chongyang tied up Zhou Botong and brought him before Emperor Duan to apologize and accept his punishment. However, Emperor Duan was obsessed with the study of martial arts, and therefore concerned more with brotherhood rather than female beauty; so he was willing to hand over Consort Liu as a gift, but Zhou Botong was determined not to accept the gesture. The memory of this event remained engraved in Emperor Duan's heart after he gave up the secular world and imperial power, and became the Zen Master Yideng:

> Master Yideng did not really mind, and continued, "When brother Zhou heard of my decision, he just shook his head. I, however, got even more angry, and said, 'If you love her, then why do you insist that you don't want to accept her? In the case that you really didn't love her, then why would you need to do this kind of thing? Although our nation of Dali is small, do you imagine that we would permit you to come in and humiliate us like this?' Brother Zhou stood there silently for a moment, and then abruptly fell to his knees and loudly kowtowed toward me several times, saying, 'Emperor Duan, regardless of whether or not it was I who made this unforgivable mistake, if you should kill me, then it would certainly be justified, and I would not dare raise a finger in my own defense.' I would never have expected him to act like that, and for a moment was completely speechless, before finally asking him in astonishment, 'How could I kill you?' He replied, 'If not, then I'll have to leave!' He then pulled a handkerchief out of his breast pocket, and handed it to Consort Liu, saying, 'Here, I'm returning this to you.' She laughed sadly, but refused to accept it. Brother Zhou let his hand drop, and the handkerchief then fell to the ground next to my feet. He remained silent, and then stalked out of the palace. He would remain away for more than ten years, and no one ever heard from him again."

(1219–1220)

In this kind of situation, in which homosocial male loyalty is stronger than heterosexual affection, we not only see Zhou Botong's act of "terminating affection" by attempting to return the brocade handkerchief, but more importantly we see his act of "terminating affection" with respect to the male homosocial bonds within this martial-arts culture, in which "brothers are like hands and feet, while wives are like mere clothing." Consort Liu is not only heartbroken by the fact that her lover throws her handkerchief to the ground, but furthermore she is devastated at the prospect of being exchanged back and forth between her sweetheart and the emperor like a mere object.

Ironically, after Zhou Botong ran away,[10] Consort Liu immediately fainted, and Emperor Duan therefore retrieved the brocade handkerchief from where it had fallen beside his feet. He saw that the handkerchief was embroidered with an image of mandarin ducks playing in water, accompanied by a Song dynasty poem entitled "The nine looms," of which the fourth stanza, or "loom," reads,

> The ducks were merely embroidered, but they were about to fly off together. It's a pity that they are still young but their hair has turned out to be white and gray. In spring waves, around green grass, in the depth of morning chill, the ducks bathed their red weathers face-to-face [...].

In this way, the object which served to bind Consort Liu's and Zhou Botong's affections came to be perceived by Emperor Duan, who also happened to constitute the third party in this love triangle. It is therefore precisely this moment of feelings of jealousy, remorse, and deep attachment for a material object that truly represents the dramatic climax of the complication of affection.

The intersection of image and text in this love object was largely the result of the way in which the figure of mandarin ducks connotes conjugal bliss. Furthermore, the line, "The ducks were merely embroidered, and they were about to fly off together" effectively encapsulates the spirit of all love tokens, not so much because its evocation of the familiar allegorical tradition of linking mandarin ducks and conjugal fidelity, but because this line contains a subtle implication at the level of the temporality of its verbs. More specifically, there is a hiatus between the first verb phrase, "were merely embroidered," and the second one, "about to fly off together." Between the past and future tenses of these two verb phrases, there lies "an instant which becomes an eternity." A fetish resembles a form of necrophilia, a mummification of desire, comparable to the instant intervening between a flash of lightning in the sky and the ensuing burst of flame on the ground. This instant, in turn, may then be abstracted into poetry and painting, thus allowing love to become eternal. The so-called "mutual promise of life and death" does not necessarily consist in literally slitting one's own throat for a beautiful woman or in dying for love and going to the underworld, but rather the love object per se can be seen as an intrinsic quality of the fetish itself, as well as a form of death which has become frozen into a perpetual stasis. Therefore, the beauty of the line "about to fly off together" lies precisely in the fact that "death" itself has been embroidered onto this pair of mandarin ducks, from which we may thereby grasp the eternity of "desiring" to fly.

The fetishistic freezing of image and text in the brocade handkerchief was also implicated in the processes of exchange and circulation by which the handkerchief comes to function as a "gift of love." According to Lacanian psychoanalysis, love itself can be seen as a kind of gift, one that uses processes of idealization and sublimation to increase the value of the person being loved. In this way, the loved one is gradually transformed from mere mortal, to abstract ideal, an impossible "non-object" of desire. The gift is thereby able to erase all of the subject's anxieties about emptiness, lack, and loss, making him or her appear to return to the period of imaginary plenitude prior to the separation from the mother.[11]

There are two levels at which we may understand the implications of this brocade handkerchief's becoming a "gift of love." On the one hand, the handkerchief functions as a metonymy for Consort Liu's heart/mind and body, both of which had been given to her idealized lover, Zhou Botong. On the other hand, there is an even more complex process of displacement and substitution between the figures of Zhou Botong and the handkerchief. Drawing on two Chinese terms that may both be translated as *object* in English, we may see Zhou as the "object" (*keti* 客體) of Liu's desire, in the sense that he represents the end point towards which that desire is directed, while the handkerchief functions as the "object" (*wujian* 物件) of her desire, in the sense that it is literally a physical, material object. In this way, the satisfactory fantasy produced during love between two individuals, I and Thou, negates the sense of lack and loss which they might otherwise feel, but when the beloved disappears or is separated from the subject, the (material) object of desire gradually comes to replace it by assuming the status of the love fetish. Accordingly, the subject is able to deny the attendant feeling of separation and loss by fixating his or her affection on the love fetish. Consort Liu embroidered the handkerchief with her own hands, and had originally hoped that Zhou Botong would wear it next to his body, thus negating the distance between them. After Zhou's disappearance, however, the handkerchief was returned to Consort Liu, and in the process becomes a concrete material emblem for their former vows of love, which otherwise only existed in their blurred and indistinct memories.

The figure of the handkerchief in both *Eagle-shooting Heroes* and *Giant Eagle* not only has romantic connotations, but also comes to connote the melancholia resulting from the loss of a child. After Zhou Botong's departure, for instance, Consort Liu gave birth to a son, and one day this son was attacked by a masked assassin. Emperor Duan originally wanted to try and heal him, but he hesitated because he was reluctant to use up his vital energy before an impending duel at Mt. Hua. However, Consort Liu's mournful pleadings succeeded in arousing his compassion:

> When she saw that I had agreed to heal him, she was so happy that she fainted. I first revived her by pressing her womb to stimulate her circulation, after which I unfastened the infant's swaddling clothes, in order to give him special massage. Who could have known that when I unfastened the swaddling clothes I would inadvertently reveal the infant's belly cloth. What I saw made me freeze in my tracks and took my voice away, was that on the belly cloth there were embroidered a pair of mandarin ducks, and next to them was stitched the lyric poem *Sizhang ji* 四張機 [The fourth loom]. As it turned out, this belly cloth was made out of the embroidered handkerchief that Zhou had returned to her so many years before.
>
> (*Eagle-shooting Heroes*, 1225)

The brocade handkerchief was originally a material token of love, and had now been made into the swaddling clothes of the child who was, in effect, the living token of that same love. While the handkerchief had originally signified a deep and intense love, in the eyes of Emperor Duan, however, it became merely evidence of an illicit affair and an illegitimate child, neither of which he was able to forgive. In an instant, Consort Liu's hair went gray from anxiety, and in desperation she stabbed the infant in the heart with her dagger in order to put it out of its misery. Furthermore, she swore that she would later use that same dagger to stab Emperor Duan himself in the heart.

As it turned out, Consort Liu (now going by the name Aunt Ying) came back ten years later to avenge the death of her child, and one of the introduction gifts that she gave to Master Yideng was that same infant's belly cloth made out of the brocade handkerchief: "The brocade had already turned yellow, but the resplendent pair of embroidered mandarin ducks still looked like new. Between the ducks there was a knife-hole, and the cloth was blackened with old blood-stains." The yellowed brocade traces the passage of time, whereas the resplendent mandarin ducks represent the frozen time of love. At the same time, this token of love also became material evidence for future retribution. What the knife hole and blood-stains between the two mandarin ducks testified to was the tragedy by which Emperor Duan broke off his love with Consort Liu in a fit of jealousy, and thereby forced her to murder her own child. These memories of love and hatred were all embodied by this handkerchief/belly cloth. For more than ten years, Consort Liu had used this handkerchief to keep the past close at hand, and in this sense it came to function as a token of absent love, bringing together the mutually opposed senses of distance and intimacy, and of separation and reassembly. At the same time, it was continuously permeated with feelings of hatred. The brocade handkerchief therefore gradually uses the materiality of its mandarin ducks image and inscription, together with its knife hole and bloodstains, to signify an attempt to resist forgetting.

The safflower handkerchief: the intersection of excorporative and incorporative love

If it can be said that the mandarin-ducks handkerchief exemplifies the nexus of hatred and desire linking Aunt Ying, Emperor Duan, and Zhou Botong, then there is another brocade handkerchief, this one embroidered with red safflowers, which similarly emblematizes the emotional turmoil associated with another love triangle. While the first handkerchief is embroidered with a pair of mandarin ducks roosting and sleeping together, this latter handkerchief is stitched with a red safflower with green leaves that mutually console and support each other. Both of these are objects which the lovers create and exchange in order to subsequently embroider them, bestow them, and wear them against their skin, in an attempt to express mutual affection without speaking. However, the way in which the brocade handkerchiefs progress from signifying love to signifying hate, turns out to be the reminder/remainder of the chilly hatred at the time, which one prefers not to recall.

In *Giant Eagle*, the witch Li Mochou becomes infatuated with the young knight-errant, Lu Zhanyuan. After Lu married another woman by the name of He Yuanjun, Li Mochou crashed Lu's wedding and made numerous threats, subsequently vowing to come and seek revenge. Sixteen years later, although Lu Zhanyuan had already passed away and his wife had also committed suicide to accompany her husband, Li Mochou nevertheless remained steadfast in her determination to exact revenge by bringing ruin to the entire Lu family. One night, the soft sound of Li Mochou's voice rang out, singing, "I ask the world, what sort of thing is sentiment, which makes the lovers promise each other life and death?" But before Li could kill Lu Zhanyuan's younger brother, Lu Dingyuan, she repeatedly hesitated, and was ultimately unable to go through with it:

> Li Mochou saw that Lu Dingyuan's martial arts skill was mediocre, and consisted only of pulling out his knife and kicking with his feet. When she turned around and found herself right next to him, however, she discovered that he was identical to Lu Zhanyuan, as she remembered him. She suddenly became disconsolate, and wanted to gaze at him some more. However, if she were to kill him, then she would never again be able to observe the "knife technique of the Jiangnan Lu family."
>
> (*Giant Eagle*, 32)

The witch Li Mochou, with her advanced martial-arts abilities and her evil ways, normally wouldn't have hesitated at the thought of killing someone, but now she would love to gaze at the "knife technique of the Jiangnan Lu family" and becomes so sentimental she cannot control herself. In watching that knife technique, she became quite nostalgic for the departed Lu Zhanyuan. What really sparked Li Mochou's nostalgia, and caused her to release Lu Dingyuan, however, was the brocade handkerchief that Lu Zhanyuan had given to Dingyuan when he was dying, and which Dingyuan had given to his niece Cheng Ying but the ripped into two pieces by Wu's wife—with one half being given to Cheng Ying and the other to Lu's daughter Lu Wushang.[12]

This particular handkerchief was one that Li Mochou had painstakingly embroidered herself, and had then given to her beloved Lu Zhanyuan as a token of her affection. Li Mochou used the Kingdom of Dali's most famous red datura flower to express herself, and capitalized on the near-homophonic coincidence of the word *green* [*lü*] and Zhanyuan's surname *Lu*, to have the green leaves signify her beloved, Lu Zhanyuan. In this way, her gesture and Consort Liu's earlier use of the brocade handkerchief with the image of the mandarin ducks, can be seen as two mutually independent but parallel techniques.

For Li Mochou, the most painful part of emotional attachment lay in its ability to make one "lose face"—falling from its creation of narcissistic self-love, to the desolation of looking in the mirror and lamenting one's lot. The novel continually describes Li Mochou as being a remarkable woman, with "beautiful eyes casting amorous glances, and peach-like cheeks with a pleasant glow," and having "bright pupils, white teeth, and light-colored skin." But after falling out of love, she is described as having "lost face" as if she had been psychologically and physically damaged by a facial disfigurement, and therefore deliberately destroyed all of her beautiful brocade and embroidery. If "excorporative" love relationships consist of trading oneself "out" without regrets, in the form of objects such as the safflower-embroidered brocade handkerchiefs without any regrets, then narcissistic, "incorporative" love relationships would use the safflower handkerchief to create a kind of illusory, specular relationship. In the latter case, the brocade handkerchief functions as a kind of "enchanted mirror" and, in the eyes of an infatuated lover, the woman in front of the mirror appears as an incomparably beautiful maiden. After their love sours, however, both she and the mirror are destroyed, and he comes to despise everything.

Therefore, the psychological breakdown of the safflower handkerchief occurs precisely as Li Mochou is forced to gaze at her own beautiful image in the mirror, but in the process is also surprised to catch a glimpse of herself as a destroyed and cast-off object. What the "red flowers and green leaves" of the handkerchief connote, therefore, is precisely both the idealized *objet a*, and Li's own "abject" experience of having been cast off. Therefore, the handkerchief momentarily preserves Cheng Ying's and Lu Wushuang's Lu family lives, yet it does not allow Li Mochou to show mercy to the two girls:

> Yang Guo once again pulled two halves of the brocade handkerchiefs from his chest pocket, and laid them out on the bedside table, saying, "Please take these away together!" Li Mochou suddenly changed expression, and with a flick of her wrist, she tossed them away. Cheng Ying and Lu Wushuang stared at each other for a second, both of them blushing furiously—because neither of them expected that the other had given their respective handkerchiefs to Yang Guo, and furthermore that he would take them both out in front of them […].
>
> Suddenly, Li Mochou ripped the handkerchiefs into four pieces, exclaiming, "What is past is past, so why must we continue to speak of it?" She continued ripping them with both hands, tossing the fragments into the air. The fragments of the handkerchiefs fluttered down like pear blossoms.
>
> (*Giant Eagle*, 599)

At this point, the two halves of the handkerchief have already been figuratively reinscribed with a new significance, as Cheng Ying and Lu Wushuang had each given their respective halves to Yang Guo, while at the same time attempting to keep this a secret from each other. Naturally, they felt so deeply about this that they would each prefer to die in order to allow Yang Guo to remain at peace. The love token that Li Mochou had originally given to Lu Zhanyuan has now become a figurative love letter that the two cousins simultaneously, and without prior consultation, used to entrust their hearts. But, as with the psychoanalytic distinction between the Lacanian *objet (petit) a* and Kristeva's notion of the "abject," is it not the handkerchief's status as an ephemeral vestige of the past, invested in the corpse-like quality of these love tokens, precisely that which ultimately causes the restless Li Mochou to rip it up?

The jadeite slipper: stealing hearts and stealing objects

The previous two sections have developed a close reading of the two brocade handkerchiefs that come to function as love tokens in the novels. In this section, I focus instead on another object that stands in a position of even greater proximity to the human body—namely, a pair of embroidered slippers. Brocade handkerchiefs are made for a loved one, and they use poems and images to affirm the sentimental bonds between the giver and receiver. Embroidered slippers—full of bodily secretions, excretions, and odors—occupy an even more overtly sexualized imaginary space. The following discussion will start from the figure of the embroidered slipper, to consider the fortuitous conjunction of the themes of stealing hearts and stealing objects, at the level of the gift. People who have lost their hearts find themselves driven to distraction, while people who have lost objects find themselves panic-stricken. An embroidered slipper, however, is able to traverse in the plot arrangement the excitement of competing for a bride, on the one hand, and the brutality of killing someone to preserve a secret, on the other. These slippers may therefore function both as a gift accompanying the marrying off of a daughter (*jianü* 嫁女), or as incriminating evidence (*jiahuo* 嫁禍).

Yang Tiexin (now going by the name Mu Yi) carried his adopted daughter Mu Nianci with him everywhere he goes, holding competitions to find her a spouse. Concerned merely with the fact that his daughter still wore her hair pinned up (signifying that she remained unmarried), he didn't necessarily aspire for the future groom to be rich, and merely hoped that he might be a young man whose martial-arts skills were greater than average. Anyone able to defeat Mu Nianci herself in hand-to-hand battle, he decided, would be allowed to have her hand in marriage. However, one day Yang Tiexin's son, Yang Kang (now known as the young prince Wanyan Kang) rode by on his horse, but failed to recognize Yang Tiexin as his father. Because he was feeling playful, he therefore agreed to take part in the competition. Initially he was a little careless, and allowed half of his brocade sleeve to be ripped off by Mu Nianci. Then, he grabbed Mu Nianci's wrist, and hugged her to his chest:

> [Mu Nianci] became anxious, and landed a flying kick to [Yang Kang's] temple, to show him that he must release her hand. The young man relaxed his right arm and lifted his hand, and then grabbed the right foot with which she was kicking him. The technique he used was one by which he was able to grab any appendage he wanted. The girl became even more anxious, and used all her strength to kick him, with which the safflower-embroidered slipper flying off her foot. In the end she managed to struggle out of his grasp, and then proceeded to sit on the ground and hang her head in shame, grasping her white socks. That young man began to laugh, and raised the slipper up to his nose to smell it.
>
> (*Eagle-shooting Heroes*, 286)

Although he won the competition, Wanyan Kang [Yang Kang] then put his brocade robe back on, placed the slipper in his breast pocket, and prepared to leave. He not only refused Mu Yi's [Yang Tiexin's] offer of marriage, but also refused to return the slipper. Everyone was shocked by his audacious behavior, and even Guo Jing, who happened to be a bystander, exhorted him to return the slipper, and then he himself proceeded to struggle with Wanyan Kang.

Regardless of how this struggle for love shifted from marital concerns to martial ones, this love token of the embroidered slipper functioned as an important catalyst for Mu Nianci's and Yang Kang's sinful destiny. Under everyone's watchful eye on the martial-arts platform, they looked like a couple of jade figures kickboxing: "The onlookers could only see the young man strolling throughout the arena, his brocade cape glittering in the light. That young woman weaving back and forth to dodge his blows, her red shirt and crimson skirt appearing to be transformed into a cloud of red smoke." What is interesting, however, is that during the competition, the objects that they each accidentally seized from each other's bodies (namely, a torn sleeve and an embroidered slipper), were precisely the same objects that would later become fetishistic tokens of their mutual affection. Furthermore, the figure of the slipper has deeper cultural and sexual connotations than do the handkerchiefs discussed in the preceding two sections. In psychoanalytic terms, for instance, shoes are one of Freud's most notorious examples of sexual fetishes (and, curiously enough, in his article on "Fetishism," Freud specifically stresses the example of Chinese women's bound feet). Furthermore, in a Chinese context, the Chinese word for *shoes* (*xie* 鞋) is homophonous with the words for *harmony* (*xie* 諧) and *togetherness* (*xie* 偕) and therefore shoes are frequently given as wedding gifts by the groom's family to the bride's, to serve as auspicious objects homophonously connoting the process of "growing old together" (*tongxie daolao* 同偕到老).

However, the sexual transaction foregrounded by this martial and marital competition consists not only of the embroidered slipper that Yang Kang took away as a trophy, because the true trophy of this competition is, of course, Mu Nianci herself, in the sense that whoever defeats her would in turn "win" her. By this reasoning, we naturally read the slippers as functioning as "love tokens" between Yang Kang and Mu Nianci—a reading that can be broadened to consider Mu Nianci herself as functioning as a "female token" being exchanged between Yang Tiexin and Yang Kang (despite the fact that, as father and son, Yang Tiexin and Yang Kang theoretically did not need to form an additional surrogate kinship relationship).

I began this essay with a consideration of Mauss' theory of the gift, together with the social relationships and emotional ties that are established when these gifts are exchanged. The first person to expand on Mauss' theory was none other than the anthropologist Claude Lévi-Strauss, whose *Elementary Structure of Kinship* took Mauss' theory of the exchange of material gifts, and extended it to the question of gender relations, illustrating how the relationships between different patrilines is grounded on the exogamic exchange of women.

In other words, we may see that that which Yang Tiexin was trying to obtain through this love duel was not lifelong happiness for his adoptive daughter, but rather his true objective was to search for his old friend Guo Xiaotian's son (Guo Jing), or some other person capable of helping him avenge his earlier humiliation. Meanwhile, the reason why Yang selected his adoptive daughter Mu Nianci to function as the "gift," was precisely in order to help establish a social bond between himself and the other man. However, the "object" being exchanged had her own perspective on these events, and she not only gives Huang Rong the inheritance left behind by her adoptive father (that is to say, the short sword with Guo Jing's name inscribed on it), but furthermore continues searching for her own beloved, and every night is spellbound watching the shadows from outside Yang Kang's window.

When Mu Nianci first opened her eyes to love, some of this tender affection remained attached to the material objects of her affection. Meanwhile, when Huang Rong saw her talking to herself and driven to distraction, she could not help but be surprised:

> Even upon hearing the faint sound of the wind in the room, her eyes would narrow to a slit, but she only saw Mu Nianci pacing back and forth in front of the *kang*, and realized that it was a false alarm. It turned out that what she had thought was an embroidered handkerchief on her shoulder was, in fact, only a ripped sleeve. She suddenly had an epiphany, saying, "This is the piece she ripped from his brocade cape that day when she and the young prince were dueling." But seeing that Mu Nianci had a smile on her lips, she realized that she was thinking back to that scene. Every now and then she would kick out her foot, and after a brief pause she would thrust out her fist. Sometimes she would raise her eyebrows and her clothes would appear to float, just like Wanyan Kang's frivolous but at the same time arrogant attitude. She remained intoxicated like this for quite a while, walking toward the edge of the *kang*.
>
> (*Eagle-shooting Heroes*, 502–503)

The embroidered handkerchief is like the torn sleeve, and from it one can return to that scene on the martial-arts platform. Only, this time, Mu Nianci herself played both roles, being simultaneously the bold suitor, as well as the bashful object of his pursuit. In wearing her lover's clothes, Mu thereby figuratively *becomes* that lover, and continues sentimentally boxing with herself. This fetishized sleeve becomes a crucial prop on this stage of love, allowing her to act it out as if it were real.

Yang Kang was profoundly moved by Mu Nianci's sincerity, and he himself soon became as muddled as she, prattling on and on about love:

> Wanyan Kang [Yang Kang] followed her with his eyes as she climbed the wall and left, after which he merely stared blankly into space. But when he saw the wind licking the tops of the trees and the countless stars in the sky, he then returned to his room, and even though the tears on the iron spear were not yet dry, and her fragrance continued to linger on her pillow and quilt, in retrospect it nevertheless seemed like a mere dream. He saw the fine strands of hair on the quilt, which she had left during their earlier struggle. Wanyan Kang picked them up, and placed them in a small pouch.
>
> (*Eagle-Shooting Heroes*, 507)

This intimacy with Mu Nianci gave Yang Kang an intoxicating rush, and the iron spear no longer represented a site of struggle between recognizing and forgetting one's ancestors and genealogy, but rather became a material object stained with the tears of his lover, to be placed with the pillow and quilt that still retained her fragrance. As for the strands of hair that he had placed in the pouch, they also function as an erotic fetish.[13] With his soul captivated by love, he was completely entranced by these objects taken from the body of his lover. He was not only able to see her through these objects, but furthermore he was able to touch her through touching them. Just as when Yang Kang found himself in trouble, he instructed Mu Nianci to engrave the words "Wanyan Kang is in difficulty, and he is on the West bank of Tai Lake, Returning-to-Cloud Village" on his belt and go to seek help. During this time of crisis, Mu Nianci continually caressed his belt, and began to fantasize:

> Thinking that it had not been long since this gold belt was still wrapped around [Yang Kang's] waist, she could merely hope that he was still all right, and would be able to wear this belt on his own body once again. More importantly, she hoped that he would remain principled and remember their vows of fidelity, and that she would be able to form marital ties, and place this belt on his body with her own hands. After thinking obsessively along these lines, she proceeded to place the belt inside her own clothes, and could not help but feel a wrenching of her heart, thinking, "Wearing this belt is as if he were embracing my waist with his own arms." She blushed for a second, and then didn't dare think more about this matter.
>
> (*Eagle-shooting Heroes*, 537–538)

Both the act of wearing a lover's clothes and putting on his belt can be seen as an amorous yearning, as well as a corporal interaction. The material aspect of amorous fantasies and the phantasmatic aspect of material objects are always already mutually intertwined.

But, no matter whether the objects in question are embroidered shoes, shirtsleeves, locks of hair, or belts, they are all unable to reverse the rough and rugged path of Mu Nianci's and Yang Kang's love. Because the two of them had once used a pair of embroidered slippers to vie for each other's love and to make their vows of fidelity, they therefore decided to have a commemorative pair of jade slippers made. But later, in a situation involving the tactic of pinning a murder onto someone else, these slippers became a crucial element in solving a crime. The crime in question involves Yang Kang's and his martial-arts master Ouyang Feng's plan to kill the Five Eccentrics of Jiangnan, and take their corpses to the tomb of the deceased wife of Huang Rong's father, Master Huang. There, they intended to arrange their corpses to make it appear as if they were five grave-robbers, and in this way they hoped to have Guo Jing and Master Huang become enemies, thus spelling disaster for Huang Rong and those close to her. But the crucial clue that ultimately resulted in the solving of the case, was the fact that when one of the eccentrics, the quick-handed scholar Zhu Cong, died, he did so grasping to his chest a tiny jadeite slipper with two characters embroidered on it (which he had grabbed from Yang Kang before he died). Fortunately, Huang Rong was very wise, and was therefore able to guess that this was a token that Mu Nianci and Yang Kang had once used to declare their eternal love, and in this way she was able to solve the murder.

When viewed from a psychoanalytic perspective, these acts of openly taking and secretively stealing are extremely revealing:

> So-called kleptomania is often traceable to the fact that a child feels injured or neglected in respect to proofs of love [...]. It procures a substitute pleasure for the lost pleasure, and at the same time takes revenge on those who have caused the supposed injustice. Psychoanalysis shows that in the unconscious of our patients there exist the same impulses to take forcible possession of the "gift" which has not been received.[14]

Here, however, we don't need to use psychoanalysis as an all-purpose hermeneutic model, but instead we may return ironically to Mauss' theory of the gift for further insight into this logic of exchange. According to Mary Douglas' introduction to Mauss' book "No Free Gift," only a gift which has been purloined from that ambiguous region between private and public space may be accepted without having to be returned.[15] As a "pure" and "free" gift, it does not produce a relationship of mutual indebtedness, nor a future exchange in return (this stands as a counterexample to the old saying that there is no free lunch). More interestingly, is not the "gift" that Zhu Cong steals from Yang Kang, precisely the figurative love letter previously exchanged between Yang Kang and Mu Nianci, as well as the "material evidence" that Huang Rong later uses to solve the murder? The jadeite slippers, therefore, served alternately as gifts, letters, and material evidence—for love, to frame someone, as well as evidence of a murder. From the perspective of fetish theory, this approach allows us to see the acts of stealing hearts and stealing objects as having similarly ambivalent connotations.

The tree-bark shirt: tombstone of heartbreak and sartorial memory

In the final section of this essay, I will pursue further this issue of the fetishistic and nostalgic dimensions of clothing, by considering an instance of sartorial memory, whereby clothing mediates not only between object and fantasy, but also between life and death. In *Giant Eagle*, Yang Guo and his martial-arts instructor Little Dragon Girl (Yang Guo called her *Aunt*) were sometimes together and sometimes apart, but even when they were separated, their hearts nevertheless remained closely intertwined. After they separated at the tomb at Zhongnan Mountain, Yang Guo set off to wander through the martial-arts world of the *jianghu*. He was not only practicing martial arts that he had learned from Little Dragon Girl, but furthermore was also wearing clothing sewn by her. Clothing necessarily grows old with time, especially in the eyes of Cheng Ying, who remained secretly in love with

Yang Guo. Therefore, she stayed up late at night sewing a finely stitched green robe for him to wear. However, when Li Mochou's Taoist robe was accidentally burned up, leaving her with only tattered clothes, Yang Guo generously gave her his new "outer layer" robe sewn by Cheng Ying, but still kept the old worn-out "inner layer" robe bestowed by Little Dragon Girl. It was in this way that Yang Guo's and Little Dragon Girl's secret use of clothing as a token of love was finally uncovered. Later, Little Dragon Girl and Yang Guo were reunited, and when Yang Guo's old robe was ripped in a fight, Little Dragon Girl immediately pulled a sewing purse out of her breast pocket and proceeded to use a pair of scissors to cut a strip of white cloth from her own gown, which she then used to mend Yang Guo's robe: "When the two of them were in Ancient Tomb and Yang Guo's clothing was torn, Dragon Girl pulled him to her like this, and mended it for him. Who knows how many times this has happened over the years" (*Giant Eagle*, 716).

Later, when Yang Guo fought with Gongsun Zhi, the demonic father of Gongsun Lü'e, in an alligator pit, this old and tattered robe that had been mended countless times was used by Yang Guo to cover Gongsun Lü'e's half-naked body. And as Yang Guo and Little Dragon Girl were about to depart together, Gongsun Lü'e wished to return the garment:

> [Gongsun Lü'e] heard him sing "With clothing, the newer the better, but with people, the older the better," and felt very sad and depressed. She then took out that old tattered shirt which Yang Guo had just taken off, and holding it in both hands carried it to him, saying, "Brother Yang, your old clothing is better than the new one." Yang Guo replied, "Thank you," and extended his hand to accept it.
>
> (*Giant Eagle*, 804–805)

"With clothing, the newer the better, but with people, the older the better." Nevertheless, the clothing is given as a gift; therefore it will be treasured even though it may be old and tattered. As the saying goes, "Brothers are like hands and feet, while wives are like clothing." Although it is not very expensive, this piece of clothing that Little Dragon Girl had sewn for him nevertheless comes to function as a bodily and material memory even more valuable to Yang Guo than his own hands and feet.

This fragile sartorial memory may be destroyed; it is nevertheless reincarnated subsequently at a different time and place. Sixteen years later, Yang Guo once again approached "Lost Love Ravine," and was heartbroken for a long time, until finally, without having found Little Dragon Girl's body, he proceeded to jump into the deep ravine. However, who could have known that at the bottom there would be a deep pool, and next to the pool there would be trees the bark of which had been peeled off by hand. Yang Guo pondered this as he walked, until he finally reached a thatched cottage:

He stepped inside and immediately recoiled in surprise when he saw that the furnishings of the room were very crude, yet the room itself was unusually clean. On the altar there were merely a single table and a small tea-stand, and otherwise there were no other objects in the room. The location of the table and tea-stand was very familiar to him, reminding him of the table and chair in the stone room in Ancient Tomb. Without giving the matter any further thought, he very casually walked over to the right, and found that there was indeed a small room there, and beyond that room was a larger bedroom as expected. In the bedroom, there was a bed, couch, table, and chairs, just like Yang Guo's bedroom in Ancient Tomb. The only difference was that in Ancient Tomb everything was made out of stone, whereas here everything was made out of wood.

(*Giant Eagle*, 1598–1599)

What surprised Yang Guo the most was that the layout of this room was a precise replica of that Ancient Tomb stone room, including the jade bed, the long rope, the book stand, as well as the shirt made out of tree bark. He then thought of how Little Dragon Girl had been forced to live in the deep ravine for sixteen years, relying not only on the Ancient Tomb sect's practices of "minimal language, minimal action, minimal happiness, and minimal sorrow," but more importantly, Bao Xiruo's former method of "spatial replication and temporal fixation." Only in this way was she able to simultaneously acknowledge and disavow the nature of the transformation, living in a space of arrested fetishization.

The Ancient Tomb had itself established this parallel between the figures of womb and tomb, but now Little Dragon Girl had re-created the space of Ancient Tomb within the depths of this ravine of lost love—working and resting just as she had formerly done in Ancient Tomb, as if time had stood still in the depths of this ravine. The child's clothing made of tree bark in the wood wardrobe expressed even more directly this condition of arrested fetishization. It is therefore not surprising that by the time Little Dragon Girl and Yang Guo were finally reunited, Yang Guo's hair had already turned grey, but in the eyes of Little Dragon Girl, he had not aged at all, but instead remained "my little Guo who has grown up." This conjunction of change and non-change, of childhood and maturity, temporal flow and stasis, is revealed even more clearly in the scene when Yang Guo, wild with ecstasy, jumps onto the tall tree and starts turning somersaults:

Little Dragon Girl pulled out a handkerchief. Back when Yang Guo turned somersaults on Zhongnan Mountain, he would happily walk back to her side, and she would pull out her handkerchief to wipe the sweat off his forehead. This time, however, when she saw him approach, he was neither flushed nor breathing heavily, so why would he have any sweat? Nevertheless, she still pulled out her handkerchief to wipe his forehead.

(Giant Eagle, 160)

Turning somersaults was a game which Yang Guo had played from a young age, just as the act of using her handkerchief to wipe off his sweat was a gesture of affection which Little Dragon Girl had long since grown accustomed to. However, whereas turning somersaults had formerly been merely a game for him, it had now become a highly refined form of martial arts, and therefore how could there be any sweat to wipe off? Similarly, how could two fully grown adults wear a child's clothing? But Little Dragon Girl nevertheless continued to use this bark handkerchief to wipe off Yang Guo's sweat, and used bark stalks to weave his clothing—with both of these actions functioning as instances of fetishized arrested development.

At this point, however, we may consider another path, one that involves not merely a constant transformation between martial arts and love, between plenitude and lack, but rather a dialectics of change and non-change to explore the differences between the materiality of martial arts and the materiality of desire. The materiality of martial arts is itself located at the level of "change," while the materiality of desire emphasizes the permanent newness of "not changing." The bright mandarin ducks, the flowers that appear to be dripping blood, the "mummification" of the fragile embroidered slippers into jadeite slippers, together with the fragile shirt which is also "frozen" into a tree-bark shirt—as the saying goes, "if the heavens had emotion, they too would grow old, and if the earth had emotion, it would also go to waste." To what extent is the fetishization of the love object the only method of searching for age and waste in a world of emotion?

Conclusion

On the basis of these various gifts, love letters, and material evidence in Jin Yong's texts, we may conclude that history, memory, and desire are all potentially materialized, and that the "unrepeatable" uniqueness of these events is thereby transformed into portable and *re*portable material objects. The history that one carries on one's body, and the memory that one witnesses with one's own eyes, are both transformed into a desire for objects that can actually be touch. It is in this that the truth and illusion of the materiality of desire and the fetishism of martial arts are all located.

Furthermore, we might build on Chris Hamm's discussion in this volume of the "canonization" of Jin Yong's fiction, and suggest that the texts of *Eagle-shooting Heroes* and *Giant Eagle* that we ourselves are currently "fondling" might also function as a kind of gift, love token, and material evidence at the level of meta-narrative. The photographs of paintings, stele inscriptions, porcelain, and wooden figurines that appear at the beginning of each volume in the Hong Kong and Taiwan edition of Jin Yong's complete works, all display a visual reminder/remainder of historicity, and perhaps might also function as a kind of border fetish underlying the narrativization of objects and events. And how are these cultural elements different from a kind of fetishism, kleptomania, together with historico-mania and archeo-mania? *Heroes* and *Giant Eagle* are both commodities with their own use value, exchange value, as well as symbolic value. In their circulation in bookstores, the popular media, the internet, as well as at academic conferences, they can also be seen as fetishes endowed with a sort of emotional value, bearing the weight of the development of memory and the projection of desire. As we enter this peculiar fascination with martial-arts romances, we must recognize that whereas we originally sought to ask "Jin Yong," What sort of thing is sentiment?—in the end the question becomes more one of the fetishization of "Jin Yong" himself.

As the preeminent cult figure in Chinese martial-arts romance writing, Jin Yong is widely acclaimed as the "Number One" Chinese writer who commands the largest readership on a global scale and who has sold more than 30 million novels around the world. Besides print copies, Jin Yong's works have also been variously adapted into films, TV dramas, comic books, and video games to make market hits for vast audience. For the Chinese society, "Jin Yong" in quotation marks, is more a brand name than a personal name, more a far-reaching cultural phenomenon than a local personality. "Jin Yong" refers not only to the writer who started his martial-arts writing in the literary supplement of a Hong Kong newspaper half a century ago, the social celebrity who has attracted both the media and academic attention since then, but also to the huge enterprise whose tremendous commercial success include the recently (as of 2000) launched "Jin Yong Teahouse," functioning as a fan magazine, as a virtual fan club website, and also as a real teahouse on the side of Hangzhou's West Lake. In light of these discursive formations, "Jin Yong" stands prominently on the stage of contemporary Chinese popular culture as both a cultural fetish and a commodity fetish. I conclude, therefore, by asking: what sort of thing is "Jin Yong"?

Notes

A version of this essay first appeared in Chinese as Chapter 5 of my book *Guaitai jiating luomanshi* 怪胎家庭羅曼史 (Queer family romance) (Taipei: Shibao chuban-she, 2000). Translated and adapted by Carlos Rojas, and reviewed by the author. All embedded translations are also by Rojas.

1 For a discussion of the origins of the romantic tradition in Jin Yong's knight-errant fiction, see Chen Mo's 陳墨 *Qing'ai Jin Yong* 情愛金庸 (Romantic Jin Yong) (Taipei: Yunlong chubanshe, 1997), 3.
2 Jin Yong 金庸, *Shediao yingxiong zhuan* 射雕英雄傳 (Eagle-shooting heroes) (Taipei: Yuanliu chuban gongsi, 1987); and Jin Yong, *Shendiao xialü* 神雕俠侶 (Giant eagle and its companion) (Taipei: Yuanliu chuban gongsi, 1989). Subsequent references to both texts will be cited parenthetically in the text.
3 Susan Stewart, *On Longing: Narratives of the Miniature, the Gigantic, the Souvenir, the Collection* (Durham: Duke University Press, 1992), *ix*.

4 Marcel Mauss, *The Gift: Forms and Functions of Exchange in Archaic Societies*, trans. Ian Cunison (New York: Norton, 1967).

5 Many critics have pointed out that in Mauss' theory of "gift exchange" there is a tendency to romanticize primitive societies, especially to underestimate the role of gift exchange as agent within the economic transactions. "Gift" and "commodity" are invariably reduced to a binary opposition between "individualization" and "reification," with the former treating as a social relations as a medium and emphasizing reciprocity and alliance, and the latter taking money as a medium and emphasizing profit and cost. Recently, however, discussions have shifted from a straightforward opposition between "gift exchange" and "commodity exchange," to an emphasis on the possible similarities between the two. See Arjun Appadurai, "Introduction: Commodities and the Politics of Value," in Appadurai, ed., *The Social Life of Things* (Cambridge: Cambridge University Press, 1986), 11–12.

6 This kind of stark opposition between people and things can not only be observed within the social logic of Western capitalism, but more importantly it has implications for the Western imperial expansion which emerged simultaneously with early capitalism. Peter Stallybrass traces the etymology of the word "fetish" back to the word "fetisso" (a commercial term that the Portuguese and Dutch used when they engaged in trade with African natives in East African's Gold Coast during the fifteenth and sixteenth centuries—the term referring to the natives' practice of using their clothes and ornaments to serve as witness to their contracts of exchange), and then proceeds to discuss the creation of the European subject from the Enlightenment forward, which he opposes to the African intermixture of people, objects, and magic: "What was demonized in the concept of the fetish was the possibility that history, memory, and desire might be materialized in objects that are touched, loved and worn" (Peter Stallybrass, "Marx's Coat," in Patricia Spyer, ed., *Border Fetishisms: Material Objects in Unstable Spaces* (New York: Routledge, 1998), 186). The European subject must be a transcendental subject, which does not stop with objects, but even obtains profit by trading gold for ships, ships for firearms, firearms for tobacco, and tobacco for cane sugar. In other words, the frightening thing about capitalism and imperial expansion lies not in their materialism, but rather in their "dematerialization," which is to say the way in which they use the abstract forms of meta-objects and meta-sensory organs to initiate value exchange. Stallybrass's fetishistic reading strategy of trying to "restore that material memory, a memory literally embodied in the commodity although suppressed *as memory*" (202) is precisely the approach I wish to adopt in this essay, although the relationship between fetish theory and China's capitalism and imperialist expansion remains to be worked out.

7 Patricia Spyer, "Introduction," in Spyer, ed., *Border Fetishisms*, 1.

8 Henri Bergson, *Matter and Memory*, trans. N. M. Paul and S. W. Palmer (New York: Zone Books, 1988).

9 Judith Butler, *Bodies That Matter: On the Discursive Limits of "Sex"* (New York: Routledge, 1993).

10 Zhou Botong's keeping women at a distance of 1,000 *li* is often discussed as an instance of a "sexual psychological deformity" (Chen Mo, *Qing'ai Jin Yong*, 25–26) or a "martial [arts] obsession" (*wuchi* 武癡). But, if we speak of a simple opposition between "romantic madness" and "martial madness," can we not then go even further and argue that the boyish skill (*tongzi gong* 童子功) emphasized in the knight-errant world is none other than a form of narcissism, with "skill" being like "libido" insofar as it cannot be wasted on other people or other objects but rather must be dedicated entirely to the enrichment of the ego. If we were to be even more provocative, we might ask whether Zhou Botong's habit of defecating every time he hears Yinggu is coming in search of him might be a kind of

arrested anal stage, just as Hong Qigong's insistence on not discussing romance could be seen as being a kind of arrested oral stage?

11 According to Lacanian theory, the subject enters the symbolic order of language and thereby becomes headless, while the idealization of love "prevent[s] the subject from apprehending his or her fundamental nothingness" (Kaja Silverman, *The Threshold of the Visible World* [New York: Routledge, 1996], 44). At the same time, the Lacanian "gift of love" takes "courtly love" as its model, and emphasizes that, because the love object has already been completely sublimated into a *petit objet*, therefore, it becomes impossible to internalize it into one's own body, to truly possess it. Under these circumstances, the distance between the subject and the *petit objet* produces a violent rupture of the symbolic order, rather than a process of abundant satisfaction. The subject does not, on account of the *petit objet*, dis/avow decapitation and lack, but rather it is the failure to obtain the *petit objet* which results in the subject's decapitation and lack. Instead, every time the subject is unable to obtain the *petit objet* and returns empty-handed, it gives the subject a sense of decapitation and lack.

12 Is not this process of being reminded of a person by seeing an object, of being reminded of old affection, precisely the role that President Clinton repeatedly played in the Lewinsky scandal? Is it not true that the tie that Lewinsky gave Clinton not only appeared at the official banquet for President Jiang Zemin, but also furthermore was worn by a certain White House steward when he appeared before the federal grand jury? And furthermore, on the morning that Lewinsky herself appeared before the federal grand jury was Clinton not wearing the same gold necktie at an event at the Rose Garden? Most curious, of course, is another of the gifts from Lewinsky's White House internship: the semen-stained dark-blue dress that she kept as a memento of their affair, and which subsequently provided the decisive DNA evidence.

13 For a discussion of hair fetish, please see my *Yuwang xin ditu* 慾望新地圖 (New cartographies of desire) (Taipei: Lianhe wenxue chubanshe, 1996), 13–14.

14 Karl Abraham, "The Female Castration Complex," in *Selected Papers* (London: Hagarth Press, 1949), 355, quoted in Adela Pinch, "Stealing Happiness: Shoplifting in Early Nineteenth Century England," in Spyer, ed., *Border Fetishisms*, 142.

15 Mary Douglas, "Foreword: No Free Gifts," in Marcel Mauss, *The Gift*, trans. W. D. Halls (New York: Routledge, 1990), vii–xviii.

13 Authorial afterlives and apocrypha in 1990s Chinese fiction

Carlos Rojas

Look at the canonical and master works in China's modern literary archive, and are there any of them that are *not* merely playing literature? It is necessary to have a sense of social responsibility! We are authors, and what kind of people are authors? They are a cut above everyone else!

(Wang Shuo, *Not Serious at All*)

" 'Tell me,' I asked An Jia, 'If someone has already eaten his fill and doesn't have anything to do, how should he pass the time?' " Thus opens Wang Shuo's 王朔 1989 novel, *Yi dian zhengjing meiyou* 一點正經沒有 (Not serious at all), with the narrator, Fang Yan, asking his wife for advice on how someone should spend his time. After they have ruled out such options as "governing the nation, fluffing cotton, or pickling pigs heads [...]," An Jia then asks Fang Yan how many Chinese ideographs the person in question knows. "Three to five thousand," Fang Yan replies dryly, "if you include the mis-written ones." "In that case," An Jia suggests, "given that he has no skills, but at the same time does not wish to be lumped together with the common people, perhaps he could try his hand at being an author."[1]

At this point the couple walk up to their bedroom dresser and, looking at each other's reflections in the mirror, proceed to have essentially the same conversation, but in reverse: " 'Tell me,' An Jia asked me, "If someone's hands are clenched into empty fists, and he has no money no power no morality and no looks, how could he, in a single evening, go from being a mere nobody to reaching heaven in a single step and completely transforming himself and so forth [...]?" After again ruling out such options as "stealing looting appropriating public funds or marrying into money [...]," Fang Yan, too, agrees that perhaps such a person should try his hand at being an author.

As the subsequent conclusion of this conversation makes clear, the unnamed acquaintance on whose behalf Fang Yan was originally asking his wife for advice was, in fact, himself. Fang Yan and his mahjong-playing friends then proceed to form an unruly cabal of anti-idealistic writers who give lip service to the May Fourth ideals of "social responsibility" (*shehui zeren* 社會責任) and "concern for country and countrymen" (*youguo youmin* 憂國憂民), while at the same time explicitly advocating the light-hearted attitude of "playing literature" (*wanr wenxue* 玩兒文學) that had already become Wang Shuo's trademark.

While writing, and specifically the writing of fiction, is presented in Wang Shuo's novel as a practice that is, in the end, "not serious at all," the novel's broader point about the changing status of literature and authorship in Chinese society is, nevertheless, very serious indeed. In particular, Wang Shuo is describing a contemporary attitude toward literature that explicitly challenges the two dominant models of authorship that characterized early twentieth century China: namely, those centered around the figure of the polit-ical author, on the one hand, and of the professional author, on the other. Or, to paraphrase Fang Yan's and An Jia's own parodic language from the beginning of *Not Serious at All*, this new attitude challenges models of authorship grounded on political activities such as "governing the nation, fluffing cotton, or pickling pigs heads" or, conversely, on economic activ-ities such as "stealing looting appropriating public funds."

Needless to say, literature in China, as elsewhere, has long been saturated with political and economic considerations. During the early twentieth century, however, these concerns began to coalesce around the two distinct (and ostensibly mutually opposed) social identities of the political and the professional author—and in particular the politically committed figure of the May Fourth author and the more professionalized figure of the Butterfly author. Over the next several decades, these two models became increasingly influential, determining not only the social identities that writers were able to assume, but also the ways in which both the general public as well as the writers themselves came to *perceive* those same identities.

These two dialectically opposed models of political and professional authorship provisionally came together in the second half of the twentieth century under the auspices of the Chinese Writers Association (*Zhongguo zuojia xiehui* 中國作家協會). Founded in 1949,[2] the Chinese Writers Asso-ciation (CWA) functioned for several decades as a guild-like organization that guaranteed its members a regular salary, while at the same time tacitly encouraging them to keep their fiction within fairly narrow bounds of what was ideologically permissible. During the 1980s, however, the CWA, and indeed China's entire literary scene, began to undergo a significant trans-formation. First, the death of Mao Zedong 毛澤東 and the formal end of the Cultural Revolution in 1976 marked the beginning of a partial depolit-icization of Chinese society and culture, undercutting the CWA's ability to maintain a strict ideological and formal homogeneity within the literary field. Second, the long-term economic development that resulted from Deng Xiaoping's 鄧小平 1978 Reforms and Openness campaign (also known as his Open Door campaign) dramatically expanded the market potential of Chinese literature. Both of these factors, therefore, contributed to the emer-gence in the 1980s of a variety of literary trends that departed significantly from the socialist realist orthodoxy of the post-1949 era, and also helped allow the market and other forces to supplant the role of the CWA in helping shape literary production.³

It was in the context of this atmosphere of economic and political liberalization that Wang Shuo roared onto the literary scene. Born in 1958, Wang Shuo published his first short story in 1978, the same year that Deng Xiaoping inaugurated his Reforms and Openness campaign. During the 1980s, he quickly established himself as one of China's best-selling and most influential authors, with a series of novels about disillusioned urban youth. These works were immensely popular, with many of them becoming best-sellers and being promptly adapted for the screen (with four major cinematic adaptations appearing in the year 1988 alone). So popular and profitable was Wang's fiction that it became common to speak of a "Wang Shuo phenomenon" to describe his ability to market and promote his works independently of the CWA or other traditional, state-controlled institutions.

Wang Shuo's fiction typically focuses on disenchanted urban youth, and features a combination of contemporary Beijing slang and "Mao-speak," a parody of the bureaucratic and political discourse that had been one of the defining characteristics of public life during the Maoist era. It was, therefore, precisely this deprofessionalized and depoliticized category of "hooligan literature" (*pizi wenxue* 痞子文學) that Wang featured and portrayed in his most explicitly "literary" novel, *Not Serious at All*. Indeed, it is ironically appropriate that Wang Shuo's challenge, in *Not Serious at All*, to what it means to be a modern Chinese writer was first published in the journal *Zhongguo zuojia* 中國作家 (Chinese writers)—one of nine periodicals and journals published under the umbrella of the Chinese Writers Association—even as the CWA was itself in the process of trying to adapt to post-Deng economic and political realities.⁴ Wang Shuo himself famously never joined the CWA, and the cynical, anti-establishment model of authorship he sketches in *Not Serious at All* is one that directly challenges everything that the CWA has traditionally stood for.

The fact that *Not Serious at All* was published in the summer of 1989 is also significant, following as it did immediately on the heels of the imminently "serious" June Fourth crackdown on Beijing's pro-democracy protesters in Tiananmen Square.⁵ Coming at the end of nearly a full decade of precipitous economic growth, the 1989 Tiananmen Square protest and crackdown marked a crucial turning point in modern Chinese history, abruptly slamming the brakes on the process of political liberalization that had been gaining momentum through the 1980s. Completed before the crackdown and published shortly after it, meanwhile, Wang Shuo's novel straddles this pivotal historical moment, and anticipates the general withdrawal from overt political engagement that characterized Chinese society in the initial years following the June Fourth crackdown. The characters in *Not Serious at All* approach writing as a whim—a source of amusement and a way of idling away time, in stark opposition to the politicized rationales that had characterized so much of twentieth-century Chinese literature. Indeed, even the name of the novel's protagonist, *Fang Yan* 方言, points to these decentralized and depoliticized tendencies in Wang Shuo's work. The name *Fang Yan* literally means "dialect" and, in linguistic terms, suggests Wang Shuo's trademark practice of incorporating considerable amounts of local slang into his works—vernacular riffs on the same Beijing dialect that also provided the model for the standard Mandarin that is now the *lingua franca* throughout China. In political terms, Fang Yan's name symbolizes Wang Shuo's attempt to mobilize a sort of political vernacular, a concern with attitudes of urban angst, disillusionment and general loss of a moral center—attitudes which are located on the margins of the orthodox politics promulgated by Beijing itself.[6]

Wang Shuo continued to write prolifically for a couple of years following *Not Serious at All*, and in 2002 published his four-volume *Wang Shuo wenji* 王朔文集 (Wang Shuo's collected works), including all of his major novels and novellas from 1984 to 1991. Not only did this collection sacrilegiously mimic the four-volume set of Chairman Mao's collected works, but further-more, in a move that was unusual at the time, Wang negotiated for himself a significant cut of the royalties of this soon-to-be best-seller. It was also in 1992, however, that he announced that he would stop writing fiction, and devote himself instead to writing for television and other venues. Even after his figurative retirement, however, Wang Shuo remained a potent symbol of the anti-establishment author who feeds off of, but at the same time systematically implodes, the dominant models of literary production that have held sway in one form or another throughout the twentieth century.

In the remainder of this essay, I will examine some dimensions of Wang Shuo's legacy, focusing on three specific moments of his figurative return to the Chinese literary scene—in 1993, 1999, and 2003, respectively. More specifically, I will put Wang Shuo's works and the more general Wang Shuo phenomenon into dialogue with works by other contemporary authors such as Mo Yan 莫言 (1955–), Jia Pingwa 賈平凹 (1952–), and Wei Hui 衛慧 (1973–), each of whom occupied a similar interstitial space between the traditional literary establishment, and the unapologetic literary com-mercialism that Wang Shuo himself helped to colonize. I am interested in these latter works not only as literary phenomena in their own right, but also for the ways in which they, like *Not Serious at All*, explicitly reflect on the predicament of the contemporary author as he or she negotiates the conflicting expectations of the politically orthodox literary establishment, on the one hand, and of the scandal-driven parasitic literary market, on the other. Collectively, these works challenge conventional assumptions about the status of contemporary authors and their relationship to their own literary creations, provocatively desacralizing traditional notions of author-ship while at the same time reinvesting them with new significance.

1993

Even after Wang Shuo stopped writing fiction in 1992, the debate over his influence, together with its implications for our understanding of the Chinese literary and cultural field, remained very much alive. One of the most significant moments in this debate, for instance, occurred in 1993, when the former Minister of Culture, Wang Meng 王蒙, published an influential essay about Wang Shuo entitled "*Duobi chonggao*" 躲避崇高 (Avoiding sublimity) in the popular literary journal, *Dushu* 讀書 (Reader).[7]

Labeled as a Rightist in the late 1950s and exiled to Xinjiang for seven years, Wang Meng was rehabilitated in 1979 and ultimately rose to the position of Minister of Culture—a position he held for three years until he was forced to resign in 1989 as a result of his disapproval of the Tiananmen Square crackdown. Although Wang Meng's three-year stint as Minister of Culture coincided with the most precipitous growth in Wang Shuo's popularity, for many years Wang Meng nevertheless carefully avoided commenting publicly on Wang Shuo's fiction or the broader socio-cultural phenomenon it reflected. In fact, it was not until January of 1993, *after* Wang Meng had already stepped down from office and Wang Shuo himself had already announced his retirement from fiction writing, that Wang Meng finally broke his public silence with the publication of his "Avoiding Sublimity" essay.

Wang Meng's essay opens with an optimistic overview of the post-May Fourth model of the politically minded reformist author:

> Although our authors have undergone many frightening schisms and struggles since the May Fourth Movement, they nevertheless have tended to remain in agreement on several basic points. Many of them feel a sense of responsibility for helping save the nation and the people, and educating their readers—goals which may be accomplished either through enlightening, healing, or uniting the people [...].

After proceeding in this vein for another couple of paragraphs, Wang Meng then takes a step back from this consecrated view of modern literary history and notes that,

> We probably never could have imagined that it was entirely possible for there to be a completely different kind of author and literature: A literature in which authors and texts do not at all consider themselves to be more impressive (more sincere, intelligent, enlightened, loving . . .) than their readers, and furthermore do not even believe that there is anything terribly impressive in the world to begin with; a literature which does not aspire to raise any questions, and has even less desire to answer them; a literature which does not write about workers, peasants and soldiers, or political cadres, or revolutionaries and counter-revolutionaries, or about historically significant figures [...].

Precisely this sort of literature has now in fact appeared, Wang Meng continues, and furthermore it has become extraordinarily popular: "These past few years, as the market for pure literature has become quite exhausted, the name of a certain young writer has become increasingly 'hot.'" So "hot" is this new author that Wang Meng then proceeds to discuss him at some length, detailing several of his major works and catchphrases, before finally conceding, two full paragraphs later: "Of course, I am speaking here of Wang Shuo."

Wang Meng's provisional erasure of Wang Shuo's name in the initial portion of the essay (he is not identified by name until nearly a third of the way into this 6,000-character essay about his work and its significance) is itself symptomatic not only of Wang Meng's own public silence on the topic of Wang Shuo up to that point, but also of the literary establishment's paranoid reaction to Wang Shuo's remarkable popularity and success. Wang Meng notes, for instance, that one influential journal vowed never even to print Wang Shuo's name, while another refused to print any news of his publications. In his own discussion, however, Wang Meng himself is surprisingly favorable in his assessment—concluding that, while Wang Shuo's writings are unquestionably unorthodox, this sort of unorthodoxy is itself *necessary* to keep the literary orthodoxy in check. Referring, for instance, to the early years of the Cultural Revolution (1966–1976) when young Red Guards enthusiastically followed Chairman Mao's injunction to destroy the Four Olds, and when the so-called Twelve Model Operas designated by Mao's wife Jiang Qing 江青 became essentially the only politically permissible forms of mass entertainment, Wang Meng muses,

> If only there had been a few more Wang Shuos, maybe there would have been a few less Red Guards running around killing and being killed while shouting "Protect Comrade Jiang Qing." Wang Shuo's playful and cynical discourse [*wanshi yanlun* 玩世言論] is particularly a reaction to the spirit of the Red Guards and Model Operas.

That is to say, Wang Meng implies that if orthodox culture does not have anything to counterbalance it, it risks becoming a destructively *hyper*-orthodox force in its own right. While Wang Meng stresses that Wang Shuo's novels are actually written much more carefully than the self-identified hooligan writer would want his readers to believe, he nevertheless stops short of claiming that the entire concept of canonicity is no longer useful. Instead, he argues more precisely that cultural orthodoxies are necessarily reliant on the existence of para- or anti-canonical cultural formations such as Wang Shuo's to keep themselves in check and prevent them from degenerating into repressive institutions.

The "Avoiding Sublimity" essay constitutes a virtual encounter between the literary establishment, on the one hand, and an iconoclast who would appear to challenge everything which that establishment represents, on the other. However, rather than presenting these two poles of orthodoxy and iconoclasm as being strictly opposed to each other, Wang Meng instead suggests that the literary establishment not only helps to spawn its own iconoclastic reaction, but furthermore is itself dependent on the existence of these disruptive elements to prevent it from becoming autocratic and repressive.

Wang Meng's 1993 essay, on the limits of "pure literature" and the challenge posed to the literary establishment by the emergence of "a completely different kind of author and literature," coincided with the release of two novels focusing quite explicitly on the shifting status of authorship in contemporary society: Mo Yan's *Jiuguo* 酒國 (Republic of wine)[8] and Jia Pingwa's *Feidu* 廢都 (Fallen capital).[9] While Mo Yan and Jia Pingwa are two of contemporary China's most influential and critically acclaimed authors, *Republic of Wine* and *Fallen Capital* are both edgy, subversive works that were censored and banned by the literary establishment—though in both cases the resulting controversies only heightened the works' subsequent popularity. It was only after *Republic of Wine* was first published in Taiwan in 1992, for instance, that a Mainland Chinese edition of the work was permitted the following year—and even then only after significant changes had been made to the text (including the deletion of the novel's original stream-of-consciousness conclusion). Also in 1993, meanwhile, the renowned "searching for roots" author Jia Pingwa published his novel *Fallen Capital* —his first work to be set in the city of Xi'an where he had been living for the past two decades, and focusing in particular on the social and cultural degeneracy that, some argue, have increasingly come to characterize contemporary urban China. Even before the novel's release, Jia preemptively censored his own work—notoriously deleting numerous sexually explicit passages and replacing them with strings of empty squares accompanied by a parenthetical note specifying precisely how many ideographs had been deleted (with the number of deleted characters of some passages running in the hundreds). Even with these deletions, however, the novel was *still* banned and recalled a few months after its initial publication (but not before it had already sold more than half a million copies). In both cases, therefore, the attempts to censor and ban the works paradoxically led to a significant increase in attention and attendant sales, facilitated by the profusion of independent sidewalk stalls selling unauthorized reprints.

Just as the scandals surrounding these two 1993 novels underscore the tensions between political and ideological orthodoxies, on the one hand, and market forces, on the other, the works themselves each examine the conflicting demands of the literary establishment and of popular demand on authors in contemporary China. It is certainly not coincidental, for instance, that both works revolve, like Wang Shuo's *Not Serious at All*, around quasi-autobiographical protagonists—celebrated authors struggling to complete a work-in-progress while wrestling with the weight of public expectations. Both protagonists, furthermore, are simultaneously shadowed by aspiring young writers who attempt to use the protagonists' authority in order to jumpstart their own literary careers.

In the case of *Republic of Wine*, the autobiographical dimension of the protagonist is quite explicit, as the work's protagonist is also called *Mo Yan* 莫言[10] (the *nom de plume of* the author, whose real name is Guan Moye 管謨業) and his fame is largely predicated on his earlier novel *Red Sorghum* (a work which appears to closely resemble the real-life Mo Yan's own 1986 novel by the same title).[11] The fictional *Mo Yan* is in the process of writing a new novel while at the same time carrying on a correspondence with a certain Li Yidou—"a Ph.D. candidate in liquor studies at the Brewer's College here in Liquorland" (21)—who was inspired by *Red Sorghum* to try his own hand at writing. Like student Bi Poli who, as Eileen Chow discusses in her essay on Zhang Henshui in this volume, aggressively petitions the fictional author Yang Xingyuan to help him publish his short story, Li Yidou similarly sends the fictional *Mo Yan* a series of his own short stories in the hope that *Mo Yan* will use his connections to help get them published in the (fictional) journal, *Guomin wenxue* 國民文學 (Citizen's literature)— described in the novel as "China's 'official' literary magazine, at the forefront of new literary trends" (56). *Republic of Wine* as a whole features several embedded layers of representation, including the text of *Mo Yan*'s work-in-progress, the text of the letters that *Mo Yan* and Li Yidou exchange regarding Li Yidou's aspirations of becoming an author, together with the text of the short stories that Li Yidou sends Mo Yan. As a result, the majority of *Republic of Wine* consists of embedded texts which *the novel itself* codes as substandard writing—ranging from Li Yidou's exuberantly unorthodox short stories, which *Mo Yan* deems virtually unpublishable, to *Mo Yan*'s own work-in-progress, which the fictional author himself abandons in frustration.

While *Mo Yan* is initially polite and encouraging in his responses to Li Yidou, he becomes increasingly bewildered by Li Yidou's seemingly anarchic and inchoate prose. The senior author nevertheless continues promising to forward Li's stories to the editor of *Citizen's Literature*, though it is clear that he holds out little hope that they will ever be accepted for publication. *Mo Yan*'s resulting struggle to reconcile himself with a style of writing that he regards as being completely opposed to his own (ironically so, given the fact that Li Yidou claims he was directly inspired by *Mo Yan*'s own fiction) parallels Wang Meng's belatedly positive appraisal of Wang Shuo in the "Avoiding Sublimity" essay. In both cases, the establishment authors Wang Meng and *Mo Yan* implicitly argue for the inherent legitimacy of a body of texts that would appear to fly in the face of everything that they value in good writing.

These parallels in the relationships between *Mo Yan* and Li Yidou, on the one hand, and Wang Meng and Wang Shuo, on the other, are further reinforced by the fact that the two Wangs are themselves prominently featured in *Mo Yan*'s fictional dialogue with Li Yidou. For instance, in response to Li Yidou's first letter and story submission, *Mo Yan* responds,

During times like this, it is fair to say that literature is not the choice of the wise, and those of us for whom it is too late can but sigh at a lack of talent and skills that leaves us only with literature. A writer by the name of Li Qi once wrote a novel entitled *Please Don't Treat Me Like a Dog*, in which he describes a gang of local punks who are deprived of opportunities to cheat or mug or steal or rob, so one of them says, "Let's go become goddamned writers."

(24)

The plot of *Please Don't Treat Me Like a Dog* (*Qianwan bie ba wo dang gou* 千萬別把我當狗) is clearly that of Wang Shuo's 1989 novel *Not Serious at All*, though the title attributed to Li Qi's work is a tongue-in-cheek allusion to *another* Wang Shuo novel from that same year: *Qianwan bie ba wo dang ren* 千萬別把我當人 (Please don't treat me like a human)[12] (which, incidentally, is cited in *Not Serious at All* itself as the title of Fang Yan's *own* work-in-progress).[13] While the real-life Mo Yan clearly admires Wang Shuo—having remarked in a 2002 interview, for instance, that

his articles are well written and he is very wise, and is someone whom contemporary literary and intellectual historians will not be able to ignore. [...] I have, from the very beginning, believed that he is one of the very few Chinese authors who have managed to truly influence an entire generation of Chinese readers with their works[14]

—the fictional *Mo Yan*, by contrast, appears to regard the fictional Wang Shuo (a.k.a. Li Qi) with considerable skepticism, though he nevertheless recommends Li Qi's novel to Li Yidou, on the assumption that the latter will identify with the maverick author's anti-establishment image. Li Yidou, however, responds that he actually *hated* the novel *Please Don't Treat Me Like a Dog*, and is particularly critical of the current Wang Shuo-inspired popularity of "playing literature" and "hooligan literature." At the same time, however, Li Yidou is equally critical of the establishment figure Wang Meng, and particularly Wang Meng's (fictional) recommendation that contemporary youth like Li Yidou voluntarily step away from the overcrowded literary field. After dismissing both Wangs, Li Yidou instead cites Lu Xun as an example of the sort of author he is attempting to emulate (for instance, he describes his own story "Meat Boy" as a "latter-day 'Diary of a Madman'" (55)).

Lu Xun is an interesting choice here because he has not only come to be regarded as *the* preeminent orthodox author of twentieth-century China, but furthermore was known for his political and literary iconoclasm. One of Lu Xun's most famous tropes, moreover, is the figure of cannibalism that he develops in "Diary of a Madman" and elsewhere. As I discuss in the introduction to this volume, Lu Xun uses this metaphorics of cannibalism not merely to comment on the involutive self-destructive tendencies of late imperial society, but also to describe the mutually parasitic relationship between orthodox and popular literature. It is therefore appropriate that cannibalism is not only a dominant theme in both the fictional *Mo Yan*'s work-in-progress as well as several of Li Yidou's short stories, but furthermore comes to provide an overarching metaphor for the relationship between *Mo Yan* and Li Yidou within *Republic of Wine* as a whole. That is to say, as the novel progresses, *Mo Yan* gradually becomes increasingly dissatisfied with the progress of his own manuscript and intrigued, in spite of himself, by the highly unorthodox stories that Li Yidou keeps sending him, to the point that *Mo Yan* ultimately abandons his own novel and resolves to travel to Liquorland and meet Li Yidou in person—thereby entering a textual space corresponding to that of the inchoate fragments of Li Yidou's own fiction. In effect, the fictional *Mo Yan* becomes cannibalistically consumed by the same textual space he had helped inspire in the first place. Or, read in terms of the novel's own explicit concerns with questions of literary orthodoxy and marginality, the establishment author *Mo Yan* becomes displaced, and even subsumed, by precisely the same iconoclastic literature which he had previously been struggling to keep at bay.

Like *Mo Yan* in *Republic of Wine*, Zhuang Zhidie in Jia Pingwa's *Fallen Capital* is a prominent novelist loosely modeled on the author himself. One of the four cultural figureheads (referred to in Wang Shuoian terms as "cultural idlers" [*wenhua xianren* 文化閑人]) in Jia Pingwa's adopted hometown of Xi'an, Zhuang Zhidie struggles throughout the work to complete his own work-in-progress, while simultaneously maintaining numerous extramarital affairs and also attempting to negotiate the public pressures which his own celebrity brings. Zhuang Zhidie is shadowed in the work by the figure of Zhou Min—a young man from the nearby city of Tongguan who, at the beginning of the novel, elopes to Xi'an with his girlfriend and then attempts to use Zhuang's celebrity to establish his, Zhou's, own career. Just as Li Yidou asks for *Mo Yan*'s help in publishing his stories in the journal *Citizen's Literature*, Zhou Min similarly uses a forged letter of introduction from Zhuang Zhidie to secure a job at the local literary journal, *Xijing Magazine* (*Xijing zazhi* 西京雜誌), where he immediately proceeds to write a biographical essay about Zhuang himself. Although the resulting essay is relatively accurate, its allusion to Zhuang's past sexual indiscretion with a local bureaucrat nevertheless results in a cluster of lawsuits from the bureaucrat in question accusing Zhuang and the journal of libel.

Not only does this racy article (together with the lawsuits it precipitates) constitute one of the central narrative threads in *Fallen Capital* as a whole, it also marks the beginning of a virtual dialogue between Zhuang and Zhou, wherein Zhuang's novel-writing is paralleled by Zhou Min's habit of retreating to Xi'an's historic city walls to play an egg-shaped wind instrument called a *xun* 塤. Zhuang Zhidie is captivated by these haunting *xun* melodies, and constantly finds himself drawn to the city walls to listen to and record the melodies, not realizing until near the end of the novel that Zhou Min is the performer. Zhou, therefore, stands as Zhuang's alter ego (one of Zhuang's most serious affairs is with Zhou Min's own girlfriend, Tang Wan'r), and his *xun* playing, functions—as Jia Pingwa himself notes—as a "keynote" of the novel as a whole.[15] While Zhuang's reputation is built on his facility with words, a crucial quality of the *xun* melodies is that they are voiceless, and furthermore that Zhou, in the process of blowing his *xun*, is quite literally rendered linguistically silent.

Zhou's *xun*-playing, meanwhile, also provides the backdrop for a virtual dialogue between Zhuang Zhidie and an even more startling voice of radical alterity—a cow owned by a local vegetable peddler called Sister Liu. This latter subplot has its origins in an interview trip Zhuang made the preceding year to the outskirts of the city, where he met Liu peddling her wares. At the time, Zhuang suggested that, rather than peddle vegetables, it might be more profitable for her to buy a cow and bring it into the city to sell milk. Sister Liu promptly took his advice and Zhuang Zhidie then became one of her regular customers, lying down and drinking milk directly from the cow's udder each time Sister Liu brought it by the Literature and Art Federation compound where Zhuang lived and worked. In a scene near the beginning of the novel, Zhuang runs into Sister Liu and her cow and, after she remarks that she hasn't seen him for a while, he proceeds to offer Liu some business advice, concluding, "Ay, just look at this cow, it is neither impatient nor restless, and looks just like a philosopher!" In the following paragraph, the narrative briefly gestures back to Sister Liu's original purchase of the cow (this time narrating the scene from the cow's perspective) and then jumps chronologically back to the current meeting:

> The cow followed Zhuang Zhidie's advice and came into Xijing [Xi'an] every day, and each time Zhuang Zhidie would lie down and use his mouth to suck its milk. The cow was very grateful for this, and as a result every time it saw him it would low in greeting. Upon hearing Zhuang remark that "the cow is like a philosopher," the animal began to regard the city with a philosophical eye, but since it couldn't speak people's language, people therefore remained unaware of what it was thinking.
>
> On this particular day, after selling milk in the morning, Sister Liu then led the cow to the base of the city wall to rest, just as Zhou Min was playing his *xun* on the top of the wall [...]. The cow filled its belly with grass, then also [like Zhou Min] lay down to ruminate, and as it was ruminating, it began to reflect.
>
> (55)

The newly philosophical cow then launches into a lengthy, first-person existentialist rumination on humanity, life, history, and other assorted topics. These philosophical reflections then recur repeatedly throughout the novel, constituting a creative *leitmotif* paralleling Zhou Min's *xun* melodies and providing a sounding board for Zhuang Zhidie's own literary efforts.

It is significant that the cow's first philosophical excursus takes place at the quintessentially liminal space of the city wall, and furthermore is explicitly juxtaposed with Zhou Min's *xun* playing. Literally marking the boundary between the structured, institutional space of the city and the comparative wilderness that lies beyond it, the city wall not only functions as a potent metaphor for the bounds of cultural orthodoxy, but also symbolizes a space of creativity and textual production. In addition, it is significant that the cow's philosophical reflections are not only associated with the geographically marginal space of the city wall, but also are born out of Zhuang's oddly perverse habit of drinking directly from cow's udder (and surely it is not coincidental that Zhuang's own wife is surnamed *Niu* [牛] which literally means *ox* or *cow*). Finally, Zhuang's habit of "suckling" (*shunchi* 吮吃) the cow's udder implicitly has the practical effect of momentarily silencing the normally prolix protagonist, even as it simultaneously helps grant the cow the power of thought and knowledge (though, significantly, *without* the corresponding power of speech and expression). Literally silent, its thoughts and reflections only knowable insofar as they are mediated through Jia Pingwa's own literary narrative, Sister Liu's cow can be seen as roughly equivalent to Gayatri Spivak's figure of the speechless subaltern, whose "voice" can only be heard as mediated through the existing academic orthodoxy.[16]

The cow's silent lucidity, therefore, mirrors the figurative silence of figures like Zhou Min and, in *Republic of Wine*, Li Yidou—both of whom hail from the institutional and geographic margins of the literary establishment (Tongguan and Liquorland, respectively), and who are struggling to use the position and influence of orthodox authors such as Zhuang Zhidie and *Mo Yan* to help make their voices heard. At the same time, however, it is not coincidental that the cow's philosophical ruminations directly parallel Zhuang's literal silencing as he buries his mouth in its udder, just as Li Yidou's unpublishable (i.e., "silent") stories mirror *Mo Yan*'s self-silencing as he ultimately decides to abandon his work-in-progress and visit Li in the quasi-fictional space of Liquorland.

Both Mo Yan's and Jia Pingwa's works underscore the paradoxical parallels between the silencing of disenfranchised voices (e.g., Li Yidou, Zhou Min, Sister Liu's cow) at the margins of the literary establishment, and the silencing of institutionally established authors like *Mo Yan* and Zhuang Zhidie. That is to say, although both Zhuang and *Mo Yan* are presented as quintessentially powerful figures within the literary field, they both feel threatened by the degree to which anonymous and decentered forces constantly usurp their ability to control the meaning of their texts and the dissemination of their own image—effectively silencing them even as their works and reputation come to assume a life of their own. In a crucial inversion, furthermore, it is precisely disenfranchised figures like Li Yidou and Zhou Min who, even as they are petitioning established authors for help in gaining entry to the establishment, are simultaneously contributing directly to the figurative hijacking of those authors' public reputations.

1999

In 1999, six years after Wang Meng broke his self-imposed silence on the topic of Wang Shuo and his fiction, Wang Shuo broke his own self-imposed literary silence with the publication of his first novel since 1992. The novel, *Kanshangqu hen mei* 看上去很美 (It looks very beautiful), featuring a group of children growing up, as did Wang Shuo himself, on a military compound in Beijing, is one of his most explicitly autobiographical works to date. The children in the novel, furthermore, turn out to be youthful versions of the characters who populate Wang Shuo's earlier fiction, with the protagonist, Fang Qiangqiang, being a youthful version of the same Fang Yan who appears in *Not Serious at All* and several of Wang Shuo's other novels.

In the novel's preface, Wang Shuo describes the work's excavation of both his personal and literary past as being

> simply a reminiscence of life from years past. A beginning. [...] The actual first day of composition can be traced back to twenty years ago, when I first considered pursuing this writing career. When I worked out the plot of my first novel, I simultaneously began mapping out the plot of this one [...].[17]

Despite having established his reputation with a series of works, like *Wanr de jiu shi xintiao* 玩兒的就是心跳 (Playing for thrills) and *Dongwu xiongmeng* 動物凶猛 (Ferocious beasts), that provocatively challenge the reliability of individual memory and self-understanding,[18] in *It Looks Very Beautiful* Wang Shuo adopts an almost confessional tone in an attempt to present the "real Wang Shuo" underlying all of his previous works. This confessional gesture, in turn, yields a work located at the intersection of an autobiographical exploration of the author's own childhood, on the one hand, and a detailed prehistory of the author's most famous *fictional* character, on the other. Underlying this project, however, is an implicit engagement with the "fictional" dimension of Wang Shuo's own identity—the degree to which his public identity is inevitably the product of a myriad of forces which remain largely outside his direct control. It is certainly not coincidental, for instance, that the title page of Wang Shuo's 1999 novel contained an unusually lengthy excerpt of the relevant Chinese copyright law, and that the volume itself was packaged with a companion CD containing the text of Wang Shuo's collected works, in an attempt to cut down on black-market reprints.[19]

A similar intertwining of autobiography and fiction can be found in the uproar that greeted the publication that same year of 27-year-old Shanghai author Wei Hui's first full-length novel, *Shanghai baobei* 上海寶貝 (Shanghai baby).[20] This sexually risqué novel features the quasi-autobiographical protagonist Coco (named after Coco Chanel) in the process of completing her new novel, while at the same time finding herself embroiled in a number of romantic and sexual relationships in contemporary Shanghai. Like Jia Pingwa's *Fallen Capital*, Wei Hui's novel was banned and recalled by the State Publishing Administration a few months following its initial publication, though this ban only whetted the public's interest in the work itself (which, like *Fallen Capital*, remained easily accessible via black-market editions, as well as on the internet).

Although *Shanghai Baby* is infamous for its sexual content, at its heart it is really a novel about authorship. Just as the protagonist Coco is clearly a projection of the author, Coco's own work-in-progress similarly revolves around a female protagonist who bears a distinct resemblance to Coco herself. Coco's work on this project, furthermore, is complicated by her increasing fascination with this fictional protagonist, as she remarks at one point that "I am falling in love with the 'I' in my novel, because in my novel I am more intelligent and more able to see the world as it really is, the emotions of love and hate, as well as implications of the shifting constellations" (366), and later explicitly compares her protagonist to herself (385). Coco's conflicted relationship with her own quasi-autobiographical protagonist, in turn, is mirrored by her increasingly ambivalent relationship with the public reception of her earlier collection of fiction *Hudie de jianjiao* 蝴蝶的尖叫 (Cries of the butterfly),[21] and particularly the way in which the public has created a fictional image of her own authorial identity based on their reading (or misreading) of her own fiction. Coco notes, for instance, that after her earlier volume came out, it was rumored that she herself was, like one of her characters, a bisexual with a proclivity for violence, and that she received a number of letters from male suitors curious as to whether she was as sexy as her fictional protagonists.

At another point, a former classmate of Coco's recalls having read her first fiction collection, *Cries of the Butterfly*, and how

> it left me with a rather extraordinary sensation, as if I had just walked into a room in which all four walls, as well as the ceiling and floor, were all covered with mirrors, such that [my] reflections were perpetually circulating from one mirror to another.
>
> (453)

This sense of being trapped in a fun-house of mirrors actually describes quite well the way in which both Coco and the author Wei Hui find themselves sandwiched between layers of fictional identity: between their loosely autobiographical fictional protagonists, on the one hand, and the fictional extrapolations their readers make about the authors on the basis of reading their work, on the other. Like *Shanghai Baby*, much of Wei Hui's other fiction up to that point is quasi-autobiographical in nature (with one of her earlier stories even being entitled "*Xiang Wei Hui nayang de fengkuang*" 像衛慧那樣的瘋狂 (Crazy like Wei Hui),[22] while in real life she simultaneously models *herself* on the larger-than-life fictional personas of her fictional protagonists. This process of recursive projection and identification is clearly evident, for instance, in the author's personal webpage, which combines aphorisms from Wei Hui's fictional works and pictures of the author herself in sexually provocative poses reminiscent of her own fictional protagonists.[23]

The classmate's mirror metaphor, furthermore, is particularly appropriate in this discussion of Coco's earlier fiction collection, given that mirroring and identity are actually central concerns of the title story of Wei Hui's actual *Cries of the Butterfly* collection on which the fictional Coco's is based. Wei Hui's title story opens with a striking mirror scene:

> I was wearing very few clothes, and stood barefoot in front of an enormous mirror, smoking my first cigarette since I quit smoking two months earlier. The light-blue cigarette smoke gently crawling over my face and eyes like the paws of a cat, enveloping my entire body in a delicate halo. I peered into the glimmering depths of the mirror, whereupon a face like a faint star gradually came into view. It was the face of that woman.
>
> (272)

This second face that appears in the mirror next to the protagonist's own turns out to be that of her roommate, Jude. Jude is herself an artist, and the narrator's ironic mirror scene at the beginning of the story anticipates her own subsequent alienated relationship with a pair of Jude's portraits.

This ironic mirror scene, in turn, anticipates a concern with issues of identification and alienation in the story's fascination with a pair of Jude's portraits. One portrait depicts the narrator herself, nude, but it is an image which the narrator finds quite alienating: "[Jude] painted very fast, and in the end completed an image which, to my eyes, completely resembled an image of a 'stranger'" (282). The second painting, meanwhile, is actually a self-portrait of Jude in the form of a butterfly (the portrait, like the story, is entitled *Cries of the Butterfly*) which Jude then hangs next to the nude portrait, and ultimately leaves behind in the narrator's apartment after she moves out. The narrator's alienation from her own portrait, therefore, is mirrored by the uncanny affinity she feels toward Jude's butterfly self-portrait—suggesting that self-understanding is intertwined with a process of displaced identification with an external node of identity.

Like Jia Pingwa's Zhuang Zhidie 莊之蝶, whose name literally means "Zhuangzi's 莊子 butterfly," the shared *Cries of the Butterfly* title of the three concentrically embedded texts (viz., the short-story collection, the short story, and the self-portrait within that short story) at the heart of *Shanghai Baby* similarly evokes *Zhuangzi*'s famous parable of the butterfly—in which Zhuangzi wakes up uncertain of whether he just dreamed that he was a butterfly, or whether he is instead currently a butterfly dreaming it is

Zhuangzi.[24] *Shanghai Baby*, like much of Wei Hui's other fiction, revolves around a dialectics of alienation and displaced identification, wherein Wei Hui's alienated protagonists (like Wei Hui herself) repeatedly identify with projected and mediated versions of themselves. The protagonists of *Republic of Wine* and *Fallen Capital*, meanwhile, confront a similar conundrum, as their self-perception is constantly challenged by the collective views which their readers have formed of them. As a character in *Fallen Capital* tells Zhuang Zhidie, for instance, "You have an enormous reputation, to the point that you are no longer merely Zhuang Zhidie the individual, but rather, more accurately, you have become society's Zhuang Zhidie" (124). Zhuang Zhidie, like *Mo Yan* and Coco, simultaneously identifies with and feels alienated from this externalized locus of identity created by his reading public. In other words, "society's Zhuang Zhidie" is Zhuang's own Zhuangzian butterfly—representing the fame and respect that he dreams of attaining, even as this same public image constantly threatens to undermine and even usurp the character's own individual identity.

More generally, these repeated allusions to butterflies in contemporary popular literature evoke not only the *Zhuangzi* parable, but also the early twentieth century tradition of Butterfly literature. As Ping-hui Liao argues in his discussion, in this volume, of Shi Shuqing's 1990s "Hong Kong trilogy" (and particularly the first volume, *Her Name Is Butterfly*, which, like *Fallen City* and *Republic of Wine*, was also published in 1993), the female protagonist identifies with a "yellow butterfly" as she "literally tries to realize her Butterfly dream and fantasy." Liao argues that Shi Shuqing, in this contemporary work, is consciously mobilizing early twentieth century Butterfly motifs and granting them new significance, using them "to represent the postcolonial conditions of Hong Kong and of Taiwan." I would argue that a similar process is at work in the Mainland Chinese novels I have examined here, which transform the earlier Butterfly/May Fourth debates over orthodoxy, popularity, and public perceptions of authorship. Wang Shuo, Mo Yan, Jia Pingwa, and Wei Hui each appeal, in different ways, to the modern discourses of literary orthodoxy and ideological rectitude that the early twentieth century May Fourth writers helped to popularize, while at the same time illustrating the degree to which the forces of the market, piracy, and projective identification continually undercut the ability of authors to control the dissemination and consumption of their own works and image.

2003

In an amusing vignette from near the beginning of *Fallen Capital*, Zhuang Zhidie and his friend Hong Jiang decide to set up a bookstall, and Hong proposes that they leverage Zhuang Zhidie's fame and prestige in order to gain the upper hand over competing stalls. Zhuang, however, objects, on the grounds that "I am a writer, and a writer relies on his works. If the outside world came to know that I had opened a bookstore, what would they possibly think?" Hong therefore suggests a ruse whereby they would take knight-errant novels by a comparatively unknown author and give them new covers with the name *Quan Yong* 全庸 on the front, in the hope that casual readers would be likely to misread the name as *Jin Yong* 金庸—the Hong Kong novelist who is one of the best-selling authors throughout the Chinese-speaking world (73).

This vignette derives its humor from the way in which it contrasts two antithetical views of the relationship between authorship and literary markets. On the one hand, Zhuang Zhidie tries to maintain an appearance of authorial autonomy (insisting that he, as a respectable author, not be publicly associated with the business of bookselling), while Hong Jiang treats authorship as a mere tool for maximizing sales (to the point of appropriating Jin Yong's name to sell completely unrelated texts). This contrast reproduces in miniature one of the central tensions at the heart of each of the three 1990s novels discussed above—namely, how each of the quasi-autobiographical protagonists struggles to reassert and maintain control over their own identity and self-image, even as a variety of outside forces (including the literary market, the literary establishment, as well as countless readers and *mis*readers) constantly challenge that control.

While early twentieth century China was characterized by the figurative birth of the figures of the political and the professional author as recognizable public identities, the final decades of the century witnessed, by contrast, a gradual fracturing of those same identities, forcing authors to confront the loss of their (ostensible) ability to control the dissemination and consumption of their own literary texts and public image. Following Roland Barthes, we might call this latter process the "death" of the author[25] —the death, that is, of the illusion that authors may maintain strict control over their identities and the meanings of their literary productions. In reality, however, what is at stake in this contemporary process is more a spectral return of the figure of the author—in which authors don't merely resist this loss of control, but instead often mobilize precisely those same destabilizing forces for their own benefit. I will conclude by considering a handful of incidents coinciding roughly with the publication of a new Wang Shuo novel in 2003—incidents which illustrate both the ways in which market and institutional forces increasingly usurp the ostensible autonomy of the author, but also the ways in which some authors may actively reappropriate those same decentralizing forces in order to reassert their own embodied authorial identity.

It was in 2003, for instance, that a book entitled *Luoyu* 裸慾 (Naked desire) appeared under Jia Pingwa's name. Ostensibly published by the same Beijing Publishing House that had published *Fallen Capital* a decade earlier, *Naked Desire* trumpets on its cover its pedigree as being "another work that, after *Fallen Capital*, will similarly shock the literary world." The inside jacket, meanwhile, includes a brief blurb about the author, concluding that "[Jia Pingwa's] representative works include *Fallen Capital*, *Baiye* 白夜 (White nights), *Feicheng* 廢城 (Fallen city) and *Luocheng* 裸城 (Naked city). *Naked Desire*, however, turns out to be a counterfeit product, ghostwritten by an unknown author or authors and falsely attributed to Jia Pingwa in an attempt to capitalize on the residual public interest in *Fallen Capital* from a decade earlier. In fact, this new volume is not even a novel at all, but rather a pastiche of short, unrelated journalistic anecdotes describing the lurid underbelly of contemporary Chinese society. Curiously, this new, counterfeit volume feeds parasitically not only on the reputation of the "real" Jia Pingwa (by borrowing his name, and presenting itself as a sequel to *Fallen Capital*), but also on the *counterfeit* public image of Jia Pingwa that shadows the real one. For instance, of the four novels cited in the "author's blurb" in the book's inside jacket, only the first two (*Fallen Capital* and *White Nights*) are actually by Jia, while the latter two (*Fallen City* and *Naked City*) are actually, like *Naked Desire* itself, counterfeit texts—fake sequels to the original *Fallen Capital*.[26] By citing them, *Naked Desire* not only capitalizes on Jia's actual fame, but furthermore implicitly reinforces the same counterfeiting industry that produced *Naked Desire* itself.

Jia Pingwa was, of course, not the only contemporary author to be confronted with this problem of identity theft. In March of the same year, for instance, Mo Yan sued three separate publishers for reprinting two of his novels without permission, and also for falsely attributing two additional works to him.[27] While this lawsuit echoes Mo Yan's strident critique, in an article entitled *"Ruanruo de shengyin"* 軟弱的聲音 (Weak voice) a year earlier, of the practice of publishing counterfeit titles under his name, it nevertheless reverses his explicit *support*, in that earlier article, for the practice of unauthorized reprints of *his own* texts.[28] Mo Yan's reasoning, in "Weak Voice," is that, while he derives no direct economic benefit from either of these two practices, the first reinforces his reputation by allowing more people to read his works, while the latter dilutes and even undermines that same reputation by encouraging readers to conflate his carefully written works with the cheap knockoffs. Mo Yan's tacit acceptance of the practical limits of his control over the production and distribution of his texts and authorial image, therefore, ironically feeds back into a process whereby he attempts to parlay precisely that same loss of control (his inability to prevent black-market reprints of his works) into a strategy for strengthening his own public image.

The logical conclusion of the paradoxical strategy which Mo Yan advocates in this 2002 essay can be found, meanwhile, in the marketing strategies behind another Wang Shuo novel. Entitled *Bu xiang shangchuang* 不想上床 (Not wanting to go to bed)[29] and advertised on the cover as "Wang Shuo's newest work," this 2003 quasi-autobiographical novel actually bears no resemblance to the style for which Wang Shuo's earlier works are famous. As it turns out, this stylistic incongruity is due to the fact that the novel is actually *not* by the author of *Not Serious at All*, after all. In a canny marketing ploy of which Zhuang Zhidie's friend Hong Jiang would surely have approved, the work was published in such a way as to give the impression that it is by the self-described "hooligan writer" himself, while in fact it is actually the debut novel of a female author who happens to share the same name as Wang Shuo (and who, furthermore, also resides in Beijing). While the act of borrowing the name and identity of an established author is, as we have seen, increasingly common in China, what makes this particular case unusual is that there is technically no actual deception involved. The female author's name actually is *Wang Shuo*, and at no point does the book explicitly identify her with her more famous namesake. It is only natural, however, that casual book buyers will be initially confused, and the book's publisher certainly doesn't make any attempt to clarify the issue (e.g., the book jacket contains no author's bio, list of previous works, etc.).

Given this ambiguity over the debut author's identity, it is doubly ironic that *Not Wanting to Go to Bed* turns out to be largely autobiographical. The female Wang Shuo, far from seeking merely to subsume herself under the more famous Wang Shuo's aura, is actually attempting to use his fame as a means of jumpstarting her own literary career (she herself published a second novel the following year).[30] *Not Wanting to Go to Bed*, therefore, not only raises intriguing legal issues,[31] but furthermore also brings into focus more general questions about an author's relationship to his or her own text. That is to say, Wang Shuo's strategy of piggy-backing on the established reputation of her more famous namesake mirrors the way in which each of the 1990s authors discussed above necessarily entered into a contestatory dialogue with *their own* established reputations—public reputations over which they themselves had already partially lost control.

Through this act of virtual transvestitism, therefore, the female Wang Shuo figuratively borrows the reputation of the "hooligan author" whose name she shares, but precisely in order to use him as a model against which she hopes to establish her own literary identity. This apparent desire to capitalize on Wang Shuo's existing fame, furthermore, is itself developed through an exploration, and provisional disavowal, of issues of *sexual* desire ("not wanting to go to bed")—thereby reprising quite precisely the early twentieth century May Fourth literature's simultaneous desire for, and disavowal of, the romantic tendencies that it originally associated with the popular body of Mandarin Ducks and Butterfly literature against which the May Fourth literary movement sought to establish its own identity and reputation.

Notes

1 Wang Shuo 王朔, *Yi dian zhengjing meiyou* 一點正經沒有 (Not serious at all), originally published in *Zhongguo zuojia* 中國作家 (Chinese writers) 1989: 4. The edition used for this essay is the one that appears in *Wang Shuo wenji* 王朔文集 (Wang Shuo's collected works) Vol. 4 (Beijing: Huayi chubanshe, 1994), 66–154.

2 The organization was originally known as the *National Chinese Literary Workers Association* (*Zhonghua quanguo wenxue gongzuozhe xiehui* 中華全國文學工作者

協會). It changed its name in 1953 to *Chinese Writers Association* (*Zhongguo zuojia xiehui* 中國作家協會).

3 For a discussion of this transformation of the CWA, please see Shuyu Kong, *Consuming Literature: Best Sellers and the Commercialization of Literary Production in Contemporary China* (Stanford: Stanford University Press, 2005), 11–36.

4 While the journal *Chinese Writers* was founded in 1985, its affiliation with the Chinese Writers Association is noted on its masthead only as of 1991. *Not Serious at All* is Wang Shuo's only major work to appear in this journal.

5 *Not Serious at All* appeared in the fourth issue of the 1989 volume of *Chinese Writers* which, at that time, was published every two months.

6 Fang Yan may be seen as one of Wang Shuo's alter egos, and appears as the protagonist of several of his novels, including not only *Not Serious at All*, but also *Wanzhu* 玩主 (Troublemakers), *Xiangpringren* (Rubberman) and *Wanr de jiu shi xintiao* 玩兒的就是心跳 (Playing for thrills).

7 Wang Meng 王蒙, "*Duobi chonggao*" 躲避崇高 (Avoiding sublimity), *Dushu* 讀書 (Reader) (1993: 1), 10–16.

8 *Jiuguo* 酒國 (Republic of wine) was actually first published in Taiwan in 1992 (Taipei: Hongfan shudian, 1992), but was not released in China (in a revised version, with a modified ending) until the following year (Changsha: Hunan wenyi chubanshe, 1993). The novel was translated into English by Howard Goldblatt: *Republic of Wine* (New York: Arcade Publishing, 2001). The edition used in this essay is that which appears in Mo Yan's collected works, under the title *Mingding guo* 酩酊國 (Republic of drunkards) (Beijing: Zuojia chubanshe (The writers publishing house), 1994).

9 Jia Pingwa, *Feidu* 廢都 (Fallen capital) (Beijing: Beijing chubanshe, 1993).

10 Throughout the following discussion, I will refer to the fictional character as *Mo Yan* (in italics), to distinguish him from the actual author of the novel.

11 See Mo Yan, *Hong gaoliang jiazu* 紅高粱家族 (Red sorghum family lineage) (Beijing: Jiefangjun wenyi chubanshe, 1987); translated into English as *Red Sorghum*, Howard Goldblatt, trans. (London: Heinemann, 1992). All of the citations used here are taken from this latter edition (though in many cases the translations have been modified slightly).

12 Wang Shuo, *Qianwan bie ba wo dangren* 千萬別把我當人 (Please don't treat me as a human), in *Wang Shuo wenji*, vol. 4 (Beijing: Huayi chubanshe, 1994), 283–481, trans. by Howard Goldblatt, *Please Don't Call Me Human* (New York: Hyperion, 2000).

13 See *Yi dian zhengjing meiyou*, 132.

14 Zhu Hongjun, *Zhongguo wenhuabao* 中國文化報 (Chinese culture daily), July 17, 2002.

15 Jiang Xin 江心, ed., *Feidu zhi mi* 廢都之迷 (The mysteries of *Fallen City*) (Beijing: Tuanjie chubanshe, 1993), 22

16 Gayatri Chakravorty Spivak, "Can the Subaltern Speak?" in Cary Nelson and Lawrence Grossberg, eds. *Marxism and the Interpretation of Culture* (Chicago: University of Illinois Press, 1988), 271–313.

17 Wang Shuo, *Kanshangqu hen mei* 看上去很美 (It looks very beautiful), (Beijing: Huayi chubanshe, 1999), 5–6.

18 See Carlos Rojas, "Wang Shuo and the Chinese Image/inary: Visual Simulacra and the Writing of History," *Journal of Modern Literature in Chinese* 3.1 (January 2000), 23–57.

19 Ironically so, given that the companion CD would have been even cheaper and easier to copy than the novel itself.

20 Wei Hui 衛慧, *Shanghai baobei* 上海寶貝 (Shanghai baby) (Shenyang: Chunfeng wenyi chubanshe, 1999); trans. by Bruce Humes, *Shanghai Baby* (New York: Pocket

Books, 2001). The edition used and cited here is that which appears reprinted in her collected works, *Wei Hui jingpin wenji* 衛慧精品文集 (Collected fine works of Wei Hui) (Kuitun: Yili renmin chubanshe, 2000), 317–516.

21 Wei Hui's own collection *Cries of the Butterfly* was also first published in 1999, only shortly before *Shanghai Baby* itself.

22 Wei Hui, "*Xiang Wei Hui nayang de fengkuang*" 像衛慧那樣的瘋狂 (Crazy like Wei Hui), in Wei Hui, *Wei Hui jingpin wenji*, 105–191.

23 See http://goldnets.myrice.com/wh/page-1-27.htm.

24 *Chuang Tzu: Basic Writings*, trans. Burton Watson (New York: Columbia University Press, 1996), 45.

25 Roland Barthes, "The Death of the Author," in Roland Barthes, *Image, Music, Text* (New York: Hill and Wang, 1977), 142–148. See also Michel Foucault, "What Is an Author?" in Paul Rabinow, ed., *The Foucault Reader* (New York: Pantheon Books, 1984), 101–120.

26 For useful discussions of this broader phenomenon, see the "Hi people" bulletin board posting by Wo Biancao 窩邊草, "*Yucheng*" *shi Jia Pingwa de zuopin?* 「慾城」是賈平凹的作品？ (Is *Yucheng* by Jia Pingwa?), February 28, 2004, posted at http://hi.people.com.cn/article/read.php?art_id=6724; and Zhou Yuanshe, "*Jia Pingwa you bei daoming*" 賈平凹又被盜名 (Jia Pingwa has again had his name pirated), in *Xi'an wanbao* 西安晚報 (Xi'an Evening News), February 7, 2006.

27 For a discussion of this case, see Peng Biao 彭彪, "*Mo Yan zhuzuoquan jiufen an liangcheyihe*" 莫言著作權糾紛案兩撤一和 (Mo Yan copyright suits: two dismissed, one settled), originally published in *Zhonghua dushu bao* 中華讀書報 (Chinese reader's news) April 17, 2003.

28 Mo Yan, "*Ruanruo de shengyin*" 軟弱的聲音 (Weak voice), in *Beijing qingnianbao* 北京青年報 (Beijing youth daily), April 4, 2002.

29 Wang Shuo 王朔, *Bu xiang shang chuang* 不想上床 (Not wanting to go to bed) (Changchun: Shidai wenyi chubanshe, 2003).

30 Wang Shuo, *Meigui yandou* 玫瑰煙斗 (Rose pipe) (Beijing: Dazhong wenyi chubanshe, 2004).

31 Yan Yang 晏揚, "'*Liang ge Wang Shuo*' *xianxiang zhide de zhongshi*" "兩個王朔"現象值得重視 (The phenomenon of the "Two Wang Shuos" should be taken seriously), in *Fazhi ribao* 法制日報 (Legal daily), April 29, 2003, posted at http://www.legaldaily.com.cn/gb/misc/2003-04/29/content_25652.htm; and Tao Lan 陶瀾, "*Ci Wang Shuo fei bi Wang Shuo tongming tongxing chushu shifou goucheng qinquan?*" 此王朔非彼王朔同名同姓出書是否構成侵權？ (This Wang Shuo is not that Wang Shuo: is publishing books with the same author's name a copyright violation?), *Beijing qingnian bao*, April 16, 2003.

Index